Global Metal Mu...

This book defines the key ideas, scholarly debates, and research activities that have contributed to the formation of the international and interdisciplinary field of Metal Studies. Drawing on insights from a wide range of disciplines including popular music, cultural studies, sociology, anthropology, philosophy, and ethics, this volume offers new and innovative research on metal musicology, global/local scenes studies, fandom, gender and metal identity, metal media, and commerce. Offering a wide-ranging focus on bands, scenes, periods, and sounds, contributors explore topics such as the riff-based song writing of classic heavy metal bands and their modern equivalents, and the musical-aesthetics of Grindcore, Doom and Drone metal, Death metal, and Progressive metal. They interrogate production technologies, sound engineering, album artwork and band promotion, logos and merchandising, t-shirt and jewelry design, and the social class and cultural identities of the fan communities that define the global metal music economy and subcultural scene. The volume explores how the new academic discipline of metal studies was formed, while also looking forward to the future of metal music and its relationship to metal scholarship and fandom. With an international range of contributors, this volume will appeal to scholars of popular music, cultural studies, social psychology and sociology, as well as those interested in metal communities around the world.

Andy R. Brown is Senior Lecturer in Media Communications at Bath Spa University, UK.

Karl Spracklen is Professor of Leisure Studies at Leeds Metropolitan University, UK.

Keith Kahn-Harris is honorary research fellow and associate lecturer at Birkbeck College, UK.

Niall W.R. Scott is Senior Lecturer in Ethics at the University of Central Lancashire, UK.

Routledge Studies in Popular Music

1 **Popular Music Fandom**
 Identities, Roles and Practices
 Edited by Mark Duffett

2 **Britishness, Popular Music, and National Identity**
 The Making of Modern Britain
 Irene Morra

3 **Lady Gaga and Popular Music**
 Performing Gender, Fashion, and Culture
 Edited by Martin Iddon and Melanie L. Marshall

4 **Sites of Popular Music Heritage**
 Memories, Histories, Places
 Edited by Sara Cohen, Robert Knifton, Marion Leonard, and Les Roberts

5 **Queerness in Heavy Metal Music**
 Metal Bent
 Amber R. Clifford-Napoleone

6 **David Bowie**
 Critical Perspectives
 Edited by Eoin Devereux, Aileen Dillane, and Martin J. Power

7 **Globalization and Popular Music in South Korea**
 Sounding Out K-Pop
 Michael Fuhr

8 **Popular Music Industries and the State**
 Policy Notes
 Shane Homan, Martin Cloonan, and Jen Cattermole

9 **Goth Music**
 From Sound to Subculture
 Isabella van Elferen and Jeffrey Andrew Weinstock

10 **Queerness in Pop Music**
 Aesthetics, Gender Norms, and Temporality
 Stan Hawkins

11 **Global Glam and Popular Music**
 Style and Spectacle from the 1970s to the 2000s
 Edited by Ian Chapman and Henry Johnson

12 **Global Metal Music and Culture**
 Current Directions in Metal Studies
 Edited by Andy R. Brown, Karl Spracklen, Keith Kahn-Harris and Niall W.R. Scott

Global Metal Music and Culture

Current Directions in Metal Studies

Edited by Andy R. Brown,
Karl Spracklen, Keith Kahn-Harris
and Niall W.R. Scott

Routledge
Taylor & Francis Group
NEW YORK AND LONDON

First published 2016
by Routledge
711 Third Avenue, New York, NY 10017

and by Routledge
2 Park Square, Milton Park, Abingdon, Oxon OX14 4RN

First issued in paperback 2017

Routledge is an imprint of the Taylor and Francis Group, an informa business

© 2016 Taylor & Francis

The right of the editors to be identified as the authors of the editorial material, and of the authors for their individual chapters, has been asserted in accordance with sections 77 and 78 of the Copyright, Designs and Patents Act 1988.

All rights reserved. No part of this book may be reprinted or reproduced or utilised in any form or by any electronic, mechanical, or other means, now known or hereafter invented, including photocopying and recording, or in any information storage or retrieval system, without permission in writing from the publishers.

Trademark notice: Product or corporate names may be trademarks or registered trademarks, and are used only for identification and explanation without intent to infringe.

Library of Congress Cataloging-in-Publication Data

Names: Brown, Andy R., editor. | Spracklen, Karl, editor. | Scott, Niall W. R., editor. | Kahn-Harris, Keith, 1971- editor.
Title: Global metal music and culture: current directions in metal studies / edited by Andy R. Brown, Karl Spracklen, Keith Kahn-Harris and Niall W.R. Scott.
Description: New York; London: Routledge, 2016. | Series: Routledge studies in popular music | Includes bibliographical references and index.
Identifiers: LCCN 2015041377
Subjects: LCSH: Heavy metal (Music)—History and
criticism. | Music—Social aspects.
Classification: LCC ML3534 .G575 2016 | DDC 781.66—dc23
LC record available at http://lccn.loc.gov/2015041377

ISBN 13: 978-1-138-06259-7 (pbk)
ISBN 13: 978-1-138-82238-2 (hbk)

Typeset in Sabon
by codeMantra

Ronnie James Dio (1942–2010)
Jon Lord (1941–2012)
Jeff Hanneman (1964–2013)
Philphy Animal Taylor (1954–2015)
Lemmy Kilmister (1945–2015)

Contents

List of Figures and Tables   xi
Acknowledgments   xvii

1 Introduction: Global Metal Music and Culture *and* Metal Studies   1
ANDY R. BROWN, KARL SPRACKLEN, KEITH KAHN-HARRIS AND NIALL W.R. SCOTT

2 Reflections on Metal Studies   22
DEENA WEINSTEIN

PART I
Metal Musicology

3 Iron and Steel: Forging Heavy Metal's Song Structures or the Impact of Black Sabbath and Judas Priest on Metal's Musical Language   35
DIETMAR ELFLEIN

4 'It's Like a Mach Piece, Really': Critiquing the Neo-Classical Aesthetic of '80s Heavy Metal Music   50
GARETH HERITAGE

5 The Distortion Paradox: Analyzing Contemporary Metal Production   68
MARK MYNETT

PART II
Metal Music Scenes

6 Voracious Souls: Race and Place in the Formation of the San Francisco Bay Area Thrash Scene   89
KEVIN FELLEZS

7 The Unforgiven: A Reception Study of Metallica Fans and
'Sell-Out' Accusations 106
ERIC SMIALEK

8 Use Your Mind?: Embodiments of Protest, Transgression, and
Grotesque Realism in British Grindcore 125
GABBY RICHES

PART III
Metal Demographics and Identity

9 The Numbers of the Beast: Surveying Iron Maiden's
Global Tribe 145
JEAN-PHILIPPE URY-PETESCH

10 The Social Characteristics of the Contemporary Metalhead:
The Hellfest Survey 167
CHRISTOPHE GUIBERT AND GÉRÔME GUIBERT

11 Un(su)*Stained Class*? Figuring out the Identity Politics
of Heavy Metal's Class Demographics 190
ANDY R. BROWN

PART IV
Metal Markets and Commerce

12 Tunes from the Land of the Thousand Lakes:
Early Years of Internationalization in Finnish Heavy Metal 209
TONI-MATTI KARJALAINEN AND EERO SIPILÄ

13 Death Symbolism in Metal Jewelry: Circuits of
Consumption from Subculture to the High Street 227
CLAIRE BARRATT

PART V
Metal and Gender Politics

14 'Getting My Soul Back': Empowerment Narratives and
Identities among Women in Extreme Metal in North Carolina 245
JAMIE E. PATTERSON

15 Gender and Power in the Death Metal Scene:
A Social Exchange Perspective 261
SONIA VASAN

16 Masculine Pleasure? Women's Encounters with
   Hard Rock and Metal Music   277
   ROSEMARY LUCY HILL

PART VI
Metal and Cultural Studies

17 Retro Rock and Heavy History   297
   SIMON POOLE

18 Transforming Detail into Myth: Indescribable Experience
   and Mystical Discourse in Drone Metal   311
   OWEN COGGINS

PART VII
Metal Futures

19 The Future of Metal Is Bright and Hell Bent for
   Genre Destruction: A Response to Keith Kahn-Harris   333
   TOM O'BOYLE AND NIALL W.R. SCOTT

20 A Reply to Niall W.R. Scott and Tom O'Boyle   343
   KEITH KAHN-HARRIS

   Notes on the Editors and Contributors   351
   Index   359

List of Figures and Tables

Figures

3.1 The Hard Rock–Metal Continuum.   35

4.1 **A Chart Showing the Harmony Used in the Chorus to 'Sabbath Bloody Sabbath'.** The group of four chords indicated with '*' are successively repeated. The jazzy harmony, unusual in early-1970s heavy metal, is apparent because of the inclusion of 7th and 9th chords.   52

4.2 **An Excerpt Showing a Portion of the Bridge's Guitar Riff from Black Sabbath's Song 'Iron Man' (1970).** Introduced by two power chords, the riff enters on a B power chord using the B blues scale with an added chromatic passing note of A# in bars 3 and 4. The function of the A# is to raise the seventh degree of the scale, thereby creating a major tonality that contrasts the blues feel of the riff.   53

4.3 and 4.4 **Two Transcriptions of the Two Organ Rises from Bach's *Toccata and Fugue in D minor, BWV 565*.** 4.3 is from bar 2, and 4.4 is from bar 10.   54

4.5 **A Transcription of the Organ Rise from Manowar's 'The Crown and the Ring'.** The organ rise is essentially an E minor spread chord ranging five octaves. The affect of the E minor chord played over this range elicits a feeling of awe not unlike the feeling evoked by Bach's 'Toccata'.   54

4.6 **The First Motivic Development in *Canon in D*.** Played on Violin I, the motif is later distributed to the 2nd and 3rd violins in canon. In this example, violin II is playing the original descending stepwise melody.   55

4.7 **The Intro Guitar Riff to 'Goodbye to Romance'.** Similar in melodic contour, Pachelbel's influence can be seen in the stepwise melodic contour and accompanying bass countermelody. Notice the pitches in the descending bass line are the same as those played by Violin II in bar 1 (4.6).   56

4.8 **A Table Showing the Harmony for *Canon in D*.**   57

xii *List of Figures and Tables*

4.9 **A Table Showing the Harmony Used during the Verse of 'Goodbye to Romance'.** Although there are differences to the harmonic structure of *Canon in D (4.8)* there are many similarities, such as the use of the Bm9, F#m7, and G6. 57

4.10 **A Table Showing the Harmony Used during the Chorus of 'Goodbye to Romance'.** 57

4.11 **The Outro Melody Heard in 'Goodbye to Romance'.** The fanfare quality is emphasized by the use of semiquavers at the end of each bar that function to introduce the succeeding notes. 58

4.12 **A Simplified Excerpt of *Adagio in G minor*'s Opening Theme.** 58

4.13 **A Transcription of the Corresponding Theme Used in 'Icarus' Dream Suite Opus 4'.** Notice Malmsteen's substitution of semiquavers for acciaccatura followed by a quaver/semiquaver/demisemiquaver flourish used as a rhythmic elaboration of the triplet in bar 2 (4.12). 59

4.14 **A Simplified Excerpt of *Adagio in G minor*'s Third Theme.** 59

4.15 **A Transcription of the Corresponding Theme Used in 'Icarus' Dream Suite Opus 4'.** Notice Malmsteen's use of similar phraseology, substituting triplet quavers for triplet crotchets and, in bar 3 (4.15), appoggiatura/quaver phrasing to simulate the second triplet (4.14). 59

4.16 **A Transcription of the Opening Nine Bars of Malmsteen's Song 'Black Star'.** Notice the use of spread chords at the beginning of almost every bar before the introduction of the harmonics at bar 9. 59

4.17 **A Table Showing the Harmony for Malmsteen's 'Black Star' Prelude.** We can see from this example that Mamsteen has written a neo-Baroque harmony around the tonic center of E minor; the Em, Em/G, Em/B, Am(sus4) are chords in this key. As is common with Baroque harmony, the tonic center is moved to give the harmony the perception of tonal modulation. Malmsteen achieves this perception by using the Em/G, E/G# as a tonic transient-modulation from E minor to E major before returning to E minor with the Am(sus4). 60

4.18 **A Transcription of the Opening Seven Bars and Anacrusis of Malmsteen's 'Far beyond the Sun'.** Notice the recurring triplet-dotted minim/triplet-crotchet motif, which is very similar to the opening motif of Beethoven's *5th Symphony*. 60

4.19 **A Transcription of the Opening Two Bars of Paganini's 'Caprice No. 5'.** 61

4.20 **A Transcription of the Opening Two Bars of Malmsteen's 'Trilogy Suite Opus 5'.** Notice the demisemiquaver scale run before coming to rest on a G major chord. Observe that the melodic shape is nigh on identical to the opening two bars of Paganini's 'Caprice No. 5'. 61

5.1	Clean Riff Sonogram (Produced Using a 8192-Point Hann Window with 50% Overlap). The majority of frequency content resides below 1.5kHz, with little within the 1.5–7.5kHz boxed region, other than brief sections reflecting the riffs higher notes.	72
5.2	Harmonically Distorted Riff Sonogram (Again 8192-Point Hann Window/50% Overlap). Compared to figure 5.1, the additional upper spectral content within the 1.5–7.5kHz boxed region is considerable.	73
5.3	Clean Guitar Riff Sonogram—Focused on Low Frequencies.	75
5.4	Harmonically Distorted Guitar Riff Sonogram—Focused on Low Frequencies.	76
7.1	'Sad but True' at the Beginning of the Chorus. Palm-muted articulations are marked, 'P.M'.	110
7.2	Country Licks from 'The Unforgiven II'. Note the whole-step bends in particular.	111
7.3	Metallica's Movement within the Field of Cultural Production.	115
7.4	A Comparison between Waveform Images of the Studio Version of *Death Magnetic* (top) and the *Guitar Hero 3* Version (bottom). Adapted from Ian Shepherd's blog.	118
7.5	Images from the YouTube Video for 'Mastered by Muppets' Depicting Ulrich and Rubin Bragging about Their Wealth in Ways Connected to Dynamic Range Compression.	119
9.1	Maiden Fans Respondents by Continent.	152
9.2	Global Clustering of Net Respondents.	153
9.3	European Clustering of Net Respondents.	154
9.4	North American Clustering of Net Respondents.	155
9.5	South American Clustering of Net Respondents.	156
9.6	Age of Iron Maiden Fans – N=4,461.	157
9.7	Residency of Iron Maiden Fans.	158
9.8	Iron Maiden Fans' Political Affiliations.	162
10.1	Listening to Other Genres of Music.	178
10.2	Hard Rock Relative Preference Based on the Level of Qualification of Festival-Goers.	182
10.3	Grindcore Relative Preference Based on the Level of Qualification of Festival-Goers.	182
10.4	Doom Metal Relative Preference Based on the Level of Qualification of Festival-Goers.	183
10.5	Black Metal Relative Preference Based on the Level of Qualification of Festival-Goers.	183
10.6	The Percentage of People from the Upper Management and Higher Professional Sectors who Listen to Subgenres of Extreme Music, as Well as the Total Number of Festival-Goers.	185

13.1 Cap, Service Dress (General) Waffen-SS with White Metal Death's Head Badge, 1934. © IWM (UNI 411). 230
13.2 Torre Abbey Jewel, *Memento Mori* Pendant. Gold and Enamel. 1540–1550, England. © Victoria and Albert Museum, London. 232
13.3 Gold and Ruby *Memento Mori* Skull Ring. 1550–1575. European. © Victoria and Albert Museum, London. 232
13.4 Pendants, Page from 2002 Catalogue. © Alchemy Carta Ltd. 237
13.5 Rings, Page from 2002 catalogue. © Alchemy Carta Ltd. 238
18.1 Front and Back Cover of *Sleep Vol. 2* (1992), with Design, Font and Title Referencing Black Sabbath Vol. 4 (1972). The back lists a Sabbath cover version recorded live, and 'Special Thanks to Black Sabbath'. 313
18.2 Last.fm Website, Genre Tags for SunnO. Screengrab, 5th November 2014. 316
18.3 Bong, *Mana-Yood-Sushai* (2012). 324

Tables

1.1	Metal Bands by Country	5
3.1	The Standard Rock Song Structure	37
3.2	Example of a Formal Structure	38
3.3	Song Structure 'Black Sabbath'. (1970)	39
3.4	Black Sabbath's 'War Pigs' (1970) and 'Iron Man' (1970)	40
3.5	Song Structures: Black Sabbath 'Paranoid' (1970), Led Zeppelin 'Misty Mountain Hop' (1971)	40
3.6	Dual Song Structures: 'Sabbath Bloody Sabbath', 'A National Acrobat', 'Sabra Cadabra', 'Killing Yourself to Live' (all 1973)	42
3.7	Dual Song Structures: Megadeth: 'Peace Sells' (1986), Slayer: 'Postmortem' (1986), Metallica: 'Fade to Black' (1984)	43
3.8	Song Structures Judas Priest: 'Tyrant' (1976), 'Stained Class' (1978), 'Steeler' (1980), 'Breakin' the Law' (1980), 'Metal Gods' (1980)	44
3.9	Song Structures Judas Priest: 'Freewheel Burning' (1984), Iron Maiden 'Where Eagles Dare' (1983), Metallica 'Phantom Lord' (1983), Slayer 'Angel of Death' (1986)	45
3.10	Song Structure Judas Priest: 'Painkiller' (1990)	46
9.1	Iron Maiden Fans' Nationality	152
9.2	Iron Maiden Fans' Level of Education	158
9.3	Iron Maiden Fans' Employment	159
9.4	Parents of Iron Maiden Fans' Level of Education	160
9.5	Parents of Iron Maiden Fans' Employment Categories	160
9.6	Iron Maiden Fans' Religious Beliefs	161

9.7	Comparison between Iron Maiden Fans and French Metalheads	162
9.8	Double Consumption of Alcohol and Drugs among Iron Maiden Fans	163
10.1	The Jobs of Festival-Goers' Fathers	170
10.2	Primary Socio-Professional Status of Festival-Goers at the Time of the Survey	170
10.3	Hellfest Audience as Part of the In-Work Population Broken down by Professions and Social Categories (compared with the In-Work French population)	171
10.4	Breakdown of Hellfest Audience by Highest Level of Qualification	172
10.5	Breakdown of Festival-Goers by Age Group (Excluding Non-Responses)	174
10.6	Breakdown of Festival-Goers Depending on their Ticket Type	175
10.7	Frequency with Which People Dress in 'Metal' Fashion (Rock-Band Tee-Shirts, Gothic Clothing, Jewelry and Accessories, Etc.)?	175
10.8	Hellfest Is First and Foremost a Way of ...	176
10.9	Pivot Table, Age against How Metal was First Experienced	177
10.10	Pivot Table, Age of the First Metal Experience against Frequency with Which People Dress in 'Metal' Fashion	177
10.11	What Type(s) of 'Extreme' Music Do You Prefer?	179
10.12	Pivot Table, Qualifications against Types of 'Extreme' Music	181
10.13	The Percentage of People from the Upper Management and Higher Professional Sectors who Listen to Sub-genres of Extreme Music, as Well as the Total Number of Festival-Goers	184

Acknowledgments

First of all we would like to thank Liz Levine, Commissioning Editor at Routledge, for encouraging us to submit a proposal on what at the time we fondly referred to as our 'big book of metal' idea! From the drafting stage to developing the thematic structure of the volume, Liz has been an encouraging and supportive voice, guiding the project forward, with a mixture of positivity and patience.

Second, we would like to thank our contributor authors for their unswerving commitment to the project over what at times has seemed a long journey and most of all for their excellent contributions, without which we would not have been able to produce such a rich, wide-ranging and coherent collection, one that truly reflects the scope and reach of metal studies scholarship at this important juncture in its development. Special thanks should also go to Deena Weinstein for generously agreeing to contribute her reflection's piece at a late stage in the book's development.

Finally, we would like to give a 'shout out' to all the metal scholars we know around the world who are not contributors to the book but who have been part of the scholarly dialogue and exchange that has richly informed the development of metal studies and our 'collective thinking', over a number of years now. A roll call that includes but is not confined to the following: Jeremy Wallach, Esther Clinton, Brian Hickam, Amber Clifford-Napoleone, Bryan Bardine, Nelson Varas-Diaz, Claudia Azevedo, Brad Klypchak, Imke von Helden, Florian Heesch, Steve Waksman, Gerd Bayer, Pierre Hecker, Magnus Nillson, Jedediah Sklower, Laura Wiebe, Paula Rowe, Marcus Moberg, Laina Dawes, Matt Donahue, Carmen Di Anna, Sara Chaker, Mikael Sarelin, Helene Laurin, Daniel Frandsen, Mark Deeks, Nicola Allett, Caroline Lucas, Dave Snell, Roderick Henry, Marcus Verne, Louis-Martin Guay, Dominic Arsenault, Albert Bell, Rosemary Overell, Michelle Phillipov, Ross Hagen and Scot Wilson.

In addition, Andy would like to acknowledge the support of Steve May and Terry Rodgers and colleagues in Film, Media and Creative Computing at Bath Spa University, and his students, past and present. He would also like to thank: Chris Griffin, Stig Manley, Julian Matthews, Bec Feasey, David Muggleton, Tim Holmes, Paul Hodkinson, Wolfgang Deicke, Andy Bennett, Mark Jones, Lee Barron, Paul Long, Pete Webb, James Saunders and Joe Bennett.

1 Introduction
Global Metal Music and Culture *and* Metal Studies

Andy R. Brown, Karl Spracklen, Keith Kahn-Harris and Niall W. R. Scott

This volume brings together a range of chapters, written by new and established scholars, that present original research and analysis into the subjects and practices that constitute the phenomenon of global metal music and culture. But what exactly is global metal music and culture? When did it begin? Is it possible to define it? Study it? And by what range of means? Following on from this, what exactly is 'metal studies'? How is it defined? Where did it come from? what is its connection to the subject it studies? This introductory chapter will explore the range of possible answers to these questions, beginning with the heavy metal music genre and its complex relationship to economic and media globalization processes, history, culture, and the academy.

Following on from this, it will outline how and why the contemporary study of this global music and cultural phenomenon ended up being called 'metal studies' and how this is itself tied up with an older history of academic neglect or conflict over the value or legitimacy of metal music and its culture(s) that has (have), in a number of ways, led to its emergence. We will then go on to set out for the reader the ways in which we have organized the book and the major themes it addresses, as well as provide an outline of each chapter and its contribution to the section theme and the wider study of global metal music and culture.

Global Metal: *From Heavy Metal World Tours to the Extreme Metal Underground*

A number of the chapters gathered here began life as research papers presented at the 2011 *Heavy Metal and Place* international academic conference. The conference was part of the *Home of Metal* project, originally a fan-initiative to create an archive of memorabilia, such as band merchandise, concert tickets, album covers, and the like, which was taken up and supported by West Midland's Capsule arts media (Trilling, 2007). The Home of Metal project was laudable in its intentions to narrate and thereby legitimate the narratives and 'stories' of ordinary fans. But inevitably, such a project was at least in part driven by a desire to reclaim heavy metal music and culture as a reflection of a particular British regional identity. Or as the *Birmingham Post* put it, 'For too long Birmingham and the

West Midlands have failed to celebrate what is rightfully theirs, to claim the city and region as home of "heavy metal"' (2008). While millions of heavy metal fans over the decades and around the globe have celebrated the bands Black Sabbath and Judas Priest[1] that emerged from this region as central to the formation of the genre style, this statement is not simply a belated endorsement of that fandom or a claim on the music's origins as traceable to a regional 'home'. Rather it echoes a recognizably contemporary discourse that surrounds the cultural politics and economics of globalization in an era of neo-liberalism, one that speaks of 'regional music scenes', of symbolic 'spaces' and 'places', national 'heritage locations', or even 'music cities' as part of a national policy of the 'global-local' (Lashua, Spracklen, and Wagg, 2014; Bennett, 2009).

According to the organizers, the HoM project was conceived as 'celebration of the music that was born in the Black Country and Birmingham' and was aimed at 'a broad audience, from music fans, social history enthusiasts to cultural tourists' (HoM, 2011).

> Loved the world over, Heavy Metal in its many forms had its roots in Birmingham and the Black Country. But you wouldn't know to visit it. Nary a plaque, tour or tea towel marked one of the region's most prolific cultural exports […] Four decades since Heavy Metal was unleashed onto an unsuspecting world, Home of Metal honors a truly global musical phenomenon (ibid.).

Daniel Trilling, reporting in the *New Statesman*, makes a similar claim to the effect that 'Heavy metal was born in the West Midlands, and has developed a global following matched only in hip-hop. It's time to stop sneering and celebrate this proud cultural heritage' (2007). But, as Gerd Bayer suggests, the globalization of metal marked a 'turning point [after which] heavy metal somehow stopped being a particular British tradition' (2009, p. 2). How are we to disentangle these apparently contradictory claims?

First, the origins of the heavy metal genre are contested, not only in respect to whether Black Sabbath is the originator of the genre but also whether the band's regional location was the significant factor in the codification of heavy metal's meta-genre characteristics.[2] While there is no shortage of claims that the urban, working class location of the band and the surrounding industrial milieu (Harrison, 2010; Phillipov, 2011, p. 55; Weinstein, 2014) gave rise to a musical style that was 'steeped in rage' (Cope, 2010, p. 97), this is a relatively recent view, one that is itself part of a retrospective re-evaluation of heavy metal. Or as Ewing put it, apparently on behalf of rock critics in general, 'How wrong we were about Black Sabbath' (2010). Reynolds, commenting on the re-release of Sabbath's 70s albums, goes further: 'Criticism always lags behind new art forms, appraising it using terminology and techniques appropriate to earlier genres [but] over the long haul Sabbath's originality and fertility have been vindicated' (2004, p. 90).

Second, and consistent with this perspective, the globalization of heavy metal has only recently been viewed as a culturally significant phenomenon. Prior to this, the international impact of the genre in territories beyond the British/North American and latterly European context was viewed unequivocally (when it was noted at all) by popular music, media, and cultural studies scholars as part of the cultural imperialism and hegemonic domination of Western media products over non-Western populations, as evidenced in the popularity of Western film, music, and television productions in international charts, cinema, and cable-television schedules (Tunstall, 1977). The subsequent shift in scholarly debates from the 'top down' cultural domination and consequent 'homogenization' (Ritzer, 1993) of local and regional cultures, to a more complex view of differentiated reception, regional variation, and evidence of local adaptation and even 'resistance' to Western hegemony (Lull, 1995; Robertson, 1995), largely ignored heavy metal in favor of studies of the global-local impact of hip-hop, punk, and electronic dance music subcultures, scenes, and neo-tribes (Mitchell, 2001; Bennett, 2000; 2015, pp. 223–225; St. John, 2009; cf. Phillipov, 2011).

Nevertheless, it is plausible to argue that the genre trajectory of heavy metal music and its global cultural impact more closely approximates the narratives of the cultural imperialism thesis and the media globalization and global-local theories that have largely replaced it than any other genre-style. For a start, heavy metal, along with 'prog rock' and singer-songwriter/ folk Americana, was one of the most successful popular music genres of the 1970s—not just in terms of record sales but also in terms of North American and international touring revenues (Brown, 2015).

This pattern, if anything, accelerated in the 1980s with bands such as Iron Maiden, on the back of successful UK and North American album releases, embarking on 'World Tours'. For example, their August 1984–July 1985 'World Slavery Tour' included over 300 shows in 28 countries, including dates in East European cities 'behind the Iron Curtain', culminating in a concert in front of 250,000 at the first Rock in Rio festival in Brazil (Wall, 2001, p. 253). Indeed, Maiden's tour of Poland was 'greeted in the metal press as proof of the existence of an international metal community' (Weinstein, 2000, p. 120). Weinstein's description of the international advance in popularity of the genre—first emergent in Germany, then the Scandinavian countries, forming smaller enclaves within, Italy, France, and Spain, then Poland because of more liberal policies on culture, but by the late 1980s spreading throughout the former Soviet bloc countries; while in the global-South it strongly emerges in South America in the mid-1980s, including Mexico, Brazil, and Argentina (op cit, pp. 118–120)—does sometimes read like strategic markers on a cultural-imperialist map; while her statement to the effect that the genre is: 'found in every part of the world where there is an industrial working class and is more ubiquitous than McDonald's' (Weinstein, 2011, p. 41), echoes but does not confirm Ritzer's thesis (1993). Certainly by the mid-'90s heavy metal's popularity was clearly to be found across the Pacific Rim countries (Indonesia, Malaysia, and Singapore, in particular) (Wallach, 2011), the Indian sub-continent, Turkey (Hecker, 2012), the Middle East (LeVine, 2008) and China (Wong, 2011).

So, has heavy metal music 'conquered the globe', inculcating a 'standardized' taste culture among youth ordinarily divided by territory, tradition, religion, culture, and language? Well, yes and no. It is certainly true to say that during heavy metal's periods of greatest commercial success, in the periods 1970–1976 and 1984–1991, metal bands not only dominated the Billboard charts at 'home' but became global commercial brands in international music markets, enabling them to headline stadium concerts and festivals and build up fan-bases around the world numbering in the millions.

The global success of big 'name' metal bands is due in no small part to being signed to major record labels, whose multi-national parent corporations dominate between 72 and 75% of international music markets, enabling them to promote their artists and products in more territories than smaller independents who are less capital rich (IFPI, 2014).[3] This is also true of the financial infrastructure, technology, and personnel needed to undertake international tours, in support of album releases unlikely to receive much radio play, in countries with low per capita income and inadequate technical resources and venue management. In this respect, big name heavy metal acts are part of the 'Anglo-international repertoire [that] has dominated sales charts […] throughout the world for a number of years' (Negus, 1996, p. 174), despite the fact that they are not part of the global-pop mainstream media.

So, does this mean that globally popular heavy metal bands are 'soft' promoters of Western capitalist values and individualist consumer identities and lifestyles? In one obvious sense they are, in that participation in metal culture, listening to recordings, and attending concerts requires a relative level of affluence that comes only with modernity, industrialization, and technological change (Weinstein, 2011). On the other hand, heavy metal is a genre that has a history of controversy in terms of its relationship to dominant ideas, institutions, and societal and political moralities, despite its commercial success. These inherent contradictions between market-logics and moral and political censorship have at times become strongly highlighted in the local reception of global tours involving heavy metal bands.

If we can argue, as Weinstein does (2011), that the international spread of metal music culture via innovative, unconventional, or non-mainstream media constitutes the first phase of the globalization of metal, then the second phase is when that global cultural export begins a complex process of contraflow; a process that is facilitated by the development of a global underground network of bands, fans, institutions, and media that largely operates outside the logic and infrastructure of the 'transnational corporate culture' of the popular music industry. Kahn-Harris (2007; Harris, 1999) has defined one such network of translocal scenes as the 'extreme metal global underground', arguing that it effectively began in the mid-1980s with the emergence of the San Francisco Bay Area thrash scene, the Florida death metal scene, the Swedish death and Norwegian black metal scenes, and the grindcore and doom metal sub-genre scenes. Following the example of the New Wave of British Heavy Metal (1979–1984), with its revivalist and avant-garde mix of hundreds of local and regional bands, recording and self-releasing demos, the extreme metal scene was largely developed by local bands in different countries 'tape trading' demo and live tracks, accompanied by letters, flyers, and 'have/want' lists; an exchange system based on the currency of the International Reply Coupon.[4]

This fluid system of musical exchange, international camaraderie, and youthful enthusiasm allowed musicians and fans to construct a pre-Internet network of reciprocal influence and competitive development, linking local scenes in metropolitan and far-flung locales—from Birmingham to Belo Horizonte, Tel Aviv to Jakarta. Arguably, as the majority of bands were un-signed, this gave many an extended period of incubation in which to develop innovative and even avant-garde stylistics, based on a mixture of influences (See Kahn-Harris, this volume).

The *International Encyclopedia of Hard Rock and Heavy Metal* records entries for only 15 bands originating from outside Europe, North America, and Australia in 1983 (Wallach, Berger, and Greene, 2011, p. 28, n. 5); by 2007 the web site *Encyclopedia Metallum* records 47,626 bands, drawn from 129 countries (op cit, p. 5). Recently, the site reached a symbolic marker of 100,000 bands, spread over 140 countries (Encyclopedia Metallum, 2015).

Table 1.1 Metal Bands by Country[5]

Country	Nmb	Country	Nmb	Country	Nmb
Afghanistan	1	Bangladesh	46	Canada	3,135
Albania	10	Barbados	1	Chile	1,559
Algeria	23	Belarus	297	China	234
Andorra	4	Belgium	1,079	Columbia	1,167
Angola	2	Belize	5	Costa Rica	170
Argentina	1,635	Bolivia	184	Croatia	363
Armenia	18	Bosnia and		Cuba	76
Aruba	1	Herzegovina	112	Curacao	1
Australia	1,983	Botswana	8	Cyprus	52
Austria	988	Brazil	4,768	Czech	
Azerbaijan	8	Brunei	17	Republic	1,221
Bahrain	10	Bulgaria	318	Denmark	822

(Continued)

Country	Nmb	Country	Nmb	Country	Nmb
Dominican Republic	24	Lebanon	40	Reunion	5
Ecuador	278	Libya	2	Romania	334
Egypt	26	Liechtenstein	11	Russia	2 902
El Salvador	113	Lithuania	151	San Morino	2
Estonia	175	Luxembourg	76	Saudi Arabia	13
Faroe Islands	12	Macedonia	90	Serbia	343
Finland	3,253	Madagascar	9	Singapore	222
France	4,329	Malaysia	496	Slovakia	481
French Polynesia	1	Maldives	7	Slovenia	231
Georgia	17	Malta	57	South Africa	152
Germany	9,414	Mauritius	1	Spain	2,851
Gibraltar	4	Mexico	2,067	Sri Lanka	29
Greece	1,690	Moldova	29	Suriname	1
Greenland	2	Monaco	6	Sweden	3,889
Guam	6	Mongolia	5	Switzerland	862
Guatemala	101	Montenegro	8	Syria	27
Guyana	2	Morocco	21	Taiwan	54
Honduras	36	Mozambique	1	Tajikistan	5
Hungary	1,011	Myanmar	2	Thailand	146
Iceland	98	Namibia	2	Trinidad and Tobago	5
India	152	Nepal	17	Tunisia	17
Indonesia	1,093	Netherlands	2,025	Turkey	454
Iran	64	New Caledonia	5	Turkmenistan	3
Iraq	11	New Zealand	301	Uganda	2
Ireland	335	Nicaragua	24	Ukraine	716
Israel	221	Norway	1,440	United Arab Emirates	23
Italy	5,543	Oman	2	United Kingdom	4,072
Jamaica	1	Pakistan	49	United States	21,344
Japan	1,584	Panama	64	Uruguay	145
Jordan	28	Paraguay	120	Uzbekistan	6
Kazakhstan	45	Peru	387	Venezuela	337
Kenya	3	Philippines	207	Vietnam	40
Korea, South	201	Poland	2,935	Zambia	1
Kuwait	6	Portugal	1,125		
Kyrgyzstan	4	Puerto Rico	136		
Laos	2	Qatar	2		
Latvia	90				

This dramatic growth of local metal music scenes around the world clearly provides empirical support for the argument that since at least the 1990s, global metal music and culture have entered a period of contraflow, where commerce and community 'centre-periphery' relations now describe a much more complex pattern of interaction between the 'west and the rest'. However, to date, only the Brazilian band Sepultura has managed the journey from economic periphery to commercial success in the European/Anglo-American music market, although there has certainly been traffic in the other direction, as we have seen. A further paradox of Sepultura success, as Harris notes (2000, pp. 13–14), is that the band's early career, releasing material on small Brazilian labels took place entirely within its home country. Yet the band's music and lyrics (painfully translated from the original Portuguese and sung in English) made no attempt to signify 'Brazilian-ness' (beyond the name)[6] as it was consciously modeled on the thrash and death styles that the band members heard via the extreme metal tape-trading underground. Bennett and Peterson's influential characterization of *translocal scenes* as 'self-conscious local music scenes that focus on a particular kind of music [while being] in regular contact with similar local scenes in distant places [with whom] they interact' (2004, p. 4), seems entirely accurate in this case. What requires further explanation is why such scenes, as Baulch (2003) puts it, 'gesture elsewhere', given their different national locations and circumstances.

Baulch's answer, arising from her pioneering study of the death/thrash metal scene in Bali, is that the *authenticity* local bands seek in performing in a global metal style is both a gesture *against* the commercial music cultures encouraged by tourism *and* local 'traditional' music cultures. However, while global death, thrash and doom metal scenes 'ha[ve] developed a more or less uniform sound around the world', black metal by contrast 'often combines the musical style and imagery of Western extreme metal with that of the traditional cultures in the regions within which it has spread' (Wallach, Berger, and Greene, 2011, p. 17). Black metal, when it first emerged in the early 1990s in Norway and Sweden, 'constructed powerful myths of nationhood from ideas of pagan, Viking and anti-Christian ancestry' while incorporating 'folk' instruments and [Western classical or baroque] styles into their music [...] in order to construct a more 'authentic' [musical] discourse that [sometimes] crossed into overt racism' (Harris, 2000, p. 20).[7]

Similarly, global/local black metal styles incorporate traditional instruments into their sound, while drawing on ancient or pre-modern myths in order to critique the perceived 'shallowness' of modern life. Or as Wallach, Berger, and Greene (2011) argue in their recent survey of global/local scene studies, the spread of transnational networks and translocal communities has led globally situated actors to question the traditions and values of their families, communities, and nations. At the same time, 'transnational capitalism has rapidly and sometimes violently transformed their cities and regions' via economic and industrial changes, leading some to turn to religious or ethnonational extremism as a source of security in uncertain times (p. 6). However, while black metal 'may draw on images of the pre-modern to critique contemporary life [its use of] distortion and crushing amplification situate it firmly within the present' (p. 17), in this way, extreme metal styles can be said to employ the technology of modernity to express their profound estrangement from it, offering a range of 'youth identities that are not burdened by religious or authoritarian pressures of conformity, traditional culture, or mainstream commercialism' (ibid.).

Metal Studies: *What's in a Name?*

This volume is sub-titled, 'Current Directions in Metal Studies'. So, why have we decided to name our area of inquiry thus and not, as Walser recently suggested, 'heavy metal music studies' (2011, p. 335)? First, as Hickam (2015), in a recent overview of the formation of the field observes:

> For many of us in the metal music and culture studies arena, we have reached the state where the number of dissertations, theses, monographs, journal articles and documentaries on metal has exceeded our capacity to keep up. It was, however, only a handful of years ago that we did not have the concept of metal studies; nor did we have any sizeable networks of metal scholars, let alone thriving global scholarly communication (pp. 5–6).

Although scholars, particularly those embarking on PhDs, were occasionally in contact with each other, sometimes meeting at conferences or tracking down references for literature reviews, the idea that metal studies could be a field of study in its own right 'was never seriously entertained until 2008, when a number of initiatives began to bring metal scholars together', most notably 'the first *Heavy Fundametalisms* conference in Salzburg', in October of that year (Kahn-Harris, 2011, p. 251). Prior to this, 'we had publications, or studies, on heavy metal, but we did not have [...] 'metal studies' (Hickam op. cit., p. 6). It is now generally agreed (Guibert and Hein, 2006, p. 8; Brown 2011, pp. 215–217; Wallach, Berger, and Greene, 2011, p. 9), that the first scholarly texts on heavy metal to have a 'significant impact' were *Teenage Wasteland: Suburbia's Dead End Kids*, by Donna Gaines, *Heavy Metal: A Cultural Sociology*, by Deena Weinstein (both 1991), and *Running with the Devil: Power, Gender and Madness in Heavy Metal Music* by Robert Walser (1993). These were followed by Bettina Roccor's fan ethnology, conducted in Germany (1998); the work of the Spanish musicologist, Silvia Martinez Garcia (1994); and the ethnomusicology of Harris Berger (1999). However, as Weinstein (this volume) recalls, 'Neither [...] I, nor those other academics writing about metal in the 1990s, had been doing metal studies. It was only after metal studies seriously got underway [...] that those earlier works were grandfathered in'. This could also be applied to the next half-decade, which saw the publication of Susan Fast's study of Led Zeppelin (2001), Mimi Schippers' study of alternative-hard rock (2002), and the first full-length study on heavy metal published in France (Hein, 2003). This work was followed by Glen Pillsbury's musicological study of Metallica (2006) and the William Irwin edited collection on Metallica and philosophy (2007).

Yet, as Hickam observes, even after Keith Kahn-Harris' (2007) ground-breaking book *Extreme Metal: Music and Culture on the Edge* was published, it was still generally believed that scholars would remain within their academic subject areas and publish in journals defined by those areas (ibid.). One of the central reasons for this was pursuing an academic career (which for many meant getting PhD approval or securing 'tenure' within an academic department, which meant publishing work in the 'right' journals). Amber Clifford-Napoleone, one of Hickam's respondents, is quoted as saying: 'I knew that I wanted to write about metal, but it had been suggested to me not to do my dissertation on metal' (p. 11). The colleague who advised her 'was looking out for her academic career' and was concerned about the 'academic respectability of studying metal' (ibid.). So what was it that changed?

The key factor appears to be the 'act of meeting up' with other scholars who were interested in metal, at an academic conference where heavy metal was its *central* theme. Another important factor was that the first conference, as part of the *ID.net* mission statement (Fisher, 2014), was interdisciplinary and non-hierarchical. In particular, there was no 'keynote', no academic status-hierarchy or subject sub-divisions. As Scott comments, 'There was openness and dialogue as nobody had an agenda and nobody was pushing for something. It was very anarchic in that sense. There was no power; there was no hierarchy' (quoted in Hickam, 2015, p. 14). It was this atmosphere that 'catalysed a kind of self-consciousness among previously isolated scholars' (Kahn-Harris, 2011, p. 251). Another factor, according to Hickam, was the 'median age' of delegates at the first Salzburg conference,

> Which [...] was mid-thirties, an age at which many academics are still on the tenure track. Academe had already opened its doors to jazz studies, hip hop studies, women's studies, and queer studies. Perhaps, we mused, there was a change in attitudes towards heavy metal, if not a trend of recognition and respect for critical analyses of the music and culture. (p. 13)

This view of the catalytic impact of that first conference and those that followed it, including 'Heavy Metal and Gender' (Köln, October 2009), the 2nd 'Heavy Fundametalism' conference (Salzburg, November 2009), 'Black Metal Theory' (New York, December 2009), the 3rd 'Can I Play with Madness? Metal, Dissonance, Madness and Alienation' (Prague, November 2010), 'Home of Metal' (Woverhampton, September 2011), Heavy Metal Generations' (Prague, May 2012) and 'Heavy Metal and Popular Culture'

(Ohio, April 2013), is echoed by Niall W.R. Scott who notes that, following the second gathering: 'the possibility of founding a society dedicated to metal studies became a goal' (2012, p. 205). Indeed, the formal announcement of the launch of the International Society of Metal Music Studies (ISMMS) was made from the conference floor at Bowling Green State University, Ohio, in April 2013. A website dedicated to the society and carrying its mission statement was launched in June 2013, and the announcement of a peer-reviewed academic journal of the society, *Metal Music Studies*, was made by its editor-in-chief, Karl Spracklen, shortly afterwards.[8]

Another critical element in the development of metal studies was the establishment of the metal studies bibliography as a central resource and focus of critical analysis and debates. The earliest version of this, *Metal Studies—a Bibliography, Compiled by K. Kahn-Harris*, was posted on the author's website in January 2004.[9] This bibliography, which also acknowledged French and German language citations, was published as Kahn-Harris, K., and Hein, F. (2006). 'Etudes Metal/Metal Studies: Une Bibliographe', in both French and English by the popular music journal, *Volume!*, as part of a special issue on 'Metal Scenes: Social Sciences and Radical Cultural Practices' (Guibert and Hein, 2006). Although Kahn-Harris continued to revise the bibliography until March 2009, as a result of meeting at the first Heavy Fundametalisms' conference, the bibliography was formally handed over to the editorship of Brian Hickam. Hickam 'expanded the scope of the bibliography to include all media, such as documentary films, and to include all works (i.e., scholarly and non-scholarly). This version of the bibliography was first published online in October 2012' (ISMMS, 2013).[10] The interim version of this bibliography (referred to as the Metal Studies Bibliography Database (MSBD)—described as 'the most complete listing of published scholarship on heavy metal music and culture to date' (Brown, 2011, p. 214)—was employed as the 'empirical base' for a critical survey of the 'emergent' themes and patterns of publication of metal scholarship, in an article published as part of the special issue 'Metal Studies? Cultural Research in the Heavy Metal Scene', in July 2011 (Spracklen, Brown, and Kahn-Harris, 2011).[11] A revised and extended version of this bibliography was re-launched on-line as a publication of the *International Society for Metal Music Studies* (ISMMS), on February 15, 2013.

The Layout of the Book: *Mapping Metal Studies*

Deena Weinstein's chapter, which follows this one, is in many ways an alternative introduction. She offers a number of considered thoughts, by a well-known metal scholar, on the rise of this 'new' field of study. She argues that media, including music magazines, films, videos, and college music DJs, played an early role in developing a discourse about heavy metal and that this conversation has continued with films like *Metal: A Headbangers Journey* and the cable TV series, *Metal Evolution*. Weinstein compares metal studies to women's studies, black studies, American studies, and queer studies, suggesting it arises out of a similar political ferment over the politics of representation. As such, metal studies is not a paradigmatic science but a study of a 'content area', one that applies multiple disciplines, multiple methods, and multiple theoretical paradigms to a particular content.

Following Weinstein's chapter, the book is organized into seven sections: Metal Musicology, Metal Music Scenes, Metal Demographics and Identity, Metal Markets and Commerce, Metal and Gender Politics, Metal and Cultural Studies, and Metal Futures. In some cases, the chapters seek to develop areas that are seen to be undeveloped in metal studies; in others, there is a sense that this new work develops entirely new ground. In still other cases, the work seeks to critique existing studies and suggest an alternative direction or new point of departure.

Metal Musicology

As Kahn-Harris has argued, the 'critical weakness in metal studies as it stands [is] the relative paucity of detailed musicological analyses' (2011, p. 252) that is able to build on Walser's (1993) pioneer work. Of course, there are the studies of Berger (1999) and Fast (2001) and Pillsbury's study of Metallica (2006). But it remains the case that studies of metal *as* music are few and far between. One direction that is signaled in recent work, particularly from Berger (1999) onwards, is to explore music making itself—how metal musicians compose music and the context in which they do so—combining a musicological analysis with an ethnographic fieldwork. While other work has explored the ways in which metal musicians have sought to employ a range of sound technologies, as well as how this pursuit of the aesthetic of timbral 'heaviness' is realized and 'recognized' in studio production sound (Berger and Falles, 2005; see also Williams, 2015), so far 'a widely accepted vocabulary for identifying the constituent musical features of metal' (Kahn-Harris, 2011, p. 252) has yet to be established, although there are signs that it is beginning to emerge.

In seeking to address this lacunae, this section offers three chapters, all of which attempt to contribute to the development of a more rigorous and multi-faceted musicology of metal music. The first piece, by musicologist Dietmar Elflein, closely examines the riff-based compositional structures of a selection of Black Sabbath and Judas Priest songs, in order to establish the compositional rules that define heavy metal as a musical language and to trace this influence to later bands, such as Metallica, Megadeth, and Slayer. Elflein's innovative methodology is to offer an analysis of well-known songs that are understood in terms of pulse length, microstructure, macrostructure, and vocal structure. In this way, metal songs are understood as made up of sequences of riffs with varying pulse lengths that are repeated in different sections of the song length, more like a series of verses than the conventional verse/chorus pop/rock pattern and duration.

Gareth Heritage's chapter makes a welcome return to the subject, first addressed by Walser, of the influence of neo-classical music on the style and compositional characteristics of 1980s heavy metal guitarists, such as Ritchie Blackmore, Randy Rhoads, and Yngwie Malmsteen. In a critique of Walser's argument, Heritage focuses on the neglect of the role of melody and harmony in well-known metal song compositions; the similarities in performance practice between '80s heavy metal guitarists and neo-classical music virtuosos; and more recent examples of the *metallization* of the Western High Art aesthetic, via a case study of the classically trained violinist, Mark Wood.

While there has been increasing recognition, in guitar tech and musician media, of the role of sound engineers, such as Martin Birch and Tom Allom, in helping to define the timbral characteristics of classic heavy metal records, the role of the record producer has most often featured negatively in metal-related media as responsible for 'softening' the sound of metal bands to render them more 'commercial' or in arguments about the 'loudness wars' (see Smialek, this volume). One of the startling points Mark Mynett makes in his chapter on contemporary metal production is that metal recordings are 'often as heavily processed as commercial pop or dance music'. But, due to the culture and aesthetics of musical authenticity and musicianship that surround the genre, the key role of the producer is not celebrated—as it is in EDM, for example—but hidden. Yet, the 'distortion paradox' as Mynett articulates it is that the pursuit of the aesthetic of timbral heaviness via the dominating role of rhythm guitars in achieving the spectral brightness that signify the heaviness of metal, means that the overall sound envelope is 'muddy' and lacking in distinction in terms of the contribution of other instruments, such as drums and bass. The role of the contemporary metal producer is to find technological solutions to 'punch through' this dense sonic blanket to make band dynamics 'clear' to the listener. Increasingly, these studio-derived solutions translate into the way that bands play live rather than the other way around.

Metal Music Scenes

Debates about music scenes, whether local, trans-local, or virtual, have dominated discussion of the post-rock landscape, as we have seen in accounts of the global metal extreme underground. Kevin Fellezs' chapter, which revisits the San Francisco Bay Area Thrash Scene, argues not only that the musical dynamics of the local Bay Area music scene have been under-emphasized in terms of explaining musical innovation but also that the 'vernacular cosmopolitanism' of the scene, in terms of the participation of Black, Latino, and Asian American musicians, has been under-emphasized or simply ignored because it does not fit the prevailing white, male, working class stereotype of metal musicians and metal fandom in this period.

Eric Smialek's chapter offers a reception study of fan accusations of 'sell out' that have accompanied the career of Metallica, from culturally consecrated underground champions of a 'thinking man's metal' to the compromises and 'betrayal' that have been seen to accompany their 'crossing-over' to mainstream commercial success, both musically and aesthetically. Drawing on a Bourdeuzian framework, Smialek charts the accumulating examples of 'sell out', from the Napster controversy to the 'loudness wars' that surrounded the release of their Death Magnetic album, suggesting that such fan discourses are located within a model of cultural production where creativity and commerce are inextricably opposed in ways that are redolent of a 19th century conception of the artistic field.

The chapter by Gabby Riches examines the continuing relevance of the extreme and grotesque realism found in the musical aesthetics of seminal British grindcore bands Napalm Death, Unseen Terror, and Extreme Noise Terror and how the politics of such music, as reflected in their anti-capitalist lyrics, is embodied in the corporeal and bodily aesthetics of the mosh pit practices to be found in the contemporary Northern British, Leeds grindcore scene, in particular the commitment to gender inclusiveness and sense of an 'imagined' community that such a metal scene makes possible.

Metal Demographics and Identity

Media images, especially those in currency in the 1980s, such as Wayne's World and Heavy Metal Parking Lot, and the demographic evidence accumulated from a number of North American school and college-based studies investigating youth delinquency and deviance in the period of the PMRC-driven moral panic, offer a remarkably consistent image of the 'typical metalhead': white, teenage working-class kids from blue-collar backgrounds. The seminal studies of Gaines (1991), Weinstein (1991), Walser (1993), and Berger (1999) that mounted a reasoned defense of heavy metal music's value and cultural significance did not contest this class profile of the heavy metal audience but tended to confirm it. However, a number of studies conducted in the 1990s and more recently in France and Germany have strongly contested what they view as a negative 'stereotype' of the poorly educated, lower-class, dysfunctional metalhead, suggesting that, on the contrary, the typical heavy metal fan is more likely to be middle class, well-educated and well-adjusted. Since then the exponential growth in global metal scene studies has further complexified this class profile, identifying upper-middle-class fans among the relatively privileged and newly formed middle-class, service-sector fans in rapidly industrializing countries, while Weinstein (2011) continues to assert that most of the metal fans constitute a 'global proletariat'.

Each of the chapters in this section directly addresses these debates and the issues that arise from them. Jean-Philippe Ury-Petesch's chapter presents evidence and analysis derived from an on-line global-survey questionnaire, conducted with over 4,000 Iron Maiden fans, drawn from 70 countries, of the 'social morphology' of this 'global tribe' in terms of age, gender, residence, education, employment, social background, marital status, religious beliefs, political affiliation, and self-reported 'risk taking', in order to compare these findings with previous European and North American studies. The chapter by Christophe Guibert and Gérôme Guibert reports the findings from a questionnaire survey conducted with over 8,000 metal fans attending the *Hellfest* festival in Western France in 2011. In this study the authors sought to gather survey data that would give them a more rounded profile of the contemporary metalhead, so they focused not only on occupation, educational achievement, age, gender, and social background but also on metal sub-genre preferences, adherence to a metal 'look', and length of time as a fan, as well as on how respondents became fans in the first place. What the results suggest is that metal fandom in the 21st century is now a well-established taste community with a strong sense of its own history and a high degree of omnivorousness in the range of sub-genre preferences. It is also quite socially heterogeneous, in terms of social class background, although it appeals perhaps more to the well-educated, there is some evidence of class patterning in sub-genre preference.

Andy R. Brown's chapter argues that, as a majority of the working class and the middle class highly 'dislike' heavy metal, a different kind of analytical measure is needed to identify the demographic profile of the metalhead within occupational and culturally classed groupings. Employing a methodology of 'class-fraction analysis', the chapter offers a re-analysis of existing studies and claims about the social class profile of the typical metalhead, suggesting that the core enduring fan base of metal is largely derived from the skilled-manual upper-working and lower-middle class, with movements 'down-market' to the lower working class more likely to occur during periods of mainstream popularity and 'up-market' movements into the middle and upper-middle classes during periods of relative unpopularity.

Metal Markets and Commerce

Although some work produced under the banner of 'post-subcultural studies' (Muggleton and Weinzierl, 2003; Bennett and Kahn-Harris, 2004), such as Brown's work on the heavy metal t-shirt (2007a) and the metal magazine (2007b), attempted to explore the role of entrepreneurship, commodities, and markets within music scenes and subcultural modes of consumption, it remains the case that this aspect of metal studies remains critically undeveloped.

The value then of the chapters by Karjalainen and Sipilä and Barratt in this section cannot be over-stated, in challenging metal scholars to reflect on their neglect of the role of commerce, design, and marketing in metal music production and consumption. For example, the chapter by Karjalainen and Sipilä examines the commercial developments and media discourses that have accompanied the 'mainstreaming' of notable Finnish metal bands and performers but also how their remarkable international success has been viewed as a process of 'exporting' Finnish culture to the wider world. By contrast, the chapter by Claire Barratt offers a historical and contemporary 'object-analysis' of the significance of death symbolism in the production and consumption of metal jewelry designs and products, such as rings and pendants. The chapter also examines how the bespoke single item of jewelry in silver, and the copies and derivatives made of lesser metals, to be found in metal and rock fan-clothing retailers and high-street stores, trace a complex cultural history of borrowings, from funerary traditions to military insignia, DIY bikers ('Hell's Angels') to rock and metal musicians, songs, and styles.

Metal and Gender Politics

As both Hickam and Wallach (2011) and Riches (2015) have argued, metal studies has not marginalized female scholars. Indeed, beginning with Weinstein and Gaines (both 1991) and continuing with Roccor (1998), Martinez Garcia (1994), Fast (2001), Schippers (2002), Halnon (2004), and Phillipov (2012), female scholars have been central to the critical development of the field. However, with the exception of Fast and Schippers, this scholarship has not privileged the politics of metal and gender. This is not the case with a new wave of female academics who are primarily concerned with this issue in particular: gender inclusion and exclusion within metal scenes that are conventionally defined as male-dominated (Vasan, 2011; Hill, 2011; Riches, 2011; Dawes, 2012; Overell, 2013, 2014) and with challenging the idea that the affective pleasures of metal music are exclusively 'masculine' (Hill, 2012).

The chapter by Jamie Patterson, based on auto-ethnography and interviews with female participants in the Raleigh, North Carolina, death metal scene, explores how the 'objective' factors of gender, class, and ethnicity fail to explain how female participants experience a sense of empowerment in a scene that is male dominated and often exclusionary. While such spaces may appear to be characterized by extreme 'masculine' expressiveness, they also offer the possibility of gender transcendence ('genderlessness') or recreational 'escape' from gender identity and gender conformity.

By contrast, the chapter by social psychologist Sonia Vasan seeks to explain why female participants in death metal scenes persist in their commitment to them when they are regularly subjected to sexism or a lack of full acceptance by males who control the scene. Vasan's answer, derived from social exchange theory, is that female participants will accept an unequal rate of exchange for their continuing membership because the subculture addresses social and psychological needs that cannot be met elsewhere in their lives, such as freedom from the constraints of domesticity and femininity.

The chapter by Rosemary Lucy Hill reflects on research conducted with female rock and metal fans that aimed to explore the listening pleasures that fandom of the music enabled. Seeking to contest the idea that such music is necessarily 'masculine' because it is predominantly performed and listened to by men, the author also seeks to highlight the ways in which female listeners, once encouraged to reflect on their personal engagement with the music, chose to extend their descriptive lexicon in ways that significantly diverged from the typically 'masculinist' adjectives of 'aggressive' and 'brutal' identified with the metal and rock scene, exploring affective emotional terms such as 'beautiful' and 'transcendent', describing musical performances as 'joyous' and the idea that 'emotionally' powerful songs offered a sense of 'companionship' between musicians and fans.

Metal and Cultural Studies

The entrée of cultural studies scholars into the emerging metal studies field was announced by the collection edited by Bayer (2009), which offered a range of interpretive studies of metal genres, song themes, and lyrics grounded in the comparative study of religions; aesthetics; comparative literary studies including classical (Campbell, 2009), gothic (Bardine, 2009), and dystopian themes (Wiebe Taylor, 2009); while another notable strand has developed analysis of death and black metal themes, drawing on post-structuralist linguistics, philosophy, and poetics (Bogue, 2004; Wilson, 2008; Masciandaro, 2010; Scott, 2014).

Simon Poole's chapter draws on the trope of the palimpsest—ancient writing written over writing that is never fully erased—to explore the 'heavy history' of metal's beginnings and renewals. In this way, as the author argues, heavy metal's continuous development, despite its deferential relationship to its past, has been achieved by both acts of allegiance and acts of renewal, over and over again. That is, heavy metal's nostalgias are nostalgias in the name of progress, each an act of engagement with a possible 'past' that is at the same time a possible 'future'.

Owen Coggins' account of the retro-progressive sub-genre of drone metal, with its acts of musical and visual homage to Black Sabbath, doom metal, and other drone bands, is one such example in contemporary metal. However, Coggins' chapter seeks to explore, through work on religion and the mystical in metal studies, as well as Michel de Certeau's work on mysticism as a mode of communication, how drone metal performance practices and listening experiences are described in terms of ritually altered senses of time, space, and the body, highlighting in particular the figure of pilgrimage. In this way, drone metal can be understood as a contemporary mystical discourse.

Metal Futures

Finally, the last two chapters in the book comprise a debate on the future of metal, conducted between Tom O'Boyle and Niall W.R. Scott on the one side and Keith Kahn-Harris on the other. Kahn-Harris in his keynote at the Heavy Metal and Popular Culture conference, and then in a series of posts to the net-magazine *Souciant*, addressed the issue of 'metal beyond metal', suggesting that the metal scene is currently experiencing, due to the Internet and other factors, a 'crisis of abundance'. Scott and O'Boyle, in their opening salvo, seek to contest this argument and its evidence base and to offer, by contrast, a picture of contemporary metal that suggests it is not backward-looking, but genre-destructive and future-oriented. In reply, Kahn-Harris, while agreeing that the debaters all share a wish for metal to progress, in turn questions the evidence base of Scott and O'Boyle, suggesting that their optimism is not grounded in a model of how creativity arises from 'scenic' constraints.

Notes

1. The HoM project chose to concentrate on these bands, as well as Led Zeppelin, Napalm Death and Godflesh: http://homeofmetal.com/the-project/about/ (accessed March 26, 2015).
2. For example, Lester Bangs and other champions of punk and garage rock argue that Detroit, Michigan ('Motor City') is the home of heavy metal and for similar reasons.
3. 'Digital Music Report 2014': http://www.ifpi.org/downloads/Digital-Music-Report-2014.pdf (accessed March 26, 2015).
4. Prompting the phrase that accompanied many letters, 'enclose IRC – or die'.
5. Data source: Encyclopedia Metallum (2015): http://www.metal-archives.com/browse/country (accessed March 26, 2015).
6. Their name is derived from Motörhead's 'Dancing on your Grave' song (Strong, 2001, p. 484).
7. Musical authenticity often meant strict adherence to a mythology of ethnic heathenism or a pure Nordic identity expunged of all 'black' (music) influences.
8. Volume 1(1) was published on October 1, 2014, and Volume 1(2) on April 1, 2015: http://www.ingentaconnect.com/content/intellect/mms/2015/00000001/00000002;jsessionid=j33beksp8n0h.alice (accessed April 1, 2015).
9. Personal communication from the author. See also: http://www.keithkahnharris.pwp.blueyonder.co.uk/metalstudies.htm (accessed March 26, 2015).
10. Metal Studies Home: http://www.ucmo.edu/metalstudies/metal_studies_home.html (accessed March 26, 2015).
11. The level of engagement and interest provoked by this journal special, and the 'heavy genealogy' piece in particular, can be gauged by the number of views and downloads it has received (currently 1100): http://www.tandfonline.com/action/showMostReadArticles?journalCode=rcuv20 (accessed March 26, 2015).

Bibliography

Bardine, B. A. (2009). Elements of the Gothic in heavy metal: A match made in Hell. In G. Bayer (Ed.), *Heavy metal music in Britain* (pp. 125–139). Surrey: Ashgate.

Baulch, E. (2003). Gesturing elsewhere: The identity politics of the Balinese death/thrash metal scene. *Popular Music*, 22(2), 195–216.

Bayer, G. (2009). Doing cultural studies with earplugs. In G. Bayer (Ed.), *Heavy metal music in Britain* (pp. 1–13). Surrey: Ashgate.

Bennett, A. (2000). *Popular music and youth culture: Music, identity and place*. New York: Macmillan.

Bennett, A. (2009). "Heritage Rock": Rock music, representation and heritage discourse. *Poetics*, 37, 474–489.

Bennett, A. (2015). The global and the local. In A. Bennett and S. Wacksman (Eds.), *The Sage handbook of popular music genres* (pp. 223–225). London: Sage.

Bennett, A., & Kahn-Harris, K. (2004). *After subculture: Critical studies in contemporary youth culture*. Basingstoke: Palgrave Macmillan.

Bennett, A., & Peterson, R. (2004). Introduction to music scenes. In A. Bennett & R. Peterson (Eds.), *Music scenes: Local, translocal and virtual* (pp. 1–15). Nashville: Vanderbilt University Press.

Berger, H. M. (1999). *Metal, rock and jazz: Perception and the phenomenology of musical experience*. Hanover: Wesleyan University Press.

Berger, H., & Fales, C. (2005). 'Heaviness' in the perception of heavy metal guitar timbres: The match of perceptual and acoustic features over time. In P. Green & T. Porcello (Eds.), *Wired for sound: Engineering and technologies in sonic cultures* (pp. 181–197). Middletown, CT: Wesleyan University Press.

Birmingham Post. (2008). Midlands should be proud of its heavy metal heritage September 8: http://www.birminghampost.co.uk/whats-on/music/midlands-should-proud-heavy-metal-3955143 (accessed March 26, 2015).

Bogue, R. (2004). Violence in three shades of metal: Death, doom and black. In I. Buchanan & M. Swiboda (Eds.), *Deleuze and Music* (pp. 95–117). Edinburgh: Edinburgh University Press.

Brown, A. R. (2007a). Rethinking the subcutural commodity: Exploring heavy metal t-shirt culture(s). In P. Hodkinson & W. Deicke (Eds.), *Youth cultures: Scenes, subcultures and tribes* (pp. 63–78). London: Routledge.

Brown, A. R. (2007b). "Everything louder than everything else": The contemporary metal music magazine and its cultural appeal. *Journalism Studies*, vol. 8(4), 642–655.

Brown, A. R. (2011). Heavy genealogy: Mapping the currents, contraflows and conflicts of the emergent field of metal studies 1978–2010. *Journal for Cultural Research*, 15(3), 213–242.

Brown, A. R. (2015). "Everything louder than everyone else": The origins and persistence of heavy metal music and its global cultural impact. In A. Bennett & S. Wacksman (Eds.), *The Sage handbook of popular music genres* (pp. 261–277). London: Sage.

Campbell, I. (2009). From Achilles to Alexander: The classical world and the world of metal. In G. Bayer (Ed.), Heavy metal music in Britain (pp. 111–124). Surrey: Ashgate.

Cope, A. L. (2010). *Black Sabbath and the rise of heavy metal music*. Farnham, Surrey: Ashgate.

Dawes, L. (2012). *What are you doing here? A black woman's life and liberation in heavy metal*. Brooklyn: Bazillion Points.

Ewing, T. (2010). How wrong we were about Black Sabbath. *The Guardian*, February 18, 2010.

Fast, S. (2001). *In the houses of the Holy: Led Zeppelin and the power of rock music*. Oxford: Oxford University Press.

Fisher, R. (2014). Vision Statement, inter-disciplinary.net: http://www.inter-disciplinary.net/about-us/vision-statement (accessed March 26, 2015).

Gaines, D. (1991). *Teenage wasteland: Suburbia's Dead End Kids*. Chicago: University of Chicago Press.
Guibert, G., & Hein F. (2006). 'Prèsentation', 'Les Scènes Metal: Sciences Sociales et Pratiques Culturelles Radicales', *Volume!*, 5(2), 5–18.
Halnon, K. B. (2004). Inside shock music carnival: Spectacle as contested terrain. *Critical Sociology*, 30(3), 743–779.
Harris, K. (2000). "Roots"?: The relationship between the global and the local within the global extreme metal scene. *Popular Music*, 19(1), 13–30.
Harrison, L. M. (2010). Factory music: How the industrial geography and working-class environment of post-war Birmingham fostered the birth of heavy metal, *Journal of Social History*, Fall, 145–158.
Hecker, P. (2012). *Turkish Metal: Music, meaning and morality in Muslim society*. Aldershot: Ashgate.
Hein, F. (2003). *Hard rock, heavy metal, metal: histoire, culture et pratiquants*. Paris: IRMA; Nantes: Mélanie Séteun.
Hickam, B. (2014). Amalgamated anecdotes: Perspectives on the history of metal music and culture studies. *Metal Music Studies*, 1(1), 5–23(19).
Hickman, B., & Wallach, J. (2011). Female authority and dominion: Discourse and distinctions of heavy metal scholarship. *Journal for Cultural Research*, 15(3), 255–278.
Hill, R. (2011). Is emo metal? Gendered boundaries and new horizons in the heavy metal community. *Journal for Cultural Research*, 15(3), 297–314.
Hill, R. (2012). Pleasure in metal: What women fans like about hard rock and metal music. In A. R. Brown & K. Fellezs (Eds.), *Heavy metal generations: (Re)generating the politics of age, race, and identity in metal music culture* (pp. 117–127). Oxford: Inter-Disciplinary Press.
Kahn-Harris, K. (2007). *Extreme metal: Music and culture on the edge*. Oxford: Berg.
Kahn-Harris, K. (2011). Metal studies: Intellectual fragmentation or organic intellectualism? *Journal for Cultural Research*, 15(3), 251–253.
Lashua, B., Spracklen, K., & Wagg, S. (Eds.). (2014). *Sounds and the city: Popular music, place and globalization*. Houndmills: Palgrave Macmillan.
LeVine, M. (2008). *Heavy metal Islam: rock, resistance, and the struggle for the soul of Islam*. New York: Three Rivers Press.
Lull, J. (1995). *Media, communication, culture: A global approach*. Cambridge: Polity Press.
Martinez Garcia, S. (1994). El fenomen musical de les tribus urbanes a Barcelona: el heavy metal. *Revista d'Etnologia de Catalunya*, n° 4, 174–176.
Masciandoro, N. (Ed.). (2010). *Hideous gnosis: Black metal theory Symposium 1*. New York: Create Space.
Mitchell, T. (2001). *Global noise: Rap and hip-hop outside the USA*. Middletown: Wesleyan University Press.
Muggleton, D., & Weinzierl, R. (Eds.). (2003). *The post-subcultures reader*. Oxford and New York: Berg.
Negus, K. (1996). *Popular music in theory*. Cambridge: Polity Press.
Overell, R. (2013). '[I] hate girls and emo[tion]s': Negotiating masculinity in grindcore music. In T. Hjelm, K. Kahn-Harris, and M. LeVine (Eds.), *Heavy metal: Controversies and countercultures* (pp. 201–227). Sheffield: Equinox.
Overell, R. (2014). *Affective intensities in extreme music scenes: Cases from Australia to Japan*. Basingstoke: Palgrave Macmillan.

Phillipov, M. (2012). *Death metal and music criticism: Analysis at the limits*. Lanham, MD: Lexington Books.

Pillsbury, G. T. (2006). *Damage incorporated: Metallica and the production of musical identity*. Routledge: New York.

Reynolds, S. (2004). Black Sabbath: The Complete '70s Replica CD Collection, 1970–78 [2001]. In B. Hoskyns (Ed.), *Into the void: Ozzy Osborne and Black Sabbath; A rock's backpages reader* (pp. 89–91). London: Omnibus Press.

Riches, G. (2011). Embracing the chaos: Mosh pits, extreme metal music and liminality. *Journal for Cultural Research*, 15(3), 315–332.

Riches, G. (2015). From cultural politics to pleasurable affects: Female metal scholarship's contribution to metal studies (Reviews). *Metal Music Studies*, 1(1), 171–176.

Ritzer, G. (1993). *The McDonaldization of society*. London: Pine Forge Press.

Ritzer, G. (2002). *McDonaldization: The Reader*. London: Pine Forge Press.

Robertson, R. (1995). Glocalisation: Time-space and homogeneity-heterogeneity. In M. Featherston, S. Lash, & R. Roberstson (Eds.), *Global modernities* (pp. 25–44). London: Sage.

Roccor, B. (1998). *Heavy metal. Kunst, Kommerz, Ketzerei*. Berlin, IP, Verlag Jeske/Mader GbR. Kunst, Kommerz, Ketzerei, IP Verlag Jeske / Mader GbR, Berlin.

Spracklen, K., Brown, A. R., & Kahn-Harris, K. (Eds.). (2011). Metal studies? Cultural research in the heavy metal scene' [special issue]. *Journal for Cultural Research*, 15(3), 209–212.

Schippers, M. (2002). *Rockin' out of the Box: Gender maneuvering in alternative hard rock*. New Brusnwick, NJ: Rutgers University Press.

Scott, N. W. R. (2012). The International Society for Metal Music Studies in Dossier <<Metal Studies>>, coordonne par G. Guibert et J. Sklower. *Volume!*, 9(2), 205.

Scott, N. W. R. (2014). Seasons in the abyss: Heavy metal as liturgy. *Diskus*, (16)1, 12–29.

St. John, G. (2009). *Technomad: Global raving countercultures*. London and Oakville, CT: Equinox.

Trilling, D. (2007). Rocking the world. *New Statesman*, July 26, 2007.

Tunstall, J. (1977). *The media are American*. London: Constable.

Vasan, S. (2011). The price of rebellion: Gender boundaries in the death metal scene. *Journal for Cultural Research*, (15)3, 333–350.

Wall, M. (2001). *Run to the hills: Iron Maiden, The authorised biography* (rev. ed.). London: Sanctuary.

Wallach, J. (2011). Unleashed in the East: Metal music, masculinity, and "Malyness" in Indonesia, Malaysia, and Singapore. In J. Wallach, H. Berger, & P. D. Greene (Eds.), *Metal rules the globe: Heavy metal music around the world* (pp. 86–105). Durham, NC: Duke University Press.

Wallach, J., Berger, H. M., & Greene, P. D. (2011). *Metal rules the globe: Heavy metal music around the world*. Durham, NC: Duke University Press.

Walser, R. (1993). *Running with the devil: Power, gender and madness in heavy metal music*. Hanover, NH: Wesleyan University Press.

Walser, R. (2011). Afterword. In J. Wallach, H. Berger, & P. D. Greene (Eds.), *Metal rules the globe: Heavy metal music around the world* (pp. 332–338). Durham, NC: Duke University Press.

Weinstein, D. (1991). *Heavy metal: A cultural sociology*. New York: Maxwell Macmillan International.

Weinstein, D. (2000). *Heavy metal: The music and its culture*. New York: Da Capo Press.
Weinstein, D. (2011). The globalization of metal. In J. Wallach, H. Berger, & P. D. Greene (Eds.), *Metal rules the globe: Heavy metal music around the world* (pp. 34–59). Durham, NC: Duke University Press.
Weinstein, D. (2014). Birmingham's post-industrial metal. In B. Lashua, K. Spracklen, and S. Wagg (Eds.), *Sounds and the city: Popular music, place and globalization* (pp. 38–54). Houndmills: Palgrave Macmillan.
Wiebe Taylor, L. (2009). Images of human-wrought despair and destruction: Social critique in British apocalyptic and dystopian metal. In G. Bayer (Ed.), *Heavy metal music in Britain* (pp. 89–110). Surrey: Ashgate.
Williams, D. (2015). Tracking timbral changes in metal productions from 1990 to 2013. *Metal Music Studies*, 1(1), 39–68.
Wilson, S. (2008). *Great Satan's rage: American negativity and rap/metal in the age of supercapitalism*. Manchester: Manchester University Press.
Wong, C. P. (2011). "A dream return to Tang Dynasty": Masculinity, male camaraderie, and Chinese heavy metal in the 1990s. In J. Wallach, H. Berger, and P. D. Greene (Eds.), *Metal rules the globe: Heavy metal music around the world* (pp. 63–85). Durham, NC: Duke University Press.

2 Reflections on Metal Studies[1]
Deena Weinstein

Metal studies presents the fundamental question to sociology: how is metal studies possible, how is metal studies constituted? In part, that question is answered by another one: what is included in metal studies? Is everything written about metal to be included in metal studies? Andy R. Brown (2011), in his exhaustive critical analysis of the scholarly work on metal and its surrounding social relations, 'Heavy Genealogy', took on this inclusive approach. He called attention to a rupture in this literature on metal between a therapeutic model and a fan-based model (p. 214). This dichotomy is akin to one that sociologists in the US some decades ago used to describe the split between behavioralism (which had an establishmentarian bent and was embraced by psychologists) and symbolic interactionism (which had a more democratic bent). Brown correctly saw my book, *Heavy Metal: A Cultural Sociology* (1991), as excluding the establishmentarian behavioralist psychological work, or at least, excluding it from being taken seriously, as I did not write about it. Not that I believe that I must remain true to material I wrote more than a quarter century ago, but I'll continue to exclude that work from metal studies. I seem not be alone in that decision—I've not seen those behavioralists at metal studies conferences or much cited in books and articles written since metal studies got underway.

Another aspect of the scope of metal studies is whether it is necessary for material to be in printed form to be included in the field. I don't think so. The raft of metal documentaries, such as *Metal: A Headbanger's Journey* (2005), *Some Kind of a Monster* (about Metallica) (2004), *Full Metal Village* (2006) (about the Wacken festival), *Heavy Metal in Baghdad* (2007), *Get Thrashed: The Story of Thrash Metal* (2008), *Global Metal* (2009) (the sequel to the 2005 film), and *Anvil! The Story of Anvil* (2009), as well as cable TV productions, such as the VH1 series, *Heavy: The Story of Metal* (2006) and *Metal Evolution* (2011) and fan footage uploaded to YouTube, should be included.[2] To the extent that such works are aimed at mass fans, via the glossy metal magazines rather than newsprint or on-line outlets, the more that hype and celebrity performances make up their content. But all of these sources contain ideas and theories nonetheless. Letting the musicians, fans, and others including journalists have their say is also surely valid. Many of those involved in creating and disseminating metal grasp their activities intellectually as well as, if not better than, academicians do.

The second part of the response to the question 'How is metal studies possible?' is a consideration of the kind of organization that metal studies has. As a more or less organized activity, what is its form? Metal studies is not organized according to some paradigm or a particular method or, like economics, the abstraction of an activity. That is, it is not a traditional discipline. It is also not transdisciplinary, as that would demand a singular form. Nor is it interdisciplinary, combining two or more disciplines in single works. Metal studies is multidisciplinary, composed of disparate approaches based in different disciplines, and includes interdisciplinarity and attempts at transdisciplinarity. It includes approaches from musicology, literature, religious studies, gender studies, anthropology, sociology, and other fields. Metal studies is not a paradigmatic science but a study of a content area. It is properly called a study—the application of multiple disciplines, multiple methods, and multiple theoretical paradigms to a particular content.

The History of Metal Studies

Like other academic study movements, such as women's studies, black studies, American studies, or queer studies, metal studies has a history, including a pre-history. It shares with the other socio-cultural studies movements a common origin in the social movements of the 1960s for justice, equality, and the democratization of culture. Those movements fought for the inclusion of hitherto-excluded voices. They were also part of a larger movement that can be described as 'cultural populism'. In the arts, for example, it included pop art and the *nouvelle vague* of French cinema. It was those same socio-cultural movements that gave rise to heavy metal itself.[3]

The revolutions of the 1960s radically democratized culture, as significantly as the French Revolution of 1789 radically democratized society. The revolutions for equality and justice haven't as yet been fully successful, and neither has the democratization of culture been achieved. The repressions of those attempts by the powers-that-be led most of those fighting for 'liberation' to take safer paths—entering established institutions to make changes within them. This was especially true in academia where the migration of activists to bureaucratic venues was referred to as The Long March through the Institutions. Women's studies was feminism instead-of-revolution, as black studies was the alternative to the black power movement, etc. Inside academia, these ideas were spread to younger generations, influencing changes in public opinion and practices.

The cultural revolution of the late 1960s entered academia in another way, too—via Cultural Theory, especially in the rise of post-structuralism, the theories of which provided an intellectual framework for these non-disciplinary academic studies, including metal studies. Cultural populism gave voice to the marginalized and suppressed. Cultural theory vindicates the political and intellectual significance of popular culture. Metal studies is situated within cultural studies and cultural theory. Both of those tendencies were subversive to academic tradition, and metal studies is exemplary of all of these subversive tendencies.

Metal studies' pre-history is found not only in academic area studies and in rock studies (often done as cultural sociology), but also in the metal-focused magazines in the 1980s, including *Kerrang!, Ardschock,* and *Metal Hammer,* and in numerous metal 'zines. Themes formative of academic metal studies are articulated and anticipated in this autochthonous literature. Metal journalists writing in those publications were in part precursors of metal studies and in part paralleled its academicians. A number of the non-academic writers were not only fans, but were also metal musicians and/or worked for metal record labels, in metal radio, at metal record stores, and with metal concerts. ('Zine writers generally did not write as a career-move or as a way of earning money. Many spent their own money to print and distribute their work, similar to so many extreme metal bands who spend their money playing live rather than making money.)

An important early metal 'zinester in the US was Brian Slagel. I first bought his *New Heavy Metal Revue* because of his cover story on Michael Schenker. At the time, Slagel was a buyer for a metal record store in Los Angeles. He soon began Metal Blade Records, and several of his publicists began their own 'zines. Another pioneer was Ron Quintana, a DJ of a metal specialty show, *Rampage Radio*, on the University of San Francisco's radio station, KUSF. He had thought of calling his 'zine *Metallica* until a metal friend of his from Los Angeles, Lars Ulrich, convinced him that *Metal Mania* was a superior name. (Ulrich made good use of the discarded name.)

Some of those writing about metal for magazines also wrote books about metal for commercial publishers. Among the first metal books were Brian Harrigan and Malcolm Dome's (1980) *Encyclopedia Metallica: The Bible of Heavy Metal,* Tony Jasper and Derek Oliver's (1983) *The International Encyclopedia of Hard Rock & Heavy Metal,* and Philip Bashe's (1985) *Heavy Metal Thunder: The Music, Its History, Its Heroes.* Those books emphasized biographies of well-known metal bands, but they also included some history and description of the genre. In the magazines too, history and subgenre depictions were interwoven with descriptions and critiques of albums and concerts and interviews with musicians.

Another non-academic precursor of metal studies was the growing number of metal DJs in the 1980s on metal specialty shows, like Ron Quintana's. The DJs not only played heavy metal records, they also informed their listeners about the music, the artists, and the meanings of their songs. They were, in the US, the equivalents of those DJs in the late 1960s on underground, free-form, progressive FM radio. Both spread a new set of values, one the counterculture, the other heavy metal culture. (I am especially indebted to a number of them in the Chicago area, especially Real Precious Metal's Paul Kaiser and Ron Simon on Triton College's station, both on FM).

Metal Enters Academia, but Not yet as Metal Studies

Metal studies was still in the future when a few academicians began to write about metal. Will Straw's 1984 article, 'Characterizing Rock Music Cultures: The Case of Heavy Metal', published in the *Canadian University Music Review*, was the first and only academic work on the genre that I encountered as I was writing my book on heavy metal. The decision to write that book wasn't stimulated by the hole in the academic literature. It was my response to the wildly outrageous accusations by the newly empowered religious right-wing in America. The PMRC (Parents Music Resource Center) was a coalition of the politically ambitious and a few greedy psychologists, appealing to parental and religious groups who saw their power over youth waning. The organization had easily been able to create a moral panic, enthusiastically spread via the mass media. Evil music, especially heavy metal, was killing, literally and spiritually, the nation's youth, so they argued.

At the time, I was a professor of sociology, specializing in social theory and mass media. I had been a participant in, and fan of, the '60s revolutions (more fan than participant) and by the mid-1980s was busily reading the French post-structuralists. Having taught a sociology of rock course for several years, I was thinking of writing a book on the topic. I was also heavily into heavy metal, listening to it incessantly on records I kept buying, on specialty metal radio, and at concerts, many concerts. I was also an avid reader of metal magazines and 'zines.

My first reaction to the anti-metal propaganda was incredulity. I had no problem with politicians spouting nonsense, but I had been too naïve not to appreciate the way that the news media were pleased enough to be their stenographers. The mainstream media follow the lead of the powerful, and, in the 1980s, President Ronald Reagan had trained them to march to his reactionary tune. I first wrote a screed, 'Maligning Metal', which I presented at a panel at the College Music Journal's annual conference (my audience replete with those specialty metal show DJs) in 1988. It was published in the British metal magazine *R.A.W.* in early in 1989. I realized that metal fans or musicians were in no position to defend the genre, so, when I was asked to write a book, I suggested one on heavy metal. The publisher was delighted with my choice to depict metal as a serious art rather than as the evil propaganda for suicide and Satanism that fueled the moral panic. The book was published in 1991, but it did not initiate metal studies.

A raft of other academic writing on metal was published in the 1990s, including Gaines (1991), Walser (1993), Roccor (1998), Martinez Garcia (1999), and Berger (1999) (see Guibert and Hein 2006). Neither Straw nor I, nor those other academics writing about metal in the 1990s, had been doing metal studies. It was only after metal studies seriously got underway, in the latter half of the first decade of this century, that those earlier works were grandfathered in. In a way, it was like Black Sabbath's early records, which were not considered heavy metal by the band or most of their fans. Fliers for early Sabbath concerts, seen at the Home of Metal museum exhibit in Birmingham in 2011, labeled the band as a prog-rock group. It was only after heavy metal crystallized as a genre, in the second half of the 1970s, that Black Sabbath 'became' heavy metal.

The Advent of Metal Studies

Why did metal studies begin when it did? There is no one answer to that question, but there are several reasons, taken together, that explain the development of this new academic study. By the middle of the first decade of the current century, there was a good deal of academic writing on metal upon which to build a literature, to teach a course, and to justify writing a PhD thesis on some aspect of metal. Academia had begun to appeal to student interests in course offerings and in selecting topics for their graduate theses.

The mass access of broadband-connected Internet 2.0 augmented and created sets of other reasons for metal studies' emergence. One set relates to making all styles and all eras of metal music widely available. Old and new music, and videos of earlier and recent concerts, became easily available for listening or downloading, with or without paying for them. Bands and labels uploaded some of their music to be freely downloaded, serving as advertisements for full albums or concert attendance. Websites abounded, which allowed bands to post information and music, and on which one could comment to anyone and everyone. There were an increasing number and variety of metal blogs, vblogs, and on-line (and on-line versions of print) magazines with their feature stories, abundant photos, and album reviews.

Although the Internet allowed metal to become known to anyone, as no one now needed a personal friend (as opposed to virtual ones) to learn about the genre, why were more and more mainly young people wanting to learn about metal? During the 1990s, there was a wider awareness of metal. Metallica's 'popped-up' *Black Album* (1991) (along with its power-hitter management and producers) broke through to mass rock fans. Metallica, at least the more commercial sounding Metallica of the 1990s, was in heavy rotation on MTV and on a variety of radio formats, especially modern rock and alternative. The band's massive success was an impetus for major labels to put some muscular promotion into other thrash bands, mainly those already signed to majors. Megadeth reached no.2 with their *Countdown to Extinction* (1992), and two years later, their next release, *Youthanasia* (1994), was at no.4 in the Billboard Top 200. Pantera's *Far Beyond Driven* hit no.1 in the same year, and their *Great Southern Trendkillers* was no. 4 in 1996. In contrast to thrash metal acts in the 1980s, each of these arena-headlining bands had songs with Gen-X lyrics recounting childhood horrors, depression, and the like (Weinstein, 2015, pp. 262–263).

A second publicity campaign for metal, this time for the then new sub-genre, black metal, came from the mayhem, *ahem*, out of Norway. The church burnings, suicide, murder, and of course the corpse-painted faces of the musicians grabbed widespread attention. *Lords of Chaos: The Bloody Rise of The Satanic Metal Underground* by Michael Moynihan and Didrik Søderlind recounted the grisly details a few years after the fact, spreading the spectacle further afield.

The Internet made metal irreversibly global by the turn of the 21st century. As a result, the fan base for metal increased, and musicians were able to create and distribute their music from anywhere at very little cost. The number of metal bands in the world proliferated geometrically in this century. Bands that could once only reach small audiences in one city could now tour the world and play at metal festivals (Wacken only being the best known among the dozens around the globe each year) where they would earn far more money in one night, playing to far more people, without further travel costs.

Especially in post-industrial countries, the Internet played a part in the significant decline of the record industry's revenue. In part, the downturn was due to file sharing (a.k.a. "piracy") by fans, but the record companies themselves were to blame for much of their fiscal decline. They had bet against rock, choosing to get short-term gains from releasing and promoting pop acts like Britney Spears, which appealed to tweenagers. As a result, in part because of the industry's production decisions, in the current century, rock is no longer the juggernaut that it had once been, certainly not in record sales or mass-media coverage. Yet large arena concerts, whose ticket prices have escalated even more than college tuition costs in the US, have featured rock groups, still on the road or recently reunited, who had received major promotional budgets decades ago. Old and very old rock acts tour well, and young people are listening to older rock, along with a diverse mix of younger rock bands.

The one style of rock that is still alive and kicking is metal. Mainstream journalists who had scorned metal or merely ignored it began to cover major metal bands more respectfully. Millennials tend toward omnivore tastes in music and are no longer 'anything but metal' in their proclivities. At metal concerts, or at Black Sabbath's main stage at Lollapalooza in Chicago in 2012, there were young, old, and older metalheads; and lots of millennials who 'like everything'. In a sense, metal has become rock's 'last man standing' and has come to approach being a metonym for rock itself.

Finally, one cannot ignore individual agency as a major initiating cause of metal studies. Several handfuls of metal scholars, mainly British, but augmented by French, Germans, Americans, and Brazilians, were responsible for organizing conferences, editing and publishing conference proceedings, initiating a society (International Society for Metal Music Studies), editing books, putting metal bibliographies on-line, and starting the journal *Metal Music Studies* (see Hickam, 2015). Without them, the study of metal would not have coalesced into an academic field. They have been instrumental in making metal studies international, not only in its object of study, but also among those inquiring into it.

The maturity of metal studies as an academic field is evinced by the appearance of a meta-discourse commenting on the field itself. The articles in a special issue of the *Journal for Cultural Research* entitled 'Metal Studies? Cultural Research in the Heavy Metal Scene' (Spracklen, Brown, and Kahn-Harris, 2011); Guibert and Sklower's (2013) 'Dancing with the Devil: Panorama des 'metal studies'' (2013); and conferences, such as the 2014 meeting in Angers, France ('Heavy Metal et Sciences Sociales'), are examples of the meta-turn, which shows a movement that has become organized 'for-itself'.

Theorizing the Resultant

Now that we've seen how metal studies developed, we can go back to the field as an organized activity. Several sets of theorists have described the form that metal studies has taken prior to the existence of the field. Its organization takes a de-centered post-modern form. Among those theorists, and most are French, who have described that form, some of the most important are:

Claude Levi-Strauss (1966) who calls the form a 'bricolage', a construction with a certain integrity whose elements have not been designed in advance to function with each other as a system. Jean-Francois Lyotard (1984) employs the metaphor of an 'archipelago', a formation of heterogeneous discourses with attenuated conceptual links between them. Gilles Deluze (1985) utilizes the term 'nomadic', a moving from one island to another, never at home. In a similar way, Jacques Derrida (1981) applies the term 'empirical wandering'. Michel Foucault (1972) grasps the form with the phrase 'discursive formation', a diverse spacio-temporally bounded articulation that addresses related questions and problematics. Finally, and there are others, Michel Maffesoli (1986) posits an 'aesthetic paradigm', one that is relatively autonomous from the state and its 'political paradigm' (akin to behavioralism). The aesthetic paradigm reveals diverse expressions of contemporary society. What these theorists have in common is that they attempted to give a form to the unsystematic. Metal studies is, in this analysis, an exemplar of the postmodern intellectual phenomena of which these theorists of decentered structures point to.

Critique and Suggestions

Let me briefly apply one of those concepts of organizational form to metal studies—Lyotard's archipelago, for example—to address some of the problems I see with metal studies as it is presently constituted and to offer solutions or some way out of the dilemma as I see it. That is, some of the islands of the archipelago that are metal studies are disciplinary ones; others erupt from concerns that have often gelled into other academic studies movements, like religious studies and gender studies. Given the heterogeneity of these islands of discourse, is there intelligibility across the archipelago?

There seems to be a Scylla-and-Charybdis set of dangerous choices for metal studies: should it be comprised of ghettoized works, fully insular, confined to single islands of defining concepts, methods, and/or practices? Or, should the works be so very general that they are not academic, that they are too general to be taken seriously? Changing metaphors to employ the physical distinction between centripetal and centrifugal forces, our aim should be to hang between a self-imposed orthodoxy or insularity, and a formless dispersion of discourse that is purely nominal. What I'm advocating here is an unforced mediation that creates a postmodern community, one that is not based on some doctrine, agenda, or paradigm. We have a common interest only in that we are all studying something called metal. How can we contain dispersal without imposing an orthodoxy?

To begin with, we need to accept that some works will be intelligible to all practitioners, and others only to one or another specialized subgroup. Yet it seems to me that the accessibility of the most insular material, confined to a single island of defined concepts, methods, and/or practices, can be facilitated by having introductory remarks on the various, more arcane aspects that would make the general ideas intelligible and would teach the rest of us about that island's intellectual culture. For example, metal musicologists have written in both ways. Some of their works are quite insular, unintelligible to those without training in music. But others have been written in ways that are both sophisticated in that field and provide those without any experience in it a way of appreciating the analysis. Synthesizing specialized and general interests is easier to do at a metal conference and perhaps in journals devoted to metal, than it is in a disciplinary musicology journal. Then there is the issue of the profusion of new material, an embarrassment of riches that no one can be expected to contain in his or her own stock of knowledge. Shouldn't we have some of these works in common? I don't mean old works from the last century, which are overly cited, in some cases ritualistically without comprehension or having read them, but the material that has been recently published.

I have some suggestions: each year one new work is selected absolutely arbitrarily, as randomly as possible, by some designated person(s), an article published on metal in any academic journal. Each of us would commit ourselves to read it and perhaps to comment on it on some blog, cite it in something we are writing, or minimally know that other eggheadbangers are familiar with it. Second, as we vet chapters, books, or even conference papers, as reviewers and editors, we should include someone from another discipline to comment on or review it.

Another problem with metal studies today is that it is under-theorized and under-methodologized. This defect can be ameliorated by academic advisors, colleagues, and reviewers of articles and books prior to publication. A related problem is that although there are several ethnographic studies of particular bands, fan groups, and scenes, there is little comparative study of the ethnographic data to extract generalizations for theory building. Awareness of the need for grounded generalizations, particularly by editors and conference organizers, would go a long way to encouraging comparative studies. Still another current flaw involves, and let me again use the Lyotardian archipelago model, the fact that some islands have become overpopulated while others are still submerged below the water's surface. Here too, some communication, in calls for papers by editors of journals or books of essays or conference organizers would be useful.

Metal Studies from the start has always been international, but language too is a problem. Many are able to write in metal's *lingua franca*, English. But what of all those who for various reasons confine themselves to a non-English language, such as when publishing in a journal in their national language? How would others even know that this work exists? The French *Volume!* has a great model, but getting material translated cannot be expected everywhere. When materials are published *not-in-English*, a summary in English should be made by the author, with the help of a person or a more-than decent computer program, and posted centrally. (I'd love to see an Encyclopedia Metallicum for Metal Studies where each author puts at least the bibliography, some keywords, and abstract in English, for all metal-related publications and conference papers.)

The prospect that metal studies will close itself into a theoretical-methodological doctrine need hardly be taken seriously. The field is already far too intellectually decentered and has too many creative sites for that to happen. Dispersion is the greater threat, and we need to devise ways in which to stay conversant with one another in unforced ways. Metal studies without an intellectual community would be a substanceless form.

We are now at a high point. Let's keep it there.

Notes

1. This chapter is a revised version of my keynote address given at the *Heavy Metal et Sciences Sociales* conference in Angers, France, in December 2014. There I was asked by Gérôme Guibert, the conference organizer, to assess metal studies from the perspective of a sociologist.
2. Editor's note: Deena Weinstein was a metal expert advisor and interviewee in the investigative documentary: *Metal: A Headbanger's Journey* (2005) and the cable channel series, *Metal Evolution* (2011).
3. For a discussion of the relationship of the counterculture to the development of heavy metal, see Weinstein (2015).

Bibliography

Bashe, P. (1985). *Heavy metal thunder: The music, its history, its heroes*. Garden City, NY: Dolphin.

Brown, A. R. (2011). Heavy genealogy: Mapping the currents, contraflows and conflicts of the emergent field of metal studies 1978–2010. *Journal for Cultural Research*, 15(3), 213–242.

Deluze, G. (1985). Nomad thought. In D. B. Allison (Ed.), *The new Nietzsche: Contemporary styles of Interpretation*. Cambridge, MA: The MIT Press.

Derrida, J. (1981[1967]). Implications: Interview with Henri Ronse (Alan Bass, Trans.). In *Jacques Derrida, Positions* (pp. 1–14). Chicago: University of Chicago Press.

Foucault, M. (1972). *Archeology of knowledge*. New York: Harper.

Guibert, G., and Hein, F. (2006). 'Prèsentation', 'Les Scènes Metal: Sciences Sociales et Pratiques Culturelles Radicales'. *Volume!*, 5 (2), 5–18.

Guibert, G., & Sklower, J. (2013). Dancing with the devil: Panorama des "metal studies". *La Vie des Idees*, http://laviedesidees.fr/Dancing-with-the-Devil.html (accessed November 5, 2014).

Harrigan, B., & Dome, M. (1980). *Encyclopedia Metallica: The bible of heavy metal*. London: Bobcat.

Hickman, B. (2015). Amalgamated anecdotes: Perspectives on the history of metal music and culture studies. *Metal Music Studies*, 1(1), 5–23.

Jasper, T., & Oliver, D. (1983). *The international encyclopedia of hard rock & heavy metal*. New York: Facts on File Publications.

Levi-Strauss, C. (1966). *The savage mind*. Chicago, IL: The University of Chicago Press.

Lyotard, J.-F. (1984). *Driftworks*. New York: Semiotext(e).

Maffesoli, M. (1986). Le Paradigme esthétique. In P. Watier (Ed.), *Georg Simmel: la sociologie et l'expérience du monde modern* (pp. 103–119). Paris: Méridiens Klincksieck.

Moynihan, M., & Søderlind, D. (1998). *Lords of chaos: The bloody rise of the satanic metal underground*. Venice, CA: Feral House.

Spracklen, K., Brown, A. R., and Kahn-Harris, K. (Eds.). (2011). Metal studies? Cultural research in the heavy metal scene [Special issue]. *Journal for Cultural Research*, 15(3), 209–212.

Straw, W. (1984). Characterizing rock music culture: The case of heavy metal. *Canadian University Music Review*, vol. 5, 104–122.

Weinstein, D. (1989). Talk this way. *R.A.W.*, no. 12(February 8–21), 4.

Weinstein, D. (1991). *Heavy metal: A cultural sociology*. New York: Macmillan/Lexington.

Weinstein, D. (2014). Birmingham's post-industrial metal. In B. Lashua, K. Spracklen, & S. Wagg (Eds.), *Sounds and the city: Popular music, place and globalization* (pp. 38–54). Houndmills: Palgrave Macmillan.

Weinstein, D. (2015), *Rock 'n America: A social and cultural history*. New York: Macmillan/Lexington.

Part I
Metal Musicology

3 Iron and Steel
Forging Heavy Metal's Song Structures or the Impact of Black Sabbath and Judas Priest on Metal's Musical Language

Dietmar Elflein

To refer to the idea of a specific musical language of heavy metal implies that this particular style of music differs from other styles and/or genres of popular music on a level open to musicological analysis.[1] Regarding a possible musical language of heavy metal, the available musicological literature focuses on tonal relationships as the principle object of study. The monographs of Walser (1993) and Berger (1999) are outstanding contributions in this respect, both finding the use of power chords, modes, chromatics, and augmented fourths to be characteristic of heavy metal music. These findings distinguish heavy metal musically from a more blues-based hard rock music. But both genres share the same ancestors and are closely related. According to Weinstein (2000) and Christie (2003), the formalization of heavy metal started when it detached itself from British blues and progressive rock—and American psychedelic rock—at the beginning of the 1970s. The genre crystallized 10 years later, via the NWOBHM, and then began the progressive stylistic differentiation that, today, is still evolving to the extent that a globalized genre is forming. Therefore, I will join Weinstein (2000, pp. 6–8) and Alan Moore (2001, p. 148) in assuming a stylistic continuum between hard rock and heavy metal.

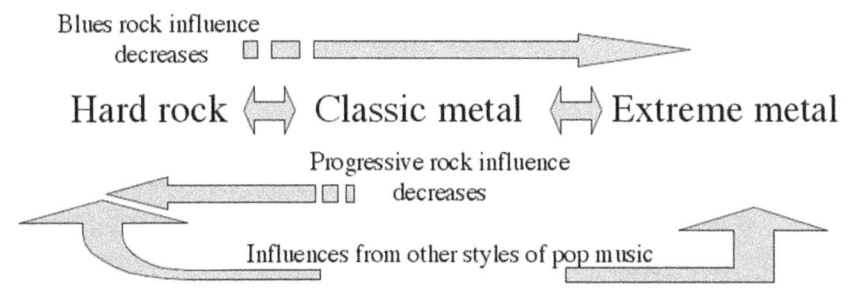

Figure 3.1 The Hard Rock–Metal Continuum.

As far as sound is concerned, the idea of a continuum helps, too. The available literature predominantly associates a distorted electric guitar sound with hard rock and heavy metal (see Walser, 1993, pp. 41–44). On the way toward extreme metal, the degree of distortion increases (see Berger and Fales 2005, p. 195) and supplements the guitar sound with distorted bass and screamed and/or growled vocals. Distorted drum sounds are few and commonly labeled as an industrial/electronic musical influence.[2] The tone color of the bass is, however, relatively unimportant, while the timbre of the vocals is so strongly differentiated within various sub-genres that there is no such thing as a timbre typical to heavy metal as a whole (Elflein, 2010, p. 305). At the same time, the use of vocals in heavy metal seems to be influenced by a regard for the virtuosic control of the voice (Berger, 2004, pp. 49–60), which can culminate in long, drawn-out screams, like the ones of Rob Halford, or in a virtuoso switch between contrasting timbres in more recent metal variations, such as metal core. Berger (2004, p. 58) differentiates this heavy metal style of voice control from a more blues-based expressive control of the voice exemplified, according to Berger, by Bruce Springsteen. I argue with Walser (1993, p. 14) that ensemble virtuosity is important to heavy metal music. Furthermore, I argue that Berger's virtuosic control of the voice in heavy metal could be used as a means to describe and analyze the formal structure of the compositions. Therefore, every little part of the composition is fixed and a matter of exact reproduction—with the exception of a few (guitar) solos. To underline my argument I will concentrate in the following on song structures by structurally analyzing and comparing several songs of the Birmingham-based metal pioneers, Black Sabbath and Judas Priest. Black Sabbath has a blues-rock background, while Judas Priest uses more progressive rock influences in their beginning. Both bands move to the metal side of the continuum cited above while bands like Led Zeppelin or Deep Purple stay on the hard rock side of the continuum.[3] By doing so, I don't argue that Black Sabbath and Judas Priest are personal innovators. In fact a lot of other bands on the psychedelic and blues-rock circuit worked on similar ideas simultaneously or even before Black Sabbath and Judas Priest. Therefore, both bands serve as good examples within the continuously flowing stream of the tradition of Heavy Metal music, because they happen to be amongst the most successful heavy metal bands of their particular era.

Song Structures in Popular Music

To talk about specific metal song structures means to argue that they differ from other song structures in popular rock music styles. It is necessary to distinguish between structures that string together structural units and periodic structures. The former could be an endless repetition of a blues structure. For example, a funk track like James Brown's 'Papa's Got a Brand New Bag', which starts with an alternation between two parts A and B (with A being a 12 bar blues structure) and stays with part B in the entire second half of the track or with a more recent electronic dance music track. Regarding periodic structures Moore (2001) identifies the "introduction, two verses, break, verse, playout" formula common to pop since the beat era' (p. 150). This structure adds an introduction and a playout to the 32 bar AABA structure of classic American Tin Pan Alley songs (Forte, 2001) with the verse fitting A and the break fitting B of the AABA structure. Terminological problems begin here, though, as the 32-bar AABA structure is commonly labeled a refrain and preceded by a single verse that differs from Moore's verse. Unfortunately, there is no such thing as a distinctive terminology regarding song structures in popular music.[4] Ken Stephenson (2002, pp. 121–143) deduced the verse-chorus structure from the Tin Pan Alley Song, with the A of the 32-bar AABA structure divided into verse and chorus while B mutates to the bridge.[5] An additional part, between verse and chorus, is commonly labeled a pre-chorus because it leads emotionally and musically to the chorus. In addition, recent commercial pop song writing thinks in terms of hooks. Pre-chorus and chorus are regarded as two hooks with unchangeable lyrics, which are supplemented by a verse with alterable lyrics (see Fitzgerald, 2007, pp. 121–122; Peterik, Austin, and Lynne, 2010, pp. 73–90).

Table 3.1 The Standard Rock Song Structure

	Structural Unit					*Source*
(Verse)	A	A	B	A		Tin Pan Alley
Introduction (I)	Verse (V)	V	Break (B)	V	Playout	Moore
I	V	Chorus (C)	V C	Bridge (B)	C C (optional)	
I	V Pre-chorus (p)	C	V p C	B	(p) C C (optional)	Stephenson
I	A	A	B	A' (optional)		Elflein
I	V Hook 1 (H1)	Hook 2 (H2)	V, H1, H2	(optional)	H1 H2 (optional)	Pop-Song

I'd like to call the highlighted structure of table. 3.1, the standard rock song structure. An introduction is followed by a main part A, which is repeated once. Then something new is happening, a contrasting part B. Finally, the standard rock song returns to a modified A built out of a selection of the already known verse, pre-chorus, and chorus parts, which are sometimes modified (e.g., vocal line of the chorus plus verse accompaniment) or mixed with new musical ideas.

Regarding the two bands in question, early Black Sabbath tends to avoid both verse-chorus structures and the clichés of the standard rock song, although these features became more prominent with the release of the third album, *Master of Reality* (1971). In contrast, Judas Priest uses both formulas throughout its career but varies them in distinctive ways. The break-through album *British Steel* (1980) abandons the more complex song structures identified with progressive rock and present on the band's earlier releases, in favor of a formal reduction of complexity, which seems to accompany or underline the change of image from hippy/psychedelia to the spikes and leather costumes now identified as one of the archetypical heavy-metal looks. Therefore, both bands learn to consciously work with rock/pop song formulas as a matter of becoming more professional and experienced musicians.

Heavy Metal Song Structures

As a musical style, heavy metal is based around riffs rather than chord progressions. Richard Middleton (1999) defines riffs as 'short rhythmic, melodic or harmonic figures repeated to form a structural framework' (p. 143). Therefore, the earlier-mentioned song structures stringing together structural units may play an important role in heavy metal song writing in addition to periodic structures. As a consequence, song structures are based on sequences of partly repeated guitar riffs.

In what follows, the formal structure of a number of song examples is presented analytically as a sequence of guitar riffs that form the microstructure of the song. The riffs are labeled in the order of their appearance a, b, c. ... A repetition of a riff is labeled with Arabic numbers, that is 2a = aa, 2ab = aab and 2(ab) = abab. Variations of riffs are indicated by superscript.[6] Since riffs differ in length, their length is measured as pulse length in order to make them comparable as structural units. If a = 8 pulses and b = 16 pulses, 2a has the same length as b. In order to simplify the resulting microstructure to a macrostructure, sequences of riffs get combined and labeled with capitals A, B, C. ... As a third analytic step, the vocal structure tries to convert the analyzed micro- and macrostructure into a periodic song structure using the following terminology: introduction (I), verse (V), pre-chorus (p), chorus (C), bridge (B), instrumental interlude (In), instrumental Solo (S), playout (Po) and short outro (O). In addition, Br indicates a harsh break between two structural units, such as a general pause.

Table 3.2 Example of a Formal Structure

Pulselength	Microstructure	Macrostructure	Vocalstructure
a = 8, b = 16,...	a 3bb^{2}Br 2(cd) ...	A B C ...	I VpC B ...

A verse is a succession of at least one riff accompanied by a vocal melody with lyrics. If only the lyrics change when the part is repeated, the structural part is again labeled a verse. If music and lyrics change the new part is labeled either pre-chorus, chorus or bridge. A chorus consists of a succession of riffs accompanying a vocal melody different from the verse with consistent lyrics while repeated. A pre-chorus is a third vocal part that follows a verse and is not a chorus. A bridge is a vocal part that follows a chorus and differs lyrically and musically from the verse.

Worship the Riff—Black Sabbath

The first song on the first record by Black Sabbath, the famous 'Black Sabbath' (1970), starts with the well-known 35 seconds of thunder and lightning later cited by Slayer's Jeff Hannemann for his 'Raining Blood' (1986) intro. The rest of the song sequences two riffs and one chord progression (labeled as riff c in the following chart as a matter of simplification).

Table 3.3 Song Structure 'Black Sabbath'. (1970)

Title	Pulselength	Microstructure	Macrostructure	Vocalstructure
Black Sabbath	6:19 $b = 12, c = 24$ $a = 32$	I 2(4a10a^2) 4a Br 20b 16c	I A A A^2 B C	I InV InV In In2 V2 S

The first riff highlights a dissonant tritone interval and starts with a power chord. It is alternated with a variation, riff a^2, that replaces the opening power chord with the single tonic. Riff a^2 is used as vocal accompaniment while the power chord version is employed as an interlude. Riff a is repeated four times (4a), riff a^2 ten times (10a^2), then the whole sequence gets repeated, which corresponds 2(4a10a^2) in the microstructure of table 3.3. The repetition is evocative of the verse repetition in the standard rock song formula. This sequence lasts about four minutes and ends in a general pause. Then the band moves to ternary time—a 12/8 beat—where the second riff b is played 20 times for about 40 seconds, which acts as a vocal accompaniment. The remaining last minute of the song is devoted to a guitar solo accompanied by a sequence of two alternating chords, labeled here as riff c. In total 'Black Sabbath' (1970) does not replicate a standard rock song structure, as the periodic closing of the structure within the play-out section does not occur. In addition, the song excises the typical 'verse-chorus' structure in favor of a sequence of verses. Therefore, the song's innovative potential in the development of heavy metal is its simple sequencing of riffs. The riffs are all centered around the tone g, to make the song more than an accidental sequencing of two hooks and a solo accompaniment. The implied tonal harmony around g is a means to achieve the goal of making a sequence of riffs a proper song.

As *Black Sabbath* (1970) is in many respects a musical model of the formal structures of early Black Sabbath songs, we can also see how such an innovative structure remained largely aesthetically unrecognized by most rock critics, such as Robert Christgau who dismissed it as 'the worst of the counterculture on a plastic platter' ([1970] 2003). Part of this judgment could have been provoked by Sabbath's decision not to employ standard rock song conventions or 12-bar blues structures or, indeed, more complex progressive rock-inspired structures. Black Sabbath's tendency to create harsh breaks between song parts in the sense of tempo, time signature, instrumentation, and sound, in spite of elegant transitions between parts, might also have had an impact on Christgau.[7] But if this judgment implies that Black Sabbath is unable to write proper songs, it misrecognizes the innovative potential of Black Sabbath's structural work.

Black Sabbath's structural work and its roots in blues structures beyond the 12-bar cliché becomes manifest in songs like 'War Pigs' (1970) or 'Iron Man' (1970), both part of the *Paranoid* album (1970).

Table 3.4 Black Sabbath's 'War Pigs' (1970) and 'Iron Man' (1970)

Title		Pulselength	Microstructure	Macrostr.	Vocalstructure
War Pigs	7:56	d,e,g,i,j = 8 a² = 12 b,c,h = 16 a,f = 24 i², k = 32	3a2a² 10b4c 2(4d8e) 4c f12gf2h 10b4c i2i²4i2i³2i⁴2j2k2k²2k 5i	A B C B² D B E	I VIn 2(In2V2) In In3S In3In4 VIn Po
Iron Man	5:56	d²,e,f = 16 a² = 24 a,b,c,g = 32 d = 64	I 2aa² 2b2b² b2b² 3c 2(2b2b² 2d) 2e8f2e4d² 2b2b² 3c Br 2a 8g	A B B² C B D B D E B C A F	I InV InV In2 2(InV V2In3) In4SIn4 In3 InVIn2 In5 Po

The microstructure of the anti-Vietnam war anthem 'War Pigs' (1970) shows that five different riffs (a to e) are sequenced before the first riff (c) gets repeated. Three more riffs (f to h) are added until two riffs, b and again c, are repeated, while the closing part of the song adds three more riffs (i to k) including variants of the first riff. Therefore, the macrostructure shows that part B is always contrasted with new material, so the overall sequence is: Intro A and then B C, B D, B E, with B being the anchor of the song. Like in 'Black Sabbath' (1970) there is neither a chorus nor a standard rock song structure. The structure of 'Iron Man' (1970) is similarly centered around such an anchor—again part B of the Macrostructure—but adds less new riffs in total.[8]

Contrasting a main riff with several new musical ideas is a blues-derived idea of song writing, stemming from the Mississippi Delta and Chicago Blues players like R. L. Burnside and John Lee Hooker (Palmer, 1982). The title song of Black Sabbath's second album, 'Paranoid' (1970), shows the idea of contrasting a main riff with different material in a very reduced form, contrasting riff b with riffs c and d in the microstructural perspective. Led Zeppelin tends to work also in this way in their riff-based songs, e.g., 'Misty Mountain Hop' (1971).

Table 3.5 Song Structures: Black Sabbath 'Paranoid' (1970), Led Zeppelin 'Misty Mountain Hop' (1971)

Title		Pulselength	Microstructure	Macrostr.	Vocalstr.
Paranoid	2:49	a = 16 b,c,d = 32	4a 2b2c 2b2d 10b 2b2c 4b	A B B² B³ B B³	I VIn VV2 In2V SIn2 VIn VIn2
Misty Mountain Hop	4:39	a = 8 c = 16 b = 32	4a²4a 2(b4ab4ac2ac6a) b4ab4ac2ac 8a³c2ac6a b4ab4ac2ac 24a	A B B B B² B A²	I VCIn VCIn VC SIn VC Po

Table 3.5 shows on the microstructural level that Jimmy Page alternates the main riff a with riffs b and c. Unlike Black Sabbath, Led Zeppelin uses the main riff as purely instrumental, while riffs b and c are accompanied by vocals. Therefore, a verse-chorus structure develops with riff b accompanying a verse and riff c a kind of chorus, while Black Sabbath uses the main riff with and without vocal accompaniment and also as a backing for the guitar solo (e.g., in Part B^3 of the macrostructure). Also, unlike Black Sabbath, Led Zeppelin normally tends to restrict the number of riffs per song, while the reduced structure of 'Paranoid' is somewhat of an exception in Black Sabbath's work. In addition, Led Zeppelin rarely uses exclusive material in the intro section like Black Sabbath does in 'War Pigs' (1970) and 'Paranoid' (1970). The intro of 'Paranoid' (1970) serves also as the first and main hook of the song.

If we return to the song structure of 'Iron Man' (1970) as shown in table 3.4, another structurally typical Black Sabbath idea is to return to the intro section after sequencing and/or contrasting several riffs. In the case of 'Iron Man' (1970), Black Sabbath moves on to the play out section G after repeating the intro A. Such a song-writing practice could be labeled a repeated or false start, as other examples, like 'Lord of this World' (1971), show that revisiting the intro section serves as a starting point to repeat several other song parts. This 'false start' has become a standard of heavy metal song writing, for example 'Exciter' (1978) by Judas Priest, as well as 'Seek and Destroy' (1983) by Metallica. In addition, heavy metal intro sections tend to consist of exclusive musical material that is not used in other parts of the song, such as the intro hook of 'Paranoid' versus the hard rock introduction of 'Misty Mountain Hop', which is the main riff of the entire song.

If we generalize this song writing idea to: let's sequence a potentially endless number of riffs or musical ideas and then repeat something already known to make it a song, this compositional idea is even more common, especially in thrash and extreme metal songs. For example, Megadeth's 'Wake Up Dead' (1986) repeats not a single musical idea, but the re-entry of the voice at the end of the song takes the part of making this particular sequence of riffs a song. Guitarist and song-writer Michael Amott reflects on this mode of composition in an interview to promote the 2011 Arch Enemy album release:

> Some of my favorite bands like Mercyful Fate and Death had unconventional song structures with some cool riffs seeming to appear from nowhere. The riffs had nothing to do with the rest of the song. When I rehearsed the old Carcass material I realized that some songs had eighteen different riffs and none of these gets repeated within the song structure [laughs].
>
> (Bittner, 2011, p. 54)

The sequencing of riffs and the harsh breaks between parts merges, especially in Black Sabbath's *Sabbath Bloody Sabbath* album (1973), into what I call *dual song structures*. The roots of these dual structures can

42 Dietmar Elflein

Table 3.6 Dual Song Structures: 'Sabbath Bloody Sabbath', 'A National Acrobat', 'Sabra Cadabra', 'Killing Yourself to Live' (all 1973)

Title		Pulselength	Microstructure	Macrostr.	Vocalstr.
Sabbath Bloody Sabbath	5:44	f = 8 d,e = 16 a,b,c = 32 b^3 = 48	6a3bb^2 6a3bb^3 5a2c Br 2(10d3cBr) 2?f	A A A^2 B B C	IVC InVC SIn2 2(InV2In3) Po
A National Acrobat	6:16	i = 8 e,g,h = 16 a,b,c,d,f = 32 j = 40	2a 2abab 2(ac) 2abab 2(ac) 22d 3ec^{2}2ff^{2}f4g 4h8ij	A B A B C D	I InV InV2 InV InV2 2(InV3) SV3 Po
Sabra Cadabra	5:56	f^2 = 8 d,f = 16 a,b,c,e = 32	4a2a^2 2(2b2b^{2}cbc) 14d2e4f 12d2e 36f12f^2	A B B C C D	I InV1V2 InV1V2 In2V3V4In3 In2V3V4 Po
Killing Yourself to Live	5:40	h = 8 b,d,e,i = 16 a,c,f = 32 g = 96	4a 2(6b2c) 8c 8d2e2f3d^2 g 15hh^{2}3hh^2 11hh^{2}3hh^2 19hh^{2}3hh^2 4i	A B B B^2 C D E	I 2(InVC) SV2 In3In4V3In3 S In5V4In5V4S

be traced back to the sudden move from riff a to b in the song 'Black Sabbath' (1970).

Songs with dual structures can be composed with or without an intro section.[9] Here, all four examples employ two main parts comprised of exclusive musical material. In fact, the first main section of the song is finished and forgotten when the second main part of the dual structure starts. On the macro structural level the second main part of 'Sabbath Bloody Sabbath' (1973) starts with section B, while the remaining three examples start the second main part with section C. No musical idea stemming from the first main part is revisited in the second main part. In addition, the break between the two main parts is often harsh, so the idea comes to mind that dual structures evolve out of an emancipation of the break part, making an AABA structure an AABB structure. But both main parts follow the standard rock song idea of repeating the verse before something new happens. Therefore, I prefer to call them dual structures. However, the songs in table3.6 differ regarding the exact point of change between the two main sections. The harsh break within 'A National Acrobat' (1973) and 'Sabra Cadabra' (1973) occurs after one-third of the song's total running time, while 'Killing Yourself to Live' (1973) changes circa the middle and 'Sabbath Bloody Sabbath' (1973) within the second half of the song.

Dual structures are also prominent in thrash and extreme metal. Table 3.7 shows examples of dual-structured songs by Megadeth, Slayer, and Metallica. The macrostructure shows that, similar to the Black Sabbath examples, both main parts of the dual structure are repeated once. Dual structures are therefore part of Black Sabbath's huge influence on metal music.[10]

Table 3.7 Dual Song Structures: Megadeth: 'Peace Sells' (1986), Slayer: 'Postmortem' (1986), Metallica: 'Fade to Black' (1984)

Title		Pulselength	Microstructure	Macrostr.	Vocalstr.
Peace Sells	4:03	$a,d^2,e,f,g = 16$ $b,d,f^2 = 32$ $c = 48$	4a 4bc 5bc 2de 3(d^2e) Br 2f2$f^2$20f 3(gf)g	A B B^2 C D D E	I VC VC In1S In2C2 S C2 S
Post-mortem	3:27	$b = 8$ $e,f,g = 32$ $a,c,d = 64$	2aba2b 4c2d 2c$c^2$2d 2aba2b 2(2e2e^2)2e^2 Br 2f2(2f2g) O	A B B A C D D	I InVCInVC I In2 V2In3 V2In3
Fade to Black	6:57	$b = 16$ $a,c,e = 32$ $d,f = 64$	I 5ab 8c2d 6c2d 4e2$e^2$2e 2$e^3$8f	I A B B C C D	I1 I2 InVIn2 SVIn2 In3V2 In3V2 In4S

Worship the Bridge—Judas Priest

While Black Sabbath's innovative potential is based on the band's avoidance of common song structures during the 'Ozzy era', Judas Priest modifies these common verse-chorus structures in certain ways to apply them to the band's preferred form of heavy metal, in that a three-part 'verse-pre-chorus-chorus' structure dominates the band's work following its image move to black leather and spikes in the late 1970s. The band logo also changed its look to a more metal-like design as a part of this image move. Regarding sound, Judas Priest develops or perfects its highly influential 'twin guitar' sound during this period while also reducing the more elaborate vocal style of Rob Halford, (e.g., the multi-track edits to be heard on 'The Ripper', 1977), to a more homogenous style of production.

Producer Kevin Shirley describes the heavy metal guitar sound that Priest develops in this period, in an interview that is part of the documentary *Heavy Metal: Louder Than Life* (Carruthers, 2007):

> There's the rumble that carries the heaviness along, and there's this really brittle top end, which has got the definition, and the really good metal stuff combines that definition with the rumbles. [...] So you have this scooped sound on the guitars, where the middle is kind of taken out and you have the bottom and the top, as opposed to the Jimmy Page guitars, the mid-range. [...] There's not a lot of bottom and not a lot of super-highs. Metal guitar really has got a sound of it's own. (transcription: D.E.)

In terms of song structure, lengthy sequencing is prominent on the preceding *Sad Wings of Destiny* (1976) and *Sin after Sin* (1977) albums, while the songs of *Stained Class* (1978), the first album promoting the new logo and image, employ riff sequencing structures as well as verse-chorus structures. The following studio albums, *Killing Machine* (1978) and especially *British Steel* (1980), are dominated by simple verse-chorus structures. Table 3.8 shows examples from these albums to underline the argument of structural simplification in order to draw attention to image and sound.

44 *Dietmar Elflein*

Table 3.8 Song Structures Judas Priest: 'Tyrant' (1976), 'Stained Class' (1978), 'Steeler' (1980), 'Breakin' the Law' (1980), 'Metal Gods' (1980)

Title		Pulselength	Microstructure	Macrostr.	Vocalstr.
Tyrant	4:28	k = 8 d,g,h,l = 16 a,b,c,e,f,i = 32 m,n,o = 32 e^2, f^3 = 48 j = 64	a 2(2a 2b2cd) cc²ff²ff³ 3g4g³4gh 2b2cd ij8kl2klmn ff²ff³ 2b2cO	A B A B C D B E C B²	IVC IVC InB S VC In2 S B VC O
Stained Class	5:19	b^3, b^4, b^5 = 8 f^3, f^4 = 8 b,c,e,f^2,i = 16 a = 32 g^2 = 48 d^2,h = 56 d,g = 64	2a Br 2($3bb^27cc^2dd^2$) 2cfgg²f²h Br 6b³4b⁴3b⁵ 3cc²dd² 2c4f³4f⁴3i	A B B C D B² E	I InVC InVC In2BIn3 S VC In2Po
Steeler	4:30	c,e = 16 a,b = 32 d = 64	4a 2(4a2b)$2b^2$ 6cBr2dd²d 4a2b Br 36c	A B B C B D	I VIn Vin S In2V2 VIn Po(S)
Breakin' the Law	2:35	e = 16 a,b,c,d,f = 32	2a 2($2bcc^22d$) 4c2f 2a6a²	A B B C A²	I VC VC B Po
Metal Gods	4:00	a,b,c = 32	I a 2(2a2b) 2c2b²2c 2a2b 2b4b³	I A A B A C	I Vp Vp CSC Vp Po

'Tyrant' (*Sad Wings of Destiny,* 1976) is an example of a sequencing structure in the old progressive rock influenced style. Fourteen different guitar riffs are used in the composition. Tyrant shows a tricky structure that implies either a long break section form C to C or two break sections (C, D and E, C) in the macrostructure because there's a normal verse-chorus progression between the two break sections. By contrast, the formal structure of 'Stained Class' (1978) is already more formulaic. Complexity is now confined to expanding the break section with a sequence of new riffs as well as using at least three riffs for verse and chorus. In comparison, the three examples from British Steel (1980) reveal a radical formal reduction: a possible break section is reduced to being only that: a break. To make the point clear: only three songs on *British Steel* work without an explicit chorus, but even these are still standard rock songs in the Moore sense, e.g., 'Steeler' (1980). Five songs employ verse-chorus structures, and one song, 'Metal Gods' (1980), shows that the B-part of an AABA structure can also be used as a chorus. Three songs, including 'Breakin' the Law' (1980), remove the guitar solo in favor of the straight verse-chorus structure.

It seems likely that the simplification of the song structures we have noted and the image shift of Judas Priest, go hand in hand. This combination of image and simplified musical structure seems to be key to the strategies of heavy metal's more 'theatrical' bands: If your songs don't fit metal structures, e.g., because of commercial reasons or because complex songs would disturb the spectators' concentration on the show, you need to metallize your image, or at least you need to have an over-the-top-image, like Kiss, Gwar, Lordi, or the entire Glam metal genre, even some black metal bands, following on from Venom. One could argue that the wish to write songs with increased commercial potential or reduced musical virtuosity has to be compensated by an increase in controversial imagery in order to retain a core heavy metal audience.

But Judas Priest continues to view itself as a metal band, musically. Therefore, in the years following the success of the new image, which according to K. K. Downing lasts until the end of the British Steel tours, Priest re-metallizes song structures by returning to the 'Stained Class' (1978) formula: a complex bridge or break section and a three part verse-chorus section with either an instrumental interlude or a pre-chorus being the third part of the section. The bridge section becomes the main part where complexity, the sequencing of riffs, is revived, while the bridge section can evolve into a miniature song-within-a-song. A prominent example is 'Freewheel Burning' (1984) from the *Defenders of the Faith* album.

Table 3.9 Song Structures Judas Priest: 'Freewheel Burning' (1984), Iron Maiden 'Where Eagles Dare' (1983), Metallica 'Phantom Lord' (1983), Slayer 'Angel of Death' (1986)

Title	Pulselength	Microstructure	Macrostr.	Vocalstr.
Free-wheel Burning	4:22	$m = 12\ g^3 = 24$ $a,b,c = 16$ $d,f,g = 32$ $h^2,i,l = 32$ $e^2 = 48\ h = 56$ $e,j,k = 64$	4a4b $2(2c2c^22b)\ dd^2eBr$ $2(2c2c^22b)\ dd^2e$ $2ff^2f^3\ gg^2g^3\ h$ $2i4i^22j2kl\ gg^2g^3\ h^2h$ $3ee^24m\ O$	A B C B C D E F E C^2	I 2(VIn)pC 2(VIn)pC In2 B S B C O
Where Eagles Dare	6:10	$a,f = 16,$ $a^2,b,c,e = 32$ $d = 64$	I4ab2a 2(2a^{2}2c) $2dd^2d^3$ 10e 4f2f^{2}2f $2dd^2d^3$ 4ab 2(2a^{2}2c) 4ab O	I A B B C D E C A^2 B B A^2	I1 I2 VCVC In1SIn2In1 I2 VCVC I2
Phantom Lord	5:01	$d,e = 8, a = 12$ $b,c,f,g = 16$ $h = 32$	I 5a4a^2 2b 2(4bc2bc2b8dBr) 2(4e4e^2)Br 8f4gBr 4hBr 2bc2bc2b12d O	I A B B^2 C D E B^3 O	I VCVC S1 In S2 VC Po
Angel of Death	4:51	$c,d^2,e^3,f = 16$ $a,b,d,e,g = 32$	6aBr 4b4c2a 4b4a Br 5dd^2 3ee^{2}fe^{3}f 2(ee^4)ee^{2}fe^{3}f 3dd^2 g4c4c^{2}2c2c^{2}4cBr 4a	A B B^2 C D C^2 E B^3	I InVpC VC In2 V2 In3 V2 In2 S C

The verse-chorus section of 'Freewheel Burning' (1984) consists of the four riffs c, b, d, and e including pre-chorus (d) and interlude (b) on the vocal-structural level while the break section presents seven new riffs (f to l) within a vocal-structure of interlude/bridge/solo and return of the bridge.

The break section turns out to be almost a little song of its own that lasts 1:50 minutes with the song clocking in at 4:22 minutes in total. Therefore, the break section covers 42% of the whole song's length—a lot more than the 25% of a middle eight section within the AABA structure.

A lot of heavy metal bands use song structures similar to Judas Priest's metal song formula. For example, Iron Maiden's 'Where Eagles Dare' (1983) employs a four-part break section with a length of 3:10 minutes, which is more than half of the entire song's length (6:10). In addition, Iron Maiden tends to construct the break section even more complexly than Judas Priest and tends to do this purely instrumentally, while Judas Priest mixes vocal and instrumental parts. Metallica uses a complex break section, e.g., in 'Phantom Lord' (1983) (see table 3:9), 'Ride the Lightning' (1984)', and 'Master of Puppets' (1986). The verse-chorus construction of Phantom Lord uses an instrumental main riff and two contrasting riffs with vocal accompaniment, a possible reminiscence of Led Zeppelin song structures, such as 'Misty Mountain Hop'. Slayer, on the other hand, normally tends to sequence riffs, but especially 'Angel of Death' (1986) could be read as relevant to the band's history as a Judas Priest cover band because of the obvious verse-chorus structure completed by a complex break-section, consisting of three instrumental and two vocal parts (op. cit.).

Table 3.10 Song Structure Judas Priest: 'Painkiller' (1990)

Title		Pulselength	Microstructure	Macrostr.	Vocalstr.
Pain-killer	6:07	$d = 8$	I 2a 2(4a2b)	A B B C D	I VCVC
		a,b,c,e = 16	$4a^22c2c^22dd^2d^3$ Br	B C^2 E	InBIn2 S
		f,h,i = 16	$2c4f3gg^24a^3$		VC InIn2
		g = 32	4a4b $2a^22dd^2d^3$		Po
			$8a^43hib^2$		

Judas Priest's *Painkiller* album (1990) is commonly regarded as the band's return to former strengths and heavy metal roots. The title song of the album announces this with a double-bass kick-drum intro followed by continuous double-bass drumming, tempo, and time-signature changes, as wells as Rob Halford's typical high-pitched screams. However, in terms of song structure, 'Painkiller' (1990) is a synthesis of the Judas Priest examples analyzed above. Verse and chorus show the *British Steel* (1980) like reduction of complexity while the break section is explicitly extended according to the *Stained Class* (1978) rules (C and D of the macrostructure). Like in 'Tyrant' (1976) there is a second break section consisting of the repetition of a shortened version of section C leaving out riff c in the microstructure. This second break-section follows the third verse and chorus and precedes the final play-out section. Therefore, the song structure is shouting 'we play metal!'

Conclusion

Both bands in question, Judas Priest and Black Sabbath, establish song structures that evolve into heavy metal clichés. They are an inspiration to countless heavy metal bands of different sub genres and decades. The song examples I have analyzed draw attention to the centrality of sequences of guitar riffs to that style. Therefore, the false start, dual structures, and extended break section are part of a possible musical language of heavy metal that is rooted in blues structures beyond the 12-bar cliché. The extended break section is also reminiscent of progressive rock's preferred more complex and neo-classical/art-music structures. Both blues-rock and progressive rock are historical forerunners of heavy metal. Therefore, if we argue about a possible musical language of heavy metal, song structures are an important part of its grammar. But song structures are only one argument in such a discussion. Similar song structures can potentially be found in other genres of popular music as well. Therefore we need to add timbre (distortion), volume (produced to evoke the 'play it loud' mythology), harmony (minor tonality or use of modes), and especially rhythm (pulse-based playing styles) to the song structures to talk about a comprehensive musical language of heavy metal. If we hear consciously or unconsciously the majority of these features we might argue that we listen to heavy metal. If we hear only the minority of these features, we might argue about a song with certain heavy metal influences.

Notes

1. A second assumption should be that the music speech metaphor is a legitimate one to describe musical differences between styles and genres of popular music.
2. Distorted drum sounds evolve in electronic music genres with mostly synthesized drums. Bands with an industrial music background, like Ministry, combine distorted drums with distorted guitars.
3. See Elflein (2010) for analyses of Led Zeppelin and Deep Purple song structures.
4. See Kaiser (2010), Appen/von Hausschild (2012).
5. Besides these song structures songwriters make use of mostly blues derived sequencing in progressive rock, adaptations of high art music structures like suites, rondos and so on.
6. Whether a specific version of a riff is still a variation of an existing riff or a new musical idea may be a question for debate.
7. See, e.g., 'Sweet Leaf' (1971), 'Into the Void' (1971), 'Supernaut' (1972).
8. 'Damage Inc'. (1986) by Metallica and 'Hammer Smashed Face' (1992) by Cannibal Corpse are just two of many examples by other bands in heavy metal music structurally working that way.
9. 'Sabbath Bloody Sabbath' (1973) and 'A National Acrobat' (1973) lack intro sections while 'Sabra Cadabra' (1973) and 'Killing Yourself to Live' (1973) feature intro sections.
10. I'd like to add a brief comment on Black Sabbath song structures of the Dio era: They have learned their craft and are now experienced songwriters and

therefore rely mostly on common verse-chorus structures with citations of their 1970s formal innovations, e.g., a dual structure can be found in the title song of the *Heaven and Hell* album (1980), while *Children of the Sea* (1980) employs a variant of the repeated start. Thus, Black Sabbath of the Dio era is not formally innovative, but its members are better craftsmen, of course.

Bibliography

Appen, R. v., & Frei-Hauenschild, M. (2012). AABA, refrain, chorus, bridge, pre-Chorus—Songformen und ihre historische Entwicklung. In T. Phleps & D. Helms (Eds.), *Black box pop: Analysen populärer Musik* (pp. 57–124). Bielefeld: transcript.

Berger, H. M. (1999). *Metal, rock and jazz: Perception and the phenomenology of musical experience*. Hannover, London: Wesleyan University Press.

Berger, H. M. (2004). Horizons of melody and the problem of self. In H. Berger & G. P. Del Negro (Eds.), *Identity and everyday life* (pp. 43–88). Middletown: Wesleyan University Press.

Berger, H. M., & Fales, C. (2005). 'Heaviness' in the perception of heavy metal guitar timbres: The match of perceptual and acoustic features over time. In P. D. Greene & T. Porcello (Eds.), *Wired for sound* (pp. 181–197). Hanover, London: Wesleyan University Press.

Bittner, R. (2011). Arch enemy: Riffs aus dem Nichts. *Rock Hard, 288*, 54.

Carruthers, D. (2007). *Heavy metal–louder than life*. DVD, MMV metropolis group/Fremantle Media 06448753719.

Christgau, R. (2003). Black Sabbath: Consumer Guide reviews, http://www.robertchristgau.com/get_artist.php?name=Black+Sabbath (accessed August 1, 2014).

Christie, I. (2003). *Sound of the beast–the complete headbanging history of heavy metal*. New York: Harper Collins.

Elflein, D. (2010). *Schwermetallanalysen: Die musikalische Sprache des Heavy Metal* Bielefeld: transcript.

Fitzgerald, J. (2007). Black pop songwriting 1963–1966: An analysis of U.S. Top Forty hits by Cooke, Mayfield, Stevenson, Robinson, and Holland-Dozier-Holland. *Black Music Research Journal, 27/2*, 97–140.

Forte, A. (2001). Listening to classic American popular songs (+ CD) New Haven: Yale University Press.

Kahn-Harris, K. (2007). *Extreme metal: Music and culture on the edge*. Oxford, New York: Berg.

Kaiser, U. (2011). Babylonian confusion: Zur Terminologie der Formanalyse von Pop- und Rockmusik' in *Zeitschrift der Gesellschaft für Musiktheorie 8/1*, http://www.gmth.de/zeitschrift/artikel/588.aspx (accessed August 1, 2014).

Middleton, R. (1999). Form. In B. Horner and T. Swiss (Eds.), *Key terms in popular music and culture* (pp. 141–155). Malden, Oxford, Victoria: Blackwell.

Moore, A. F. (2001). *Rock: The primary text* 2nd ed. Aldershot: Ashgate.

Palmer, R. (1982). *Deep blues: A musical and cultural history of the Mississippi Delta*. New York: Penguin.

Peterik, J., Austin, D., & Lynn, C. (2010). *Songwriting for dummies* 2nd ed. Hoboken: Wiley.

Stephenson, Ken. (2002). *What to listen for in rock: A stylistic analysis*. New Haven: Yale University Press.

Walser, R. (1993), *Running with the devil: Power, gender and madness in heavy metal music.* Hanover, London: Wesleyan University Press.
Weinstein, D. (2000). *Heavy metal: A cultural sociology.* Cambridge, MA: Da Capo Press.

Discography

Black Sabbath. (1970). Black Sabbath. On *Black Sabbath.* Vertigo.
Black Sabbath. (1970). Iron Man, Paranoid, and War pigs. On *Paranoid.* Vertigo.
Black Sabbath. (1971). Into the void, Lord of this world, and Sweet leaf. On *Master of reality.* Vertigo.
Black Sabbath. (1972). Supernaut. On *Vol. 4.* Vertigo.
Black Sabbath. (1973). A national acrobat, Killing yourself to live, Sabbath bloody sabbath, & Sabra cadabra. On *Sabbath bloody sabbath.* Vertigo.
Black Sabbath. (1980). Children of the sea & Heaven and hell. On *Heaven and hell.* Vertigo.
Cannibal Corpse. (1992). Hammer smashed face. On *Tomb of the mutilated.* Metal Blade Records.
Iron Maiden. (1983). Where eagles dare. On *Piece of mind.* EMI.
Judas Priest. (1976). The ripper & Tyrant. On *Sad wings of destiny.* Gull Records.
Judas Priest. (1977). *Sin after sin.* CBS.
Judas Priest. (1978a). Exciter & Stained class. On *Stained class.* CBS.
Judas Priest. (1978b). *Killing machine.* CBS.
Judas Priest. (1980). Breakin' the law, Metal gods, & Steeler. On *British Steel.* CBS.
Judas Priest. (1984). Freewheel burning. On *Defenders of the faith.* CBS.
Judas Priest. (1990). Painkiller. On *Painkiller.* CBS.
Led Zeppelin. (1971). Misty mountain hop. On *Led Zeppelin IV.* Atlantic.
Megadeth. (1986). Peace sells & Wake up dead. On *Peace sells ... but who's buying.* Capitol Records.
Metallica. (1983). Phantom lord & Seek and destroy. On *Kill 'em all.* Music for Nations.
Metallica. (1984). Fade to black & Ride the lightning. On *Ride the lightning.* Music for Nations.
Metallica. (1986). Damage Inc. & Master of puppets. On *Master of puppets.* Music for Nations.
Slayer. (1986). Angel of death, Postmortem, & Raining blood. On *Reign in blood.* Def Jam Recordings.

4 'It's Like a Mach Piece, Really'
Critiquing the Neo-Classical Aesthetic of '80s Heavy Metal Music

Gareth Heritage

In the cult movie *This Is Spinal Tap* (1984), actor/director Rob Reiner paints a satirical picture of a number of heavy metal clichés attributed to the fictitious heavy metal band. Amongst the comedy and true-to-life mishaps, Reiner includes a scene that jokes about heavy metal's neo-classical sound. The scene in question involves the band's lead guitarist (Nigel Tufnel) who is filmed playing a sequence of chords on a piano. When asked by Reiner to describe what he is composing, Tufnel replies that he is strongly influenced by the music of W. A. Mozart and J. S. Bach and that his piece is a meeting of these two composers' styles: 'It's like a Mach piece, really' (Reiner, 1984). The scene's comic value becomes apparent when Tufnel tells Reiner that his song is entitled 'Lick My Love Pump' (ibid.).

Since the late 1960s, rock bands have fused the timbres of heavy guitars, drums, and basses, with pseudo-operatic singing styles, orchestral arrangements, and virtuosic performance practices.[1] The trend of classicizing rock and heavy metal in this way became common practice during the 1980s. Referencing a leading guitar magazine, which in 1986 stated that 'the single most important development in rock guitar in the 1980s was 'the turn to classical music for inspiration and form', Walser states that heavy metal in the 1980s underwent a period of classicization (1993, p. 57). Since Walser's noteworthy *Eruptions: Heavy Metal Appropriations of Classical Virtuosity* (1993), little has been written about the neo-classical sound of heavy metal. This noticeable lack of musicological research should come as no surprise given that, for the vast majority of laypeople, heavy metal is stereotyped as a cacophonous language, indistinguishable from noise because of gritty timbres emitted through heavily distorted guitars, screaming vocals, pounding drums, and thumping basses (Bangs, 1992, p. 459). Yet, on closer examination '80s heavy metal bears many of the musical hallmarks generally considered the preserve of Western High Art music.[2]

Middleton (1990) attests that 'there is a relatively high syntactic correlation' between rock[3] and Baroque music, noting that both 'use conventional harmonic progressions, melodic patterns and structural frameworks' (p. 30) as the basis for musical composition. Despite Middleton's insight into the compositional similarities between rock and Western High Art music, Walser downplays heavy metal's use of melody, harmony, and structure, advocating instead the significance of performance practice and pedagogy as the principal reasons for '80s heavy metal's neo-classicization. For example, in reference to the neo-classical aesthetic of Randy Rhoads, Walser (1993) notes that because of 'his classical allusions and his methods of study [...] Rhoads brought to heavy metal guitar a new level of [pedagogical] discipline and consistency' (p. 84).

Methodology

To elucidate the significance of composition and performance in the neo-classicization of '80s heavy metal, this chapter employs methods of musicological analysis to decipher the music underpinning the aesthetic. It examines the way Western High Art composition techniques and virtuosic performance practices were used by '80s heavy metal bands/artists in classicizing their sound, and this is achieved in the following three ways. First, the research analyzes to what extent and in what ways Western High Art music inspired the composition of '80s heavy metal melody and harmony; second, it examines the similarities in performance practice between '80s heavy metal guitarists and Western High Art music virtuosos; third, it investigates the *metallization* of the Western High Art aesthetic in the late '80s/early '90s. The purpose of analyzing '80s heavy metal in these three ways is to provide an informed critique of the music, whilst placing the musicological analysis in a wider aesthetic/historical context. Yet, it is important to note that one must use musicological analytical methodologies with caution. As noted by Leichtentritt (1973) pure analysis of the music 'cuts music off from its natural connection with the spiritual and material world' (p. xii),[4] whereas Adorno (1969) warns that conclusions obtained as a result of pure analysis can prove to be illegitimate, due to the fact that these conclusions are the perceptions of the musicologist and do not necessarily reflect the intentions of the composer (p. 162). It is necessary to bear in mind, therefore, that musicological analysis forms only part of a wider methodology when studying the aesthetics of music.

Neo-classicism in Discourse: A Musicological Conundrum

Heavy metal bands that use elements of High Art music in their aesthetics have been labeled 'neo-classical' (Fly, 2007)[5] by fans. Strictly speaking, however, neo-classicism is a musicological specific term used to describe 'the conscious use of techniques, gestures, styles, forms, or media from an earlier period' (Griffiths, 2014) in the music of 20th-century composers such as Stravinsky. However, because of the way musical styles and genres naturally develop over time, Whittall (2014) posits the 'probability that composers who seem radically expressionistic today will seem neo-classical tomorrow' (n.p.). Whittall's theory does not strictly apply to popular music as he writes in relation to 20th-century composers. However, as a conjunct of the notion that music classification paradigms are evolutionary, and that no musicological terminology is fixed,[6] there is merit in applying the term 'neo-classical' to '80s heavy metal.

Further validation for the application of the neo-classical label pertains to the notion of 'legitimate culture' (Eliot, 1948). In cultural theory, Mannheim (1940, quoted by Eliot, 1948, p. 37) states that a legitimate culture comprises voices from both the high arts and popular arts, whereas Laermans (1992) notes that the concept of a legitimate culture is based on a reproduction hierarchy (p. 252), meaning that the high art contributors hold greater 'symbolic authority' (ibid.) than the low art contributors. Laermans' suggestion that an authenticity hierarchy exists between legitimate culture's high and low cultural contributors fits well with Eliot's theory that high culture and popular culture complement and nourish each other as part of a wider societal cycle of influence (p. 37). Despite being a style of popular music, with the vast majority of bands producing what was fundamentally heavy pop music, heavy metal's '80s neo-classical contributors brought the High Art aesthetic to the metaphorical table. Whether this was for reasons to do with 'professional producers [trying] to find consumers for their' music (Laermans, 1992, p. 250), or simply heavy metal bands/musicians experimenting with new aesthetic formulae is subject to further investigation.[7] However, what is clear is that the meeting of both popular art and High Art under the same stylistic umbrella qualifies '80s heavy metal as a legitimate culture, and it is for this reason that the neo-classical label can be legitimately applied.

A Brief Historical Overview of the Musical Contexts Responsible for the Neo-Classicization of '80s Heavy Metal

Heavy metal's late-1960s musical genesis relied on blues and, to a lesser extent, jazz influences for its composition (Walser, 1993, p. 57). Bands such as Led Zeppelin utilized the standard I-IV-V blues chord progression in songs such as 'Rock & Roll' (1971), whereas Black Sabbath experimented with jazz harmony in its song 'Sabbath Bloody Sabbath'[8] (1973) (see fig. 4.1). However, the most noticeable connection that early heavy metal had with blues music can be found in the extensive use of pentatonic and blues scales for the construction of guitar riffs, licks, and solos (Brown, 2015; Wilton, 2014) (see fig 4.2).

Am9*	Am9*	G/D*	G/D*	Am9	Am9	GM7/D	GM7/D	Am7	Am7

Figure 4.1 A Chart Showing the Harmony Used in the Chorus to 'Sabbath Bloody Sabbath'. The group of four chords indicated with '*' are successively repeated. The jazzy harmony, unusual in early-1970s heavy metal, is apparent because of the inclusion of 7th and 9th chords.

Figure 4.2 **An Excerpt Showing a Portion of the Bridge's Guitar Riff from Black Sabbath's Song 'Iron Man' (1970).** Introduced by two power chords, the riff enters on a B power chord using the B blues scale with an added chromatic passing note of A# in bars 3 and 4. The function of the A# is to raise the seventh degree of the scale, thereby creating a major tonality that contrasts the blues feel of the riff.

As the 1970s progressed, heavy metal's blues-inspired sound gradually changed as bands began to incorporate more sophisticated performance techniques and compositional devices into their songs. During the early-1970s, Ritchie Blackmore pioneered a sound that combined Western High Art-inspired melodies and harmonies with blues riffs as heard in songs such as 'Demon's Eye' (1971) and 'Highway Star' (1972). By the mid-1970s, Thin Lizzy was experimenting with harmonizing guitar passages, using antiphonal motifs in the guitar solo to 'Emerald' (1976), and in the late-1970s, Eddie Van Halen established a neo-classical heavy metal sound by using modes and a performance skill known as the two-hand 'tapping' technique[9] in his song 'Eruption' (1978).

By the 1980s, heavy metal was at the zenith of its commercial popularity and bands were economically free to diversify their repertoire. One particular group who experimented with their sound was Def Leppard, who embraced the creative use of melody and harmony over speed and thrashing tempos. Walser (1993, p. 92) attributes Def Leppard's attention to music detail to the musical education of guitarist Steve Clark, who recognized the importance of music theory to inform the writing of melody and harmony when composing. Speaking in a television documentary Def Leppard's lead singer (Joe Elliott) testified that Def Leppard's decision to create a musically informed aesthetic was attributable to the fact that the band members wanted to preserve the commercial success of being an '80s heavy metal band, on the one hand, whilst distancing themselves from musical superficiality on the other: 'I never felt comfortable being called a heavy metal band because we did more than that, we harmonized' (Elliott, 2006).

A Brief Explanation of Harmony and Its Significance in Determining the Origins of a Neo-classical Aesthetic

Of all the musical qualities that delineate between general historical music and High Art music, the informed use of harmony is widely considered to be the most significant (Dahlhaus et al., 2014). Harmony is to a High Art composer what a hallmark is to a silversmith; it is the primary identifiable characteristic of a piece's origins. Idiomatically authentic harmonies, therefore, are central to any neo-classical composition. However, the vast majority of '80s heavy metal songs were written using power chords,[10] and the tonal limitations of power chords did little to perpetuate '80s heavy metal's neo-classical aesthetic. In order to find examples of idiomatically specific harmony writing in '80s heavy metal, one must examine the harmonies of songs that were not overly reliant on power chords.

Manowar's 'The Crown and the Ring (Lament of the Kings)' (1988)[11] is an example of a neo-classical '80s heavy metal song with a rich, Western High Art-influenced harmony. Substituting the distorted electric guitar for synthesized pipe organ and male voice choir, 'The Crown and the Ring' borrows its harmonic construction from Bach's 'Toccata' from *Toccata and Fugue in D minor, BWV 565* (c.1708). Evidence of this can be seen in the way that both pieces develop from two distinct broken chords played on the pipe organ. The organ rise in Bach's 'Toccata' is built on notes from a C# half diminished chord, with a D pedal, that functions to introduce two separate melodic themes (see figs 4.3 and 4.4). Similarly, the organ rise in 'The Crown and the Ring' (0.17 and 0.30) is constructed from notes in an E minor triad that precedes the introduction of the choir at 0:33 (see fig. 4.5).

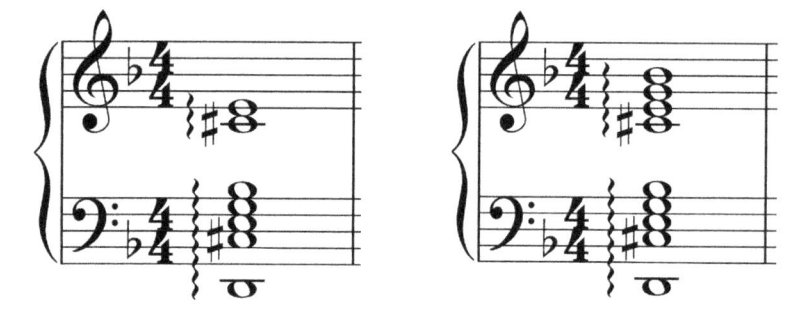

Figures 4.3 and 4.4 **Two Transcriptions of the Two Organ Rises from Bach's** *Toccata and Fugue in D minor, BWV 565*. 4.3 is from bar 2, and 4.4 is from bar 10.

Figure 4.5 **A Transcription of the Organ Rise from Manowar's 'The Crown and the Ring'**. The organ rise is essentially an E minor spread chord ranging five octaves. The affect of the E minor chord played over this range elicits a feeling of awe not unlike the feeling evoked by Bach's 'Toccata'.

'The Crown and the Ring' is just one example of an '80s heavy metal song that replaced heavily distorted guitars with clearer sounding instrumentation, thereby enabling the listener to appreciate the rich harmonic quality of the music. However, unlike Bach, who was expert at writing intricate, highly communicative harmonies—many of which were liturgically composed[12], Manowar combined pipe organ and choir instrumentation with pseudo-religious lyrics—that due to their fantastical/mythical context[13] give the piece an aura of hyperreal religiosity—to simulate the aesthetic of Western sacred music. By composing music that was sonically similar to Bach's liturgical organ music, Manowar was able to simulate an aesthetic synonymous with Western sacred music in a neo-classical context. In doing so, Manowar embraced the popularity of neo-classicism to perpetuate the mythology that the band's neo-classical/pseudo-sacred music was the only 'true metal' music at a time where the commercial success of heavy metal meant that bands seized any opportunity, regardless of how ridiculous it made them look, to compete for fan attention.

Composing Harmony and Melody: Analyzing the Neo-classical Aesthetic of Ozzy Osbourne's 'Goodbye to Romance'

'80s heavy metal compositions are stereotyped as having simple vocal melodies, screaming guitar solos, and heavy power chord harmonies. Yet despite these preconceptions, evidence of High Art musical influences can be seen throughout the genre. Walser (1993) notes that the Ozzy Osbourne and Randy Rhoads ballad 'Goodbye to Romance' (1981) 'adapted the harmonic progression' of Pachelbel's *Canon for three violins and continuo*[14] (*c*.1680) (p. 79). However, Walser does not provide a comparison between the two pieces to show this. In response to Walser's recognition of Rhoads' adoption of Pachelbel's musical influences, my analysis will expose some of the compositional techniques used by Rhoads to create a neo-classically inspired heavy metal ballad.

The opening guitar motif of 'Goodbye to Romance' closely resembles the first motivic development of Pachelbel's *Canon in D*. The calming aura of *Canon in D* is retained by Rhoads as he emulates the core melody, played on a clean electric guitar, during the song's introduction.

Figure 4.6 **The First Motivic Development in *Canon in D*.** Played on Violin I, the motif is later distributed to the 2nd and 3rd violins in canon. In this example, violin II is playing the original descending stepwise melody.

Figure 4.7 **The Intro Guitar Riff to 'Goodbye to Romance'.** Similar in melodic contour, Pachelbel's influence can be seen in the stepwise melodic contour and accompanying bass countermelody. Notice the pitches in the descending bass line are the same as those played by Violin II in bar 1 (4.6).

Despite the differences in pitch, the stepwise movement of this introductory melody is a contemporary reflection of the melodic contour originally written by Pachelbel. The texture accompanying both melodies reinforces the feeling of serenity as both are accompanied by a steady countermelody. In *Canon in D,* the second violin plays four descending crotchets, whereas in 'Goodbye to Romance' the bass guitar plays the exact same notes, in a lower register, but as minims. A similar all-quaver stepwise melody is reintroduced during the song's interlude at 2:14 and again at 2:28 where Osbourne sings a vocal passage with each note having a corresponding word. The downheartedness of the words is emphasized by the downward melodic contour of notes from the Phrygian mode. The significance of this melodic reprise indicates Rhoads' understanding of the role of melody to convey the emotiveness of the words. In much the same way Western High Art vocal music is written with an intention for the melody to express the piece's emotiveness, Rhoads similarly succeeded when composing for Osbourne—a singer unrenowned for having a naturally melodious voice—a tuneful, emotionally moving vocal passage in the interlude.

The use of melody in *Canon in D* also functions in an initiatory way. The melodic excerpt exemplified in fig. 4.6 is first played by violin I, passed to violin II and then to violin III as the canon develops. Its purpose, therefore, is to introduce the first of three successive melodic developments to perpetuate the canonic structure of the piece. By the same token the stepwise melody played by the guitar during the song's introduction—where it functions to introduce the piece—and in the vocals during the interlude—where it functions to introduce the guitar solo at 2:40—illustrates Rhoads' ability to write neo-classically inspired melodies, strategically exposed at critical junctures in the song's configuration, that have a crucial function in developing the song's structure.

In conjunction with the melody, Rhoads uses a similar harmony to emphasize the emotive aesthetic of the song. *Canon in D* is a simple canonic repetition of eight chords in D major (see Fig. 4.8), whereas 'Goodbye to Romance' is a ballad, using a verse/chorus structure, based on a similar eight-chord progression also in D major (see Figs 4.9 and 4.10). The tonality of the two pieces, therefore, is almost identical. However, *Canon in D* has a stronger sense of being in a major key—a suitable tonality given the celebratory context in which it is believed the piece was composed[15]—whereas the tonality for 'Goodbye to Romance' is stylistically nuanced to reflect the melancholic qualities of a rock ballad.

| D | A | Bm | F#m | G | D | G | A |

Figure 4.8 A Table Showing the Harmony for *Canon in D*.

| DM7 | F#m | Bm9 | F#m7 | G6 | G6 | A7(sus4) | A7(sus2) |

Figure 4.9 A Table Showing the Harmony Used during the Verse of 'Goodbye to Romance'. Although there are differences to the harmonic structure of *Canon in D (4.8)* there are many similarities, such as the use of the Bm9, F#m7, and G6.

| D | A/C# | Bm | Bm(add4)/A | G6 | G6 | A7(sus4) | A7 |

Figure 4.10 A Table Showing the Harmony Used during the Chorus of 'Goodbye to Romance'.

Although colored by alterations and inversions, the harmony of 'Goodbye to Romance' is an implied mirror of *Canon in D*, with only minor deviations at bars two, six and seven in the chorus and bars four, six, and seven in the verse. Rhoads' use of chord extensions and inversions is a clear modernization of Pachelbel's original harmony, the effect of which results in the song having a contemporary tonality and wider emotional spectrum. Rhoads diminishes the joyousness of Pachelbel's harmony by modifying the I-V (D-A) chord change in bars 1 and 2 with an I-iii (D F#m) chord change in bars 1 and 2 of the verse. By replacing the A with an F#m, Rhoads has written a more soulful harmony that is suited to the melancholic subtext of the accompanying lyrics.

The lyrics in verse three (3:49–4:12) are more optimistic than in the previous verses. Here the song's sorrowful message has been replaced with a subtext of optimism as the protagonist speaks of leaving the past behind. Verse three is followed by a final chorus before the song's outro begins at 4:43. At this point, another composer might have changed the outro's harmony to reflect the confident outlook of the lyrics in verse three. However, Rhoads does not change the outro's harmony. Instead, he cleverly writes a new melodic motif in the style of a fanfare, played using a synthesized trumpet timbre, as a celebration of the protagonist's inclination to forget about the past and look positively toward

58 *Gareth Heritage*

the future. The fanfare quality of the concluding motif is emphasized by two semiquaver notes at the end of each preceding bar that introduce the core melody in each proceeding bar. Although in no particular Western High Art musical style, the fanfare is aptly suited to the emotional metamorphoses the song's protagonist has undergone during the course of the piece.[16]

Figure 4.11 **The Outro Melody Heard in 'Goodbye to Romance'.** The fanfare quality is emphasized by the use of semiquavers at the end of each bar that function to introduce the succeeding notes.

We will perhaps never know what Rhoads might have gone on to achieve in developing this style due to his tragic early death in 1982. Zakk Wylde, his second successor as lead guitarist in Ozzy Osbourne's band, described him as having 'unbelievable technique' (Bosso, 2012), and Walser (1993) testifies that Rhoads' legacy is one where people will remember him as 'the first guitar player of the 1980s to expand the classical influence [of heavy metal]' (p. 78).

Performing Virtuosity: Analyzing the Neo-Classical Aesthetic of Yngwie Malmsteen

Another '80s heavy metal guitarist who used Western High Art musical influences is Yngwie Malmsteen. Born in Stockholm in 1963, Malmsteen (2011) first learned to play blues music but was dissatisfied with its limitations. Having performed in commercially unsuccessful bands during the early 1980s (Berelian, 2005, p. 208), Malmsteen released the Yngwie Malmsteen band's first album in 1984. Upon its release, *Rising Force* (1984) presented a neo-classical aesthetic like no other in the history of heavy metal music. From the outset *Rising Force* is steeped in Baroque and Classical influences as heard in 'Evil Eye', the introduction of which is essentially an arrangement of the theme from J. S. Bach's 'Bourrée' from the *Lute Suite in E Minor BWV 996* (*c.*1708–1717), and 'Icarus' Dream Suite Opus 4', a piece that bases its opening two and a half minute allemande on the theme from Albinoni's *Adagio in G minor* (*c.*1708).

Figure 4.12 A Simplified Excerpt of *Adagio in G minor's* Opening Theme.

Figure 4.13 A Transcription of the Corresponding Theme Used in 'Icarus' Dream Suite Opus 4'. Notice Malmsteen's substitution of semiquavers for acciaccatura followed by a quaver/semiquaver/demisemiquaver flourish used as a rhythmic elaboration of the triplet in bar 2 (4.12).

Figure 4.14 A Simplified Excerpt of *Adagio in G minor*'s Third Theme.

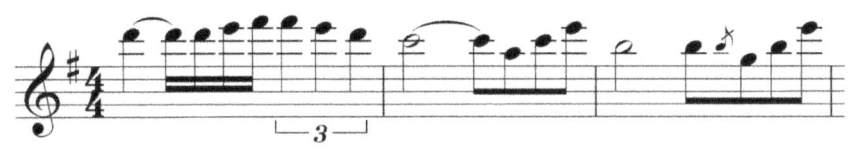

Figure 4.15 A Transcription of the Corresponding Theme Used in 'Icarus' Dream Suite Opus 4'. Notice Malmsteen's use of similar phraseology, substituting triplet quavers for triplet crotchets and, in bar 3 (4.15), appoggiatura/quaver phrasing to simulate the second triplet (4.14).

Rising Force opens with the instrumental track 'Black Star'. More overtly neo-classical than 'Goodbye to Romance', 'Black Star' may have been the very first time many heavy metal fans would have heard a High Art inspired heavy metal song. Malmsteen achieves a neo-classical sound by opening 'Black Star' with a prelude reminiscent of Baroque guitar pieces, such as Visée's (*c.*1655–*c.*1732-3) *Suite No. 12 in E Minor* (1686) and Sanz's (1640–1710) 'Pavanas' (1675), played on a nylon string guitar.[17] The use of ornamentation via trills, spread chords, and harmonics[18] characterizes the 'Black Star' prelude as a neo-classical song that combines Baroque and contemporary influences.

Figure 4.16 A Transcription of the Opening Nine Bars of Malmsteen's Song 'Black Star'. Notice the use of spread chords at the beginning of almost every bar before the introduction of the harmonics at bar 9.

60 *Gareth Heritage*

Although the timbre and ornamentation contribute to the Baroque sound, the neo-classical aesthetic of the 'Black Star' prelude is primarily achieved through the use of Baroque inspired harmony.

| B/F# | Em | B/F#. A | Em/G | E/G# | Am(sus4) | F#/A# | Em/B B A |

Figure 4.17 **A Table Showing the Harmony for Malmsteen's 'Black Star' Prelude.** We can see from this example that Mamsteen has written a neo-Baroque harmony around the tonic center of E minor; the Em, Em/G, Em/B, Am(sus4) are chords in this key. As is common with Baroque harmony, the tonic center is moved to give the harmony the perception of tonal modulation. Malmsteen achieves this perception by using the Em/G, E/G# as a tonic transient-modulation from E minor to E major before returning to E minor with the Am(sus4).

Another neo-classical song on *Rising Force* is 'Far Beyond the Sun', which further attests to Malmsteen's ability to essentially rearrange recognizable motifs from famous High Art pieces in a heavy metal style. In the introduction of 'Far Beyond the Sun' (1984), Malmsteen uses a triplet/dotted-minim/triplet/crotchet motif similar to the opening, and subsequently repeated, motif written by Beethoven in his renowned *Symphony No. 5* (1808). Although borrowing the main motif from Beethoven's 5th, Malmsteen's skills as a virtuosic performer allow him to blend the theme into his lightning-fast phrases, effectively camouflaging Beethoven's motif with elaborate scale runs. The process of revealing a musical theme one moment and concealing it the next could be described as musical trickery.

Figure 4.18 **A Transcription of the Opening Seven Bars and Anacrusis of Malmsteen's 'Far beyond the Sun'.** Notice the recurring triplet-dotted minim/triplet-crotchet motif, which is very similar to the opening motif of Beethoven's *5th Symphony*.

The purpose of this trickery has enabled Malmsteen to exploit the familiarity of Beethoven's motif, thereby catching the ear of an audience who would recognize this famous piece of Classical music and, off the back of this free publicity, market himself as a mainstream heavy metal guitarist playing neo-classical music. This trickery, however, reveals Malmsteen's aesthetic to be influenced by an ability to play virtuosically rather than compose artistically. In a television interview, Jens Johannson, Malmsteen's musical collaborator and keyboardist, testified that Malmsteen preferred playing with the speed of Paganini rather than the complexity of Bach: 'We would often sit and get drunk just listening

'It's Like a Mach Piece, Really' 61

to Paganini, that was like his favorite, and I was like nah, Paganini sucks Bach is much better, listen to this [Malmsteen would reply] that is better but this is faster' (Johannson, 2011).

The influence of Paganini is recognizable throughout Malmsteen's repertoire. One particular piece that exemplifies Paganini-inspired playing is 'Trilogy Suite Opus 5' from *Trilogy* (1986). Using a harmonic minor scale, Malmsteen opens 'Trilogy Suite Opus 5' with a scale run just short of two octaves before playing a G major chord. This theme is repeated a further three times, with each successive theme ending on a different chord. Malmsteen proceeds to develop these themes throughout the song's allemande accompanied by a drum kit, bass guitar, and synthesized harpsichord timbre. However, if any of these opening themes is compared with themes used by Paganini in 'Caprice No. 5' from *24 Caprices* (*c*1809), it is instantly apparent that Malmsteen has borrowed heavily from Paganini's style whilst adding little creative value of his own.

Figure 4.19 A Transcription of the Opening Two Bars of Paganini's 'Caprice No. 5'.

Figure 4.20 A Transcription of the Opening Two Bars of Malmsteen's 'Trilogy Suite Opus 5'. Notice the demisemiquaver scale run before coming to rest on a G major chord. Observe that the melodic shape is nigh on identical to the opening two bars of Paganini's 'Caprice No. 5'.

From a performance perspective, Malmsteen is considered to be one of the most important heavy metal guitarists in heavy metal music's history. His virtuosic style has earned the respects of many amateur and professional guitarists, including George Lynch, who in a 2014 Internet poll nominated him as one of the world's greatest guitarists (Lynch, 2014). Yet from a compositional angle, Malmsteen's inability to write 'even a single memorable song' (Berelian, 2005, p. 208) marks him as a failed heavy metal musician in the eyes of metal traditionalists: 'Yngwie Malmsteen [is] a tedious virtuoso [who as a performer was] too precise, especially in an era when the best music tended to lack precision. [Yngwie Malmsteen] embodied a sterile egocentric strain of metal that collapsed on itself' (Christe, 2003, p. 108).

Mark Wood and the Metallization of the High Art Aesthetic

Although guitarists are widely accredited for spearheading the neo-classicization of '80s heavy metal, other musicians such as Steelheart's singer Miljenko Matikevic[19] and Poison's drummer Rikki Rockett[20] are examples of technically proficient performers with the necessary skills to classicize their aesthetic. However, few High Art musicians have looked to heavy metal for inspiration. Yet in an aesthetic role-reversal, the classically trained violinist and luthier, Mark Wood, did just that in the late 1980s/early 1990s. For example, his album *Voodoo Violince* (1991) fuses violin playing with heavy metal instrumentation to generate a sound that is indistinguishable from that of other late-'80s/early-'90s heavy metal instrumental albums.[21]

Voodoo Violince opens with the song 'Monkeybats' (1991) which, due to Wood's use of performance techniques such as 'speed bowing' and arpeggio sweeps, is musically comparable to the virtuosic playing of Malmsteen. These performance practices, combined with the fact that Wood is a classically trained musician, help establish Wood's neo-classical aesthetic. Ironically, the ability to bow notes enabled Wood to naturally create articulations that the '80's neo-classical guitarists could only simulate. Because guitarists are unable to naturally create the sound of bowing,[22] and given that violin timbres and articulations are synonymous with Western High Art music, heavy metal's neo-classical guitarists simulated the sound of the violin by playing what are known as 'violin notes'.[23] By simply bowing a note, as all violinists not playing pizzicato do, Wood is able to naturally create the artificial 'violin notes' that Malmsteen, for example, plays in 'Icarus Dream Suite Opus 4' (3:07–3:30).

As 'Monkeybats' develops, Wood's phrasing becomes progressively less well defined to the point that at 2:14 it is not at all clear what notes are being played. At 2:30, Wood's violin solo uses levels of virtuosic speed that are comparable to Malmsteen's guitar solos, but that lack the clarity and technical execution of the notes. Between 2:31 and 2:40, Wood's performance becomes shrill and exponentially distorted the faster he bows until 2:41, at which point the sound becomes cacophonous and notes blend together creating a sonorism more aptly suited to the string timbres of avant-garde pieces such as Penderecki's *Threnody to the Victims of Hiroshima* (1960). These discordant passages do not reflect a lack of technical prowess; they are instead symptomatic of the violin's limitations. As a way of compensating for these limitations, whilst bringing the look of the violin in conformity with heavy metal guitar iconography, Wood redesigned the instrument.

Engineering his violin to have the aesthetic shape and practical functionality of the superstrat,[24] Wood effectively built a 'superviolin' that looked pointy and had a body made from a solid piece of wood fitted with electric guitar pickups, two fretted necks, machine heads, and a bolt-on bridge. In sum, Wood's 'superviolin' was his self-customized aesthetic paintbrush. It enabled him to play in a similar virtuosic way and look the same as the neo-classical guitarists who influence his aesthetic.

Wood's music can be viewed as something more than a duplicate of '80s heavy metal neo-classicism. Wood is both an impeccable musician and a cultural pioneer whose willingness to change clichéd attitudes toward not only the violin but Western High Art music in general sets him apart from almost any other neo-classical musician in heavy metal's history; as Wood succinctly puts it: 'People associate the violin with such tasteful sophistication, I want to ruin that' (1991).

Conclusion

In the movie *This Is Spinal Tap* Nigel Tufnel refers to his music as being inspired by J. S. Bach and W. A. Mozart. However, during the movie's 80-minute duration, Tufnel never once plays a single piece of music that could be compared to the music of Bach or Mozart. As this chapter has shown, classically trained musicians, such as Yngwie Malmsteen and Randy Rhoads, experimented with Western High Art musical formulas to create a modern, High Art-inspired popular music that is today widely thought of as neo-classical. Interestingly, Walser (1993) never once refers to Western High Art-inspired heavy metal music as neo-classical. Perhaps this is because Walser realized that neo-classicism has a specific musicological meaning. If this is the case, Walser is prudent to avoid this loaded label in order to retain the clarity of his ontology.

The prevalence of neo-classical heavy metal in the modern era means that the term is more widely used in metal music discourse than ever before. The 1980s were a seminal transitional period in the evolution of heavy metal music. Yngwie Malmsteen and Randy Rhoads established the compositional and performance practices that would later inspire the power metal and symphonic power metal bands of the nineties and noughties, and it is for this reason that the neo-classical label has stuck.

Regardless of whether the Western High Art influence makes heavy metal neo-classical or not, the term will continue to be used in the discourse because, now more than ever, bands are using Western High Art influences as core musical components in their aesthetic. It is unlikely that the power chord will be entirely replaced by Western High Art music-inspired harmony writing, but heavy metal music is evolving, and one of these evolutionary traits is the neo-classicization of heavy metal's visual and sonic aesthetic. It is clear that further research is needed to clarify how heavy metal's neo-classical aesthetic developed during the past two decades, and it is going to be interesting to see how the neo-classical aesthetic of heavy metal further develops into the 2020s.

If certain heavy metal subgenres continue to be labeled 'neo-classical', and if Whittell's theory is true of heavy metal as it is true of 20th-century music, the future of heavy metal's neo-classical sound is now, more than ever, a defining musical characteristic of contemporary mainstream metal styles. Furthermore, if historic trends repeat themselves and the symphonic metal aesthetic as we know it today is the future equivalent of the blues rock aesthetic of heavy metal's yesteryear, there is a possibility that High Art music may become normative in the heavy metal aesthetic of tomorrow. If so, it is prudent for metal music scholars to become familiarized with the methodologies of musicological analysis, as future Nigel Tufnels are highly likely to compose 'for real' in the styles of Mozart and Bach.

Notes

1. One notable example is Deep Purple's *Concerto for Group and Orchestra* (1969).
2. The term 'Western High Art music' as opposed to 'classical music' will be used throughout this paper to reference music from the Baroque to the Romantic and to avoid periodic ambiguity.
3. Due to the symbiotic relationship between rock and heavy metal, Middleton's observations apply as much to heavy metal bands as they do to rock bands.
4. Here Leichtentritt is simply saying that there is more to an aesthetic than just the music.
5. Fly's *Brief History* about neo-classical metal music on the Ultimate-Guitar.com website contains factual errors including a sentence that suggests Beethoven's *Symphony No. 5* was composed by Mozart.
6. As a way of reflecting heavy metal's profound stylistic change over the past 30 years, the heavy metal label has changed to describe new metal subgenres.
7. The neo-classical guitarist Yngwie Malmsteen is noted by Walser (1993, p. 99) as having denounced his heavy metal credentials. Since his arrival on the scene in the mid-1980s, Malmsteen has regularly stated that he is a High Art musician who has been misclassified as a heavy metal performer by the metal music fraternity.
8. 'Sabbath Bloody Sabbath' is unusual in the repertoire of early heavy metal bands, in so much as the sound of the verses' power chords are sharply contrasted with the choruses' jazz chords.
9. The two-hand technique allows a guitarist to tap notes on a guitar's fretboard. The benefit of this technique is that it allows a guitarist to use multiple fingers to play more notes than using a plectrum to pick the strings alone. Walser (1993, p. 70) compares Van Halen's two-handed technique to a similar keyboard technique innovated by J. S. Bach to allow for the smooth performance of his complex keyboard pieces.
10. A power chord is essentially a perfect fifth interval, often with the octave added above the fifth.
11. Referred to as 'The Crown and the Ring' forthwith.
12. The fundamental purpose of which was to enrich the experience of prayer and bring worshipers closer to God.
13. 'The Crown and the Ring' is about the last fight of a warrior king who, like the warrior kings of Norse mythology, would ascend to Valhalla when killed in battle.
14. Referred to as *Canon in D* forthwith.
15. It is hypothesized the *Canon in D* was composed for the wedding of Johann Christoph Bach (1671–1721) (Pachelbel's Canon, 2014).
16. Osbourne has described this song as a 'farewell to Black Sabbath'. The concluding fanfare signifies a break with the past and celebrates the pursuit of pastures new (Osbourne, 1997, p. 3).

17. Malmsteen uses an arrangement of the 'Black Star' prelude—'Farewell'—to close *Rising Force*.
18. A technique typical of '80s heavy metal guitar playing that requires guitarists to lightly place their fingers over a fret and play the note. The resulting 'harmonic' is a resonating frequency devoid of the overtones that characterize notes.
19. In 'She's Gone' (1990) Miljenko frequently ornaments his phrases with acciaccatura and sings a G5.
20. Walser describes Rockett as an 'excellent musician' (Walser, 1993, p. 128).
21. Wood's violin solo 'The Howling' would likely fool the most astute metaler's ear into believing that this was actually a solo guitar piece played in the style of Vai's *Passion and Warfare* (1990).
22. Guitarists can use an electromagnetic device called an E-bow to simulate the sound of a violin bow.
23. Violin notes are essentially volume swells, often played with the little finger manipulating the guitar's volume knob, which smooths the attack of picked notes.
24. A streamlined version of the Stratocaster, superstrats were built for speed and range, having low action and a 24-fret neck. It was the instrument of choice for the vast majority of '80s heavy metal guitarists (Bacon & Wheelwright, 2014).

Bibliography

Adorno, T. W. (1969). On the problem of musical analysis (Max Paddison, Trans.). In Leppert, R. (Ed.). (2002). *Essays on music* (pp. 162–180). Berkley, CA; London: University of California Press.

Bacon, T., & Wheelwright, L. (2014). Electric guitar. *Grove Music Online. Oxford Music Online*. Oxford University Press, http://www.oxfordmusiconline.com/subscriber/article/grove/music/A2256412 (accessed October 15, 2014).

Bangs, L. (1992). Heavy metal. In A. DeCurtis & J. Henke (Eds.), *The Rolling Stone illustrated history of rock and roll*, 3rd ed. (pp. 452–454). New York: Random House.

Berelian, E. (2005). *The rough guide to heavy metal*. London, New York: Penguin.

Bosso, J. (2012). Interview: Zakk Wylde on Randy Rhoads. Available at: http://www.musicradar.com/news/guitars/interview-zakk-wylde-on-randy-rhoads-534858 (accessed October 11, 2014).

Brown, A. R. (2015). 'Everything louder than everyone else': The origins and persistence of heavy metal music and its global cultural impact. In A. Bennett & S. Wacksman (Eds.), *The Sage handbook of popular music genres* (pp. 261–277). London: Sage.

Christe, I. (2003). *Sound of the beast: The complete head banging history of heavy metal*. New York: HarperCollins.

Dahlhaus, C., Anderson, J., Wilson. C., Cohn, R., Hyer, B. (2014). 'Harmony'. *Grove Music Online. Oxford Music Online*. Oxford University Press. http://www.oxfordmusiconline.com/subscriber/article/grove/music/50818 (accessed December 23, 2014).

Eliot, T. S. (1948). *Notes towards the definition of culture*. Reprint (1983). London: Faber.

Elliott, J. (2006). Interviewed by Dave Fanning for *Talks with Dave Fanning*. Sky Arts 1 Television (broadcast March 14, 2013).

Fly, D. (2007). Neo-classical metal music. Available at: http://www.ultimate-guitar.com/lessons/music_styles/neo-classical_metal_music.html (accessed September 30, 2014).

Griffiths, P. Neo-classicism. (2014). In A. Latham (Ed.), *The Oxford Companion to Music*. Oxford: Oxford University Press. http://www.oxfordmusiconline.com/subscriber/article/opr/t114/e4701 (Accessed September 30, 2014).

Johannson, J. (2011). *Metal evolution. Part 10: Power metal*. Sky Arts 1 Television (broadcast September 22, 2012).

Laermans, R. (1992). The relative rightness of Pierre Bourdieu: Some sociological comments on the legitimacy of postmodern art, literature and culture. *Cultural Studies*, 6(2), 248–260.

Leichtentritt, H. (1973). *Music, history and ideas*, 15th ed. Cambridge, MA: Harvard University Press.

Lynch, G. (2014). Thirty great guitarists—Including Steve Vai, David Gilmour and Eddie Van Halen—Pick the greatest guitarist of all time. Available at: http://www.guitarworld.com/30–30-greatest-guitarists-picked-greatest-guitarists?page=0,5 (accessed October 12, 2014).

Malmsteen, Y. J. (2011). *Metal evolution. Part 10: Power metal*. Sky Arts 1 Television (broadcast September 22, 2012).

Middleton, R. (1990). *Studying popular music*. Philadelphia: Open University Press.

Osbourne, O. (1997). Goodbye to romance. On *The Ozzman cometh: The best of Ozzy Osbourne* [CD liner notes]. New York: Sony Music.

Pachelbel's Canon. (2014). *Wikipedia*. Available at: http://en.wikipedia.org/wiki/Pachelbel's_Canon (accessed October 13, 2014).

This Is Spinal Tap. (1984). Directed by Reiner, R. [DVD] (2004). Los Angeles, CA: Metro-Goldwyn-Mayer.

Walser, R. (1993). *Running with the devil: Power, gender and madness in heavy metal music*. Hanover, NH: Wesleyan University Press.

Whittall, A. (2014). Neo-classicism. *Grove Music Online. Oxford Music Online*. Oxford: Oxford University Press, http://www.oxfordmusiconline.com/subscriber/article/grove/music/19723 (accessed September 30, 2014).

Wilton, P. (2014). Heavy metal. In A. Latham (Ed.), *The Oxford Companion to Music*. Oxford: Oxford University Press, http://www.oxfordmusiconline.com/subscriber/article/opr/t114/e3192 (accessed September 30, 2014).

Wood, M. (1991). Rising stars. *Turn up the volume 1*. Directed by C. Foglio & W. Isham [DVD] (2000). Huntingdon: Quantum Leap.

Discography

Black Sabbath. (1970). *Iron man*. iTunes [Download]. Available at: http://apple.com/uk/itunes/ (accessed September 30, 2014).

Black Sabbath. (1973). *Sabbath bloody sabbath*. iTunes [Download]. Available at: http://apple.com/uk/itunes/ (accessed October 1, 2014).

Johann Pachelbel. (2009). Canon for three violins and continuo. On *The 50 greatest pieces of classical music,* performed by London Philharmonic Orchestra and David Parry. iTunes [Download]. Available at: http://apple.com/uk/itunes/ (accessed October 1, 2014).

Johann Sebastian Bach. (2009). Toccata and fugue in d minor, BWV 565. On *The most essential classical music in movies*, performed by Klemens Schnorr. iTunes [Download]. Available at: http://apple.com/uk/itunes/ (accessed October 1, 2014).

Manowar. (1988). The crown and the ring (Lament of the kings). On *Kings of metal* [CD]. New York: Atlantic Recording Corporation.

Mark Wood. (1991). *Monkeybats*. iTunes [Download]. Available at: http://apple.com/uk/itunes/ (accessed October 13, 2014).

Niccolò Paganini. (*c*.1809). Caprice No. 5, performed by Shlomo Mintz. *Violin Piano*. YouTube: Available at: http://www.youtube.com/watch?v=amfCqFUMBkY (accessed October 16, 2014).

Ozzy Osbourne. (1997). *The Ozzman cometh: The best of Ozzy Osbourne* [CD]. New York: Sony Music.

Tomaso Albioni. (*c*.1708). Adagio in g minor. *eddiexplorer*, You Tube: Available at: http://www.youtube.com/watch?v=XMbvcp480Y4 (accessed October 12, 2014).

Yngwie Malmsteen. (1984). *Black star*. iTunes [Download]. Available at: http://apple.com/uk/itunes/ (accessed October 7, 2014).

Yngwie Malmsteen. (1984). *Far beyond the sun*. iTunes [Download]. Available at: http://apple.com/uk/itunes/ (accessed October 12, 2014).

Yngwie Malmsteen. (1984). *Icarus dream suite opus 4*. iTunes [Download]. Available at: http://apple.com/uk/itunes/ (accessed October 13, 2014).

Yngwie Malmsteen. (1986). *Trilogy suite opus 5*. iTunes [Download]. Available at: http://apple.com/uk/itunes/ (accessed October 15, 2014).

5 The Distortion Paradox
Analyzing Contemporary Metal Production[1]

Mark Mynett

'The most important music of our time is recorded music. The recording studio is its principle musical instrument' (Case, 2007, p. xix). Despite this, the role of the producer and the changing uses of recording technologies is a subject that has received comparatively little attention in musicology and popular music studies, until quite recently (Frith and Zagorski-Thomas, 2012; Zagorski-Thomas, 2014). This comparative lack of academic exploration of the aesthetics and techniques of sound production in metal music recordings is particularly important given the centrality of distortion-producing technologies to the signature sound of the genre (but see Wallach, 2003; Berger and Falles, 2005; Williams, 2015).

Arguably, in comparison to other genres, metal is the least acceptable when delivered with poor production, as the music's defining quality of 'heaviness' will inevitably be vastly compromised. Furthermore, due to the frequent complexity and technicality of composition, production clarity is essential for the listener to be able to clearly perceive and understand these qualities—and as Izhaki notes, 'Intelligibility is the most elementary requirement when it comes to sonic quality' (2007, p. 5).

Capturing and presenting intelligibility whilst simultaneously retaining metal music's heaviness is a distinct and fundamental production challenge facing the contemporary metal producer. Despite the fact that the harmonically distorted guitar embodies the primary identity of metal music; too much distortion will inappropriately neutralize the guitar's dynamic content. This has the impact of obscuring the note onset and therefore the guitar's note definition, thereby masking the clarity of the riffs on which the music is frequently based. Additionally and importantly (as this chapter will explore) the increased spectral energy and density resulting from the guitar signal's harmonic distortion casts a sonically dense blanket over the majority of the other instruments and sounds involved. This is often referred to as spectral masking. Alexander Case explains,

> The harmonic energy associated with distortion can cause masking of other signals. That is, a vocal that is perfectly intelligible and a snare drum that formerly cut through the mix can both become more difficult to hear when distortion is added to the electric guitar. Distortion affects the instruments that occupy similar spectral regions. (2007, p. 100)

Therefore, within these harmonically distorted sounds, the listener's ability to understand these other signals will tend to be heavily obscured, with a diminished perception of how affective they are. To be intelligible and therefore enhance the production's overall heaviness, these other signals need to punch and cut through this sonically dense blanket.

For these reasons, harmonically distorted rhythm guitars provide a framework that requires a vastly different production ethos than other genres—whose textures are usually far less dense. To provide the drums, bass, and vocal signals with the qualities that will enable them to remain intelligible, a significant level of processing and 'technological mediation' is often required. As a result, modern metal music productions are often as heavily processed as commercial pop or dance music regularly is (Mynett, 2012, p. 110). However, due to the culture and aesthetics of musical authenticity and musicianship that surrounds the metal genre, the significant role of production technologies in the creation of the music is most often downplayed or effectively disguised. This can be contrasted with electronic dance music, for example, where such technological influence is often valued and clearly revealed.

The radical harmonic distortion of contemporary metal's rhythm guitar timbres therefore presents a paradox. Although this form of signal modification embodies metal music's primary identity, this attribute simultaneously presents a significant challenge to successfully producing this style of music. This chapter analyzes this paradox, examining the link among harmonic distortion, perception, and heaviness; the signal modification provided by distortion; and the challenges that this modification presents to definition and intelligibility.

The Distortion Paradox Explored

Within popular music, the term 'heavy' can be used to describe a variety of sounds and performance characteristics within a wide range of styles. However, for many, this adjective is solely reserved for metal music and mainly used to depict the perceived 'weight' and frequency density displayed by acts from this style. Regardless of whether it is traditional or contemporary metal, from Black Sabbath's (1970) self-titled debut album (generally considered heavy metal's first) right through to Machine Head's (2014) 'Bloodstone and Diamonds' and everything in between, 'heaviness' is metal music's defining feature.

Harmonic Distortion

Although contemporary metal artists will often explore different dynamics, styles, and expressions within one song (Hoffstadt and Nagenborg, 2010, p. 41), 'the most important aural sign [of heavy metal] is the sound of an extremely distorted electric guitar' (Walser, 1993, p. 41). Very simply, if a groups' sound doesn't contain this vital component, it is highly unlikely that it would be considered a metal band. At this stage of the genre's development, there are no other sounds, or performance attributes, that are pre-requisites for the 'metal band' moniker to be applicable and valid. However, the quality of distorted guitar timbres does not in itself automatically qualify a sound as metal (Eddie Van Halen's solo on Michael Jackson's 'Beat It' obviously didn't make this eligible for the 'metal' label). Clearly, there are further sonic characteristics relating to the way the music is composed and performed that are required for it to be defined as metal. Nevertheless, harmonically distorted guitar tones can be viewed as embodying the primary identity of metal music, consequently providing coherence to its numerous subgenres. It is therefore important to briefly discuss the relationship between human perception and distortion, as this connection could be considered as being at the very core of the music's appeal.

Distortion and Ecological Perception

The origins of the word 'distort' can be traced back to the late 15th century Latin verb '*distorquere*', meaning 'to twist'. However, relevant definitions of distortion in modern dictionaries tend to stress the altered form of a sound wave or electrical signal during amplification or other processing. Interestingly, the most tangible and influential experience humans gain from distortion is not as a result of amplification or processing, but through ecological perception.

The ecological approach emphasizes the relationship between organisms and their environment. It proposes the theory of direct perception, due to inherent interpretations formed from certain kinds of stimuli or environment. By doing so, the contention of potentially countless individual interpretations that can be associated with secondary cultural associations can be averted. As Alan Moore (2012) proposes: 'Much detailed writing on music contents itself with sophisticated description, and analysis […] but it is also worth keeping an eye on pragmatic reality' (p. 285). It is this 'pragmatic reality' with which ecological perspectives are concerned.

James J. Gibson (1979) initially formulated the concept of ecological perception, principally through his publication *The Ecological Approach to Visual Perception*. In this respect, Gibson proposes arguments of direct realism and perception, rather than the indirect realism associated with cognitive, information-processing style perspectives. Eric Clarke (2005) reconceived Gibson's ecological approach and related this to musical analysis and discourse in his publication *Ways of Listening*. Discussing these invariant properties that relate to sound, Moore suggests:

> Ecological perception can be characterized most simply by the phrase invariants afford through specifications. An ecological approach identifies invariants that are perceived in the environment. In the case of music, this environment is purely sonic. Such an approach then observes what responses these invariants afford, and it thus promotes action on the basis of the source the sound is (not necessarily consciously) interpreted as specifying. (2012, p. 12)

Zagorski-Thomas (2012) similarly proposes that certain facets of a world with consistent physical laws, as interpreted through our bodies, are 'immutable and universal because the experience of existing within a human body forces some types of interpretation upon us' (p. 2). Here, as Tagg (1992) highlights, the experience of existing within a human body is largely shaped in our formative years. Babies are endowed with nonverbal vocal talents totally out of proportion to other aspects of their size, weight, and volume: they have inordinate lung power and vocal chords of steel, it seems, capable of producing high decibel and transient values.

Most humans start to hear four months before birth, following which our aural capabilities are already highly developed. These aural abilities enable the successful early use of pedagogical methods involving music and melody. Examples here include the effective enhancement of mathematics and alphabet retention through the use of rhythm and melody and nursery rhymes that are used not only as a creative activity, but also to teach vocabulary through meter and rhyme. Therefore, given that a functioning voice box and speech capabilities are present, the way we listen to and interpret music and its myriad timbres is heavily bound to this knowledge and experience of oral sound. These ideas are supported by Wallach (2003), who refers to a 'model of culture that views linguistic signification as the primary determinant of cultural experience' (p. 36). Additionally, Moore states, 'The way listeners listen is greatly determined by whatever bodily knowledge they have of producing music' (op. cit., p. 4), and Middleton refers to 'the voice, in its commonly understood significance as the profoundest mark of the human' (1990, p. 262).

During early stages of development, non-verbal sounds are essential, and it is here, under normal circumstances, that an inherent association between volume and distortion will start to be formed. As the capabilities of human vocal chords are transcended, normally through excessive volume or power, audible vocal distortion is produced (Walser, 1993, p. 42). This excessive volume often accompanies high degrees of energy and emotionality. In many associated instances, such as those related to pain, hunger, or separation anxiety, infants will experience these high degrees of emotionality as intense. In subsequent years, as soon as a concept of aggression is understood, associations between distortion and aggression will also be made. Hence, from an early age, distortion starts to function as a sign of volume, power, energy, aggression, intensity, and emotionality. In this respect, Case (2007) proposes: 'Fans of many, if not most, styles of popular music react positively to distortion almost instinctively. When a device is overloaded, something exciting must be happening [...] there is something visceral and stimulating about distortion that makes the music more exciting (pp. 97–150). Case's account of our instinctive reaction to distortion is positive and relates this to exciting attributes. This correlates with the core appeal that metal music has provided for almost half a century.

Frequency Content—Proximity and Density

Distortion has a considerable, and highly significant, impact on the frequency content of electric guitars. Distortion makes the complex direct injection (DI) signal coming straight from a guitar's quarter-inch jack output significantly more complex. Not only does it amplify and attenuate spectral regions in the sound being processed, it also constructs entirely new frequency components by generating musically related harmonics *above* and *below* the fundamentals and overtones of the guitar's signal. In simple terms, 'harmonics' are frequencies that are whole number multiples of the fundamental frequency, which in the instance of guitars relates to the pitch of the note being played, i.e., a guitar to dropped B = 61.735Hz.

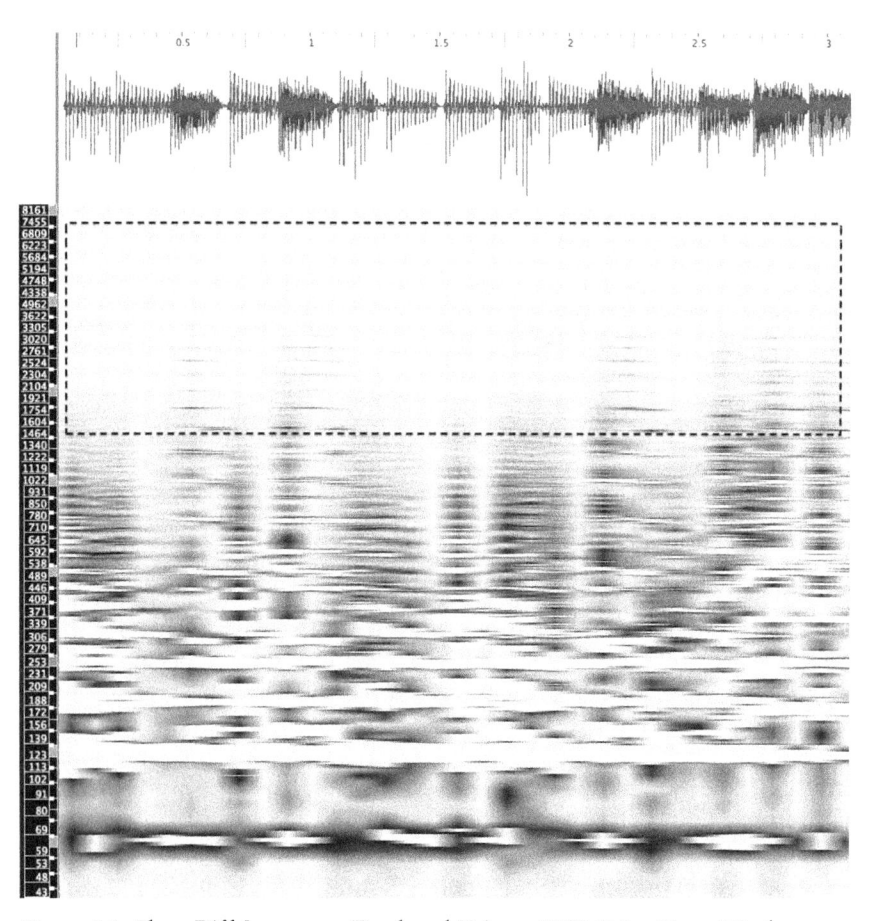

Figure 5.1 **Clean Riff Sonogram (Produced Using a 8192-Point Hann Window with 50% Overlap).** The majority of frequency content resides below 1.5kHz, with little within the 1.5–7.5kHz boxed region, other than brief sections reflecting the riffs higher notes.

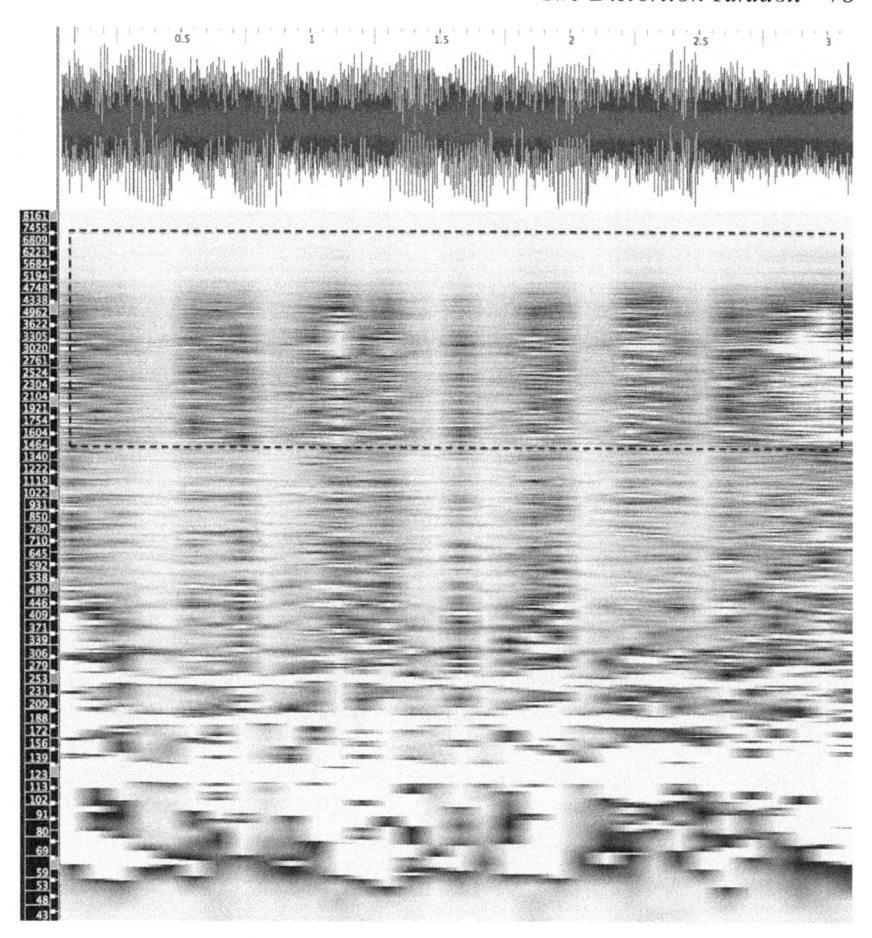

Figure 5.2 **Harmonically Distorted Riff Sonogram (Again 8192-Point Hann Window/50% Overlap).** Compared to figure 5.1, the additional upper spectral content within the 1.5–7.5kHz boxed region is considerable.

It is within a guitar's high frequencies that distortion's impact is most significant. Drastically more content is generated in the region above 1.5kHz, especially up to 7.5kHz. The above two sonograms demonstrate this principle. The first (Fig. 5.1) represents the resulting frequency spectrum of a DI guitar-riff signal routed through a valve amp and loudspeaker cabinet, but with the amp parameters set up so that the sound is entirely clean. The second sonogram (Fig 5.2) represents the same DI guitar-riff signal routed through the same valve amp and loudspeaker cabinet, but this time with the amp parameters set up so that the sound is representative of a typical contemporary metal rhythm sound.

Vitally, when additional spectral information in the form of high frequency energy is introduced to guitar timbres, they are perceived as heavier (Berger and Fales, 2005, pp. 193–194). Very importantly, the increase of high frequency energy makes a guitar appear to be closer to the listener. This is essential, as the concept of proximity is a vital part of metal music and metal music production. High frequency sounds dissipate considerably with distance and are absorbed at a faster rate than low frequencies as they propagate through the air. Conversely, the energy created by low frequencies is powerful enough to go straight through solid objects and can therefore reach us from great distances. However, when sounds are perceived as emanating from a greater distance, they are observed as softer and less intense. Clearly, a decrease in intensity, with sounds being perceived as softer, contradicts the core requirements for heavy metal music.

Conversely, largely due to the 'in your face' perception of proximity that harmonic distortion provides, these sounds are perceived as more intense, somehow harder, and therefore heavier. Thus, if a sound source contains a considerable degree of high frequency energy, the brain infers an apparent lack of air absorption, therefore an apparent lack of distance, and thereby perceives the sound as being close/proximate to the listener. Zagorski-Thomas (2012) even suggests that intense high frequency content 'can be used to make something seem closer than the loudspeaker it emanates from' (p. 8). This relationship between high frequency content and heaviness is frequently overlooked, and this association similarly extends to many of the other sounds involved, particularly the high frequency energy emphasis of the metal genres bass drums (often referred to as 'clickiness'). Unlike rock music, where a sense of depth is regularly conveyed by providing a sense of 'textural foreground, middle-ground and background' (Moore, 2001, p. 121), this is less relevant to contemporary metal production, where the principal focus is foregrounded sounds.

However, harmonic distortion also increases the density of the frequencies *at* and *around* the fundamental. Frequency density relates to how the energy of a guitar signal is distributed across the frequency range—in this instance being modified so that it is highly concentrated at and around the fundamental. In combination with the intensified harmonic content between 1.5kHz and 7.5kHz, this increases the perception of the apparent 'solidity' of a guitar timbre, providing a strong and focused impact.

Figures 5.3 and 5.4 are spectrograms (produced using a 16384-point Hann window with 50% overlap) employing the same guitar signals used for figures 5.1 and 5.2 (i.e., clean and distorted amp sound respectively), but this time with the spectrogram more closely focused on low frequencies. The boxed region in each highlights spectral content between 50 and 120 Hz (i.e., at and around the 65.407 Hz fundamental). Figure 5.4 evidences harmonic distortion dramatically increasing the magnitude and density of this band of low frequency energy. This considerable emphasis of frequency content toward the lower and upper ranges of human hearing means that contemporary metal's sounds are perceived as occupying considerable height on the vertical plane.

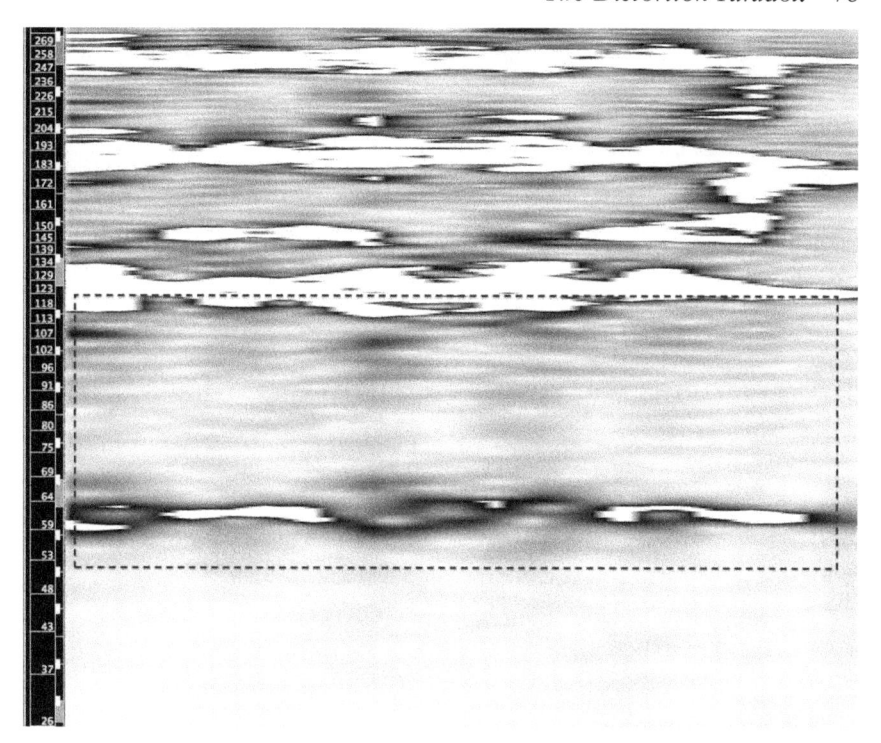

Figure 5.3 Clean Guitar Riff Sonogram—Focused on Low Frequencies.

Signal Stability and Volume

In addition to the physical associations of distortion with proximity, volume, power, aggression, energy, and intensity, the impact of distortion on the dynamic content of an electric guitar timbre enables similar associations. Distortion introduces a highly effective form of dynamic range reduction to electric guitars (evident when comparing the waveforms at the top of figures 5.1 and 5.2). For rhythm guitars, the impact of distortion, as Berger and Fales argue: 'simulates the conversion of the guitar from an impulsive to a sustained or driven instrument, and this transformation may be part of the acoustic correlate to the perceptual experience of heaviness' (2005, p. 194). In effect, distortion provides the rhythm guitar with a flatter dynamic envelope and with it an almost infinite sustain, providing a great capacity for sonic power and expression (Walser, 1993, pp. 42–43). As exertion is normally required for sustaining any physical activity, distorted electric guitar sounds also signal energy and power 'through this temporal display of unflagging capacity for emission' (op. cit., p. 42).

Furthermore, capturing or enhancing high (as well as low) frequencies in this manner will often result in sounds being perceived as louder than they actually are. The reason for this is that human hearing is exponentially more

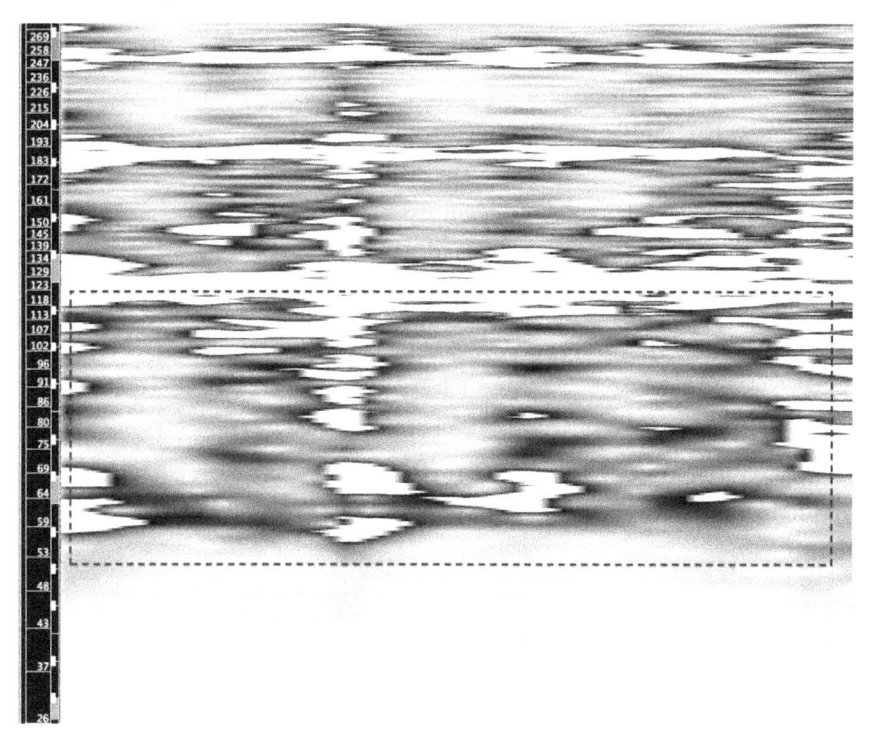

Figure 5.4 Harmonically Distorted Guitar Riff Sonogram—Focused on Low Frequencies.

sensitive to low and high frequencies the louder they are in volume (Senior, 2011, p. 62). This is the basic principle of the 'loudness' button sometimes found on hi-fi amplifiers, whereby low and high frequencies are accentuated to emulate how they would be perceived at a higher volume level. These frequencies at the extremes of the audio spectrum significantly contribute to our somatic perception of sound, due to their ability to cause vibrations in skin and internal organs (Zagorski-Thomas, 2014, p. 72).

Harmonic Distortion and Note Definition

Having emphasized the benefits that distortion provides, it is probably quite obvious why sufficient gain needs to be provided to contemporary metal's guitar sounds in order to enable density of timbre and a high perception of proximity, as well as enhanced harmonic content and signal compression. Importantly, though, too much distortion will inappropriately neutralize the guitar's dynamic content, hence obscuring the note onset and therefore the guitar's note definition. Note definition, in relation to harmonically distorted rhythm guitar sounds, can be considered as the pitch clarity of notes and chords and the ability to detect this pitch when the guitar sound is placed in the context of a mix. Note definition reflects strong qualities in the guitar's sound envelope characteristics, an appropriateness of spectral content, particularly in the low frequencies around the fundamental, the minimal bearing of unmusical resonant frequencies, and the appropriateness of influence that distortion has on dynamic range.

Too much increase in a guitar's high frequency content can result in a highly abrasive timbre, with the usually pleasing range of presence frequencies (generally speaking 4 kHz–6 kHz) sounding harsh and rasping. This can easily counteract and obscure the listener's perception of the guitar's note definition, as well as its low frequency content. Similarly, an excessive amount of low frequency content, or inappropriate low frequency content, can cause the guitar to have a muddy, 'droning' quality, which can also obscure the guitar's note definition. Controlling and spectrally sculpting these regions is therefore essential to note definition, and this is especially so with rhythm guitar performances featuring fast subdivisions.

Bass Distortion

It is important to note that in addition to the radical harmonic distortion in its guitar timbres, contemporary metal is likely to present a number of other audio sources with distorted characteristics. Elements of highly distorted bass signals are a regular feature within overall bass sounds, where its use can provide additional harmonic content and an enhanced perception of proximity, thereby enabling a timbre that is more appropriate to the context provided by the rhythm guitars. As with guitar timbres, though, it is significant to note that there is a finite degree to which distortion can be applied to bass sounds before the law of diminishing returns comes into play, and retaining the note definition of the bass should always take priority. For example, although Troy Sanders from Mastodon employs bass distortion for most of his sounds on the (2014) *Once More 'Round The Sun* album, bass signal clarity is still retained (the bass line for the main riff of 'The Motherload' remaining entirely intelligible is just one example).

Vocal Distortion

Although the term 'heavy' is most frequently associated with characteristics relating to drums, bass, and guitar, the subjective perception of heaviness can also be impacted by vocal timbre. Although in contemporary metal, there is an aesthetic-association between heaviness and *the degree to which* vocal melody is avoided (Kahn-Harris, 2007, p. 32), vocals eschewing melody additionally need to be combined with vocal distortion in order to contribute to a production's sense of heaviness. Contemporary metal's vocal styles (e.g., Aaron Matts on 'For Untold Reasons' (2009) *Oubliette* EP) communicate a sense of considerable physical effort and aggression, and as a consequence are often so distorted and guttural as to fail to present any distinguishable note or pitch (Berger, 1999a, p. 164).

Aggressive vocal techniques can be somewhat simulated with processing, and this can provide a more appropriate vocal texture for the context of the music. However, it is more likely that a high level of vocal aggression provided at the performance stage would contribute to a production's sense of heaviness, rather than processing to emulate this. For example, Al Jourgenson's vocal sound on the vast majority of Ministry's (1991) 'Psalm 69' features a liberal application of distortion processing. Nevertheless, this far from results in Jourgenson's vocal sound communicating the levels of physical effort and aggression conveyed by Aaron Matts.

The Distortion Paradox Resolved

It is a given that metal music's guitar timbres have become heavier and heavier over time. This has been facilitated by way of developments in high-gain, valve guitar amplification technology (e.g., Peavey 5150, Mesa Roadster, EVH MkIII 5150, Engl Savage 120, etc.), which is adept at delivering pleasing even order musical harmonics when overdriven. With characteristics better suited to down tuning, this new breed of valve amplifiers has provided the ability for musicians and producers to achieve significantly heavier and denser rhythm guitar timbres whilst still retaining the vital quality of note definition. However, this progression toward higher-gain, heavier timbres with considerable high frequency energy has a clear impact on the context within which the rest of the instruments and vocals are placed.

As we have noted, the energy and density created by contemporary metal's radical harmonic distortion has a high tendency to mask/obscure other instruments and sounds and particularly those that have essential frequency content in regions where these guitars also have significant content. A useful analogy is that contemporary metal's harmonically distorted rhythm guitars create a dense wall of sound with wide foundations, through which the other signals must penetrate and 'punch' through. Failing to do so will not only result in these other musical statements, and the relevant artists' intentions, being left unclear, but will also result in these elements failing to properly fulfil their potential to contribute to the production's heaviness. This is at the very core of the challenges involved with contemporary metal music production.

For contemporary metal music, 'punchiness' is normally a fundamental obligation for this style of production and most particularly for the drums. This is first due to the manner in which size and weight, partly enabled by punch, contributes to the music's heaviness and sonic weight. Principally, though, the most effective way the drums can be clearly heard and understood within the context of the dense wall of rhythm guitars is through qualities relating to 'punchiness'. The entirely subjective terms 'punch' and 'punchiness' are commonly used within a wide range of music production styles and most often used to describe the perceptual attributes of the rhythm section within the mix. Punch generally refers to a high level of energy, density, weight, and power within a particular duration of time. This often results in these sources being perceived as having significant 'size' and 'mass'. Importantly, the attribute of punch is frequently enhanced through the capabilities of technology.

However, the 'size' and 'weight' associated with 'punch' needs to be informed by the speed of the relevant subdivisions involved. Clearly, sound sources with considerable size and weight take up a greater amount of 'space' in a production. If this space is not available due to the speed of subdivisions involved, then the size and weight of the source will be perceived as excessive, and this will likely obscure not only the energy and intensity of the performance, but also the clarity of other elements. Therefore, in instances of contemporary metal drum performances featuring fast subdivisions, the 'punch' required is often more concerned with emphasizing the transient attack of the sound source than with emphasizing size and weight. An example would be Behemoth's (2009) *Evangelion* album, where the drums have a very sharp attack, fast decay, and are quite 'thin' with minimal sonic weight, especially the kick drums. This can be contrasted with the drum sounds on Mastodon's (2014) *Once More 'Round the Sun* album, which have a greater emphasis on sonic weight and size, mainly due to there being more space within the production for these attributes to reside.

Definition and Intelligibility

Frith suggests that academics have a duty to make value judgments, rather than evade them, proposing that: 'Popular cultural arguments [...] are not about likes and dislikes as such, but about ways of listening, ways of hearing, about ways of being. The importance of value judgment for popular culture thus seems obvious, but it has been quite neglected' (1996, p. 8). Numerous writers have also highlighted the dichotomy in popular music between artistic/authentic/aesthetic values versus commercial concerns. For example, Moore refers to 'the opposition between the authentic and the commercial' (2002, p. 211), and Frith discusses the rhetoric between art and commercial values being kept apart (1996, p. 42). However, for contemporary metal music, when represented in recorded and mixed form, this dualism is largely removed.

The technicality of musical composition and performance complexity often displayed in this style of music represents a fundamental authentic/artistic perspective. This proficiency and sophistication is often afforded high value and esteem by artists and enthusiasts alike (Purcell, 2003, pp. 12–14), as Phillipov argues: 'Technical complexity is often claimed as a virtue in and of itself, with fans and musicians often claiming a level of prestige for the music based on its technical difficulty' (2012, p. 64).

Clearly, contemporary metal music culture places high value on genuine virtuosity and musicianship. Many of contemporary metal's most successful bands (for example Gojira, Fear Factory, Machine Head, Lamb of God,

Slipknot, etc.) that are held in esteem by both fans and other artists, combine performance energy and intensity with complexity and technicality of composition. However, for the listener to be convinced of virtuosity and advanced standards of musicianship in a production, a high level of clarity needs to be provided. If this clarity is not provided, the often-complex performative gestures are rendered largely unintelligible, and the ability to receive or perceive the virtuosity involved becomes obscured.

As highlighted, emphasizing the definition and intelligibility of contemporary metal's sounds tends to simultaneously enhance a production's perceived heaviness. An important element of this correlated increase of heaviness with improved intelligibility relates to the need to accentuate the energy of the performative gestures within the studio production. Importantly, this enhances and exaggerates the feelings of performance physicality required to produce these highly embodied sounds with the principal aim of evoking a synesthetic response in the listener. In this respect, as Wallach (2003) argues, the production sound is perceived as 'audiotactile', in that it aims to literally move the listener (p. 42). Similarly, Corbett (1994) discusses embodied presence in music recordings as tracing visual presence (pp. 41–44). This would appear to be particularly true of metal music where cultural understandings, often gained through the lived experience, become embedded in the perception of audio experience. An example of such cultural understanding would be the actions that are performed to create certain sounds. In many instances when guitars are perceived, the actions and emotional associations behind the relevant sounds are simulated. Wallach refers to sound waves' ability to create this experience as 'copresence' (2003, p. 36). In metal music, this notion of copresence is largely achieved through the intelligibility of the various sound sources, the emotional associations of which, therefore, contribute to a production's perceived heaviness. The author therefore proposes that productions presenting a lo-fi approach, with reduced sound source intelligibility, are not as subjectively heavy as those are where the performative gestures of the musicians are more intelligible. An example of this would be contrasting the 'lo-fi' approach of Darkthrone's (1994) 'Transilvanian Hunger', where the transients of the drum performance are largely unintelligible, compared with the high-fidelity/high production standards of Dimmu Borgir's (1999) 'Spiritual Black Dimensions'.

Although definition and intelligibility are often considered to be similar in meaning, they can be differentiated from each other. The term 'definition' refers to what it is about a single sound that makes it easy to perceive and understand. In other words, what characteristics that a sound source contains will allow it to be decipherable? Definition refers to what it is about each of the individual drum sounds heard during the brief solo drum fill from 3'43'–3'45' of Lamb of God's (2006) 'Blacken the Cursed Sun' track that allow the fast subdivisions to be decipherable and clearly understood. If the drum sounds on this production lacked the required definition, for instance if they had a dull and flat attack combined with a long resonant sustain, it would be much harder for the listener to make sense of what Chris Adler was playing here. Without definition, the impact of this drum fill would therefore be largely lost, as would Chris Adler's intentions when playing this part.

Whilst definition contributes to intelligibility, intelligibility refers to the ease of perception and understanding of a particular instrument or sound source within the perspective of the mix as a whole. So, for instance, intelligibility refers to not only how easy it is to understand what the notes and subdivisions of a complex guitar riff are playing, but also how easy it is to understand this riff when it is heard within the context of fast double kick drums, down tuned bass guitar also playing fast subdivisions, and a further guitar playing an entirely different part. An example of this exact scenario would be the fast subdivisions of the rhythm guitar riff from 3'20'–3'41' of Machine Head's (1994) 'Davidian'. Despite the density and concentrated nature of the other instrumentation during this section, the rhythm guitar riff and its respective notes remain intelligible.

If a contemporary metal production delivers poor definition and intelligibility, then the performances, particularly those that are complex, are rendered largely unintelligible. This results in the listener's ability to perceive the energy and intensity involved becoming obscured or lost. To use an analogy, when contemporary metal is produced with poor levels of definition and intelligibility, it is the sonic equivalent of a photo being so out of focus and badly printed that the image it attempts to portray is hard to decipher. Conversely, strong definition and intelligibility means that the image is clear. Therefore, the musical role of each and every element of the production serves its purpose, thereby supporting the intent of the musician. Obviously, sounds can only contribute to a production if they can actually be heard, and a clear production means that *every sound source* that *needs* to be heard *can* be heard. Bands whose performances involve a high level of musicianship and/or fast subdivisions have a considerable requirement for their production to deliver a high level of definition and intelligibility. This is simply because these qualities will enable the intent of the musicians to be properly represented.

However, not all contemporary metal bands will require clarity for every element of their production. The clarity of the vocal performances is one such example. In a vast majority of the world's music genres, vocal intelligibility is a fundamental requirement, mainly so that the message and emotion of the lyrics can be plainly understood. Of relevance here, though, is that in some genres, for example, German/Italian/foreign language opera, the listener often won't be able to understand the lyrics even if they are intelligible. Nevertheless, many of contemporary metal's vocal performances shun the traditional melodic role, and are often so guttural and feature so much vocal distortion that, regardless of the level of the vocal within the mix, the lyrical content is indecipherable. In these instances, although presenting the emotion and energy of the vocal performance is key, there is a lessened requirement for vocal intelligibility. A case in point would be the production of the post black metal band Deafhaven's (2013) album *Sunbather*. There is strong intelligibility to the beats and patterns of the drums, and the notes and chords of the guitars and bass are clearly defined, providing an overall production that is far from 'lo-fi'. However, a far lessened requirement for vocal intelligibility is represented on this album, due to the aggressive texture/non-melodic role of the vocal. This can be contrasted with the production requirements of, say, Killswitch Engage, whose choruses frequently present a requirement of a more typical intelligible quality. A correlation can easily be drawn, therefore, between the melodic content in contemporary metal's vocals and the need for vocal intelligibility.

Signal Processing and Technological Mediation

Compared to other popular music styles featuring similar instrumentation, contemporary metal music production has a greater fundamental requirement for the use of drum samples. Dunkley and Houghton (2011) even go as far as to say that the use of drum samples is the only way to get the drums to punch through the sonic wall of guitars. This is mainly due to the required density, weight, attack, and consistency of dynamics for the drums to cut through the harmonic distortion of the guitars and thereby contribute most effectively to the production's heaviness.

Despite this, it is important to highlight that the over-use, or misuse, of drum samples tends to sterilize and homogenize the raw energy, aggression, and intensity of a drum performance—and these qualities provide a vital contribution to a contemporary metal production's heaviness. This is because no matter how you go about employing drum samples, the interaction between the very first part of the signal chain (the performance itself) and the *natural* dynamic and timbral variations of the acoustic kit are inevitably obscured to some degree through their use. In simple terms, this means that the over-use, or misuse, of drum samples increasingly results in the perceived performance sounding less authentic and less believable, and therefore less likely to be associated with the organic energy of a genuine performance.

However, it is important to emphasize that even when a high quality drum sound and performance has been well recorded, thereby largely negating the need for *corrective* drum sample use, the *creative* benefits provided by drum samples can still prove essential. This is due to drum samples enabling greatly enhanced control. They can be provided with radical EQ boosts, which if carried out on the equivalent acoustic signal, would usually result in the unwanted emphasis of spill, and importantly, radical EQ boosts, particularly in the higher frequencies, are invariably required in order for the drums to cut through the dense upper frequency harmonic content of the guitars.

For anyone new to signal processing, compression (more precisely for these purposes of dynamic range compression) is the practice of reducing the disparity between the peaks and valleys of an audio signal. There are some music genres, for instance classical or jazz, where the control of dynamics is not particularly important to the required production approach. The wide dynamic range in the overall performance ethos to these styles regularly allows quieter sounds to still remain intelligible. Needless to say, though, dynamic range reduction clearly has significant relevance to a genre where high levels of consistent power and volume—from both a performance and production perspective—are a central tenet. The perception of loudness, which with many of the signals involved is largely enabled through the manipulation of compression processing, therefore tends to play a major role in the sound of a high standard contemporary metal production.

However, compression tends to be the most misunderstood, misused, and frequently overused processing tool during the mix stage of this style of music. Novice mixers often underestimate how challenging it is to get this aspect of a mix right, particularly as compression use will largely determine a production's fundamental sonic impact. Indeed, appropriate and effective application of compression across the relevant signals of the multi-track will often be the single factor that separates a truly great production from the merely average.

Important for this style of music, though, simply narrowing the dynamic range of a signal can be considered straight forward, whereas sculpting certain sounds so that they most effectively punch through the dense wall of harmonically distorted down-tuned rhythm guitars and remain intelligible within this context becomes a distinct challenge. For these reasons, compression use for contemporary metal music production is usually motivated as much by sound modification as for level control.

Additionally, the right make of compressor (for example, the Teletronix LA-2A [optical compressor] or the Urei 1176 [FET compressor]) providing appropriately radical gain reduction, can deliver elements of timbral coloration—often akin to a form of mild musical distortion. This often-overlooked quality generates musically related harmonic content, which delivers psychoacoustic information for perceptions of higher performance volume levels. For instance, more energetic and aggressive performances on the drums, bass, or vocals (or in fact most musical instruments) will impart additional overtones and frequencies from the instrument itself—with these qualities allowing the listener to thereby comprehend the increased performance energy and volume. Importantly, then, augmented harmonic content from compression heightens the perceived volume and energy of the performance event, enabling the drums, bass, and vocals to be more appropriate to, and more intelligible within, the harmonic distortion of the rhythm guitars.

Regardless of its sometimes less-prominent role and mix level, the importance of the bass guitar is frequently underestimated and misunderstood within this style. Although every project will have its own specific bass requirements, failing to present a dense and punchy bass sound with strong note definition will inevitably result in a production that has deficient sonic weight, heaviness, and overall clarity. A cursory listen to a number of high-standard contemporary metal productions will confirm that these attributes are common sonic denominators of the bass sounds presented.

Clearly, bass guitar tonalities have a considerable bearing on a productions' sense of heaviness, and these can be viewed as being heavy when their impact gives the sense of having sonic weight, density, and depth, as well as being proximate to the listener. However, one of the challenges created by the wall of down-tuned harmonically distorted guitars is getting these sounds to sit together, from a frequency-content perspective, with the bass. Rhythm guitars are generally considered as needing to occupy the midrange; however, here, the down-tuned guitars have a fundamental frequency that is occupying the area normally allocated to the bass drum and bass guitar. Therefore, it can often be the case that bass sounds that ordinarily, in isolation, embody the qualities of weight, size, and depth will not work within the context of the rhythm guitars, and therefore the mix overall.

From a bass engineering perspective then, enough rich harmonic content across the appropriate frequency spectrum needs to be generated, and captured. A common misconception is that equalization can be used for these purposes. However, in reality, equalizers are not capable of generating frequencies, or harmonic content—they can only amplify or attenuate those that already exist within any given signal. Therefore, the foremost engineering approach for capturing sonically heavy bass sounds is strengthening the coverage of frequencies through the layering of sounds. A signal layer of heavily distorted bass is a regular feature, which during the mix stage tends to have its frequency content heavily band limited.

Radical compression and EQ processing is also required of contemporary metal's vocal performances. This can be considered as providing a dynamic range that is more in keeping with the rhythm guitars, and with usually radical high frequency EQ boosts that inevitably should enable the vocals to be perceived as being as bright as the rhythm guitars. In many instances, largely dependent on the vocal characteristics in question, distortion processing will be employed. As well as generating additional harmonic content, this form of processing can bridge the gap between the radically distorted rhythm guitars and the vocals, which can sometimes be perceived as somewhat detached from each other.

Conclusions

Despite the fabricated soundscape that this considerable level of signal processing and technological mediation provides, this is not one that could be referred to as abstract. The impact of a high sonic standard metal production creates its own highly effective reality, whereby the highly controlled characteristics combined with sounds that are very close, but of great apparent size, are compressed into a single blended space. This is not hard for the listener to make sense of, as the sounds are not manipulated in any extraordinary way, and mostly, are all perceived as coming from the same location. However, the manner in which these sounds are presented can only exist in the production's artificial environment.

Note

1. The arguments developed in this chapter draw on material in my forthcoming book *Metal Music Manual: Producing, Engineering, Mixing and Mastering Contemporary Heavy Music* (to be published in January 2016 by Focal Press).

Bibliography

Berger, H. (1999). Death metal tonality and the act of listening. *Popular Music*, 18(2), 161–178.

Berger, H., & Fales, C. (2005). 'Heaviness' in the perception of heavy metal guitar timbres: The match of perceptual and acoustic features over time. In P. Green & T. Porcello (Eds.), *Wired for sound: Engineering and technologies in sonic cultures*. Middletown, CT: Wesleyan University Press.

Case, A. (2007). *Sound FX: Unlocking the creative potential of recording studio effects*. Burlington, MA: Focal Press.

Clarke, E. (2005). *Ways of listening: An ecological approach to the perception of musical meaning*. New York: Oxford University Press.

Corbett, J. (1994). Free, single and disengaged: Listening pleasure and the popular music object. In *Extended play: Sounding off from John Cage to Dr. Funkenstein* (pp. 32–55). Durham, NC: Duke University Press.

Dunkley and Houghton. (2011). Cutting Edge Drums. *Sound on sound* (online) March. Available at: http://www.soundonsound.com/sos/mar11/articles/cutting-edge-drums.htm (accessed August 2014).

Frith, S. (1988). Video pop: Picking up the pieces. In S. Frith (Ed.), *Facing the music: A Pantheon guide to popular culture* (pp. 88–130). New York: Pantheon Books.

Frith, S. (1996). *Performing rites: On the value of popular music*, Cambridge, MA: Harvard University Press.

Frith, S., & Zagorski-Thomas, S. (2012). *The art of record production: An introductory reader for a new academic field*. Farnham: Ashgate.

Gibson, J. (1979). *The ecological approach to visual perception*, Boston: Houghton Mifflin.

Hoffstadt, C., & Nagenborg, M. (2010). You're too fuckin' metal for your own good! Controlled anger and the expression of intensity and authenticity in post-modern heavy metal. In N. W. R. Scott & I. von Helden (Eds.), *The metal void: First gatherings* (p. 41). Oxford: Inter-Disciplinary Press.

Izhaki, R. (2007). *Mixing audio: Concepts, practices and tools*. Oxford: Elsevier Science Ltd.

Kahn-Harris, K. (2007). *Extreme metal: Music and culture on the edge*. Oxford and New York: Berg.

Middleton, R. (1990). *Studying popular music*. Buckingham: Open University Press.

Moore, A. F. (2001). *Rock: The primary text*. Burlington, VT: Ashgate Publishing.

Moore, A. F. (2002). Authenticity as authentication. *Popular Music*, 21(2), 214–218.

Moore, A. F. (2012). *Song means: Analysing and interpreting recorded popular song*, Farnham: Ashgate.
Mynett, M. (2012). Achieving intelligibility whilst maintaining heaviness when producing contemporary metal music. *Journal on the Art of Record Production* (6): http://arpjournal.com/achieving-intelligibility-whilst-maintaining-heaviness-when-producing-contemporary-metal-music/.
Phillipov, M. (2012). *Death metal and music criticism: Analysis at the Limits*. Lanham, MD: Lexington.
Purcell, N. (2003). *Death metal music: The passion and politics of a subculture*. Jefferson, NC: McFarland and Company.
Senior, M. (2011). *Mixing secrets for the small studio*. Burlington, Oxford: Elsevier.
Tagg, P. (1992) Subjectivity and soundscape, motorbikes and music. In H. Järviluoma (Ed.), *Soundscapes. Essays on vroom and moo* (pp. 48–66). Tampere: Department of Folk Tradition.
Wallach, J. (2003). The poetics of electrosonic presence: Recorded music and the materiality of sound. *Journal of Popular Music Studies*, 15(1), 34–64.
Walser, R. (1993). *Running with the devil: Power, gender and madness in heavy metal music*. Hanover, NH: Wesleyan University Press.
Williams, D. (2015). Tracking timbral changes in metal productions from 1990 to 2013. *Metal Music Studies*, 1(1), 39–68.
Zagorski-Thomas, S. (2012). Musical meaning and the musicology of record production: http://geb.unigiessen.de/geb/volltexte/2013/10095/pdf/Popularmusikforschung38_S135_148.pdf (accessed April 2015).
Zagorski-Thomas, S. (2014). *The musicology of record production*. Cambridge: Cambridge University Press.

Discography

Behemoth. (2009). *Evangelion*. Compact Disc. Nuclear Blast NB 2344–2, 27361 23442.
Darkthrone. (1994). *Transilvanian hunger*. Peaceville Records. VILELP43PMI.
Deafhaven. (2013). *Sunbather*. Deathwish. DW146.
Dimmu Borgir. (1999). *Spiritual black dimensions*. Nuclear Blast. NB 349–9.
Lamb of God. (2006). *Sacrament*. Epic Records. 721155.
Machine Head. (1994). *Burn my eyes*. Roadrunner Records. B000000H6G.
Mastodon. (2014). *Once more 'round the sun*. Reprise Records. B00K06PZ72.

Part II
Metal Music Scenes

6 Voracious Souls

Race and Place in the Formation of the San Francisco Bay Area Thrash Scene

Kevin Fellezs

> I really believe that Metallica invented thrash metal. I really believe that thrash metal did not exist until *Kill 'Em All* came out. You know, there [were] pockets of bands in L.A. and pockets of bands in New York that played heavy metal. But it was Metallica that brought it up to the next level. And it happened in San Francisco [...] Metallica was kicked out of L.A. because they weren't understood. I'm sure that after the fact it was really convenient for people to say, 'Oh, yeah, it started in L.A'. But, no. *It started in San Francisco.*
>
> —Kirk Hammett (Ernst, 2008)

American thrash metal was forged in the early 1980s in California, primarily by bands located in San Francisco and Los Angeles. Indeed, three of the so-called Big Four of thrash hail from California—Metallica, Slayer, and Megadeth—while the fourth band, Anthrax, originates from New York. Danny Lilker, bassist in Anthrax, adds support to Hammett's origin narrative in the film documentary, *Get Thrashed: The Story of Thrash Metal* (Ernst, 2008), confessing, 'Yeah, Metallica influenced Anthrax. We were like, holy shit. We saw those guys rehearse in the Music Room in Jamaica [Queens, NY] and it was very intense'. The two bands met while Metallica was in New York to record the band's debut, *Kill 'Em All* (Megaforce, 1983).

It is not my intention here to defend or denounce any particular origin narrative; this chapter is not a specific historical argument regarding thrash metal's origins. Rather, I begin with Metallica guitarist Kirk Hammett's pronouncement regarding the location for the launching of Metallica's eventual global success in order to think about the importance of place in locating thrash metal culture. Varas-Díaz at al. (2014) and many others (see Wallach, Berger and Greene, 2011) have produced convincing studies in which a particular geographic location set within its own array of spatialized imaginaries, colonialist histories, and hybrid populations—Puerto Rico in Varas-Díaz's case—contain the conditions of possibility that allow for a particular type of metal scene and, in some cases, metal music as well. I am interested, in this chapter, in questions and issues particular to outlining the specific 'contexts' for 'originary sites' by thinking through the case study of thrash metal. How do locale and location articulate Hammett's narrative of Metallica finding 'their audience' in San Francisco after the band was 'kicked out' of Los Angeles 'because they weren't understood' in the Southern California scene? Why might San Francisco *matter*?

I aim to show that thrash metal's hybrid aesthetic can be heard as an articulation of the San Francisco Bay Area's history of racial and ethnic diversity, cultural openness, and artistic experimentation, which had long characterized the city's rock musicians. While the term thrash metal can be aptly applied to Venom's music on the 1981 release, *Welcome to Hell*, or Mötörhead's 1980 recording, *Ace of Spades*, neither of the bands nor their records were described as such on their release. There were early scenes external to the San Francisco Bay Area in New York, Brazil, and Germany in which overlapping local heavy metal and punk scenes shared audiences, musicians, and taste hierarchies; indeed, the Los Angeles scene is often seen as a 'rival' to San Francisco, in terms of bragging rights over thrash's origins, but this relationship is only one marker of a scene, as delineated by Jeremy Wallach and Alexandra Levine (2013, p. 130; see also Brown, in press). Still, in terms of shaping the formation of 1980s thrash metal, nothing achieved the iconic status of the San Francisco Bay Area.[1]

In many ways, it is thrash's sonic articulation in California bands Metallica, Megadeth, and Slayer that became the sound of 21st century metal, particularly in terms of drumming styles and the highly compressed 'crunch' distortion timbre of the rhythm guitar. Phil Anselmo of Pantera asserts, 'Metallica was all about the brilliance of that crunchy fucking guitar. Before anyone else had it, *they had it*'. Hammett is not shy to claim Metallica 'took [metal] to the next level' (Ernst, 2008).

The aesthetics of San Francisco Bay Area thrash metal, which merged the heavy sounds of the New Wave of British Heavy Metal (NWOBHM) with the aggressive speed of hardcore punk, was a sonic rapprochement between metal and punk, which were seen to be poles apart politically, ideologically, and aesthetically. In addition, popular music in the San Francisco Bay Area's various scenes had long demonstrated the local area's cultural hybridity in which Asian, Latino, and Black contributions to the local cultural vitality were reflected in the audiences, music ensembles, and programming. As with any other cosmopolitan urban 'scape, there were musical performances of European, Asian, African, and South American music ensembles offered in multiple locations on any given evening, from the Davies Symphony Hall to the nightclubs of the North Beach neighborhood.

The local hard rock and metal scene was anchored by clubs such as the legendary East Bay local metal club, Ruthie's Inn, San Francisco's The Stone, The On Broadway, and Mabuhay Gardens, as well as Metal Mondays at the Old Waldorf. Audiences could also tune into the eclectic deejay-driven programming at KUSF, the University of San Francisco's college radio station, which built on a legacy of local 'free-form' FM radio stations such as KSAN and would feature the *Rampage Radio* show with heavy metal fans Ron Quintano (who also founded the *Metal Mania* fanzine), Ian Killen, and

Howie Klein, beginning in 1982. Local concertgoers had also enjoyed decades of eclectic programming in the concerts produced by local music impresario Bill Graham in which, for example, jazz trumpeter Miles Davis shared bills with the Grateful Dead at the Fillmore, the San Francisco concert hall.

Because thrash appeared to celebrate an individualist autonomy, it appealed to musicians interested in heavy metal who might otherwise have felt hesitant to participate in a genre racialized as white, meaning a presumed cohort of white musicians creating music listened to by an exclusively white audience. The assumption that the audiences for metal are comprised exclusively of suburban, working- and middle-class white males rests on the racial black-white binarism that permeates US American discourse regarding music genres (Weinstein, 2000 [1991] 2009; Walser 1993; Arnett, 1991; Binder, 1993). With few exceptions such as Latin music, which is racially and ethnically marked in specific ways, US American popular music is divided into black and white genres despite the hybrid, transracial constituencies and musical elements at play (and totally disregards any Asian influence or participation). While there are several facets to this binarism, including a significant historical involvement of early recording industry players such as Ralph Peer, who institutionalized the racialized distinction between 'race records' and 'hillbilly records' (Miller, 2010), I want to remain focused on the fact that the black-white binary effectively excludes other kinds of racialized bodies. Asian, American Indian, and other 'brown' ethnicities disappear before the logic of a black and white sounding world.

As George Lipsitz argues, 'Whiteness is everywhere in American culture, but it is very hard to see [...] *As the unmarked category against which difference is constructed, whiteness* never has to speak its name, *never has to acknowledge its role as an organizing principle in social and cultural relations*' (1995, p. 369, emphasis added). As a result, non-white musicians have felt generic limitations more dearly than their white counterparts who could easily perform in a variety of styles without losing credibility and whose relative ability to shrug off questions regarding authenticity reflected whiteness's cultural power and dominance (Miller, 2010; Small, 1998a).

Thrash metal, however, held a liberating vision of radical autonomy for musicians across the racial spectrum and was one of the reasons Black, Latino, and Asian American musicians began forming or joining thrash bands in the San Francisco Bay Area. This aspect of the thrash metal story has been largely ignored—even Kirk Hammett's Filipino background largely escapes notice (but see Wallach and Clinton, 2014, p. 2)—yet the contributions of these musicians formed a core element of thrash metal. Rather than provide an historical rundown of bands or musicians, I aim to challenge the *doxa* (to borrow Pierre Bourdieu's term for a widespread 'common sense' or the seemingly self-evident, even unconscious, ideological assumptions that tend to reinforce given social hierarchies) in which the racialization of thrash metal as a 'white genre' ignores the racial and ethnic diversity of the San Francisco Bay Area thrash scene itself. While I marshal historical evidence to support the claim that non-white working-class participation in the scene helped shape thrash metal's aesthetics and ideological orientation, my focus is on the ways in which that dominant perspective has served to eclipse the facts of hybridity, categorical transcendence, and a vernacular cosmopolitanism offered from the 'bottom up', that are central to understanding it.

Vernacular Cosmopolitanism

Combining the heaviness of NWOBHM bands with the speed of hardcore punk, thrash musicians both discarded and privileged various aspects of more mainstream hard rock performativities and aesthetics. As Steve Waksman (2009) notes in *This Ain't the Summer of Love*, his magisterial study of the connections between punk and metal: 'Often considered in oppositional terms, metal and punk have crossed into one another as often as they have been starkly differentiated [...] Metal and punk have enjoyed a particularly charged, at times even intimate sort of relationship that has informed the two genres in terms of sound, image, and discourse' (p. 7).

Additionally, as Jeremy Wallach, Harris M. Berger, and Paul D. Greene point out in *Metal Rules the Globe*, metal is a 'key site in which social agents publicly think about and debate modernity's wrenching social changes' (2011, p. 8). Building from these insights, I argue that the Filipino, Latino, Black, and American Indian metal musicians of the San Francisco thrash metal scene sought to carve out spaces of radical autonomy by forging a vernacular cosmopolitanism that pointedly ignored given cultural hierarchies with its attendant racializations.

In the 1987 video for 'Voracious Souls', the Death Angel song from which the title of this chapter is taken, a series of images is shown throughout the brief instrumental introduction: the band skateboarding in Aquatic Park in the Fisherman's Wharf area of San Francisco; sauntering along various San Francisco streets; hanging out at a bonfire on a beach—followed by a live performance, which occupies the majority of the video. In the introduction, there is also a brief segment showing the band members cavorting in a graveyard, jumping in and out of the cemetery, and goofing around at a gravestone, but as the introduction ends, band members stride aggressively past the gravestones. The metaphor I want to draw out here is one in which the performance of the song corresponds with the series of social policies that occurred throughout the 1980s under the Reagan administration, adversely affecting youth, particularly those from aggrieved communities, through 'tough on crime' policies that increased the surveillance and incarceration of these youth. This increase in the policing of youth of color was coupled with federal policies explicitly targeted to reduce government spending on public education and institutions dedicated to alleviating the quality of life and concerns of the poor and working classes, which complemented an increasing lack of employment opportunities for these same youth (Beckett and Sasson, 2004; Blanchard, 1987; Wilson, 2008, 2009).

In the 1990s, debates surrounding the theorization of cosmopolitanism circulated within anthropology and postcolonial studies. Scholars sought to strip the term of its Eurocentrism, and a number of qualified uses of cosmopolitanism were theorized. As Pnina Werbner notes,

> Vernacular cosmopolitanism belongs to a family of concepts, all of which combine in similar fashion apparently contradictory opposites: cosmopolitan patriotism, rooted cosmopolitanism, cosmopolitan ethnicity, working-class cosmopolitanism, discrepant cosmopolitanism [...] Vernacular cosmopolitanism is perhaps the most ambiguous of these conjunctural terms: are we talking about non-elite forms of travel and trade in a postcolonial world [...] or of non-European but nevertheless high cultures produced and consumed by nonwestern elites? (2006, p. 497)

Werbner's question unveils the contradictory sense of cosmopolitanism within contemporary globalization. There is an elite cosmopolitanism in which, as Stuart Hall describes, 'global entrepreneurs following the pathways of global corporate power and the circuits of global investment and capital, who can't tell which airport they're in', circulate (cited in Werbner 2008, pp. 346–347). Hall goes on to contrast this with another, a 'cosmopolitanism from below [of] people who have no choice as to whether or not to become cosmopolitans. They have to learn to live in two countries, to speak a new language and make a life in another place, not by choice but as a condition of survival' (ibid.).

The thrash musicians considered here are the diasporic children of these uprooted 'cosmopolitans from below', people who emigrated to the United States—or, in the case of American Indians, an internal displacement from 'home'—for reasons of survival. While most of the thrash musicians in San Francisco were working class, some raised in extreme poverty, their attraction to metal music can be heard as embodying aspirations of social equality on individualist terms, distinct from the normative disciplining of conventional political activity. While utopian and unrealized in many ways, thrash metal held out the promise of a cosmopolitan access to a larger world beyond the neighborhood or ethnic enclave for many young metal musicians on the scene. As then-14-year-old drummer for Death Angel, Andy Galeon, confessed in 1987, 'San Francisco is pretty cool but I'd like to check out some other cities. US or Europe or anywhere. Just to go, and play, and skate other territories',[2] a comment that speaks to metal's 'global turn' and a growing recognition of 'other territories' beyond the United States and Europe at the time.

In contemplating race within the San Francisco thrash metal scene, metal musicians such as Chuck Billy (Pomo American Indian) of Testament; Kirk Hammett (Filipino) of Metallica; Mike Coffey, Anthony Starks, and Darren Tompkins (all Black Americans) in Stone Vengeance; as well as the original members of Death Angel, Filipinos Rob Cavestany, Dennis Pepa, Gus Pepa, and Andy Galeon, did more than simply participate in a scene out of which a superstar band such as Metallica emerged—they helped to constitute it as racially diverse scene; one that undermines a narrative of white, working-class suburban male domination of metal scenes (Fellezs, 2013). Ryan Moore (2009), for example, assumes this narrative in tracing a genealogy of heavy metal from Black Sabbath to grunge and Nirvana that rests on an assumption of working- and middle-class US American white suburban male participation. While I agree with Moore that post-industrialization and downward social mobility are key factors in metal's often incoherent or, better perhaps, non-programmatic (a)political ideological underpinnings, I would like to complicate the racialization of thrash metal as a 'white musical style'. As Glenn Pillsbury asks at the conclusion of his study of Metallica, in which he dissects Metallica's articulation of white masculinity, 'How does the addition of bass player Robert Trujillo, who comes from a Spanish-American and Hispanic background, fit in the context of the constructions of whiteness so important to Metallica's reception history?' (2006, p. 188).

One possible answer might be found in the diverse population living in San Francisco throughout the 1980s. While Whites dominated at a little over 59%, there was a sizeable Black and Asian/Pacific Islander population (12.7% and 22%, respectively); add in a 'Spanish Origin' (taken to mean 'non-White Latina/o') population of 12.4%, and the Bay Area was almost evenly divided between Whites and non-Whites in 1980 (Metropolitan Transportation Commission, 2009, n.p.). While a diverse population is not necessarily mirrored by participation rates within a particular scene, many San Franciscan scenes enjoyed a diverse set of participants.

The Bay Area Scene(s)

The popular music scene throughout the early 1980s in San Francisco and California as a whole was much wider than thrash metal, which remained largely an underground phenomenon until Metallica managed to break into mainstream rock consciousness. While subculture and scene are often used interchangeably, I prefer scene, following Richard A. Peterson and Andy Bennett (2004), who, building on Will Straw's (1991) conception,

> view a local scene to be a focused social activity that takes place in a delimited space and over a specific span of time in which clusters of producers, musicians, and fans realize their common musical taste, collectively distinguishing themselves from others by using music and cultural signs often appropriated from other places, but recombined and developed in ways that come to represent the local scene. (p. 8)

Peterson and Bennett find the term subculture less useful as the 'term presumes that a society has one commonly shared culture from which the subculture is deviant [and] presumes that all of a participant's actions are governed by subcultural standards' (p. 5).

As Wallach and Levine's (2013) comparative study of metal scenes in Jakarta, Indonesia, and Toledo, USA, demonstrates, 'metal scenes generally do not emphasize ideological purity, as do punk and hardcore scenes' (p. 124). Their study not only explicitly marks the global reach of metal culture beyond a white male suburbia but also delineates four core functions as well as six generalizations of metal scenes that mirror Straw's demarcations (1991). I want to draw attention in particular to their second and third functions; namely, that scenes 'provide gathering places for collective consumption [and] for local performance and artifactual production' (Wallach & Levine, 2013, p. 119) of a particular musical formation. Indeed, as Waksman and others have described, the rich cassette trading culture in which knowledge about bands in distant scenes became known across the globe, inadvertently created a translocal network of fans, clubs, and record stores that metal bands would tap into in their attempts to reach beyond their local fan bases.

San Francisco is located on a geographically tiny peninsula, hemmed in by water on three sides, confined to a box-like 49 square miles. The scene, in other words, was easily accessible by many of its musicians and fans in a city with a transportation system that allowed even those without personal vehicles the means to attend concerts, rehearsals, and other related events. This spatial geography translated into a dynamic live scene involving active participants in a small, delimited urbanscape, allowing a rich cross-pollination of genres to develop. So, while the burgeoning metal scene was beginning to form around a number of local bands, venues, and record stores, there was also a nascent funk-rock fusion movement by bands such as Primus, Fishbone, and the Red Hot Chili Peppers, which shared performance venues and somewhat overlapping audiences with punks and metalheads (and which would soon explode into the rock mainstream). Within the local punk scene, there were sub-scenes, including straight edge and hardcore punk scenes, particularly in the East Bay, which grew out of the activities of punk bands such as Romeo Void, the Dead Kennedys, Flipper, the Mutants, and the Nuns. Additionally, there was a vibrant funk and R&B scene, particularly in the Black and Chicano neighborhoods of San Francisco and Oakland. While Sly and the Family Stone, Tower of Power, the Pointer Sisters, Maze, and Cold Blood were the most visible funk bands, there were dozens of funk and soul bands performing in bars and nightclubs throughout the San Francisco Bay Area.

Dominating all of these scenes and bands, however, especially in the local press and on the national charts, were the pop-rock groups out of which highly successful bands such as Huey Lewis and the News emerged. There were dozens of local pop-rock acts, including Eddie Money, the Greg Kihn Band, Pearl Harbor and the Explosions, Bonnie Hayes and the Wild Combo, Tommy Tutone, and the Rubinoos. There were also hard rock bands such as Montrose, whose guitarist, Ronnie Montrose, would go on to form progressive rock group Gamma, Y&T (originally named Yesterday and Today), and local Hendrix impersonator, Randy Hansen. Art rockers, The Tubes, were somewhat in a category of their own with their elaborate stage shows and hard rock sensibilities as were The Residents, an 'anonymous' art rock group. Additionally, overriding all of these rock groups were internationally known groups such as Journey, Jefferson Airplane/Starship, Santana, and the Grateful Dead, though with the exception of the Dead and its various members' offshoot groups, these superstar groups rarely played in the area unless part of large national or international tours.

Ironically, these superstar bands featured veterans of the earlier hippie countercultural scene associated with San Francisco's Haight-Ashbury district, though by 1967—a year in which both the 'summer of love' and the November 'funeral for the hippie' transpired—the failure to reconcile the contradictions within the hippie movement with its mix of communal, anti-capitalist counterculture and bourgeois, even entrepreneurial, individualism was already beginning to disperse the early Flower Children from the neighborhood. 'Haight-Ashbury', however, would continue to index a cluster of ideas regarding, among other issues, sexual mores and drug use that continued resonating within (and outside) rock culture, reflected in the phrase 'sex, drugs, and rock and roll', even in music that sounded nothing like period 'acid rock' or was produced by artists otherwise antagonistic to 'hippie values' (e.g., Velvet Underground, Frank Zappa).

Outside of rock, jazz has enjoyed a long history in San Francisco, which, at the time of thrash metal's emergence, boasted internationally known local musicians such as vibraphonist Bobby Hutcherson, drummer Billy Higgins, drummer Eddie Marshall, alto saxophonist John Handy, pianist Denny Zeitlin, and drummer Tony Williams, all of whom could be seen performing in local jazz clubs. In fact, the jazz scene enjoyed a rich legacy of clubs such as the Blackhawk and the Hungry i from the 1950s and 1960s that was continued in the 1980s by the Keystone Korner and Pearl's, both of which were located in the historically Italian neighborhood of North Beach. In addition, there were numerous restaurants, cafes, and neighborhood bars where jazz continued to be performed. Across the Bay Bridge in Oakland, there was the high profile jazz club nestled into a Japanese restaurant at Yoshi's, as well as jazz performances in numerous restaurants and bars throughout Oakland and Berkeley.

Given the large Latino population in San Francisco, there was a dynamic Latin music scene centered at clubs like Bajone's and Cesar's Latin Palace in the Mission district. There were also smaller scenes such as the West Coast Western Swing bands in which Norton Buffalo's Stampede and Asleep at the Wheel gave evidence of the rich cross-genre (jazz and country, in this case) sensibilities of the San Francisco Bay Area. There was also the 'new dawg' movement of David Grisman and his cohort, which updated bluegrass with a virtuosity that was informed by the jazz stylings of Django Reinhardt as much as by traditional bluegrass conventions.

Though not part of scenes per se, there were bands that continued to draw on the legacy of earlier periods of San Franciscan musical movements such as neo-surf heartthrob Chris Isaak, the psychedelic-surf band the Mermen, and perennial scenesters the Flamin' Groovies, all of which kept the sounds of older styles of rock alive in San Francisco clubs. There were a small number of ska bands of which The Uptones were the best known nationally. Similar to large metropolitan areas throughout the United States, there were numerous reggae, country, and blues bands adding their sounds to the rich musical soundscape heard throughout the greater San Francisco Bay Area.

This brief overview of the various popular music scenes is meant to provide a broader context against which thrash metal emerged in the San Francisco Bay Area. While this survey is certainly not complete or comprehensive, scenes are often written about as if they were formed in isolation or only in conjunction with or opposition to a purported mainstream (notable exceptions are Barry Shank's (1994) *Dissonant Identities* and Harris Berger's (1999) *Metal, Rock, and Jazz*). I mean to highlight the fact that underground scenes are often jostling for visibility with a number of other subcultures/scenes and therefore must be considered co-constitutive elements in a broader local or regional popular music culture.

Deviance or Agency?

As Andy R. Brown's (2011) research indicates, academic work on heavy metal was initially produced by psychologists and sociologists wanting to 'measure' levels of 'deviance' within heavy metal youth subculture (see also Walser, 1993a). Deviance was defined as the underage consumption of alcohol and other drugs, truancy, delinquency, and other forms of 'anti-social' behavior. Many of these studies were conducted in the late 1980s, simultaneous with the consolidation of thrash as a commercially viable genre, when anxieties regarding metal and rap music reached a 'fever pitch' due to the reporting of 'record' suicides rates among metal fans and the moral panic surrounding gangsta rap lyrics (Litman and Barberow, 1994; Brown and Hendee, 1989; Arnett, 1991; Bennett, 2002; Binder, 1993; Brown, 2013).

These studies reinforced the 'public outcry' against these two youth music cultures, fomenting a 'tough on crime' rhetoric by political legislators. But as Amy Binder (1993) points out, the outcry took a decidedly racialized turn:

> Writers who were concerned about heavy metal lyrics and rap lyrics did not address the content of the music alone; embedded in their discussions were reactions to differences in the demographic characteristics of the genres' producers and audiences—music made by and for working and middle-class white youth versus music they perceived as predominantly by and for urban black teenagers [...] rap music—with its evocation of angry black rappers and equally angry black audiences—was simultaneously perceived as a more authentic and serious art form than was heavy metal music, and as a more frightening and salient threat to society as a whole than the 'white' music genre. (p. 754)

Heavy metal music was heard as simultaneously threatening and comical, a threat by musical no-talents whose caricature in the comedy film, *This Is Spinal Tap* (1984), engendered knowing nods and chuckles from both metal fans and musicians as well as from the music's detractors—and often for the same reasons—including overweening pretense, misguided virtuosic tendencies, and bellicose posturing. I raise Binder's insight in order to point to two main assumptions regarding heavy metal during this period: one, it is a white genre and therefore while occasionally accused of fueling aberrant white male behavior, is not considered a threat to social cohesion that rap, a 'black' genre, represents; and two, it is not a 'serious' musical genre worthy of scholarly consideration.

Leaving aside, momentarily, the impact of race on metal, I want to take up the notion of agency and its powerful rhetorical and signifying practice within metal music culture. Metal musicians, regardless of the type of metal music they perform, indulge in the forbidden (coincidentally the name of one of the better-known Bay Area thrash bands) as a means to not only acquire autonomous power but also to practice wielding it, establishing rituals and other symbolic means for performing individual as well as collective agency.

In particular, I want to suggest that the 'mosh pit' that emerges as a key symbolic practice in the Bay Area scene is an expression of this self-control, a space in which unwritten codes determine the extent of performative violence that allows participants to dance in a collective expression of power while controlling their movements *just enough* in order to keep actual physical harm to a minimum (Lull, 1986).[3] This balancing of abandonment and control is at the heart of understanding thrash metal as well as other extreme forms of metal music as agentive performance rather than deviant aggression. As another instance of the ways in which punk and metal fans interacted in the San Francisco Bay Area at the time, the preferred term was not 'moshing' but 'slam dancing'. Metal fans borrowed the term from the Northern California skate punk hardcore scene in which punk 'pogo-ing' had morphed into the more aggressive arm twirling, leg kicking movements that appeared more like fighting than dancing. The point, however, was not to intentionally hurt one another (though that certainly occurred often enough) but, as with stage diving, participants observed unwritten codes prohibiting actual fighting, policing each other and keeping fellow dancers from real harm. Admittedly, the rhetoric of metal music is often directed toward individual empowerment, often in the face of larger structural if mystified forces, but I want to keep our attention on the performance of individual empowerment in collective spaces such as concerts and the equilibrium sustained between violence and community caught within the mosh pit.

Color-blind or just blind?

Psychologists attempted to explain deviance by surveying heavy metal audiences and assisted in fueling various moral panics associated with the purported ill effects of heavy metal musicking (often, as mentioned, accompanied by comparisons to rap music). Indeed, Robert L. Gross (2004) writes, 'Most metal cultists [note the term!] come into this subculture with preconceived notions that this is a group in which there are others who share their feelings of isolation, anger and a dissatisfaction with life' (p. 126). Although Gross concluded that 'many of today's hard core metal fans will no doubt grow up to be outstanding community leaders' (ibid.), the stereotype of the typical metal fan as an alienated and inarticulate suburban working-class male remains a powerful caricature (e.g., Linxwiler and Gay, 2000).[4]

Despite the challenge to the prevailing moral panic about metalheads as anti-social delinquents mounted by the seminal studies of Deena Weinstein (2000 [1991]), Donna Gaines (1991), and Robert Walser (1993a), which emphasized the value of the music and the culture(s) of metal, their emphases on whiteness, heteronormative masculinity, youth, and exurbanity bore only a slight resemblance to the 1980s metal scene in the San Francisco Bay Area, as we have seen.[5] San Francisco is often characterized, even caricatured, by its 'anything goes' attitude toward alternative lifestyles, political views, and social relations that is reflected in the wide diversity of races, sexual orientations, and self-identified social positionings that its residents claim, perform, and enact. Thrash metal emerged in the wake of second wave feminism, gay liberation, black power, and a lingering hippie counterculture still fully resonant and visible throughout the Greater Bay Area. These social movements not only marked San Francisco as one of the more visible spaces for social experimentation and progressive political discourse but also gave room to artistic exploration that was not confined to historically bohemian enclaves such as North Beach with its legacy of the Beats or the Haight-Ashbury district with its remaining vestiges of the hippie counterculture. Particularly for thrash musicians, the lingering resonance of earlier rock experiments with leading exponents from San Francisco such as those found in acid rock (e.g., the Grateful Dead, Jefferson Airplane, Quicksilver Messenger Service, Moby Grape) that would eventually become larger trends within popular music paved the way for encouraging experimentation and exploration by rock musicians throughout the area. This also fed the idea that an underground movement could yield commercial success without compromising other ideals associated with rock music such as anti-commercialism, leftist politics, and anti-bourgeois sensibilities (Zimmerman, 2008; Fellezs, 2014).

In terms of race, there were a number of models of non-black, non-white musicians participating in various popular music genres, such as Filipino jazz pianist, Joseph 'Flip' Nuñez, whose career never achieved much visibility beyond jazz cognoscenti. Somewhat concurrent with the thrash scene was the emergence of the Asian American jazz movement, which was also initially centered in the San Francisco Bay Area with baritone saxophonist Fred Ho, tenor saxophonist Francis Wong, pianist Jon Jang, and bassist Mark Izu, among others (Dessen, 2006; Fellezs, 2007; Kajikawa, 2012). In terms of rock music, there was Carlos Santana and his brother, Jorge, who led Malo, another Latin rock band, as well as the Escovedo family, from *paterfamilias* Pete, who led the brilliant Latin rock band, Azteca, to his daughter, Sheila E., who was enjoying widespread success due to her association with Prince during this time period, as well as the already-mentioned metal musicians. My main point here is that San Francisco provided not only a racially and ethnically diverse population but had also enjoyed a long history of Asian and Latina/o musicians, both native-born and immigrant, who were active not only in local scenes but had achieved national and international stature as well.

Within this larger musical and cultural context, then, the appearance of a band of Filipino musicians such as Death Angel is not particularly extraordinary. However, at the time, as I have detailed above, the metal world still assumed an environment exclusively racialized as white and Death Angel or American Indian vocalist Chuck Billy of Testament did little to trouble such assumptions, and again Kirk Hammett's own Filipino background was little noted at the time. Indeed, in an early promotional video for Death Angel, vocalist Mark Osegueda and drummer Andy Galeon disavow that their music has anything to do with their Filipino background. However, this can be seen in light of two central issues: young second-generation Asian-Americans are typically inured to racial discrimination, viewing it more as a problem for blacks or Latina/os than for their communities, despite what they may experience, often through internalizing the model-minority myth; and, they may have chosen to downplay race in an effort to avoid tokenism and be evaluated on their 'music alone', a common strategy for musicians of color working in white-identified musical genres (Jung, 2012). In her study of Asian American musical production, for example, ethnomusicologist Grace Wang (2014) notes that contemporary discussions of color-blind universalism in music circles obscures the role of whiteness in the formation of standards and norms, which:

> helps explain why Asian American musicians working in both classical and popular music might express pride in their ethnic heritage while downplaying the impact that race and/or racism play in their professional lives or seek to commodify their ethnic identity while disowning the existence of racial barricade. (p. 15)

Unlike Osegueda and Galeon's early dismissal regarding the impact of race on their musicking, vocalist Chuck Billy of Testament frequently raises issues related to American Indians in his lyrics, notably 'Trail of Tears' (*Low*, 1994), 'Allegiance' (*The Gathering*, 2000) and 'Native Blood' (*Dark Roots of Earth*, 2012) and publicly announced his belief in American Indian spiritual practices as a result of their role in helping him overcome germ cell seminoma cancer (Billy, 2012). It is worth noting, however, that the first of these songs, 'Trail of Tears', was recorded nearly a decade after the heyday of the thrash metal scene in San Francisco. Still, contrary to the allegations of metal music's debilitative effects, Billy was honored by the California State Assembly through Assemblyman Jim Frazier's efforts in recognition of Billy's 'positive influence' on American Indian youth and the general public in 2013 (Shrum, 2013).

Conclusion

To return to the 1980s, the diversity of the Bay Area thrash scene was due to the heterogeneity of the Bay Area beyond the metal club stage and rehearsal studio. Indeed, as the Black American members of thrash band, Stone Vengeance, attest, while there was little room for Black American thrash musicians beyond the local San Francisco scene, particularly in terms of the commercial music industry, the local scene embraced them.[6] This inclusive plurality gave thrash metal its particular shape—a willingness to merge two disparate genres, heavy metal and punk, being the most conspicuous signifier of thrash metal's cultural openness. Mixed race band memberships as well as bands without white members at all were further indications of thrash metal's pluralistic origins and ideological thrust. While arguably having moved away from a strict definition of thrash metal, the scene's most visible and commercially successful band, Metallica, can still boast of having a Filipino lead guitarist, Kirk Hammett, and a Chicano bassist, Robert Trujillo, continuing the racial inclusiveness of the original San Francisco Bay Area metal scene.

Was it a perfectly integrated scene? It would be disingenuous to assert that the thrash scene was a perfect social experiment in racial harmony. However, my point in this chapter has been to underline the idea that an aesthetic that mixed musical genres and was formed within a heterogeneous, even proudly diverse, urbanscape, embracing members from a variety of racial and ethnic groups, is underserved and misrepresented by a discourse that roots heavy metal—and thrash metal, in particular—in white masculinist stereotypes. As the Black American thrash band, Stone Vengeance, sings in 'Higher Now': 'I listen to the wisdom now/I am, "Show me how"'. It is in this spirit of open-mindedness that thrash metal, for all its dark, violent imagery, invites a reconfiguration of the *doxa* that privileges and centralizes white masculinity within metal music culture—its challenge continuing to reverberate within various styles of extreme and progressive metal throughout the often rancorous chambers of metal music culture.

Notes

1. San Francisco as thrash metal's originary scene is also the underlying argument of the film documentary, *Get Thrashed: The Story of Thrash Metal*. If one uses debut recording release dates as an indication of a scene's visibility beyond the local, then the appearance of Metallica's debut in 1983 is months, sometimes years, before the debut recordings of other contenders to thrash's origins and thus seems to trump those other claims. Additionally, while Los Angeles

had its own thrash scene, providing Brian Slagel the impetus to found Metal Blade Records, an important label for thrash, this chapter will focus on the San Francisco Bay Area scene. I concede that there are other ways to measure the importance of a particular scene or to support a claim for site of origin of a musical style or tradition.
2. Quoted in *Death Angel*, promotional video, 1987. The Death Angel promotional video is available for viewing on YouTube: https://www.youtube.com/watch?v =0kwpwWTvva4 (accessed July 6, 2014).
3. A participant-observer ethnography on the San Francisco area conducted by James Lull places 'thrashing' within the punk scene, see, in particular, pages 241–243, in which he details 'thrashers' at live shows. Interestingly, there is no mention of metal in the article. I want to thank Andy R. Brown for alerting me to Lull's essay.
4. While recent studies show that heavy metal fans, particularly outside of North America, are drawn from middle-class backgrounds (see Brown, this volume), early research focused on the ways in which heavy metal preference was indicative of limited educational and employment potential. See Bryson (1996).
5. Waksman (2009) provides an alternative to this general trend in his chapter-long study of The Runaways, an all-female band that he reveals was much more agentive than it was often given credit for.
6. According to Stone Vengeance leader, Mike Coffey, white San Francisco metal music radio disc jockey andscene booster, Ron Quintana, was instrumental in recording Stone Vengeance's first LP.

Bibliography

Arnett, J. (1991). Adolescents and heavy metal music: From the mouths of metalheads. *Youth Society,* 23(1), 76–98.

Arnett, J. (2002). The psychology of globalization. *American Psychologist,* 57(10), 774–783.

Bayer, G. (2009). *Heavy metal music in Britain.* Surrey: Ashgate.

Beckett, K., & Sasson, T. (2004). *The politics of injustice: Crime and punishment in America.* New York: Sage Publishing.

Bennett, A. (2002). Researching youth culture and popular music: A methodological critique. *British Journal of Sociology,* 53(3), 451–466.

Berger, H. (1999). *Metal, rock, and jazz: Perception and the phenomenology of musical experience.* Middletown, CT: Wesleyan University Press.

Billy, C. (2012). Testament's Chuck Billy talks to LRI about health, happiness, dark roots and Dublin death. *Legendary Rock Interviews:* http://www.legendaryrockinterviews.com/2012/09/17/chuck-billy-of-testament-talks-to-lri-about-dark-roots-dublin-death-patrol-and-embracing-life/ (accessed July 11, 2014).

Binder, A. (1993). Constructing racial rhetoric: Media depictions of harm in heavy metal and rap music. *American Sociological Review,* 58(6), 753–767.

Blanchard, O. J. (1987). Reaganomics. *Economic Policy,* 2(5), 15–56.

Brown, A. R. (2011). Heavy genealogy: Mapping the currents, contraflows, and conflicts of the emergent field of metal studies, 1978–2010. *Journal for Cultural Research,* 15(3), 213–242.

Brown, A. R. (2013). Suicide solutions? Or, how the emo class of 2008 were able to contest their media demonization, whereas the headbangers, burnouts or 'children of Zoso' generation were not. In T. Hjelm, K. Kahn-Harris, & M. LeVine (Eds.), *Heavy metal: Controversies and countercultures* (pp. 17–35). Sheffield: Equinox Publishing.

Brown, A. R. (in press). Thrash/Speed metal. In J. Shepherd, D. Horn, & D. Laing (Eds.), *The continuum encyclopedia of popular music of the world (Vol 8: Genres)*. New York and London: Continuum.

Brown, E. F., & Hendee, W. R. (1989). Adolescents and their music: Insights into the health of adolescents. *Journal of the American Medical Association*, 262(12), 1659–1663.

Bryson, B. (1996). Anything but heavy metal: Symbolic exclusion and musical dislikes. *American Sociological Review*, 61(5), 884–899.

California Postsecondary Education Commission. (1985). Population and enrollment trends: 1985–2000: The third in a series of background papers for the commission's long-range planning project. *Commission Report*, March 4, 85–16.

Cavestany, R., & Osegueda, M. (1986). *Voracious souls*. I.P.F.S. Rejected Youth/La Rana Music (BMI).

Coffey, M. (1998). *Higher now*. Stone Vengeance Music (BMI).

Dessen, M. (2006). Asian Americans and creative music legacies. *Critical Studies in Improvisation*, 1(3), 1–15.

Ernst, R. (2008). *Get thrashed: The story of thrash metal*. Saigon1515 Productions: Warner Bros.

Fellezs, K. (2007). Silenced but not silent: Asian American jazz. In M. T. Nguyen & T. L. N. Tu (Eds.), *Alien encounters: Popular culture in Asian America* (pp. 69–108). Durham: Duke University Press.

Fellezs, K. (2013). Black metal soul music: Stone Vengeance and the aesthetics of race in heavy metal. In T. Hjelm, K. Kahn-Harris, and M. LeVine (Eds.), *Heavy metal: Controversies and countercultures* (pp. 182–200). Sheffield: Equinox Publishing.

Fellezs K. (2014). The sun and moon have come together: The fourth way, the counterculture, and Capitol Records. In T. S. Brown & A. Lison (Eds.), *The global sixties in sound and vision: Media, counterculture, revolt* (pp. 151–166). New York: Palgrave-Macmillan.

Frith, S. (1998). *Performing rites: On the value of popular music*. Cambridge, MA: Harvard University Press.

Gross, R. L. (2004). Heavy metal music: A new subculture in American Society. *Journal of Popular Culture*, 24(1), 119–130.

Jung, S. (2012). Left or right of the color line? Asian Americans and the racial justice movement. *ChangeLabinfo.com* http://www.changelabinfo.com/research-paper/left-or-right-of-the-color-line/#.VDrG6edf-Dc (accessed July 11, 2014).

Kajikawa, L. (2012). The sound of struggle: Black revolutionary nationalism and Asian American jazz. In D. Ake, C. H. Garrett, & D. I. Goldmark (Eds.), *Jazz/Not jazz: The music and its boundaries* (pp. 190–216). Berkeley: University of California Press.

Linxwiler, J., & Gay, D. (2000). Moral boundaries and deviant music: Public attitudes toward heavy metal and rap. *Deviant Behaviour: An Interdisciplinary Journal*, 21, 63–85.

Lipsitz, G. (1995). The possessive investment in whiteness: Racialized social democracy and the 'white' problem. *American Quarterly*, 47(3), 369–387.

Litman, R. E., & Farberow, N. L. (1994). Pop-Rock music as precipitating cause in youth suicide. *Journal of Forensic Sciences*, 30(2), 494–499.

Lull, J. (1986). Thrashing in the pit: An ethnography of San Francisco punk subculture. In T. Lindlof (Ed.), *Natural audiences: Qualitative research on media uses and effects* (pp. 225–252). Norwood, NJ: Ablex.

Metropolitan Transportation Commission (MTC) and the Association of Bay Area Governments. (1990). Bay Area Census: San Francisco City and County Decennial Census Data. http://www.bayareacensus.ca.gov/counties/SanFranciscoCounty70.htm (accessed July 11, 2014).

Miller, K. H. (2010). *Segregating sound: Inventing folk and pop music in the age of Jim Crow*. Durham: Duke University Press.

Moore, R. M. (2009). *Sells like teen spirit: Music, youth culture, and social crisis*. New York: New York University Press.

Peterson, R. A., & Bennett, A. (Eds.). (2004). Introducing music scenes. In *Music scenes: Local, trans-local, and virtual* (pp. 1–15). Nashville: Vanderbilt University Press.

Pew Research Center. (2013). The rise of Asian Americans. Updated edition: April 4, 2013.

Pillsbury, G. (2006). *Damage incorporated: Metallica and the production of musical identity*. New York and London: Routledge.

Shank, B. (1994). *Dissonant identities: The rock 'n' roll scene in Austin, Texas*. Middletown: Wesleyan University Press.

Shrum. (2013). Testament: Chuck Billy honored by California State Assembly! *New Noise Magazine,* June 7, 2013 http://newnoisemagazine.com/testament-chuck-billy-honored-by-california-state-assembly/ (accessed July 11, 2014).

Small, C. (1998a [1987]). *Music of the common tongue: Survival and celebration in African American music*. Hanover, NH: Wesleyan University Press.

Small, C. (1998b) *Musicking: The meanings of performing and listening*. Hanover, NH: Wesleyan University Press.

Straw, W. (1984). Characterizing rock music cultures: The case of heavy metal. *Canadian University Music Review,* 5, 104–122.

Straw, W. (1991). Systems of articulation, logics of change: Communities and scenes in popular music. *Cultural Studies,* (5)1, 368–88.

Varas-Díaz, N., Rivera-Segarra, E., Rivera Medina, C. L., Mendoza, S., González-Sepúlveda, O. (2014). Predictors of communal formation in a small heavy metal scene: Puerto Rico as a case study. *Metal Music Studies,* 1(1), 87–103.

Waksman, S. (2009). *This ain't the summer of love: Conflict and crossover in heavy metal and punk*. Berkeley, Los Angeles, and London: University of California Press.

Wallach, J., & Clinton, E. (2014). Recoloring the metal map: Metal and race in global perspective. Unpublished paper.

Wallach, J., & Levine, A. (2013). I want *you* to support local metal: A theory of metal scene formation. In T. Hjelm, K. Kahn-Harris, & M. LeVine (Eds.), *Heavy metal: Controversies and countercultures* (pp. 117–126). Sheffield: Equinox Publishing.

Wallach, J., Berger, H. M., & Greene, P. D. (Eds.). (2011). *Metal rules the globe: Heavy metal music around the world*. Durham: Duke University Press.

Walser, R. (1993a). Professing censorship: Academic attacks on heavy metal. *Popular Music Studies,* 5(1), 68–78.

Walser, R. (1993b). *Running with the devil: Power, gender and madness in heavy metal music*. Hanover, NH: Wesleyan University Press.

Wang, G. (2014). *Soundtracks of Asian America: Navigating race through musical performance*. Durham: Duke University Press.

Weinstein, D. (2000 [1991]). *Heavy metal: The music and its culture*, (rev. ed.). New York: Da Capo.
Weinstein, D. (2009). The empowering masculinity of British heavy metal. In G. Bayer (Ed.), *Heavy metal music in Britain* (pp. 17–31). Surrey: Ashgate.
Werbner, P. (2006). Vernacular cosmopolitanism. *Theory, Culture and Society*, 23(2–3), 496–498.
Werbner, P. (2008). Cosmopolitanism, globalisation and diaspora: Stuart Hall in conversation with Pnina Werbner, March 2006. In P. Werbner (Ed.), *Anthropology and the new cosmopolitanism: Rooted, feminist and vernacular perspectives*. Oxford: Berg.
Wilson, W. J. (2008). The political and economic forces shaping concentrated poverty. *Political Science Quarterly*, 123(4), 551–571.
Wilson, W. J. (2009). Toward a framework for understanding forces that contribute to or reinforce racial inequality. *Race and Social Problems*, 1(1), 3–11.
Zimmerman, N. (2008). *Counterculture kaleidoscope: Musical and cultural perspectives on late sixties San Francisco*. Ann Arbor: University of Michigan Press.

7 The Unforgiven
A Reception Study of Metallica Fans and 'Sell-Out' Accusations[1]

Eric Smialek

During the 1980s, as Metallica grew in popularity, their quick tempos and complex song structures became markers of distinction from other metal bands, suggesting that they were able to achieve popularity without conforming to popular song-writing norms. Metallica's apparent refusal to compromise resulted in an aura of authenticity that would inflate the band's underground prestige throughout the 1980s.

The next decade of Metallica's career included a series of moves that increasingly alienated many of the band's fans, tarnishing its reputation to the point where high-profile metal musicians voiced opposition to the band (Christe, 2003, pp. 307, 312–313), and some writers spoke of Metallica's inauthenticity as though it were a truism. Deena Weinstein (2000), for instance, after detailing many of the changes that fans reacted against, casually referred to a 1998 Metallica concert as a 'sell-out show' in her historical summary of metal in the 1990s (p. 290).

These reactions would only intensify into the new millennium with Metallica's lawsuit against Napster, a legal battle that explicitly pitted the band against many of its fans in a way that made Metallica seem antagonistic, ungrateful, and hypocritical—and perhaps most importantly, as I will later argue, conspicuously wealthy. Controversy surrounding Metallica has lasted well over two decades, touching on multiple issues of sensitivity for fans, including the significance of genre and its relationship with categories of identity, the effect of commerce on musical creativity and artistic motivation, and the expectations placed on musicians regarding stylistic change, notions of loyalty, beliefs about authenticity, and the process of aging within a subculture that prizes rebellion. This chapter aims to demonstrate how these concerns impacted Metallica's increasingly controversial reception, deploying Pierre Bourdieu's theories of cultural production to explain how fans' frustrations became compounded over time and how their judgments were informed by broader social belief systems within metal subculture.

The Canonization of Early Metallica, or Metallica and Authenticity

Although the desire to be independent from mass culture is by no means unique to metal, several studies on metal music and fans have argued that individualism represents a common value for metal fans (Berger, 1999, pp. 264–269, 286–290; Kahn-Harris, 2007, p. 42; Purcell, 2003, p. 132). While this is most apparent in the kinds of transgression valued by audiences of extreme metal (Kahn-Harris, 2007, pp. 27–49, 127–129*ff.*), Metallica's ability to convince fans and critics during the 1980s that they were complex, in control, and independent from the hedonism and overt sexuality of glam metal (Pillsbury, 2006, pp. 57–98, esp. 88–98), a symbol of mass culture for many metal fans of the time, played a central role in their subcultural consecration. For many fans and critics, these qualities were most evident in the band's lyrics. Several contributors to *Metallica and Philosophy* devote considerable attention to the emphasis they find in Metallica's lyrics toward individuality (Nys, 2007), freedom (Fosl, 2007, p. 78; Sotos, 2007), and the rejection of 'normalcy and conformity' (Wisnewski, 2007, p. 55). Musically, Metallica communicated these ideals through lengthy, complex songs that emphasize power and control using amplified, high-gain distortion and an emphasis on ensemble virtuosity.[2] As Pillsbury (2006) has argued, these stylistic factors played an important role in marketing Metallica as a kind of 'thinking man's metal' (pp. 57–98, esp. pp. 88–98), a stylistically coded affirmation of metal subculture's tendency to value whiteness over blackness (notable in critics' celebrations of metal's independence from the blues), masculinity over femininity, and related dichotomies such as the mental over the corporeal and the rational over the emotional. When put this way, there is clearly a conservative element informing the subcultural consecration of early Metallica, one carried over from broader, entrenched societal value systems. This conservative element at least partially explains how the individuality that metal fans paradoxically share is one that is relatively constrained within subcultural norms related to fashion, speech, behavior, and one's apparent independence from certain symbols of mass culture associated with abject identity categories (Huyssen, 1986, pp. 47–53).

This relatively constrained notion of individuality led many fans to feel betrayed when confronted with Metallica's increasing popularity beyond metal subculture. For them, Metallica's shifts away from subcultural markers of authenticity were compounded by their suspicions toward the band's growing mass audience. As Sarah Thornton memorably explained, the phrase 'selling out' stands in for this kind of reaction:

> 'Selling out' refers to the process by which artists or songs sell beyond their initial market which, in turn, loses its sense of possession, exclusive ownership and familiar belonging … 'selling out' means *selling* to *out*siders. (Thornton, 1996, p. 124; original emphasis).

For many 1980s thrash fans, Metallica represented an underground opposition to undiscerning outsiders responsible for saturating MTV's daily request charts with glam metal. Metallica's departure from the symbols of individuality and transgression most widely recognized by metal audiences broadcast an unwelcome message that audiences of underground metal could no longer claim ownership over the band.

Especially considering the band's underground reputation, Metallica's '80s albums have sold exceptionally well. *Ride the Lightning* (1984), *Master of Puppets* (1986), and *… And Justice for All* (1988) peaked at Nos. 100, 29, and 6 respectively in the *Billboard* Top 200 with respective sales currently at over 6, 6, and 8 million units.[3] To some extent, these figures suggest a degree of popularity at odds with the subcultural consecration of these records as 'a distinguished trilogy of albums' (Pillsbury, 2006, pp. 36–39). At the same time, at least two factors complicate this opposition of economic success with subcultural prestige. For one, the total sales do not necessarily indicate how popular the albums were when they were first released. The albums' canonical reputation undoubtedly boosted sales since the 1990s. Secondly, the popularity of a wide variety of music labeled 'heavy metal' in the 1980s suggests that the Trilogy's audience was never limited to an underground subculture. As David Brackett (2014) explains, the popularity of heavy metal toward the late 1980s allowed 'bands like Metallica [to] simultaneously maintain 'underground' status and experience mass popularity …' (p. 400). With *… And Justice for All*, this situation would change in a way that would profoundly impact the band's record sales and relationship with fans.

Mass Media Recognition, Musical Changes, and Sell-Out Accusations

And Justice for All marked Metallica's first exposure to televised media recognition through 'One', the band's first music video and first Grammy Award winning song. Describing the fan discourse surrounding the release of the 'One' video, Pillsbury notes how, despite the lack of supporting evidence, fans insisted that drummer Lars Ulrich denounced MTV and denied that Metallica would ever make a video (2006, pp. 152–153). He cites one fan for whom Metallica's supposed disavowal of music videos acts as a symptom of the band's shifting values toward the mass-media culture of MTV: 'Metallica went from being the harshest, meanest fucking metal band, to some Alteri-metal happy MTV shit. […] They said they'd never do a video, that MTV sucked. Look at them now' (p. 152). Regardless of the falsity of such accusations, they gain momentum through each speaker and listener, resulting in more and more fans' interpreting Metallica's videos as symbols of hypocrisy and mainstream media, and thus betrayal.

Fans often cite the *Metallica* album (commonly called 'The Black Album') as the beginning of an ongoing selling out process. *Metallica* would become the first in a series of four Metallica albums to achieve a peak *Billboard* 200 chart position of No. 1. It also boasted five singles that charted on the *Billboard* Hot 100 with the song 'Enter Sandman' peaking as high as No. 16. According to the Nielson Music 2012 Year-End Music Industry Report, *Metallica* has become the highest selling album since the implementation of SoundScan.[4] To put this into perspective, the 15,845,000 units sold of the *Metallica* album nearly doubles the sales of Metallica's next best-selling record, ... *And Justice for All*, and exceeds the sales of post-1990s releases by Shania Twain (*Come on over* [1997] 15,524,000), Alanis Morissette (*Jagged Little Pill* [1995] 14,806,000), the Backstreet Boys (*Millennium* [1999] 12,209,000), and the Beatles' compilation of no. 1 hits, *Beatles 1* ([2000] 12,139,000).[5] Astonishingly, the market success of the *Metallica* album suggests that a metal record has outsold the best-selling records of such mass-media-oriented genres as country pop, singer-songwriters, and boy bands.

To a limited extent, one could explain the sales of the *Metallica* album by its stylistic changes from its predecessors. While most of Metallica's earlier songs foreground ensemble virtuosity, the *Metallica* album significantly reduces the importance of that aesthetic. Metallica's previous emphasis on ensemble virtuosity is now drastically cut in favor of 'heaviness', a different signifier of aggression and power. For instance, Metallica reintroduced the middle-frequency range to its guitar timbres in contrast to the previously 'scooped' guitar sound.[6] In response to a *Guitar World* interview question about scooping the mids, Kirk Hammett replied, 'Well, we used to do that [...] but while making [the] *Metallica* [album], we rediscovered mid-range and how much louder and fuller our guitars sound with it in there' (Quoted in Kitts and Tolinski, 2002, p. 196). Metallica also emphasized lower frequencies and slow, plodding rhythms in order to evoke a feeling of thickness or hulking weight. During the chorus of 'Sad But True' (figure 7.1), for instance, the technique of palm-muting attenuates the higher frequencies of the guitar, resulting in a restrained attack that emphasizes the guitar's lowest possible register (Pillsbury, 2006, pp. 11–12, 160, 167). Hetfield and Hammett even create the illusion of lower frequencies than are actually heard on the recording by playing some power chords as perfect fourths, implying a lower root than would be possible within their current tuning. These techniques have an even more dramatic impact when played by instruments tuned a full step below standard tuning (op. cit., 166), using echo and reverb effects, at the very slow (for thrash metal) tempo of 86 bpm.

Hetfield's approach to singing also noticeably changes, largely due to the singing lessons he undertook in preparation for the *Metallica* album. With this album and all the band's material that follows, Hetfield deepens his vocal timbre and adds melismatic endings to his phrases. These characteristics would become more pronounced throughout his career, becoming caricatured in online amateur CD reviews and musical parodies (e.g., the vocal style of Beatallica's Jaymz Lennfield).

It seems unlikely, however, that stylistic changes alone would threaten the aura of authenticity that Metallica had built throughout the 1980s. Stylistic changes over a band's career are common enough, and the aesthetic reactions they provoke rarely reach a consensus among fans. In Metallica's case, however, angry fans were able to blame these changes on a single scapegoat. Prior to the *Metallica* album, all of Metallica's albums were produced by Metallica and Flemming Rasmussen. The distinct sound of the *Metallica* album followed the hiring of Bob Rock, an experienced rock producer with

110 *Eric Smialek*

Figure 7.1 **'Sad but True' at the Beginning of the Chorus.** Palm-muted articulations are marked, 'P.M'.

a reputation for cultivating commercial appeal. Fans blamed Bob Rock to such an extent that by May 2008, 20,107 signatures had been added to an online petition that called for Rock's dismissal.[7] Such a widespread reaction would be unlikely had Rock only produced the *Metallica* album. However, Rock would produce Metallica's next three albums, recordings that no longer merely reinterpret musical aggression from thrash metal to 'heaviness', but now represent a complete crossover to other musical genres.

Connected by their similar titles and packaging, the albums *Load* and *Reload* represent a period in Metallica's history that many fans denounce as the realization of earlier sell-out signs. With the band's new haircuts came magazine covers that showed each member in eyeliner, suggesting a rock star persona far removed from their earlier, torn-jeans subcultural image.[8] In *Load* and *Reload*, Metallica's earlier focus on rhythmic saturation through repeated palm-muted attacks of the open lowest string and syncopated power-chord accents[9] gives way to a more groove-oriented hard-rock guitar style with regularly emphasized down beats, long string bends, and lead guitar call-and-response licks. Similar string bends characterize Hammett's guitar solos, which previously derived their expressive qualities from speed and well-timed scale runs. Rather than blazing through diatonic minor scales, carefully crafted in advance to fit overtop Hetfield's chromatic power chords, Hammett's solos now linger across pentatonic blues patterns that have an improvised feel, and they now occur over diatonic chord progressions.

In addition to similarities with the blues, Pillsbury cites rock critics who called 'Mama Said' from *Load* a 'bona fide country song' and 'a fully successful stab at country-blues' (2006, p. 162).[10] A striking example that supports these descriptions occurs near the beginning of 'The Unforgiven II' on *Reload*. At 0:22, the track introduces a solo clean-tone guitar accompanied only by a hi-hat. More to the point, it includes two strong markers of country music: a country lick involving a B-bender, a guitar accessory that facilitates the rapid whole-step bends and pre-bends of country music, and a harmonized guitar melody that mimics a pedal-steel guitar through its processed timbre, smooth slides, and bends (figure 7.2). While *Reload* does retain some moments of aggression that recall the 'heavy' aesthetic of *Metallica* (especially heard on 'The House Jack Built'), it never returns to the thrash metal paradigm of the Trilogy.

Figure 7.2 **Country Licks from 'The Unforgiven II'.** Note the whole-step bends in particular.

Although the animosity toward Metallica appeared at first to be limited to nostalgic fans, on April 14, 2000, it expanded far beyond the metal subculture when the band sued the popular online music sharing service, Napster (Eliscu and Thigpen, 2000). Metallica further attracted attention by suing two universities that had not blocked the service (Carlson, 2000) and by demanding that 370,000 users who had downloaded their music be banned (Pillsbury, 2006, p. 154).

As Pillsbury explains, Metallica's position was deeply imbedded in nineteenth-century ideals of authorship and control of one's art (pp. 137–38, 155). A widely quoted Metallica press release states, '[I]t is therefore sickening to know that our art is being traded like a commodity rather than the art that it is' (Pillsbury, 2006, 155; Carlson, 2000). At times, Ulrich tempered this overtly elitist stance by emphasizing how the lawsuit would protect other bands and artists with less influence than Metallica, but when asked to summarize his position during a televised debate, he appeared to be more concerned with protecting his own interests as an *auteur* in control of his work. Ulrich responded, 'In essence it's about control. It's about controlling what you own'.[11] Depending on the wording of this line of thought—whether Ulrich speaks of personal ownership or elitist distinctions between art and commodities—it may seem somewhat odd that Metallica's case against Napster provoked the kinds of widespread outrage that it did. To wit, the notions of artist-as-genius and the valuation of originality implicit in Ulrich's stance seem widespread enough that one might expect his arguments to elicit more sympathy than they did. Yet Ulrich's actions and arguments were met with CD smashings, a network of anti-Metallica websites, and online cartoons that demonized the band through accusations of greed.[12] These reactions are not merely attributable to the frustrations of Napster users. I would argue that the mounting complaints, based on subcultural and musical values, raised with each of their previous albums directly impacted the magnitude of the Napster public relations backlash. To explain its enormity, I turn to Bourdieu.

Polarized Perceptions of Authenticity

Bourdieu's model of cultural production is especially valuable for understanding Metallica's reception because of its ability to connect seemingly disparate phenomena and explain their impact on one another. Bourdieu ([1983] 1993) speaks of several cultural fields (e.g., the educational, political, literary, and artistic fields) where polarized groups struggle for control over prestige, power, wealth, and a variety of cultural currencies (pp. 37–38; Thomson, 2008, pp. 76–81). The ability for various agents to thrive within their social limitations within the field depends on their capacity to accrue various forms of symbolic capital—symbolic forms of power analogous to the power of monetary currency—that vary in importance according to one's position in the field. Particularly important examples for my purposes are forms of cultural knowledge prized by certain groups ('cultural capital') and social connections desired in certain circles ('social capital'). The ability to accrue symbolic capital depends on making choices according to often subtle and unspoken cultural rules. In order to gain respect and feel comfortable within a social group, one must recognize the taste-based distinctions of certain peer groups, such as choosing particular clothing or knowing which genres and bands tend to be perceived by one's peers as legitimate choices. Crucially, Bourdieu argues that the collective belief in the value of certain choices is arbitrary in that it is socially conditioned and historically specific rather than natural, inevitable, or eternal ([1992] 1996, p. 169; [1986] 1993, p. 81). Yet these collective beliefs are often misrecognized as absolute truths in a way that obscures the ideological interests in cultural domination behind them.

Fans and sympathetic critics who describe Metallica's later albums as having evolved or matured, usually by referring to increasingly introspective and autobiographical lyrics and an emphasis on meaningful simplicity (Pillsbury, 2006, pp. 160–165), align themselves with Metallica within a segment of the cultural field that values artist-audience directness over technical complexity—ideals of folk authenticity characteristic of singer-songwriters, country musicians, and certain strains of rock, such as Southern rock (Booth and Kuhn, 1990, pp. 417–418, 421, 437; Frith, 1996, pp. 39–41; Keightley, 2001, pp. 121, 135–137). Conversely, fans wishing to escape mass culture through metal tend to value these ideals less than they do the musical and lyrical signifiers of individualism I outlined at the beginning of this chapter. Fans for whom thrash metal represents an underground opposition to mass culture are more likely to associate Metallica's folk-rooted material with commercial success and thus compromise. As Bourdieu puts it, these metal fans 'identify with [a] degree of independence from the economy, seeing temporal failure as a sign of election and success as a sign of compromise' (1993, p. 40). To such fans, Metallica's wider audience and increased economic capital indicates their failure as artists to value autonomy over commercial success.

These negative associations between mass culture and Metallica become reinforced by Metallica's appearance at Grammy Awards ceremonies, collaborations with mainstream artists, and friendships with high profile stars. Bourdieu describes these kinds of alliances as homologies 'between positions occupied in the space of production, with the correlative position-takings, and positions in the space of consumption' (ibid., p. 45). A fan quoted by Pillsbury writes, 'Jason [Newsted], what's new in hip hop? James [Hetfield] ... If you think rubbing elbows with Garth [Brooks] is cool I've got to say adios' (2006, p. 180). A more insidious example, revealing of the gendered and racially charged hierarchies within metal as a cultural field, is given by Jason Ferguson, author of *Orlando Weekly*'s 'Why Metallica Sucks' contest, who summarizes the winning entry by saying, 'Metallica's slut-easy willingness to collaborate with such middling talents as Ja Rule (just because they're 'down') is a prime indicator of how low the group has fallen. Should Metallica hate rap? No. But should they make rap records? No' (2003). With Bourdieu's discussion of homologies in mind, it is clear that these examples do not merely reflect a distaste toward country and hip hop. They also represent a reaction toward those genres' perceived positions nearer to the mass-market segment of the cultural field, a segment that has longstanding associations with alterity and devalued social groups (Huyssen, 1986), with which Metallica is now aligned.

Thinking this way about Metallica's history of sell-out accusations and the band's increasingly strained relationship with fans of its older recordings—that is, as a gradual reduction of the band's social and symbolic capital within the metal scene—helps to better understand the backlash that followed Metallica's *St. Anger* (2003) album, the band's first studio album after the Napster scandal. One can partly explain the controversy surrounding *St. Anger* in terms of further reductions in social capital. Metallica lost a great deal of social credibility by hiring Phil Towle, a therapist or 'performance coach' tasked with helping the band around the time of *St. Anger* and its documentation in the film, *Some Kind of Monster* (2004). Despite the unflattering ways in which Towle was depicted in the DVD, his very presence resulted in criticism from Metallica's ex-bassist, Jason Newsted, as well as Slayer-guitarist, Kerry King (Pillsbury, 2006, pp. 186, 219, n. 6). Stylistic similarities with nu metal were another factor, but they would not likely have generated such vehement opposition were it not for each previous loss in symbolic capital that gradually fostered animosity between the band and its fans. In other words, the distance within the cultural field between Metallica and its fans had become so great, with so much of Metallica's symbolic capital lost, that many fans *expected* to dislike *St. Anger* before they encountered it.

Metallica was also quite sensitive to fans' apprehensions to the point where sell-out accusations appear to have noticeably influenced the band's artistic decisions. Through its use in Metallica's DVD *Some Kind of Monster*, *St. Anger*'s music can reasonably be heard as a response to years of sell-out accusations. Most noticeably during *Some Kind of Monster*, Hetfield sings the lyrics to 'Shoot Me Again' ('All the shots I take/What difference did I make?/All the shots I take/I spit back at you'.) immediately after Ulrich discusses his frustration with the Napster scandal. Elsewhere in the DVD, Ulrich proposes 'Frantic' as a title to what would become the *St. Anger* album only to have the band's manager strongly advise against it due to his worries that 'Frantic' may communicate desperation. Moments like these in *Some Kind of Monster* publicize the high degree of self-consciousness behind the making of *St. Anger*. The filming of Metallica's therapy sessions and the extensive documentation behind the band's struggles to generate ideas made several of Metallica's vulnerabilities public at a time when skepticism toward the band's artistic motivations and abilities was at its highest.

To clarify each historical stage of Metallica's changing reputation as well as my interpretation of the band's career according to Bourdieu's field theory, figure 7.3 sketches Metallica's shifts within the field of cultural production following Bourdieu's own analytical diagrams (1984, pp. 128–129; 1993, p. 49).

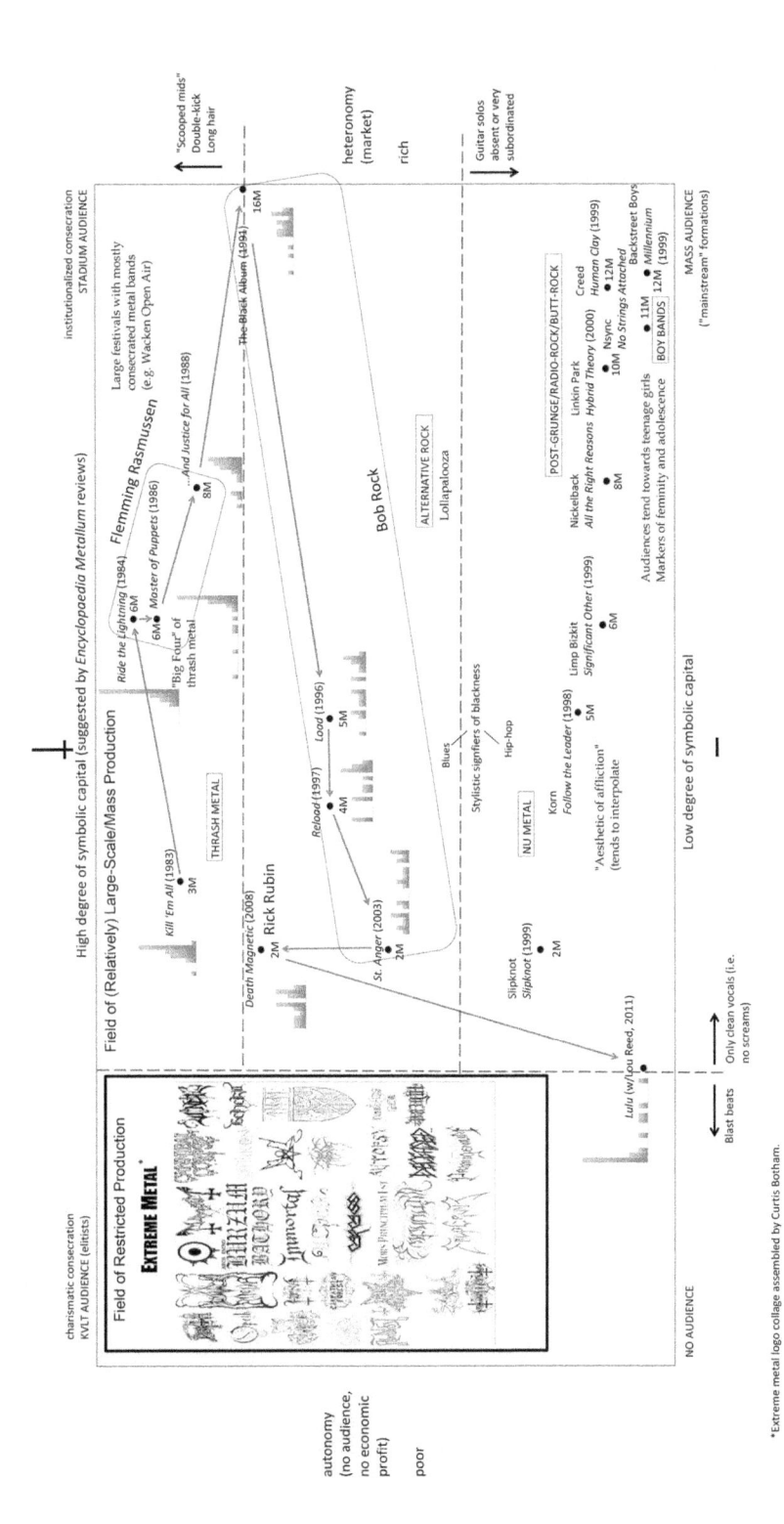

Figure 7.3 Metallica's Movement within the Field of Cultural Production.

116   *Eric Smialek*

In its most basic sense, the diagram mostly charts various albums in terms of record sales (the horizontal axis) plotted against each album's relative amount of prestige, or symbolic capital, within the metal community (the vertical axis). Recordings with tremendously high sales figures, according to RIAA certification records, appear on the right of the chart. They then appear nearer the top of the diagram depending on their relative level of consecration within the metal discourses that I have researched.[13] Each Metallica album's position is based on how many million sales it generated in North America against the average-review-score it received on *Encyclopaedia Metallum*, a globally popular Anglophone website whose extremely detailed policy on which bands deserve inclusion on the website speaks volumes about the importance the site's users place on symbolic capital with respect to metal music.[14]

Following Bourdieu's example in *Distinction*, I appended histograms to the chart beside every Metallica album to show at a glance the relative levels of consensus or controversy surrounding each album in the online reviews. Considering that reviews on *Encyclopaedia Metallum* assign a percentage score to each recording, the logic of the histograms may be immediately familiar to educators who receive statistical breakdowns of grades online: the histograms display clusters of similar review scores together so that each bar represents the total number of reviews that lie within five percentage points. Thus, *Ride the Lightning* (1984) shows a sharp spike on the far right, indicating an overwhelming consensus of positive reviews. Metallica's collaboration with Lou Reed on *Lulu* (2011) shows a different kind of consensus, this time with a histogram skewed toward the far left indicating very negative responses (notwithstanding a few more generous reviewers). With the exception of *Lulu*, the arrows connecting each Metallica album chart a path from a general consensus of consecration for Metallica's '80s recordings (each increasing in mass market popularity), through a period of turbulent reception during Bob Rock's tenure as Metallica's producer, marked by a spread of variation in the histograms indicative of controversy (i.e., the era of 'sell-out' accusations), toward a warmer but somewhat ambivalent reception given to *Death Magnetic* (2008) that I shall discuss further below.

Lastly, I have attempted to sketch the relative positions of certain genres and tendencies related to audience demographics. These annotations reflect metal scholars' awareness of tensions within the metal scene toward identity-based differences regarding gender (namely femininity), race (principally blackness in the United States), and adolescence. Nu metal, for instance, is shown in a position of relatively low subcultural consecration in a way that reflects metal fans' frequent statements of suspicion toward rap. The diagram positions hip hop near the blues, and in so doing, connects the negative reception of Metallica to racial tensions in metal discourses: one thinks of metal critics' eagerness to praise the elimination of blues elements in '80s metal (Walser, 1993, pp. 8–9; Wells, 1997, pp. 51–52; Fellezs, 2011, p. 181; e.g. Sharpe-Young, 2007, pp. 8–9) as well as Lars Ulrich's uneasiness toward an interviewer's description of '90s Metallica as 'bluesy' (Pillsbury, 2006, pp. 170, 175–176). Broadening the scope of the chart this way will, I hope, facilitate connections between Metallica's reception history and broader issues of social discrimination and aesthetic value in metal.

Death Magnetic, The Loudness Wars, and Bourdieu's Useful Anachronism

Several factors suggest that *Death Magnetic* has been widely received as at least a partially successful 'comeback' effort or a return to Metallica's stylistic past during the 1980s. Many reviews, both positive and negative, speak of the album directly in terms of an attempt at a stylistic return, with titles such as 'Goddamn, talk about great come backs! - 90%', 'Putting the 'metal' back in Metallica! - 83%', and 'A band trying to be something they are not. - 51%'.[15] Within the chart, the album's position leaps up the vertical axis, reflecting its significantly higher review scores at *Encyclopaedia Metallum* in comparison to its three 'sell-out' era predecessors. The histogram (figure 7.3) alongside this position indicates much less controversy than the previous three albums, now showing two main camps of reviewers (shown by the two large bars) that both give the album relatively high scores (the first bar represents the 70–74 score range; the second bar shows scores between 85 and 89).

Shortly following the release of *Death Magnetic*, a large number of fans began complaining about the album's extreme amount of dynamic range compression, an effort at the mixing stage to increase the overall loudness of the CD. According to a trail of blog posts by Ian Shepherd, a mastering engineer whose discussions of *Death Magnetic*'s role in the 'loudness war' became widely cited by international news syndicates, the album's mix engineers drastically reduced the dynamic range of the recording (i.e., the difference between its quietest and loudest components) by increasing the amplitude of the quiet components far beyond ordinary industry standards (Shepherd, 2008).[16] As a result, the high-frequency sound components, most noticeable in the hi-hat, cymbals, and snare drum, became buried amongst all the other parts of the mix. Additionally, certain parts of the overall sound suffered from an audible form of distortion associated with digital clipping.[17] The effects of this are apparent in figure 7.4, which reproduces sound waveform images taken from Ian Shepherd's blog.[18]

The bottom image shows an earlier version of a song from *Death Magnetic*, used for the video game *Guitar Hero 3*, that did not suffer from clipping problems. In comparison, the top image shows how the waveform of the studio version appears stretched, indicating increased loudness. One can also see how segments of the top (album-version) waveform are cut off, or 'clipped', at the outer edges. The differences in sound between the studio release and *Guitar Hero* versions further kindled the controversy surrounding *Death Magnetic*'s sound quality, sparking a series of online comparisons

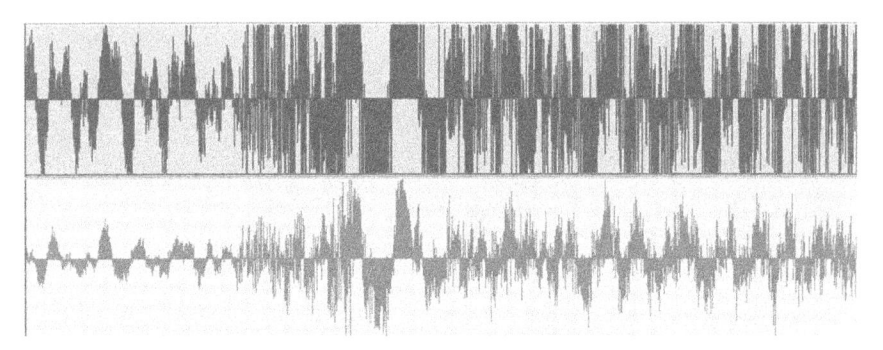

Figure 7.4 **A Comparison between Waveform Images of the Studio Version of** *Death Magnetic* **(top) and the** *Guitar Hero 3* **Version (bottom).** Adapted from Ian Shepherd's blog.

between the two versions and torrent sharing of alternate mixes from the game or by fans themselves.

In some striking ways, the controversy surrounding *Death Magnetic* seemed to mirror Metallica's prior history of 'sell-out' accusations. For instance, in a move reminiscent of the petition against Bob Rock, fans began to gather online signatures to petition Metallica's management company, Q-Prime to re-mix *Death Magnetic*, resulting in 22,553 signatures by the time of this writing.[19] When asked to respond to the petition, Lars Ulrich gave a dismissive response reminiscent of his antagonistic remarks during the Napster scandal:

> The Internet gives everybody a voice, and the Internet has a tendency to give the complainers a louder voice. Listen, I can't keep up with this shit. Part of being in Metallica is that there's always somebody who's got a problem with something that you're doing: 'James Hetfield had something for breakfast that I don't like'. That's part of the ride.[20]

Although the members of Metallica were away on tour when *Death Magnetic* was being mastered, Ulrich's unsympathetic response to complaints about the album confirmed for many fans the band's complicity in the loudness wars, a trend widely associated with the prioritizing of commercial over artistic goals.

The connections to the previous history of sell-out accusations become even clearer in a widely distributed parody song by Clipping Death, 'Mastered by Muppets', the YouTube video of which focuses primarily on producer Rick Rubin and the band's desire for sales above sound quality. Throughout the video, which presents a slideshow of comedic images alongside parodic lyrics, Rubin's face is superimposed over Metallica record covers or included in photos altered to lampoon the process of dynamic range compression. Most tellingly from a Bourdieusian perspective, two of the video's slides depict Ulrich and Rubin bragging about their wealth in a way that connects the album's production qualities to their financial success (see figure 7.5).

Figure 7.5 Images from the YouTube Video for 'Mastered by Muppets' Depicting Ulrich and Rubin Bragging about Their Wealth in Ways Connected to Dynamic Range Compression.

The left image refers to Ulrich's hobby of collecting expensive paintings, a pastime depicted in *Some Kind of Monster* where Ulrich auctions most of his collection for sums upwards of $5.5M. Notably, Ulrich's same exaggerated grimace appears on Shepherd's blog to accompany Ulrich's dismissal of the petition. It would seem that in various instances, online reactions to *Death Magnetic*'s audio quality and the band's statements about it have collectively associated wealth, indifference toward fan opinion, and obnoxious attitudes with Metallica (and especially Ulrich) in ways that recall the alienation fans felt during the Napster scandal.

The at least partial unfairness of these associations seems to point to a reason Bourdieu's theories remain useful for analyzing mass-media culture despite the valid criticisms that media scholars have made toward Bourdieu's relative disinterest in that segment of the cultural field (Hesmondhalgh, 2006, pp. 211, 217–219). In an article evaluating the potential of applying Bourdieu's analytical framework to contemporary media (i.e., television, video games, Internet video streaming, etc.), Hesmondhalgh (2006) explains that much of the ambivalence media scholars have expressed toward Bourdieu is due to his relative disinterest in the mass-audience portion of the cultural field as well as his silence regarding profound changes that have occurred in the ways culture is produced and distributed since the mid-twentieth century (pp. 217–221). Hesmondhalgh also raises the possibility that Bourdieu's emphasis on two polarized economic logics—the profit-driven economy of the marketplace that tends to value economic capital and the prestige-driven cultural economy of the field of restricted production that tends to value symbolic capital—may not adequately account for the overlapping and fluid relationships between various market niches in contemporary media. In other words, without careful adaptation, there is a risk of inappropriately applying to twentieth-century mass-mediated popular culture theoretical ideas that Bourdieu did not necessarily intend for it.

To my mind, however, the attitudes expressed by Metallica's critical fan base appear to match Bourdieu's competing principles of hierarchization (the autonomous and the heteronomous, or the valuation of economic vs.

symbolic capital) quite nicely. The tendency for fans to unfairly blame Rick Rubin alone for *Death Magnetic*'s poor sound quality, despite how responsibility for the mix could conceivably be attributed to multiple personnel on the album's credits (including the band), suggests that many fans share with Bourdieu a potentially outdated, simplistic model of cultural production, stemming from the 19th century.[21] Indeed, Pillsbury argues convincingly that the notion of selling out as it is generally expressed by fans 'depends heavily upon a multifaceted relationship of creativity and commerce conceived in the early years of [the 19th] century' (2006, p. 137). In other words, if Bourdieu's theoretical model does not account for the nuances and complexities of labor and marketing brought on by the culture industries, it usefully does not do so in much the same way that fans' imaginations of cultural production do not. If, in popular music media since the 1960s, 'prestige and popularity are not necessarily so much in contradiction as in Bourdieu's schema' (Hesmondhalgh, 2006, p. 222), the segments of Metallica's fan base most concerned with subcultural forms of symbolic capital do not seem to recognize it. The suspicions fans have repeatedly voiced that Metallica's motivations might be commercially rather than artistically driven suggest that for many metal fans, prestige and popularity are still very much opposed.

Conclusions

The width of the schism between Metallica and the band's detractors cannot be explained through any single instance of subcultural transgression or even a hierarchal reception history that emphasizes certain accusations over others. Rather, I would like to suggest that each of these functions interdependently. Objections directed at Metallica's musical changes and subcultural charges of symbolic betrayal inform each other teleologically through the progression of time and retrospectively through memory. When Metallica's Napster lawsuit erupted into a public relations nightmare, fans recalled earlier controversies that became catalysts for their rage. Despite the musical returns to aggression of *St. Anger* and *Death Magnetic*, the controlled orchestration of sympathy through the edited candor of *Some Kind of Monster*, and the firing of Bob Rock, fans have not dismissed the two decades of frustration they have felt. The widespread outrage felt by Metallica fans toward a band that they once consecrated is remarkable in its endurance and publicity. The flexibility of Bourdieu's model allows for a better understanding of the motivations behind metal aesthetics and their role within what has undoubtedly become the highest-profile case of 'sell-out' accusations in metal history.

Notes

1. For their comments on drafts of this chapter, I would like to thank David Brackett, Andy R. Brown, Karl Spracklen, Laura Risk, Mimi Haddon, Sean Lorre, Farley Miller, Melvin Backstrom, Claire McLeish, Curtis Botham, and

Maria-Alexandra Francou-Desrochers. Thanks also go to Glenn Pillsbury for guidance with copyright permissions procedures.
2. Pillsbury's term, 'ensemble virtuosity' (Pillsbury, 2006, p. xii) derives from Robert Walser's description of thrash metal's 'fast tempos, meter changes, and complicated arrangements with precise ensemble coordination' (Walser, 1993, p. 14). A striking instance occurs during the climax of 'One' from ... *And Justice for All*. Here machine-gun-like rhythms, played by the entire band, alternate between brief pauses of silence that intensify both the sense of tight coordination amongst the band as well as the lyrics' dramatic enactment of a disfigured soldier's horror.
3. Sales data were retrieved through an RIAA database search at: http://www.riaa.com/goldandplatinumdata.php?content_selector=gold-platinum-searchable-database (accessed July 28, 2014).
4. Soundscan is a barcode-like technology used in *Billboard* magazine's sales charts. It was implemented in March 1991 to replace the subjective 'conversion procedures' by *Billboard* employees and potentially manipulable reports from music retailers (Sernoe, 2005, pp. 639–642).
5. http://www.businesswire.com/news/home/20130104005149/en/Nielsen-Company-Billboard%E2%80%99s-2012-Music-Industry-Report#.U8XVG5RdWGl (accessed July 15, 2014).
6. For previous albums, Metallica's guitar sound involved completely reducing the middle-frequency range while boosting both low and high frequencies. This technique, variously achieved through the tone settings of a guitar amplifier or during the mixing stage of a recording, is frequently referred to by guitarists as 'scooping the mids'. For more on Metallica's scooped mids with ... *And Justice for All*, see Pillsbury, 2006, p. 75.
7. http://www.petitiononline.com/SaveMet/petition.html (accessed May 7, 2008). A small percentage of the entries represent supportive fans of Rock's production who unwittingly added their names with their rebuttals.
8. See for example, *Rolling Stone* June 27, 1996.
9. Pillsbury demonstrates Metallica's earlier guitar writing by inserting these techniques into riffs from 'Cure' and '2X4' and comparing them with transcriptions of the original version (Pillsbury, 2006, pp. 167–169). One can also hear this style within the verse section of 'Enter Sandman'.
10. On the subject of country music, one reviewer at *Encyclopaedia Metallum* draws a particularly amusing—and compelling—comparison between the verse of '2X4' and Shania Twain's 'Man! I Feel Like a Woman' ('Ibanezmancons' [pseud.], 'Not worthy. 66%', June 7, 2013).
11. A transcript of this debate from the *Charlie Rose Show* between Ulrich and rapper Chuck D is available online at http://la.indymedia.org/news/2003/09/81777.php (accessed August 3, 2014).
12. Although long defunct, http://www.killmetallica.com maintained an index of similar archived sites when it was in operation (accessed January 2, 2007). The best-known satirical cartoon, 'Napster Bad!' can be seen on *Some Kind of Monster*.
13. Much of the research I have undertaken for the reception of the genres along the bottom of the diagram comes from my dissertation chapter titled, 'Extreme Metal and Its Others'. See also Smialek (2014a) and Smialek (2014b).
14. The policy can be found at http://www.metal-archives.com/content/rules by clicking on the 'Heavy Metal Only' tab and selecting the option titled,

'Long-ass, rambling, read-before-complaining-only version'. (Accessed July 19, 2014.) For practicality's sake, I have used a flexible scale along the horizontal axis. Near the edges of the field, the scale collapses so that the extreme cases could fit. If the field were drawn to scale at those points, *Metallica* (The Black Album) would actually be located much further away than all the other albums charted here.
15. http://www.metal-archives.com/reviews/Metallica/Death_Magnetic/204927/ (accessed July 23, 2014).
16. The loudness war is a term widely used by audiophiles and recording technicians to refer to a decades-long trend of increasingly loud recording mixes made in an effort to compete with other recordings.
17. Clipping occurs during attempts to amplify an audio signal beyond an amplifier's maximum capacity. The parts of the signal that are lost in this process are 'clipped'. This kind of clipping distortion should not be confused with the ordinary use of electric guitar distortion in metal.
18. Ian Shepherd, 'Metallica 'Death Magnetic' Yes, it IS clipping', *Mastering Media Blog* (September 18, 2008) http://mastering-media.blogspot.ca/2008/09/metallica-death-magnetic-yes-it-is.html (accessed July 25, 2014).
19. http://www.gopetition.com/petitions/re-mix-or-remaster-death-magnetic.html (accessed July 24, 2014).
20. The interview was originally reported at http://www.blender.com/Blender BlogNewPost09292008/Blender-Blog/blogs/1168/42090.aspx. Although the URL is no longer available, the interview is widely cited elsewhere. See, for example, Ian Shepherd, 'Metallica 'Death Magnetic'—Distortion is deliberate, say band', *Mastering Media Blog* (September 29, 2008) http://mastering-media.blogspot.ca/2008/09/metallica-death-magnetic-distortion-is.html (accessed July 25, 2014).
21. Responding in support of Rick Rubin's Grammy Award for his production work on *Death Magnetic*, Ian Shepherd reminded readers of his blog that a producer's role often involves coaching tasks related to matters of 'composition, performance, arrangement, subject, feel, mood, motivation, pace, [and] atmosphere' rather than those of a sound engineer (Ian Shepherd, 'Does Rick Rubin Deserve the 'Producer of the Year' Grammy Award?' *Mastering Media Blog* [February 8, 2009] http://mastering-media.blogspot.ca/2009/02/why-rick-rubin-deserves-his-producer-of.html (accessed July 24, 2014). For a sensitive cultural explanation of the different, and often overlapping, roles between producers and engineers, see Albin J. Zak III, 2001, pp. 163–183.

Bibliography

Berger, H. (1999). *Metal, rock, and jazz: Perception and the phenomenology of musical experience*. Hanover, NH: Wesleyan University Press.
Booth, G. D., & Kuhn, T. L. (1990). Economic and transmission factors as essential elements in the definition of folk, art, and pop music. *Musical Quarterly*, 74, 411–438.
Bourdieu, P. (1984). *Distinction: A social critique of the judgement of taste* (R. Nice, Trans.). Cambridge, MA: Harvard University Press.
Bourdieu, P. (1986). The field of cultural production, or: The economic world reversed. In R. Johnson (Ed.), *The field of cultural production: Essays on art and literature* (R. Nice, Trans.). Cambridge: Polity Press.

Bourdieu, P. (1986). The production of belief: Contribution to an economy of symbolic goods. In R. Johnson (Ed.), *The field of cultural production: Essays on art and literature* (R. Nice, Trans.). Cambridge: Polity Press.

Bourdieu, P. ([1992] 1996). *The rules of art: Genesis and structure of the literary field* (S. Emanuel, Trans.). Stanford, CA: Stanford University Press.

Bourdieu, P. (1994). *Practical reason: On the theory of action.* Stanford, CA: Stanford University Press.

Brackett, D. (Ed.). (2014). *The pop, rock, and soul reader.* New York: Oxford University Press.

Carlson, S. (2000). Metallica sues universities and Napster, charging that students engage in music piracy. *The Chronicle of Higher Education,* 46(34), April 28, A50(1).

Christe, I. (2003). *Sound of the beast: The complete headbanging history of heavy metal.* New York: Harper Collins.

Eliscu, J., & Thigpen, D. (2000). Metallica slams Napster. *Rolling Stone,* May.

Fellezs, K. (2011). Black metal soul music: Stone Vengeance and the aesthetics of race in heavy metal. *Popular Music History,* 6(1/2), 180–197.

Ferguson, J. (2003). Why Metallica sucks. *Orlando Weekly,* July 10 http://www.orlandoweekly.com/music/story.asp?id=4741 (accessed August 1, 2014).

Frith, S. (1996). *Performing rites: On the value of popular music.* Cambridge, MA: Harvard University Press.

Fosl, P. S. (2007). Metallica, Nietzsche, and Marx: The immorality of morality. In W. Irwin (Ed.), *Metallica and philosophy: A crash course in brain surgery* (pp. 74–84). Malden, MA: Blackwell Publishing.

Hesmondhalgh, D. (2006). Bourdieu, the media and cultural production. *Media, Culture & Society,* 28(2), 211–231.

Huyssen, A. (1986). *After the great divide: Modernism, mass culture, postmodernism.* Bloomington, IN: Indiana University Press.

Kahn-Harris, K. (2007). *Extreme metal: Music and culture on the edge.* New York: Berg.

Keightley, K. (2001). Reconsidering rock. In S. Frith, W. Straw, & J. Street (Eds.), *The Cambridge companion to pop and rock* (pp. 109–142). New York: Cambridge University Press.

Kitts, J., & Tolinski, B. (Eds.). (2002). *Guitar World presents the 100 greatest guitarists of all time!From the pages of* Guitar World *Magazine.* Milwaukee, WI: Hal Leonard.

Nelson, P. (2014). Newport Folk Festival, 1965. In D. Brackett (Ed.), *The pop, rock, and soul reader* (pp. 157–159). New York: Oxford University Press.

Nys, T. (2007). Through the mist and the madness: Metallica's message of nonconformity, individuality, and truth. In W. Irwin (Ed.), *Metallica and philosophy: A crash course in brain surgery* (pp. 41–51). Malden, MA: Blackwell Publishing.

Pillsbury, G. (2006). *Damage incorporated: Metallica and the production of musical identity.* New York: Routledge.

Purcell, N. J. (2003). *Death metal music: The passion and politics of a subculture,* Jefferson, NC: McFarland.

Sernoe, J. (2005). Now we're on the top, top of the pops: The performance of 'non-mainstream' music on *Billboard*'s album charts, 1981–2001. *Popular music and society,* 28(5), 639–662.

Sharpe-Young, G. (2007). *Metal: The definitive guide.* London: Jawbone Press.

Shepherd, I. (2008). Heavy metal mix-up. Interview by Joel Moors. BBC Radio 4. http://www.bbc.co.uk/radio4/youandyours/items/01/2008_41_fri.shtml (accessed July 24, 2014).

Shepherd, I. (2008–2009). *Mastering media blog* http://mastering-media.blogspot.ca. (accessed July 25, 2014).

Smialek, E. (2014a). Metal taxonomies: Parallel universes of genre. Paper presented at *Music and Genre: New Directions Conference*, Montréal, QC, September 27–28.

Smialek, E. (2014b). Extreme metal and its others: Metal audiences' hostility towards adolescence. Paper presented at the *American Musicological Society Annual Meeting*, Milwaukee, WI, November 6–9.

Sotos, R. (2007). Metallica's existential freedom: From we to I and back again. In W. Irwin (Ed.), *Metallica and philosophy: A crash course in brain surgery* (pp. 85–97). Malden, MA: Blackwell Publishing.

Thomson, P. (2008). Field. In M. Grenfell (Ed.), *Pierre Bourdieu: Key concepts*, Durham, UK: Acumen.

Thornton, S. (1996). *Club cultures: Music, media, and subcultural capital*, Hanover, NH: Wesleyan University Press.

Walser, R. (1993). *Running with the devil: Power, gender, and madness in heavy metal music*. Hanover, NH: Wesleyan University Press.

Weinstein, D. (2000). *Heavy metal: The music and its culture*. New York: Da Capo Press.

Wells, J. (1997). Blackness 'scuzed: Jimi Hendrix's (in)visible legacy in heavy metal. In J. Fossett (Ed.), *Race consciousness* (pp. 50–63). New York: New York University Press.

Wisnewski, J. J. (2007). The metal militia and the existentialist club. In W. Irwin (Ed.), *Metallica and philosophy: A crash course in brain surgery* (pp. 55–64). Malden, MA: Blackwell Publishing.

Zak III, A. J. (2001). *The poetics of rock: Cutting tracks, making records*. Berkeley, Los Angeles: University of California Press.

8 Use Your Mind?
Embodiments of Protest, Transgression, and Grotesque Realism in British Grindcore

Gabby Riches

> The Well, a metal venue in Leeds, was heaving with people cheering, whistling, shouting, and near the front a chorus of voices were chanting 'Napalm Death! Napalm Death!' with such force that it drowned out Barney's voice as he attempted to address the fans. The crowd was a mixture of metal fans, crusties,[1] punks, older fans headbanging alongside metal newcomers, women colliding into men in the pit ... People were moving closer to the stage, bodies swaying in anticipation for Napalm Death's next song. Barney growled abrasively into the mic 'Suffer the Children' and a pit immediately erupted. Several people clambered onto the stage and tossed themselves off the edge into a throng of moving bodies adorned in black band t-shirts, tattoos, patched vests and long hair. People were being thrown, tossed, pushed, and pulled in multiple directions, and I was caught up in this maelstrom of aggression. There were quite a few women in attendance, some of them I saw weaving themselves in and out of the chaos while others were being carried across the room as they stage dived and crowd surfed. Metal horns pierced the air and a cacophony of hollers rang in my ears as Barney delivered various political anecdotes with the audience between songs. He urged us to remain skeptical of the 'system', that Nazism and any other form of racist and bigoted thinking should and will not be tolerated, that organized religion is the catalyst for terror, and most importantly, he encouraged us to keep thinking for ourselves. ... (Author's field notes October 4, 2012)

Why Grindcore, Why Now?

Grindcore is a subgenre within the extreme metal umbrella that developed within an anarcho-punk environment in Birmingham during the 1980s. During this time grindcore bands were heavily influenced by the radical politics of nihilism and 'aesthetic negation' and the rudimentary song structures of British hardcore and Anarcho-punk bands such as Crass (Dee, 2009). Dee (2009, p. 57) argues that unlike other extreme metal subgenres, such as thrash and death metal, which adopted the 'stripped back speed of hardcore punk', grindcore's extremity developed *from* punk, which detached the subgenre from the continuation of heavy metal virtuosity. As a result of this ideological and stylistic alignment with the UK Anarcho-punk scene, many grindcore musicians share a commitment to and affiliation with various political and ethical causes such as animal rights, environmental groups, and anti-war initiatives. As a dynamic and amalgamated style of music, grindcore incorporates death metal's guttural vocals, fast drumming, and extreme volumes and fuses these with punk's blatant satire and political orientation (Overell, 2010). With its radical-left politics, grindcore portrays a different lyrical and political orientation in comparison to other extreme metal genres with many bands tackling global inequality in their lyrics and offering, rhetorically at least, anarchist or socialist revolution as the only suitable solution (Napalm Death, 1989; Overell, 2014; Unseen Terror, 1987).

Within the Leeds grindcore scene, the junctures of anarcho-punk and metal are evident as audiences are comprised of crusty punks and metal fans, and the gender ratio is less disparate compared to typical extreme metal gigs. Grindcore bands usually play short, fast songs, characterized by heavy distorted, down-tuned guitars, high-speed tempos, unfathomable blast beats, and vocals ranging from guttural growls to high-pitched screams. The subgenre was popularized in both the United States and Western Europe; bands such as Napalm Death, Discharge, and Extreme Noise Terror are credited with laying the groundwork for the style (Mudrian, 2004). Notably the members of the Birmingham-based band, Napalm Death, are considered by many to be the forefathers of grindcore as they played critical roles in shaping the subgenre's stylistic demarcations and nomenclature (Brown, forthcoming). Overell (2014) contends that grindcore's aggression is directed toward the 'machinations of late capitalism, and identities that are seen as complicit with dominant culture' (p. 2). It was this sort of politically conscious aggression that enabled grindcore to flourish in the working class milieu of the Midlands in the mid to late 1980s in Britain. The deep unpopularity of Thatcher's conservative administration, coupled with high youth unemployment, attacks on workers' rights and public service cutbacks provided the context for the formation of this ear-splitting subgenre, which rapidly became a vehicle to express and embody political and social discontent.

Similar to other extreme metal genres, grindcore operates on a DIY ethos where independent, more underground methods of musical production, distribution, exchange, and performance are highly valued. Of all the subgenres of extreme metal, grindcore has probably received the most positive attention from music critics because of its fiercely political orientation. The highly influential DJ John Peel often played grindcore and death metal on his 'Top Gear' show on BBC Radio 1 (Kahn-Harris, 2007; Mudrian, 2004). For Peel, there was something unique about 1980s grindcore in Britain; he found bands like Napalm Death, Carcass, and Extreme Noise Terror exceptionally visceral and exciting, and he admitted that 20 years after Napalm Death made its first appearance on his show he was still 'wandering the record shops, still standing amongst the boys searching the racks marked 'metal', still hoping to hear something that will thrill me and make me laugh out loud' (cited in Mudrian, 2004, p. 18). Many fans and popular music critics saw Napalm Death as a subcultural trailblazer of a new underground youth movement that was shocking, unique, and controversial; consequently, the band was afforded front page coverage by the NME (*New Musical Express*) and received a surprising amount of attention in the BBC Arena art's program special on Heavy Metal, which aired in 1989 (Brown, forthcoming). Yet over three decades later grindcore still deeply resonates with metal fans and remains a popular subgenre within local British metal scenes, especially in the north of England. Although grindcore has received some scholarly attention within metal music studies, most discussions have emphasized its origins, political significance and affective qualities of belonging for male fans, while women's participation and experiences within the subgenre remain largely ignored (Dee, 2009; Mudrian, 2004; Overell, 2010, 2011). Drawing upon my ethnographic experiences of attending various gigs and interviewing female metal fans in Leeds's grindcore scene, I argue that the subgenre has a significant and dedicated female fan base. This chapter aims to address the aforementioned gaps in the literature by focusing on the ways in which grindcore politics are produced and made meaningful through gendered, corporeal performances within Leeds's grindcore scene. This conceptual shift from the discursive to the corporeal moves us beyond normative understandings of what extreme metal means and opens up new theoretical and methodological spaces to explore how extreme metal and its politics are *felt* (Driver, 2011).

Methods

Drawing upon Phillipov's work on the implications of politically oriented music criticisms and Overell's (2010, 2014) research on the affective dimensions of grindcore sociality, I argue that grindcore's political significance is manifested in fans' embodiment of extreme and grotesque realism (Halnon, 2006; Taylor, 2009). By referring to the lyrics of three UK grindcore bands: Napalm Death, Extreme Noise Terror, and Unseen Terror; utilizing ethnographic interviews from female grindcore fans and musicians; and drawing on ethnographic field notes from my experiences in the Leeds grindcore scene (February 2012–August 2013), I suggest that grindcore opens up spaces for social critique and is a form of corporeal politics and pleasure for its fans. Frith (1981) argues that using a lyrical analysis approach to understanding the meaning and value of popular music is limiting because 'words are sounds we can feel before they are statements to understand' (p. 14). He goes onto say that the words in rock songs, if they are noticed at all, are absorbed after the music has made its mark. Accordingly, I argue that a multi-method approach, as outlined above, alongside the examination of lyrics and album artwork, offers a more nuanced rendering of grindcore aesthetics. There has been very little written about the political significance of grindcore and even less on the bodily pleasures experienced by female metal fans. While other authors have discussed contemporary grindcore bands that are known for their gory imagery and misogynistic and violent lyrics

(Overell, 2014), this chapter focuses specifically on the songs of politically oriented bands in order to consider to what extent they can be considered to produce a form of protest music. In particular, I will examine how discursive transgressions, such as the use of dystopia and extreme, grotesque realism in grindcore lyrics are embodied and played out in the UK grindcore scene by female metal fans.

Limitations of Extreme Metal Politics: Grindcore as Protest Music

Although grindcore has a self-evident political orientation, it is important to place the sub-genre within the broader context of the politics and aesthetic of the global extreme metal scene. Kahn-Harris (2007) considers all forms of extreme metal as being part of a marginal, underground scenic-infrastructure, where individualism and anti-conformity are privileged over the commercial interests of mainstream heavy metal. Although extremity has become a pervasive and ambiguous concept in contemporary popular culture, Kahn-Harris argues that the concept of transgression captures the 'extremity' of extreme metal and its practices: 'they are excessive, testing and breaking boundaries, invoking the joys and terrors of formless oblivion within the collective, while simultaneously bolstering feelings of individual control and potency' (2007, p. 30). Two forms of transgression that are important to, and shape the political ideologies of, the extreme metal scene, concern the interrelationship between discursive and bodily transgressions.

Extreme metal groups discursively transgress conservative sensibilities by exposing, through lyrics, album artwork, song titles, and publications, the darker aspects of the human condition such as death, violence, war, the occult, and suffering. Demonstrating a sense of self-awareness and an acknowledgement that no certainties exist in relation to our fragile existence, it can be argued that the extreme metal scene is a reflexive community. However, Kahn-Harris points out that the term 'politics' and practices of political and social reflexivity operate precariously in the extreme metal scene. He argues that for many extreme metal members, 'music connotes the scene and politics connotes that which is outside the scene. Discourses that emerge from spaces outside the scene are seen as threatening and members attempt to keep them at bay' (p. 154). Furthermore, Kahn-Harris asserts that scene members are frequently criticized if their commitment to politics supersedes their perceived commitment to the music. Extreme metal musicians and bands that have challenged power relations most effectively have generally been those with a close affiliation to the more overtly political hardcore punk scene: the subgenre of grindcore. Grindcore bands such as Napalm Death, Extreme Noise Terror, Unseen Terror, and Nu Pogodi! exemplify the ways in which grindcore music is inseparable from politics. Yet, there is a delicate balance between embodying and expressing political views that are both overt and indirect.

Going back to the vignette at the beginning of this chapter, part of Napalm Death's musical success is due to the ways in which they foster social and political dissidence by encouraging their fans to 'think for themselves' and remain critically cognizant of their surroundings, instead of offering their audiences identifiable, ready-at-hand solutions (Taylor, 2009). It is through album artwork, lyrics, scenic discourses, and on-stage banter that anarchic political sensibilities are situated directly *within* the grindcore scene, defining its subcultural boundaries, and these political orientations are made visible inside and outside the scene through particular embodied practices. Within the UK grindcore scene, corporeal practices such as moshing, excessive drinking and drug use, tattooing, piercing, dreadlocks, dietary lifestyles (veganism, vegetarianism), and more alternative forms of dress are bodily expressions of anarchist philosophies that distinguish grindcore from other extreme metal genres such as death metal, black metal, and thrash metal.

Political discourses and embodiments within the grindcore scene are produced by and reflect underlying social conditions and class backgrounds. For example, Nilsson (2009) claims that the *existence* of working class subcultures is politically significant in itself because they create accessible, transgressive spaces, away from mainstream regulation and control, that 'constitute a necessary precondition for emancipatory political action' (p. 176). Political action in British heavy metal, according to Nilsson, is actualized through subcultural practices whereby individual experiences of class alienation, inequality, and subordination are transformed into a collective experience of solidarity, empowerment, protest, and resistance. Although Nilsson does not refer to grindcore specifically, his discussion of the political potential of heavy metal in Britain suggests why one of the prevailing themes in grindcore lyrics is social and political protest.

Yet, if grindcore's common lyrical theme is protest, why is it not always 'heard' as such? First, for many fans it is grindcore's 'sound-as-physical-assault' (Dee, 2009), its ability to physically, sensually, and aurally transform a venue space through dissonance and vocalized aggression, that makes it compelling. As Frith (1981) argues, 'We can identify with a song whether we understand the words or not [...] because it is the voice—not the lyrics—to which we immediately respond' (p. 12). Second, the majority of protest songs are not heard as protest songs due to a lack of lyrical intelligibility or misinterpretation (Weinstein, 2006). Third, even if people can make out the lyrics, they may be misread because grindcore lyrics are often ambiguous, abstract, and oblique, leading to many 'outsiders' failing to pick up on the sarcasm, use of metaphors, and subcultural references. On the other hand, a protest song can attain a longer shelf life if it is 'indirect, since it can be heard generations later merely as a song relieved of the baggage of a protest that may no longer be relevant or popular' (Purcell, 2003, p. 12). In a similar way, I argue that grindcore continues to play a pertinent role in the lives of young people because its lyrics are not focused on a particular time period or event; rather the music is seen to express a sense of longevity in its ability to articulate strong feelings of discontent across different time periods and to new and older fans. What should also be emphasized is that grindcore is not only about resisting mainstream ideals, healing through aggressive music, or 'fighting' out social conflicts, it is a resistance to superficiality and deception, to pressure to conform, and to biased judgments.

In her analysis of how extreme metal has been situated within popular music criticisms, Phillipov (2012) argues that a preoccupation with the political value of music obscures the pleasures of extreme metal listening practices and overlooks affectivities of metal fandom. But as Dee (2009) suggests, by upholding serious political views in its lyrics, evoking a visceral extremism in its music and intense performances, and by inciting affective mosh pit experiences that work to strengthen a sense of 'self', 'grindcore opens up spaces for a sustained non-commodified experience beyond the dominating identity of avant-pop and the mainstream culture industry' (p. 67). In this way, grindcore performers and listeners, due to their working-class dispositions and awareness, occupy a potentially conscious and critical position in the maintenance of a radical and democratic space beyond the abject reality of capitalism (Dee, 2009; Nilsson, 2009; Overell, 2014).

Human Error: Dystopia and Extreme, Grotesque Realism in UK Grindcore

The covers of Napalm Death's early albums were offensive, jarring montages of political injustices, offering a prototype for subsequent grindcore acts like Terrorizer. Typical graphics included multinational corporate logos superimposed over images of Holocaust victims or images of skulls piled up from those killed by fascist politicians (Dee, 2009). Taylor (2009) asserts that for metal fans there is a pleasure enjoyed, and an embodiment of power experienced, in metal music and its catastrophic narratives and imagery, arguing that pleasure in metal is multi-dimensional and complex, stemming from a range of sources such as 'the honesty of music that exposes the harsh realities of the world or the physical stimulation of extreme tempos, distortion, and amplification' (p. 89). The revelation of harsh realities and skepticism toward future possibilities that define the dystopian sci-fi narrative tradition, which includes H. G. Well's *War of the Worlds* (1898), Aldous Huxley's *Brave New World* (1932), and George Orwell's *Nineteen Eighty-Four* (1949), have been highly influential for heavy metal (Taylor, op. cit.). For example, many early representations of apocalyptic and dystopian realities are to be found in Black Sabbath, Judas Priest, and Bolt Thrower, who have employed the 'vocabulary of science fiction, apocalypse and dystopia to expose the horrors that may lie in our futures' (Taylor, 2009, p. 90). This literary tradition continues in British grindcore, where bands make use of harsh lyrics, sound, and visual imagery to express critical concerns about human actions, decision-making, and fears about the future. For example, Unseen Terror's album *Human Error* (1987) features someone holding a crystal ball that depicts an ominously dystopian city engulfed in flames, ravaged by chaos, and littered with decomposing bodies, all of which are the result of human actions. The majority of the songs included on the album critically expose topics such as mass employment, racial and gendered divisions in society, and the implications of war and governmental conspiracies. Dystopian themes in grindcore are important because a dystopian narrative, for Taylor, never entirely excludes the possibility for hope and change; instead, it serves as a warning, a 'reawakening' rather than an impending death sentence.

Grindcore is distinctive in relation to other extreme metal genres in drawing attention to the ways in which the metal scene and its fans are continually entangled in relations of power, globalization, and capital. This connection was made evident during the late 1980s when UK grindcore bands, through their aural, rhythmic, and lyrical extremism, depicted the effects of industrial capitalism (Dee, 2009). As Great Britain dealt with the melancholic decline in prospects of jobs-for-life, increased mass underemployment, and shrinking welfare support under Thatcher's government, grindcore bands such as Napalm Death, Unseen Terror, and Extreme Noise Terror became important vehicles for representing public discontent and frustration. According to Lee Dorrian, who sang for Napalm Death between 1987 and 1989, the late 1980s was a special time in metal music in England because during this period the grindcore scene was 'very anti-establishment and it did join a lot of people from different backgrounds together' (cited in Mudrian, 2004, p. 134). The use of 'slogan' songs where a repeated phrase is aggressively uttered throughout a song, such as the opening phrase 'Multinational corporations, genocide of the starving nations' (Napalm Death, 1987), can be considered a stylistic reflection of discontent. This form of slogan-politics (Brown, forthcoming) is embedded within the dystopian tradition as the repeated phrase alerts listeners to their hostile surroundings and is a practice of grotesque realism in that these utterances, which were overlaid by a cacophony of guitar feedback, transgress conventional metal song structures. Extreme, grotesque realism and dystopian tropes are visually and lyrically prominent in Napalm Death's album *From Enslavement to Obliteration* (1988). The focus of the album cover is a distraught, terrified man holding his head in his hands as he attempts to mentally block out, or fathom, the grotesque reality that exists around him. The overlapping images of decaying corpses, wounded soldiers, corrupted politicians, rows of unmarked coffins, and starving black children work to construct an affective dystopian vision that is difficult to ignore. The title track of the album draws attention to how capitalism works to maintain and reinforce social and racial inequalities. As working-class men desperately search for prosperity and economic mobility within a political system that flourishes on hierarchy and disparity, their aspirations actually become the 'tools of [their] own oppression' (Dorrian, 1988). Napalm Death asserts that in our fight for 'stronger positions' within a profit-driven society, we actively retain hegemonic relations of power that exacerbate existing gender, racial, and class divisions.

In other words, people living under capitalism are 'committed to a life of slavery' (Dorrian, 1988), an existence of enslavement that tragically leads to mental and physical obliteration. These lyrics evoke a dystopian and grotesque picture of Britain where young men are slaves to minimum-wage factory work, desperately competing in the endless rat race in order to reap the benefits of employment and possibly obtain a more lucrative future than their predecessors. For many commentators the term grindcore is actually a description of the rhythmic 'grind' of down-tuned, low-pitched guitars (Brown, forthcoming), which echoes the soundscapes of monotonous factory life. Napalm Death was one of the first grindcore bands to explicitly voice working-class frustrations and speak out about the dire socio-economic conditions of key parts of Britain during that time. It is Napalm Death's politically conscious lyrics and punchy, aggressive rhythms that have sustained the band's popularity. But like other pro-feminist and anti-capitalist grindcore bands, such as Agathocles, Napalm Death's ability to question, challenge, and confront pervasive gender inequalities and hegemonic power relations makes the band attractive to female metal fans who might already feel marginalized and oppressed, within the extreme metal scene and in society more broadly (Dee, 2009). Although I discuss this in more detail later on in the chapter, I want to focus next on the notion of 'grotesque realism' within British grindcore and how it is made intelligible through bodily performances.

In her discussion of heavy metal carnival, Halnon (2006) argues that this form of spectacle can be considered a politics of grotesque realism in which fans and musicians rebel against 'potentially everything that is moral, sacred, decent or civilized' (p. 35). Drawing upon Bakhtin's notion of the carnival-grotesque, Halnon explains that the metal carnival open up spaces where difference from the predictable, managed, impersonal, and commercialized mainstream is celebrated and seeks to challenge the structural and moral orders of everyday life through comedic, satirical exaggerations that are excessive and transgress social norms (Halnon, 2004, 2006). Dee (2009) also notes that the 'extreme realism' of grindcore, generated from its northern England working-class milieu, and its radical experimentalism, derived from anarcho-punk, are manifest in the performance aesthetic of 'corporeal brutality' (p. 55). Accordingly, forms of rebellion and critique that are found in the lyrics and album artwork of grindcore bands are made meaningful through physical movements of the body where fans transgress social conventions by moshing aggressively, stage diving, crowd surfing, drinking alcohol, headbanging, and performing. Grotesque realism becomes intelligible through the grotesque body that transgresses the ordinary limits between itself and other bodies. Extreme Noise Terror (ENT), in its song 'Use Your Mind' (*A Holocaust in Your Head*, 1989), emphasizes the liminal and bodily politics of grindcore, which are seen as incompatible with more 'conservative' scenes, such as straight edge hardcore and punk. Multiple interpretations can be derived from this song, but what I want to focus on here is the apparent tension between the excessive and 'straight and narrow' political embodiments found within the metal scene. On the one hand, ENT positions grindcore as more 'authentic' than straight edge because it addresses 'real' issues, instead of being preoccupied with superfluous concerns, such as fashion. ENT asserts that it would rather be 'fucked' than 'straight' and openly questions the extent to which tattooing an X on one's hand is an effective way to incite social change. On the other hand, ENT embraces an excessive yet apathetic political stance: as struggling working-class musicians with no hopes for the future they would rather force down pills and drink excessively because they've 'got nothing to lose'. However, near the end of the song they suggest that in order to 'break down the barriers' within society and within the scene, we have to use our *minds*. Paradoxically, ENT is encouraging fans to engage in critical thinking by using their minds whilst endorsing excessive drinking and corporeal self-destruction in order to form alliances among scene members. Frandsen (2010) considers self-destructive behaviors such as moshing, excessive drinking, and sometimes drug use, as well as listening to heavy metal at loud volumes, as integral to extreme metal culture. Yet these behaviors could be understood as practices of corporeal politics whereby fans and musicians are expressing a discontent and frustration with modern society, through their bodies. Feelings of alienation and absurdity are reconciled through excessive and transgressive bodily performances. These ostensibly self-destructive behaviors shape metal fans' identities in contrast to mainstream society. During a grindcore performance, bodies are typically colliding, fans are holding onto the edge of a small stage as the band launches into a plunging riff, sweat is dripping onto other dampened bodies while beer sprays out in all directions as a pint is knocked over from the chaotic movement; people feel part of a community that is made concrete and sensual through these corporeal practices. Therefore, in accordance to Halnon's (2006) discussion, mosh pit practices and intimate performances from grindcore bands may be the most transgressive and politicized aspects of the grindcore spectacle as it actively creates a subversive 'reality' that is accomplished through bodily practices, ultimately opposing a society that places primacy on autonomy, personal boundaries, control, self-interest, and individualism.

Use Your Mind?: Corporeal Politics and Bodily Pleasures in Grindcore

This section expands upon the argument put forth by Scott (2012), who argues that metal can generate a philosophy and a politics that is produced not merely through intellectual debates, but also through bodily *performance*. He suggests that metal's political positionings are embodied and expressed in a variety of ways, such as utterances, lifestyles, performances, and gestures. Scott's participation in the highly volatile and aggressive mosh pit at a Hatebreed gig illustrates how metal's philosophy and politics are understood and made meaningful through the body. A combination of the lyrical and performative, this metal moment was a corporeal assemblage of politics, challenges, catharsis, reflection, and contemplation that exceeds the physical boundaries of the metal venue. Taking Scott's argument further, grindcore then can be conceptualized as a politics in the deeper, corporeal sense of its *being* political. It affords metal fans the opportunity to challenge social and gendered norms and garner a sense of collective social action through bodily practices. Within popular music and heavy metal scholarship there have been some notable studies that have looked at the relationship between embodiment and music (DeNora, 2000; Overell, 2010, 2014), but there has been a lack of research on how women specifically embody subcultural politics through bodily performances. Frith (1981, p. 15) argues that the response to music is, to a large degree, physical. However, in rock, or in this case grindcore, pleasure is a cultural as well as a physical matter, and the meaning of the music is not fixed. Thus, grindcore is a result of an ever-changing combination of independently developed musical elements, each of which carries its own cultural message and meaning.

The political ideologies that are articulated in grindcore lyrics are expressed and made meaningful through corporeal practices such as moshing. This is illustrated in Overell's account of her initial mosh pit experiences within the grind scene: 'I loved going in to the mosh pit and dancing, jumping and feeling the music course through my body. I loved the communal experience of the mosh […] It is usually a euphoric experience of shared enjoyment of grindcore music' (2014, p. 5). The fast, aggressive rhythms of grindcore and its abhorrence toward the machinations of late-capitalist culture (Overell, 2010) penetrate the skin and are actualized through embodied performances. In his research about the hardcore music scene, Simon (1997) argues that because the majority of punk and hardcore bands are politically driven, there is potential for social change to be enacted within the pit and that slam-dancing can be understood as 'an expressive performance which serves to comment on the society at large' (p. 152). According to Hancock and Lorr (2013), mosh pit practices can be understood as embodied political strategies for punks to be noticed and taken seriously because they feel that their voices and opinions are excluded from mainstream political debates. Within the punk scene, Leblanc (1999) highlighted how moshing practices were a direct manifestation of punk philosophy. Indeed, for some female punk fans involved in straight edge scenes, mosh pits are sensual spaces that afford them the opportunity to vent frustrations and anger; embodiments of a communal rebellion that challenges and resists conventional understandings of femininity (Tsitsos, 1999). Therefore, grindcore is not just about the voicing of political ideas but is the embodiment of resistance and grotesque realism. In the next section, I focus on women's participation in the UK grindcore scene and argue that women are drawn to grindcore because it challenges personal boundaries and offers a space for the legitimacy and articulation of gendered experiences. While acknowledging the potentialities of political expression, I also wish to draw attention to the limitations of grindcore's transgressive and radical characteristics.

'Fuck My Womb': Women's Participation in the Grindcore Scene in Leeds, UK

> I'm frantically grabbing onto the monitor, trying to maintain my position at the front of the stage as people repeatedly jostle into me from behind. I'm at the 1in12 Club, a DIY, not-for-profit music collective, in Bradford headbanging along to a Leeds based d-beat, grind group, Nu Pogodi! Villa, the guitarist and lead singer, rapidly and aggressively spits out the lyrics at the top of her lungs into the swaying microphone, her grotesque neck tattoos makes her look intimidating. Talia's dual raspy vocals echo throughout the room as she heavily strums her bass. Blast beats are thundering out from behind the obscured drum kit, producing a wall of noise that feels like its tearing open my insides for all to see. And just as the first song comes to an abrupt finish Villa seizes the mic and screams, 'Being female is beautiful but sometimes having a womb sucks, fuck my woooooomb!' (Author's field notes February 22, 2013)

For promoter and musician Trevor,[2] the Leeds extreme metal scene is well known for its production and promotion of grindcore bands. He maintains that the subgenre thrives in northern England because 'it's so grim up here', the music aptly reflecting Leeds's working-class background and industrialized landscape. He goes on to say that, 'if you put on a grindcore gig in Leeds you're guaranteed to get a good turnout compared to other metal genres like thrash or power metal'. Although the Leeds grindcore scene is dominated by male fans, musicians, and promoters, grind/hardcore punk acts like Nu Pogodi! (at the time of the band's first interview it was an all-female group but recently incorporated a male drummer) have been successful both locally and internationally. Well known within hardcore punk, riot grrrl, and grindcore circles in Leeds, Nu Pogodi! does not shy away from radical politics. In the band's lyrics and stage banter the members openly address taboo topics such as stigmas around mental health, the abuse of power by authorities, female genital mutilation, poverty, and gender-related violence. They explain that politically focused lyrics have always played an important role in defining the band, and they make a conscious effort to voice their opinions in a positive, less 'pushy' manner. Villa, the lead vocalist and songwriter, admits: 'I think my aim was always to do it in a positive way, like fuck this is fucking happening, let's fucking change it, we can do it, like we can and we will [pounds her fists on the table]!' Even though Nu Pogodi! is exposing the dark underbelly of human existence the members still remain hopeful and optimistic that social change is *possible* through collective scenic action.

Dee (2009) argues that male domination and masculinist tropes have been challenged in grindcore through less hegemonic displays of masculinity on stage, in lyrical content, and on album covers, which could explain why grindcore tends to have a more gender-balanced audience and more participation by female musicians. Members of Nu Pogodi! highlight the differences in reception from male and female metal fans. They observed how men were generally surprised at how loudly, fast, and aggressively they played, whereas women would approach them and reveal how they resonated with their lyrics. Villa claims that female grind/punk fans view Nu Pogodi 'as a bit of a stand or they feel like they're part of it and they're not sort of watching it they feel more involved'. The idea that female fans feel that they are taking a political stand by attending grindcore gigs and consider themselves active participants in the performance demonstrates a corporeal politics of resistance. For music scholars like Scott (2012) and Halnon (2006), metal generates a politics of dissent and dissatisfaction that is embodied and expressed through bodily practices such as moshing and metal performances. Villa's remarks also illustrate how grindcore performances and spaces are important in giving dissenting voices and alternative performances of femininity, legitimacy, visibility, and authority.

Within the broader British grindcore scene Napalm Death has been the most outspoken all-male band in critiquing conventional forms of masculinity and questioning the gendered relations within the grind scene through songs like 'It's a M.A.N.S. World', 'Cock-Rock Alienation', and 'Musclehead', all of which are from their album *From Enslavement to Obliteration* (1988). According to Dee (2009), this attitude is consonant with the anarcho-punk roots of grindcore, where the 'reality of patriarchal capitalism is something to be vehemently critiqued rather than apolitically 'exposed' and thus tacitly legitimated' (p. 60). However, in Griffin's (2012) research about gendered performances in the DIY punk and hardcore music scene, she found that most local hardcore and punk scenes are dominated by men, meaning that they control the 'voice' and discourse of the scene through music production and gig promotion; thus, dictating which bands are worthy of playing. Due to this gender imbalance 'there is a risk that women's voices remain hidden and their contributions overlooked, even where attempts are made to challenge gender norms' (Griffin, 2012, p. 71). This concern is pertinent when thinking about the limits of political progression within grindcore music. These concerns were brought up by one female metal musician and fan who is active in the Leeds extreme metal scene:

> I think it's cause it's [metal] got to confront itself. You know you can have 101 people going 'yah, fuck the major corporations' but then when you turn around and say, 'yah, well what have *you* done to stop people being sexually abused today?' They'll go 'yeah fuck off' you know.

> Umm that's possibly a reason why I don't know, but punk has been more ... because the political metal bands have been more about the wider politics whereas punk has been more about the personal politics.
> (Carry)

Kahn-Harris (2007) asserts that the extreme metal scene 'needs to be 'opened up' both so its own practices are challenged and that the wider world can learn from it' (p. 163). In relation to Carry's comment, grindcore's ability to challenge and confront itself is severely limited if grindcore musicians and fans *already* believe that they are being politically progressive by exposing the harsh 'truths' of reality. In the Leeds metal scene the majority of grindcore musicians and fans are white, heterosexual, working-class men, and these demarcations place restrictions on the types of political discourses and performances that can be openly expressed and taken seriously.

Unseen Terror, a grindcore band from Shropshire who remained active for only four years (1986–1990), vehemently speaks out about the ways in which political expression is constrained within the extreme metal scene. In the short, minute-and-a- half song, 'Ignorant Scene' (*Human Error* 1987), Unseen Terror critiques metal scene members, along with mainstream society, for being 'one sided' and derisive toward the philosophical views, practices, and lifestyle choices of grindcore scene members. For Unseen Terror, these 'ignorant' relations undercut subcultural solidarity and the potential to make a difference. The band goes on to say that because everyone is affected by hegemonic structures of inequality, 'we should stick together not fight each other'. For many outsiders, grindcore is still viewed as a breeding ground for anger and purposeless aggression more often than it is recognized for any of its political achievements, affirmations, and consolations. Yet for Taylor (2009), anger itself can be conceptualized as 'a militant emotion, not a resigned one, and may plant a seed for resistance that need not be nihilistic or reactionary' (p. 105). Unseen Terror's lyrics could also be interpreted as the metal scene accusing outsiders (i.e., metal scholars and critics, employers, parents, non-metal fans) of being ignorant and dismissive of grindcore music. Phillipov (2012) outlines how metal scholars criticize extreme metal for being too nihilistic, for not transforming its social and economic disgruntlements into tangible political goals, and for embracing conservative sensibilities by celebrating narcissistic performance of male power and sexuality. The lack of 'real' engagement with politics is also a concern within the Leeds extreme metal scene, but as Steph, whose sister sings in an extreme metal band, explains, extreme metal is a way for women to be taken seriously as political and subcultural agents:

> People get freaked out about politics once you start raising a topical subject they go 'oh, oh it's political oh, oh' [disgusted facial expression] and they seem to back off don't they and it's like well you wouldn't be where you are today now if it wasn't for politics, but women's role

> in extreme metal bands offer them an opportunity to sound off about politics, it's a way to deal with being a woman [smiles].
>
> (Steph)

Steph's comment reflects the notion that 'discourses that emerge from spaces outside the scene are seen as threatening' and fans tend to keep them at bay (Kahn-Harris, 2007, p. 154). Discourses around femininity, womanhood, and sexuality, if taken seriously, can potentially destabilize and undermine the masculinist discourses that have come to define extreme metal. Thus, opening up political dialogues around gender, sexuality, and race within grindcore could have real implications for female fans in the subgenre, potentially resulting in their being further marginalized within extreme metal.

On the other hand Jenny, a self-identified grind fan who organizes grindcore and goregrind gigs in London, has noticed that most women who are into grind are more 'tomboyish', less feminine compared to the women who attend death metal and black metal gigs. Jenny considers grindcore to be different from other styles of extreme metal in terms of its political positionings, freakish stage performances, and 'don't-give-a shit' attitude; therefore, it opens up a space where social pressures to adhere to certain behaviors and norms associated with normative-femininity are less prominent. Jenny's comment reflects the ways in which extreme realism in grindcore carves out new avenues for women to engage in and embody grotesque realism through bodily critiques of gender norms. Although gender divisions still exist within the grind scene, there remains a large female audience drawn to grind because of the sensations that are derived from its extreme brutality:

> I like fast, fast drumming and I like low guttural vocals so you'll generally find that to be a pretty common occurrence throughout grindcore. I like the feeling of grindcore. You know people make fun of me because I don't want to be called a metalhead, I'm a grindfiend, right [laughs].
>
> (Marie)

Marie's comment also echoes Unseen Terror's sentiments in 'Ignorant Scene' in that she has experienced taunts and ridicule from metal scene members for identifying as a 'grindfiend' rather than a regular metal fan. Marie adds that grindcore's playfulness and energy are distinctive elements to the subgenre, making it unique from other genres of extreme metal: 'Part of the reason I love grind so much is because it makes me laugh, I have fun listening to grindcore, I jump around my room inhaling grindcore, squealing into a hairbrush'. Other musicians, fans, and music critics have commented on the multifarious experience of listening to and engaging in grindcore music; it is simultaneously 'thrilling, dangerous and hilarious, without the latter cancelling out the former' (Dee, 2009, p. 66). The playfulness and absurdity of grindcore are attributes of its visceral extremism, and this creates an atmosphere at live gigs that enables female fans to experiment and play with different gendered identities and bodily dispositions.

Grindcore's aggressiveness, brutality, sincere message, and ability to push social and personal boundaries are also important affective qualities for female fans such as Rider:

> The first time you've heard something really deep and really loud and then once you start listening to, I don't know, say umm, like brutal death metal then you got the gutturals, which you know to most people sounds petrifying, and you haven't ever heard anything like that before, and you kind of get a bit fascinated with it and you start to search around the subject and see what similar bands are doing and what kind of boundaries of yours they are pushing.

Rider's pleasure in seeking out extreme metal bands that push personal and social boundaries relates to Overell's (2010) observation where she found that her grindcore participants took pleasure in the shocking and unsettling aspects of grindcore. In this way, the transgressive elements of grindcore aesthetics work at the representational and affective level. They produce sensations that transform scene members into 'grind fiends' or 'freaks' that feed on the intense energy and corporeal pleasures that grindcore performances and listening practices generate.

Uncertainty Blurs the Vision ...

> *So here I am, sweat is dripping down my face, my hair is tangled from hours of headbanging and moshing, my body aches, my heart beat is pounding in my ears, and Napalm Death have come back on stage for an encore. Throughout the show they encouraged us to practice critical thinking, circumvent the formation of divisions, and remain sceptical of institutions that continue to oppress and further marginalize vulnerable populations. 'Barney' jumps in the air and chaos immediately breaks out in front of the stage. In the pit I crash into Carry, we punch our fists upwards into the air in unison, we charge headlong into the male-dominated crowd that swallows us up in a whirlpool of collective movement.* (Author's fieldnotes, October 4, 2012)

In this way grindcore is 'a demand for community, freedom, and equality and an opportunity to surface, release, and transform everyday frustrations and aggressions' into a positive and cooperative form of corporeal political resistance, even if the moment is fleeting (Halnon, 2006, p. 46). Despite on-going criticisms from popular music and metal scholars about extreme metal's political indifference (Phillipov, 2012), political action in the British grindcore scene is manifested through subcultural practices and performances where seeds for social change are embedded in the vulgar guitar riff, socially cognizant lyrics, female dominated mosh pits, and commitment to living life a little bit differently.

Conclusion

By focusing on the subgenre of British grindcore, which is widely recognized for its political orientations, I have offered here a more multidimensional understanding of how gender, politics, resistance, and corporeality operate within and outside the scene. Paying attention to particular embodied practices within a grindcore context, such as the mosh pit, challenges us to think differently about the significance of certain subgenres, and this brings us back to 'Barney's' political iteration at the beginning of the chapter. It is critical to ask not only how female fans are involved in scenic activities but also how scenes and subgenres are felt and experienced differently. It is this corporeal lens that allows us to explore the messy intersections of embodied practices, gender performances, subgenre development, and political ideologies and how these intersections are shaped by and reflect the ever-changing cultural, social, and political landscape in which it is produced. In his review of Napalm Death's *From Enslavement to Obliteration*, Horsley (1999) explains that this album was influential because it signaled 'the genre's perilous rite of passage through Britain's post-industrial urban landscape' (p. 54). Bands like Nu Pogodi!, Napalm Death, and Extreme Noise Terror are performing particular worldviews through their utterances, lifestyles, gestures, and bodily practices. In this way grindcore presents 'a way of looking at the world and being in the world; it is a philosophy that is shown, not just argued in language' (Scott, 2012, p. 221). Even though some metal scene members view political posturing as interfering with musical pleasure, extreme metal and the scene can never be isolated from flows and structures of power and capital; hence, an apolitical scene is almost impossible. All extreme metal scenes are enmeshed in relations of power, despite their relative marginality and independence as a musical field (Kahn-Harris, 2007). Yet for grindcore musicians and groups who overtly challenge ideas of power, oppression, gender politics, and capital they can be considered a threat to the wider extreme metal scene because they expose metal's paradoxical nature in that it simultaneously challenges hegemonic power and gendered relations whilst reifying them. Thus, it could be argued, that we still live in an ignorant scene.

Notes

1. Crustie is a colloquial term in extreme metal and punk circles to refer to people who are associated with anti-establishment views, political protests and squatting and are sometimes unemployed. Typical style of dress includes an unkempt appearance, dreadlocks, piercings, tattoos, and patched denim jackets and trousers.
2. To protect the identities of all research participants all formal names have been changed.

Bibliography

Brown, A. R. (forthcoming). Grindcore. In J. Shepherd, D. Horn, & D. Laing (Eds.), *The Continuum encyclopedia of popular music of the world* (Vol 8: Genres). New York, London: Continuum.

Dee, L. (2009). The brutal truth: Grindcore as the extreme realism of heavy metal. In G. Bayer (Ed.), *Heavy metal music in Britain* (pp. 53–69). Surrey, UK: Ashgate.

DeNora, T. (2000). *Music in everyday life*. Cambridge: Cambridge University Press.

Driver, C. (2011). Embodying hardcore: Rethinking 'subcultural' authenticities. *Journal of Youth Studies*, 14(8), 975–990.

Extreme Noise Terror. (1989). *A holocaust in your head*. Ipswich, UK: Head Eruption Records.

Frandsen, D. (2010). Live for music, die for life. In R. Hill & K. Spracklen (Eds.), *Heavy fundamentalisms: Music, metal and politics* (pp. 9–17). Oxford: Inter-Disciplinary Press.

Frith, S. (1981). *Sound effects: Youth, leisure and the politics of rock*. London: Constable.

Griffin, N. (2012). Gendered performance: Performing gender in the DIY punk and hardcore music scene. *Journal of International Women's Studies*, 13(2), 66–81.

Halnon, K.B. (2006). Heavy metal carnival and dis-alienation: The politics of grotesque realism. *Symbolic Interaction*, 29(1), 33–48.

Halnon, K. B. (2004). Inside shock music carnival: Spectacle as contested terrain. *Critical Sociology*, 30(3), 743–779.

Hancock, B. H., & Lorr, M. J. (2013). More than just a soundtrack: Towards a technology of the collective in hardcore punk. *Journal of Contemporary Ethnography*, 42(3), 320–346.

Horsley, J. (2009). Essential albums|Europe. *Terrorizer Magazine*, 180, 54.

Kahn-Harris, K. (2007). *Extreme metal: Music and culture on the edge*. Oxford: Berg.

Leblanc, L. (1999). *Pretty in punk: Girls' gender resistance in a boy's subculture*. New Brunswick, NJ: Rutgers University Press.

Mudrian, A. (2004). *Choosing death: The improbable history of death metal and grindcore*. Los Angeles: Feral House Publications.

Napalm Death. (1988). *From enslavement to obliteration*. Nottingham, UK: Earache.

Napalm Death. (1987). *Scum*. Nottingham, UK: Earache.

Nilsson, M. (2009). No class? Class and class politics in British heavy metal. In G. Bayer (Ed.), *Heavy metal music in Britain* (pp. 161–179). Surrey: Ashgate Publishing.

Overell, R. (2010). Brutal belonging in Melbourne's grindcore scene. *Studies in Symbolic Interaction*, 35, 79–99.

Overell, R. (2011). '[I] hate girls and emo[tion]s': Negotiating masculinity in grindcore music. *Popular Music History*, 6(1–2), 198–223.

Overell, R. (2014). *Affective intensities in extreme music scenes: Cases from Australia and Japan*. Basingstoke: Palgrave Macmillan.

Phillipov, M. (2012). *Death metal and music criticism: Analysis at the limits*. Lanham: Lexington Books.

Purcell, N. J. (2003). *Death metal music: The passion and politics of a subculture*. Jefferson, NC: McFarland and Company.

Scott, N. W. R. (2012). 'Politics?! Nah, fuck politics man!' What can we expect from metal gods? In N.W. R. Scott (Ed.), *Reflections in the metal void* (pp. 215–222). Oxford: Inter-Disciplinary Press.

Simon, B. S. (1997). Entering the pit: Slam-dancing and modernity. *Journal of Popular Culture*, 31(1), 149–176.

Taylor, L. W. (2009). Images of human-wrought despair and destruction: Social critique in British apocalyptic and dystopian metal. In G. Bayer (Ed.), *Heavy metal music in Britain* (pp. 89–110). Farnham: Ashgate.

Tsitsos, W. (1999). Rules of rebellion: Slamdancing, moshing, and the American alternative scene. *Popular Music*, 18(3), 397–414.

Unseen Terror. (1987). *Human error*. Nottingham, UK: Earache.

Weinstein, D. (2006). Rock protest songs: So many and so few. In I. Peddie (Ed.), *The resisting muse: Popular music and social protest* (pp. 3–16). Farnham: Ashgate.

Part III
Metal Demographics and Identity

9 The Numbers of the Beast
Surveying Iron Maiden's Global Tribe[1]

Jean-Philippe Ury-Petesch

In *Les Nouvelles Tribus Urbaines* (1999), Valérie Fournier argues that most of the contemporary examples of youth tribes or subcultural 'styles' are identified by their relationship to music genres. This chapter will focus attention on the *Iron Maiden* tribe, who can be considered a representative segment of the global heavy metal tribus, who were encountered via an Internet survey carried out between December 2007 and July 2009. Over four thousand (4,456) computer literate Maiden fans, from 70 countries, answered the 135 questions that made up the 'Ironthesis' on-line questionnaire survey, in this period. Accordingly, the aims of this chapter are threefold. First, to describe how this global survey was conceived and conducted, paying attention to the issues of gathering large social data sets via the Internet and, in particular, how to overcome geographical and language barriers, so that the survey could be as representative as possible. Second, to describe and illustrate the global scale of the survey in terms of the number of fans that participated, their nationalities, and their countries of residence. Third, to record the social morphology of these fans, in terms of age, gender, residence, education, employment, social background, marital status, religious beliefs, political affiliation, and so on and to discuss this data in relation to previous national and regional survey findings and debates about heavy metal fandom, particularly but not exclusively in France, Germany, and North America.

Ironthesis: Seven Languages to Speak to Maiden Fans around the World

In this section, we discuss the target population we wished to survey, the writing of the questionnaire itself, and the process of developing the e-version (including the host website where it would be made available), in relation to existing heavy metal research and debates about social science methodologies.

Qualitative researchers generally prefer to be in close or direct contact with the populations they study, especially when they are employing observational methods or conducting interviews. One of the consequences of this is that participant sample sizes are often quite small, are derived from particular geographical areas and economic, social, and cultural groups. The advantages of such methods are that they can gather rich and possibly important or insightful data. The disadvantages are that this data is small and may not be representative of the target population or group the research is trying to investigate. Quantitative methods, particularly social surveys involving structured questionnaires, do not have these limitations, as a wide sample of respondents can be reached, traditionally by post or through door-to-door surveys. However, such research-at-a-distance needs to have a very clear idea of the target survey population it wants to gather data about and how a sample can be gathered from the group that can be viewed as representative, i.e., that will reflect in proportion the key features or characteristics of the larger population of which it is a part.

Previous research into heavy metal has been divided very much along these traditional lines of qualitative (small) and quantitative (big) data gathering studies (see Brown, this volume). For example, almost all of the studies conducted in Britain in the 1970s and North America in the 1980s, with mainly school and college students, have been quantitative (questionnaire surveys sometimes correlated with sample interviews). Indeed the predominant or at least most well-known social and cultural profile of the 'typical metalhead' is one largely derived from these data sets (although studies conducted in Europe, mainly in France and Germany, have widened this picture somewhat, as we will discuss). By contrast, the majority of contemporary research into metal fandom, such as the many studies reported in *Metal Rules the Globe* (Wallach, Berger, and Green, 2011) are qualitative, often ethnographic in nature or based on a small group of interviewees who are assumed to be representative in some key respects of the wider population of metal fans of that country or region or internationally.

Limits and Bias of the Approach

Fournier, in her study, notes that: 'In order to approach a field like this, participant observation seems the best method. A questionnaire-based survey turns out to be impossible in an environment where liberal professions are not well represented, research work coming from a university organ arouses little interest, or even suspicion' (1999, p. 13).[2] With a questionnaire, we fail to follow one of the main teachings of anthropology: knowing how to watch and to listen while remaining as neutral as possible. If, as Hein (2003) and Walzer (2007) claim in respect to France, metalheads are educated and qualified people, we thought it likely they would be inclined to take part; across the Atlantic, as Weinstein (2000, pp. 113–117) indicates, they are more likely to be 'blue collar' or proletarian (see also Brown, this volume). However, Le Bart (2000) speaks of how fans want to talk about their passion and let other people know about it. So, we were optimistic fans would participate.

The beaconing by the investigator is also another problem, as the questions he asks go in the direction of confirming or invalidating his/her hypotheses. By only asking about what interests him, thanks to a closed questionnaire, he deprives himself of an interesting exchange with the population studied; the latter could help him to go beyond his prejudice. Nevertheless, the social morphology of a group is based on elements that do not require a direct exchange between the investigator and the population studied. The lack of qualitative data compared to quantitative data is a major limit of a multiple-choice questionnaire as it deprives the investigator of the transcription of what Hennion (2007) would call the 'words of passion'. But there is no perfect method at the level of a sole researcher because both methods present pros and cons.

The imperfection of a multiple choice question survey appears at two levels: the questions and the suggested answers. One of the main faults, indeed the most common one, is when meaningful questions are missing. For example, we did not ask the Maiden fans about their haircuts when clearly long hair is part of the metal *bricolage*. The way questions are formulated also generates problems as each person has a different sensibility that can lead to misunderstanding. And when the survey is conducted on a global scale, the lack of knowledge of other cultures inevitably leads to ethnocentric questions that do not make sense for people coming from a different cultural substratum. The same remark applies for answers that sometimes do not correspond to the life and the experience of the polled people. The lack of choice is the other main problem: *either* options have been omitted or they are too limited and do not enable the polled people to give a satisfactory answer. The possibility of skipping the question is also an option in case of no suitable answer.

The length of the questionnaire can also be a factor if potential respondents think that their time could be spent on something more entertaining or immediate in reward. With a long questionnaire, one can be quite sure that some respondents will be lost along the way. Also, the anonymity of the Internet is a double-edged sword because either the respondent feels perfectly at ease, therefore trustful, and will honestly answer all the questions, even the sensitive ones about religious beliefs, political affiliation, etc,. or he can be a total mythomaniac inventing a false or fake persona.

A lengthy questionnaire can therefore be a good tool to discourage the second type of response; only 'die-hard' fans will be willing to spend up to half an hour on something that does not bring them instant reward. In addition, we forewarned potential participants of our right to delete questionnaire returns that looked doubtful in their veracity.

Using an online survey also raises the question of the representativeness of the sample. It is extremely difficult, not to say impossible, to determine the representativeness of an Internet-derived sample. However, gaining an exceptionally high number of returns does offer validity in terms of the sheer number of respondents. Despite this, we do not know how many fans found the link to the questionnaire but did not complete it.

Population Studied

Unlike many studies that are geographically limited, we wanted to reach as many countries and nationalities as possible. A conventional postal or paper survey would simply not have made this possible.[3] The Internet appeared to be the best tool for our purposes, even if its use introduced a first bias or limitation in gathering our sample: the survey would only be able to reach computer-literate fans, those with access to the Internet, or fans with friends ready to assist them in answering the survey. Despite the persistence of the 'digital divide' in global Internet access, from the late '90s the use of Internet technologies has grown exponentially, and so we were reasonably confident we would be able to reach a wide fan base and age range, between 12 and 55 years.

Despite the fact that Iron Maiden is a British band, coming to prominence as one of the leading bands of the New Wave of British Heavy Metal (NWOBHM) in the mid-1980s, the success of the band's records and concerts has led to world tours and a global fan following. It was the success of the *Number of the Beast* (1982) album and subsequent world tour that cemented its reputation as a major live act, breaking many records for concert attendance figures.

The 2008 *Somewhere Back in Time World Tour* (documented in the film *Iron Maiden: Flight 666*, [2009]), took in India, Australia, Japan, the USA, Mexico, Cost Rica, Columbia, Brazil, Argentina, Chile, Puerto Rico, and Canada, while *The Final Frontier* (2010) album achieved a number-one chart placing in over 21 countries worldwide (Kerrang! 24 September 2010, p. 8). So the band was an obvious choice for us as one that had a large and loyal global fandom but also a fandom that would be 'representative' of the demographic and social characteristics of global metal fandom.

As the Internet enabled us to reach far away populations, we did not want English to be a discriminating factor. Indeed, fans do not necessarily need to understand the language of the lyrics in order to appreciate the music and the songs. So the population studied can be divided into three categories:

- Native English speakers who have direct access to the band's music and lyrics;
- Non-native English speakers who have more or less direct access to the band's music and lyrics but always with the perspective of a different culture;
- Non-English speakers who appreciate the music and the band's lyrics thanks to on-line translation of the lyrics.

Because we wanted to gather a lot of data, we knew that the survey would be quite long and that only 'die-hard' fans would take the time to answer questions about the object of their passion. In addition, these more 'active fans' would also belong to one or several of the on-line communities where the survey was advertised. So not only did fans have to be computer-literate but they also had to belong to an Internet tribe.

Writing of the Survey

Out of our research and study into metal media and academic texts on metal, we generated approximately 300 questions. At this initial stage we did not censor ourselves as we knew that those rough ideas would eventually be boiled down into a more thematic and logical selection. If the idea of conducting a survey on a global scale can be exhilarating and can make one daydream, the difficulty of how we would analyze such data brought us back to reality. As we expected a great many fans to answer our survey, it was clear that a set of open questions—where fans could say as much or as little as they wanted—would be impossible to administer, so we decided quite early on that it had to be a multiple choice questionnaire survey, in order for us to handle the data when the collecting was over.

While always keeping in mind the type of questionnaire we had chosen, we gathered similar questions and deleted some preposterous ideas, which enabled us to reduce the number of questions by half. Further proofreading by a survey specialist helped us to reduce the size of our questionnaire. Finally, programming the electronic version led to the deletion of 10 more questions to finally arrive at a 115-question survey (to which 20 more questions were added, whose aim was to draw out the social and cultural morphology of the sample).

Once we had arrived at a satisfactory version, we programmed an English and a French version and then set about pre-testing it with volunteer respondents.[4] We wanted to measure the time that respondents typically needed to answer the questions, and we also wanted to get some feedback about the intelligibility of each question. We found that between 12 and 28 minutes were typically needed to complete the questionnaire, and we also were able to identify questions that were problematic in their meaning to our initial respondents. Once we had rectified these questions, we conducted a further test with two high-school students. This time things went smoothly, and so we concluded that the French and English versions were ready.

However, as we wanted to conduct a global survey, English and French were not sufficient to reach the range of nationalities we hoped to reach, so other languages were needed. One advantage of a multiple choice question survey is that the analysis of the data is the same whatever language it is in, as the coding system is the same for each of them. However, the high cost of translations (because our native or core languages were French and English) forced us to make choices. Here is the list of the languages we chose and why we did so:

- German: Germans are world-renowned for their love of heavy metal music.
- Spanish: not only did we want to reach the Spanish fans but we also realized that this language would give us access to Spanish-speaking respondents in Latin America.
- Portuguese: this choice was similar to the Spanish one, even more so given the huge crowds that Maiden had drawn in the Rock in Rio concerts in Brazil.

- Japanese: Iron Maiden was hugely successful in this country, like many major metal acts.
- Italian: Iron Maiden is a famous act in Italy, and it is also the country where Iron Maiden's tribute bands are the most numerous.

We regret that Eastern European languages were not included in the survey, especially Russian, Polish, and Czech versions of the questionnaire, but the limitations of funding caused us to limit ourselves to seven languages.[5] We also had to exclude Scandinavian countries; even though Sweden, Norway, Finland, and Denmark have very large fan bases per capita, total numbers still only approximated a third of the German sample. Also, we relied on the quality of their education system, where pupils and students are expected to master English or German as second language, thereby allowing them to access a version of the survey. In terms of country per capita populations, then China's one billion three hundred million people, would make it the largest sample of global metal fandom. Certainly, metal exists there, and a taste for different genre and subgenre styles, as well as bands, is growing, but we were not certain that there would be a large enough sample of Maiden fans to justify the translation. However, in the case of the Indian sub-continent and the middle East, we knew there was strong evidence of Maiden fandom, but we simply did not have the resources to support a wider range of world languages.

Electronic Versions

In order to avoid any problems due to human error, it was better to generate the different HTML[6] versions of the survey with scripts that were easier to check for accuracy. Those computer-generated questionnaires were linked to a square SQL[7] database. The different versions of the questionnaire were tested in France, Japan, and Argentina, and as no particular problems emerged, the survey was ready to be advertised. Fifty active websites of Iron Maiden fans were found; nine of them had a forum that required a registration, which was done under the name 'Iron Thesis'. In order to introduce the least amount of bias in our selection, we only posted the following brief message:

> Great academic study on IRON MAIDEN and their fans.
> If you feel like being one of the band's genuine fans, please answer the questionnaire at the following link: http://www.Ironthesis.org/
> THANKS in advance. Jean-Philippe PETESCH
> University of Versailles Saint-Quentin-en-Yvelines

As this message was ready in the seven languages of the survey, we posted it accordingly. Because the Iron Maiden official forum was only accessible to members of the fan club, it was impossible to promote our research there. Fortunately, 'Gore', a Greek member, found our initiative interesting and created a thread about it. In addition to that post, we also sent the message in the appropriate language to the webmasters of all the active sites we had identified.

Creation of the Host Website

In order to make the survey available, we had to create a dedicated website. We chose a Linux-run server with 1,500 Mb storage space in order to make sure that we would not suffer from a lack of space. We also chose a large bandwidth to be sure that the data transfer would be fast and smooth. We chose the domain name <Ironthesis.org> and not <Ironthesis.com> as we wanted to avoid any commercial association in the mind of the fans. The name came from the simple *assemblage* of 'Iron' from Iron Maiden and 'thesis', the aim of the research. Suggesting to the fans that the survey was part of academic research we hoped would encourage them to contribute, especially given that the heavy metal music genre has been misrepresented in the past as 'unintelligent'. Clearly, the use of 'iron' is part of the lexical field of heavy metal sounds and imagery. So the name was likely to catch the fans' attention and incite them to answer the questions.

The welcome pages invited the fans to choose their mother tongue or the language with which they were the most at ease. That welcome page was linked to a visit counter whose results will be presented in the next part. Rather than sending the fans directly to the questionnaire, we wanted to give some details about the survey first. We introduced our identity, the university, and the supervisors of this work. This introduction also contained a warning about the possible invasive nature of some questions. It also underlined the required and expected honesty of respondents in answering the questions as well as assuring of the anonymity and confidentiality of the survey. The time necessary to complete the survey was also mentioned and thanks given in advance. Finally, we added a small picture to enable the fans to get an idea of who was behind the whole project.

Survey Analysis

Before presenting some of the results of Ironthesis, here is an overview of survey participation by continent and nationality. Their geographic locations are given thanks to the maps provided by our tracker. As mentioned earlier, we put a counter on the welcome page: it recorded 9,318 visits, but in the database only 4,860 validated questionnaires were found. So, we believe that 52% of the fans who visited the site took part in the

152 *Jean-Philippe Ury-Petesch*

survey. Some fans may have been curious about the number of participants and come back to check the counter, so we cannot be exactly sure about how many fans have visited the page. We also have to mention that 178 questionnaires did not show any answers to the questions concerning the 'social morphology' of the population studied. Either those questionnaires were blank or they had been filled in by fans who did not play by the rules and did not provide this essential information. Furthermore, 206 questionnaires were recorded twice or more, and we do not know if this was due to human or computer error. So we decided to delete 384 questionnaires (7.9% of the total), leaving us with 4,476 judged valid for our study.

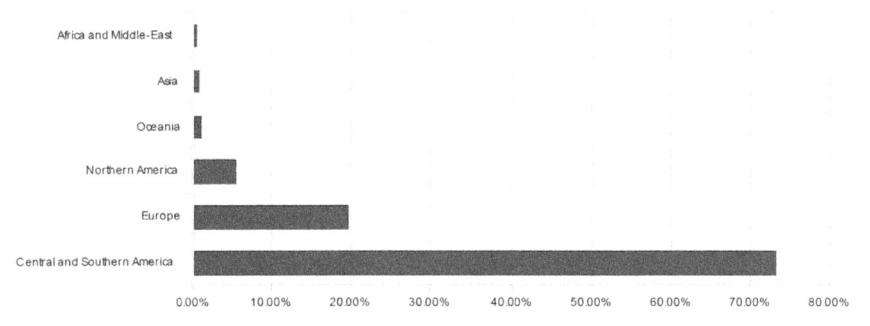

Figure 9.1 **Maiden Fans Respondents by Continent.**

Seventy nationalities living in 72 countries participated in the survey; the difference can be explained by the fact that 186 fans (4.16% of our sample) had left their homeland to live in another country. As Steve Harris has noted on a number of occasions, there is a huge concentration of Iron Maiden fans in South America who are incredibly passionate about the band. So it was not a surprise to us to see that three- quarters of the fans who responded to the survey were from Central and South America, whereas Europe is represented by one out of five fans. Clearly, though, the disproportionate number of South-Americans fans does suggest that they are over-represented in the survey, and this needs to be borne in mind when interpreting some of the evidence.

Table 9.1 Iron Maiden Fans' Nationality

| Iron Maiden Fans: distribution by nationality N = 4,476 ||||||
Nationality	n	%	Nationality	n	%
Brazilian	2,892	64.61	Argentinian	54	1.21
French	177	3.95	Portuguese	52	1.16
British	173	3.87	German	51	1.14
American	173	3.87	Australian	39	0.87
Colombian	164	3.66	Spanish	39	0.87
Danish	109	2.44	Mexican	36	0.80
Italian	64	1.43	Bolivian	32	0.71
Canadian	61	1.36	Costa Rican	32	0.71

The Numbers of the Beast   153

Iron Maiden Fans: distribution by nationality N = 4,476

Nationality	n	%	Nationality	n	%
Swiss	29	0.65	Macedonian	2	0.04
Swedish	29	0.65	Puerto Rican	2	0.04
Norwegian	24	0.54	Singaporean	2	0.04
Chilean	21	0.47	Uruguayan	2	0.04
Japanese	20	0.45	Andorran	1	0.02
Dutch	18	0.40	Armenian	1	0.02
Finnish	16	0.36	Cyprus	1	0.02
Austrian	15	0.34	Czech	1	0.02
Ecuadorian	14	0.31	Dominican	1	0.02
Belgian	11	0.25	Algerian	1	0.02
Greek	11	0.25	Estonian	1	0.02
Irish	11	0.25	Georgian	1	0.02
Venezuelan	11	0.25	Greenlander	1	0.02
Israeli	10	0.22	Iranian	1	0.02
Polish	10	0.22	Islander	1	0.02
Indian	9	0.20	Cambodian	1	0.02
New Zealander	6	0.13	Lithuanian	1	0.02
Croatian	5	0.11	Luxemburger	1	0.02
Peruvians	5	0.11	Nicaraguan	1	0.02
Romanian	5	0.11	Panamanian	1	0.02
Guatemalan	3	0.07	Pakistani	1	0.02
Filipino	3	0.07	Russian	1	0.02
Paraguayan	3	0.07	Slovenian	1	0.02
Bulgar	2	0.04	Slovak	1	0.02
Faroese	2	0.04	Salvadorian	1	0.02
Hungarian	2	0.04	Turkish	1	0.02
Moroccan	2	0.04	Yugoslavian	1	0.02
			Total	4476	100

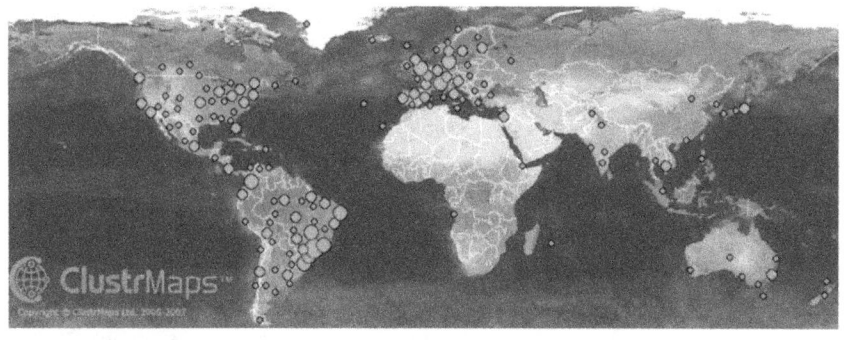

Figure 9.2 Global Clustering of Net Respondents.

154 *Jean-Philippe Ury-Petesch*

Maps

While we had 4,820 saved questionnaires in the database, ClustrMap™ [8] showed 4,655 visits. This difference of 165 visitors can be explained by the fact that the tracker uses the IP address to count the number of visits, whereas questionnaires validated from the same IP address are only counted once. This global map shows us that net surfers from some countries have been more inclined to take part in the survey than are those from others.

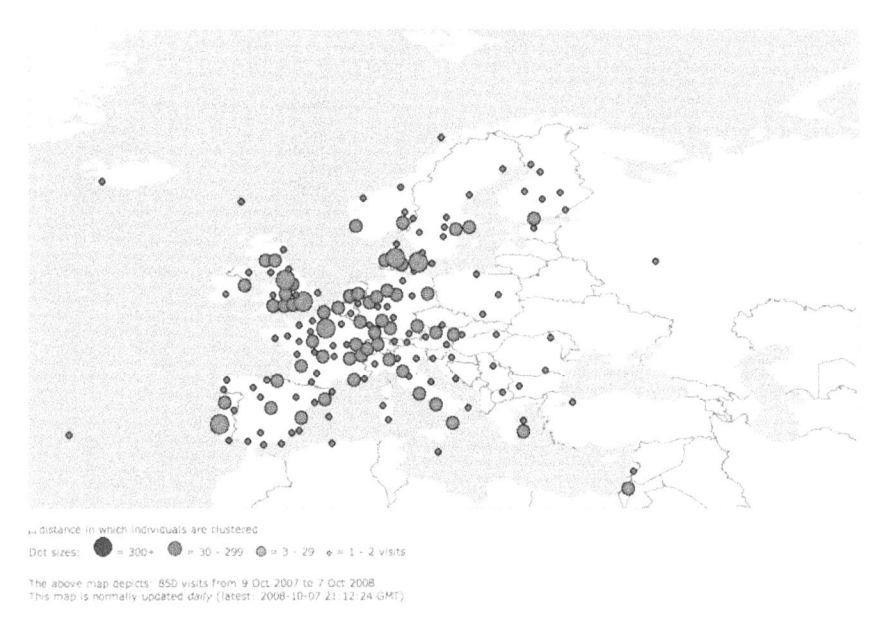

Figure 9.3 **European Clustering of Net Respondents.**

Europe

The distribution of survey respondents is quite homogeneous in Western Europe and more scattered in Scandinavia. Important concentrations appear in the United Kingdom, Denmark, and Switzerland. Fans responded from all over France, Spain, and Italy. The further east we go, the fewer the participants with almost no respondents in the former Soviet bloc.

North American Continent

ClustrMap™ provided two separate maps for the American continent: one for Northern America and one for South America. However, a problem of overlapping exists: participants from Southern Mexico, Cuba, Guatemala, Costa Rica, Salvador, Honduras, and Venezuela are counted twice. It was mainly fans living in large towns who answered the survey. From West to East coasts, here are the cities that we can recognize: Vancouver, Seattle, San Francisco, Los Angeles, Edmonton, Phoenix, Guadalajara, Mexico,

Figure 9.4 **North American Clustering of Net Respondents.**

Winnipeg, Dallas, Minneapolis, Chicago, Detroit, Miami, Toronto, Ottawa, Montreal, Quebec, Washington, Baltimore, Philadelphia, New York, and Boston. This may also be explained by the fact that Internet provider servers are located in urban zones, and the web tracker might have located and recorded them. However, we can note that participation is relatively proportionate to population densities: the densely populated coasts show a large number of participants while mountainous and agricultural zones, almost none. Finally, one unique visit from Greenland was recorded.

South American Continent

With 3,313 participants, the South American continent represents almost two thirds of our sample but some disparities in this geographic zone appear. The map shows heavy participation by Brazilian fans. We can also see important concentrations in Costa Rica, Columbia, and Argentina, less significant ones in Venezuela, Bolivia, Ecuador, Paraguay, Peru, and Chile. While participants in Uruguay, Guatemala, Salvador, Nicaragua, and Cuba are minimal.

Asian Sub-continent

The Asian map shows Lebanon and Israel as locations. We can also see the only Russian participant, from Djibouti. Then comes Pakistan, India,

⊢⊣ distance in which individuals are clustered

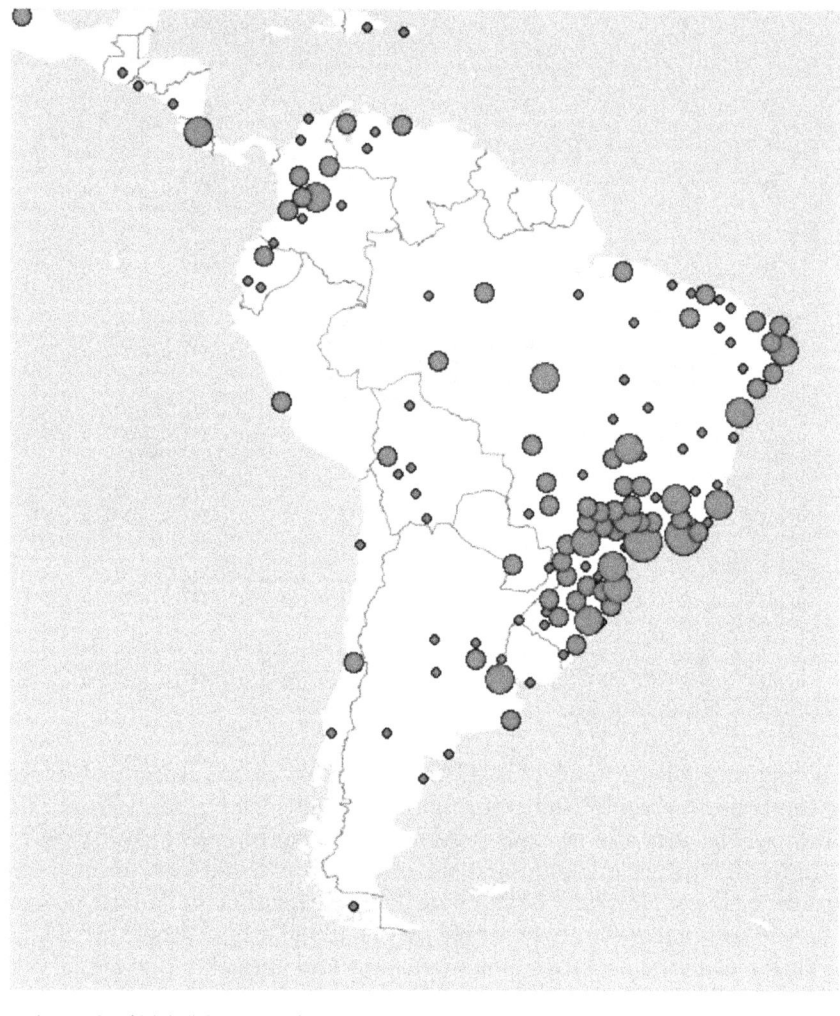

Dot sizes: ● = 300+ ● = 30 - 299 ◉ = 3 - 29 ○ = 1 - 2 visits

The above map depicts: 3,313 visits from 9 Oct 2007 to 7 Oct 2008
This map is normally updated *daily* (latest: 2008-10-07 21:12:24 GMT)

Figure 9.5 **South American Clustering of Net Respondents.**

Singapore, China, Philippines, South Korea, and Japan. The important concentration in Cambodia is due to our pre-survey tests conducted there.

Oceania

On the Oceania map, we can see participants from Australia and New Zealand. Unfortunately, we were not able to collect data from the important Indonesian metal tribe.[9]

Africa and the Middle East

Africa and the Middle East are the areas where participation was the lowest with only a dozen fans coming from Israel, Réunion, Angola, Algeria, and the Canary Islands. This is likely, as with Eastern Europe, to be partly due to language restrictions as well as Internet access.

The Iron Maiden Tribe

In this section, we present the data we collected from the survey. In particular, we focus on the social morphology of our sample and do so via a comparative analysis of the data found in in the studies conducted by Fournier (1999), Hein (2003), and Culat (2007) in Europe and Arnett (1993) and Weinstein (2000) in North America.

Age

The age of the fans who answered ranged from 10 to 60 years old, which corresponds to three generations. As Steve Harris has remarked: 'We just get millions of fans all the time. It's amazing. It's three generations of the fans out there. Some of the fans were not even born when we did the first album. It's pretty scary. [...] I suppose they probably passed albums into the hands of brothers, even their kids' (Dance of Death DVD). The average age is 26, whereas it was 24 for the three French surveys. This can be explained by the fact that Iron Maiden is an 'old band' that has been releasing LPs since 1980. Not only does the band have the power to attract a young public (a quarter of the sample is less than 19 years old), but their musical and artistic consistency allows them to keep the fans of the 'golden age' of their career.[10]

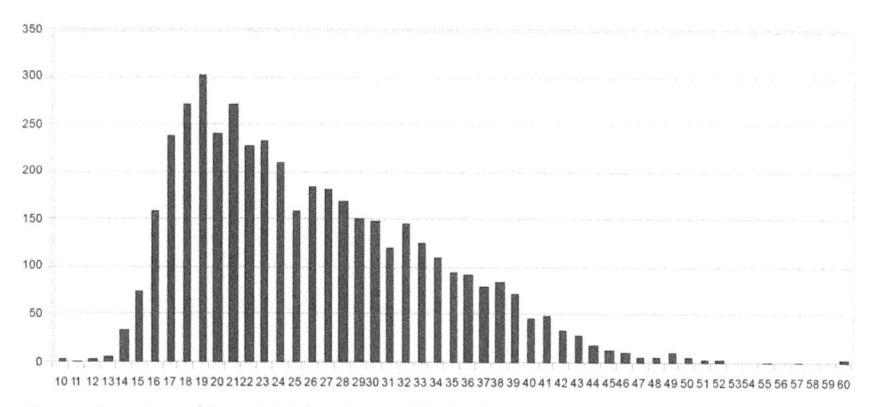

Figure 9.6 **Age of Iron Maiden Fans – N=4,461.**

Gender

Although a study conducted by GEMA[11] showed that metal audiences were a third female (Hein, 2003, p. 178), the results of our survey are closer to

158 *Jean-Philippe Ury-Petesch*

the studies conducted by Culat (14.13%). The fact that Iron Maiden plays a more traditional or 'classic' heavy metal explains the fact that female fans represent less than 10% in our study (see also Weinstein, 2000, pp. 102–105).

Residence

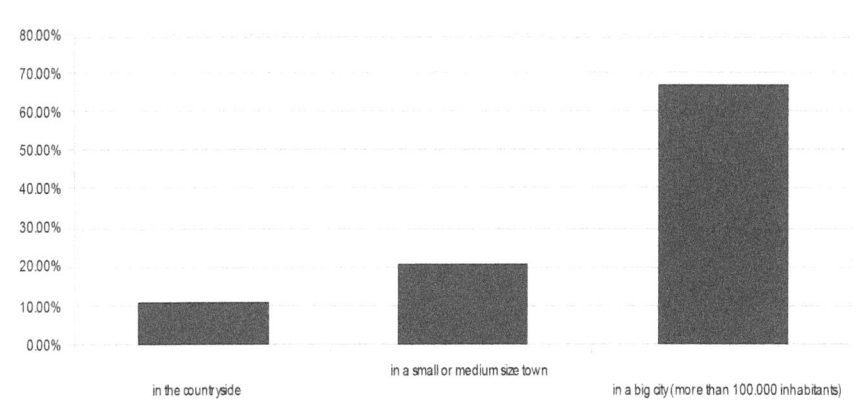

Figure 9.7 **Residency of Iron Maiden Fans.**

The North American ClustrMap™ indicated that the majority of respondents came from cities. This patterning turned out to be accurate: 9 out of 10 fans who answered the survey come from urban areas with two-thirds from a big city.

Education

Considering the fact that the average age is 26, it is not surprising that three-quarters of the fans have at least a high-school diploma. What is striking is the important number of post-graduates: almost 1 out of 10. This echoes Fabien Hein's work who concluded that metalheads 'make up a qualified social group' (2003, p. 226).

Table 9.2 Iron Maiden Fans' Level of Education

Iron Maiden Fans' distribution by level of studies – N = 4,418		
Level of studies	N	%
No degree	224	5.07
G.C.S.E./Junior certificate, fifth form	288	6.52
Vocational diplomas	197	4.46
Sixth form, eleventh grade, final year	422	9.55
A-level, high-school diploma	842	19.06
Advanced vocational training certificate, diploma taken after two years at an institute of technology, university diploma taken after 2 years	798	18.06
Bachelor's degree, diploma taken after 3 years	742	16.79

Iron Maiden Fans' distribution by level of studies – N = 4,418

Level of studies	N	%
Master's degree, diploma taken after 4 years	465	10.53
Postgraduate diploma, diploma taken after 5 years and more	369	8.35
PhD, doctorate	71	1.61
Totals	4,418	100.00

Employment

In previous French studies, pupils and students represent a significant number of polled fans. The fact that the survey was conducted through the Internet is another reason this group is well represented: almost 1 out of 3 fans. The interesting figure in the table is the very low rate of unemployed people. In this respect our results confirm those reported by Bettina Roccor (2002, p. 150), Fabien Hein (2003, p. 229), and Nicolas Bénard (2008, p. 88), that metal fans belong more to middle and upper middle classes, being well-educated. These findings contrast with those found in the North American research (Walser, 1993, pp. 16–17; Weinstein, 2000, pp. 113–117; see Brown, this volume).

Table 9.3 Iron Maiden Fans' Employment

Iron Maiden Fans distribution by socio-professional groups – N = 4,386

Socio-professional group	n	%
Student, pupil	1,584	36.11
Executive, upper intellectual profession, independent, engineer	1,121	25.56
Employee, clerk	813	18.54
Intermediate profession, primary school teacher, foreman, supervisor	300	6.84
Worker	300	6.84
Craftsman, shopkeeper, company manager	143	3.26
Unemployed	119	2.71
Farmer	6	0.14
Totals	4,386	100.00

Social Background

The table shows that if we do not take technical degrees into account, then females do better up to B.A. level. However, males are over-represented from master's degree level on. If we compare Maiden fans' level of education in comparison to their parents', we note that the percentage of high-school diplomas is higher on the children's side; the cumulated percentage reaches 74.4% for fans versus 59.11% on the fathers' side and 57.41% on the mothers' side. We also note the low percentage of Iron Maidens fans with 'no degree' (5.07%) compared to their parents (14.08% for fathers and 13.26% for mothers). In summary, we can say that Iron Maiden fans are better educated than their parents, which was also noted by Roccor and Hein.

Table 9.4 Parents of Iron Maiden Fans' Level of Education

Presentation of the levels of study of Iron Maiden fans' parents N = 4,277, N = 4,300 et N = 4,418

Level of studies	Fathers N	%	Mothers n	%	Sample n	%
G.C.S.E./Junior certificate, fifth form	602	14.08	570	13.26	224	5.07
Vocational diplomas	507	11.85	606	14.09	288	6.52
Sixth form, eleventh grade, final year	344	8.04	266	6.19	197	4.46
A-level, high-school diploma	338	7.90	389	9.05	422	9.55
Advanced vocational training certificate, diploma taken after two years at an institute of technology, university diploma taken after 2 years	593	13.86	758	17.63	842	19.06
Bachelor's degree, diploma taken after 3 years	356	8.32	375	8.72	798	18.06
Master's degree, diploma taken after 4 years	501	11.71	563	13.09	742	16.79
Postgraduate diploma, diploma taken after 5 years and more	448	10.47	428	9.95	465	10.53
PhD, doctorate	351	8.21	206	4.79	369	8.35
Total	237	5.54	139	3.23	71	1.61
Level of studies	4,277	100.00	4,300	100.00	4,418	100.00

Table 9.5 Parents of Iron Maiden Fans' Employment Categories

Presentation of socio-professional group of Iron Maiden fans N = 4,184, N = 4,208, N = 4,386

Socio-professional group	Fathers n	%	Mothers n	%	Sample n	%
Farmer	75	1.79	17	0.40	6	0.14
Craftsman, shopkeeper, company manager	494	11.81	283	6.73	143	3.26
Executive, upper intellectual profession, independent, engineer	1,355	32.39	613	14.57	1,121	25.56
Intermediate profession, primary school teacher, foreman, supervisor	448	10.71	792	18.82	300	6.84
Employee, clerk	832	19.89	788	18.73	813	18.54
Worker	706	16.87	424	10.08	300	6.84
Unemployed	268	6.41	1,271	30.20	119	2.71
Student, pupil	6	0.14	20	0.48	1,584	36.11
Totals	4,184	100.00	4,208	100.00	4,386	100.00

The striking figure in the above table is that of unemployed mothers: 30.20%. Such a high figure may be explained by the 1,028 mothers recorded in the South American sample. If this number were excluded, the percentage would drop to 20.44%, which is very close to the 22.4% recorded by Hein (2003, p. 228). We also note the 'Intermediate profession, primary school teacher, foreman, supervisor' category is most representative on the fathers' side, with 1 out of 3 belonging to that category.

Marital Status

Seven out of 10 fans in our survey are single, but we should not forget that 11.71% of our sample is less than 18 years old. If we exclude the under-18s, the predominance of singles is slightly tempered at 67.83%.

Religion

Table 9.6 Iron Maiden Fans' Religious Beliefs

Iron Maiden fans' distribution by religious beliefs – N = 4,338		
Religious beliefs	*n*	*%*
None	1,586	36.56
Catholic	1,397	32.20
Other faith	894	20.61
Protestant	240	5.53
Buddhist	65	1.50
Christian Scientist	32	0.74
Satanist	28	0.65
Jewish	24	0.55
Orthodox	19	0.44
Druid	15	0.35
Animists	12	0.28
Hindu	9	0.21
Jehovah's Witness	9	0.21
Muslim	7	0.16
Taoist	1	0.02
Totals	4,338	100.00

The main religions claim 4 out of 10 fans, while a third declare not having any religious belief. However, there was a flaw in our survey: the lack of an 'agnostic' category (recorded at 7.79% in Culat's survey (2007, p. 230). The same author proposed an 'indifferent' category that we combined with atheist under the 'none' (religious belief) label. To get a better picture of Iron Maiden fans' religious beliefs, it is interesting to compare their profile with those in Culat's study.

162 *Jean-Philippe Ury-Petesch*

Table 9.7 Comparison between Iron Maiden Fans and French Metalheads

Comparative table of Iron Maiden fans and French metalheads N = 552, N = 4,338		
Religious beliefs	French metalheads N = 552	Iron Maiden fans N = 4,338
Believers	15.22%	32.80%
Atheists + indifferent (non)	59.06%	34.65%
Agnostics	7.79%	—
Satanists	4.89%	0.62%
Other	7.25%	24.18%
No answer	5.80%	3.25%

Despite the differences in sample size, a number of features stand out: compared to French metalheads, the number of religious fans in the Iron Maiden tribe is almost twice as large. This can be explained, in many ways, by the large proportion of Brazilian respondents; a country that is strongly Catholic. The number of Satanists is only 0.65% (28 people out of 4,322) whereas they were almost 1 out of 20 for French metalheads. Finally, other beliefs are three times as well represented in our sample.

One needs to be cautious about the percentage of atheists and those who are 'indifferent' as they represent more than half of Culat's sample, while they are only a third of our sample. Moreover, if we add in agnostics, then two-thirds of French metalheads do not have any religious beliefs. All things considered, it seems that Iron Maiden fans (particularly in South America) are less opposed to traditional religious beliefs than the average metalhead.

Political Affiliation

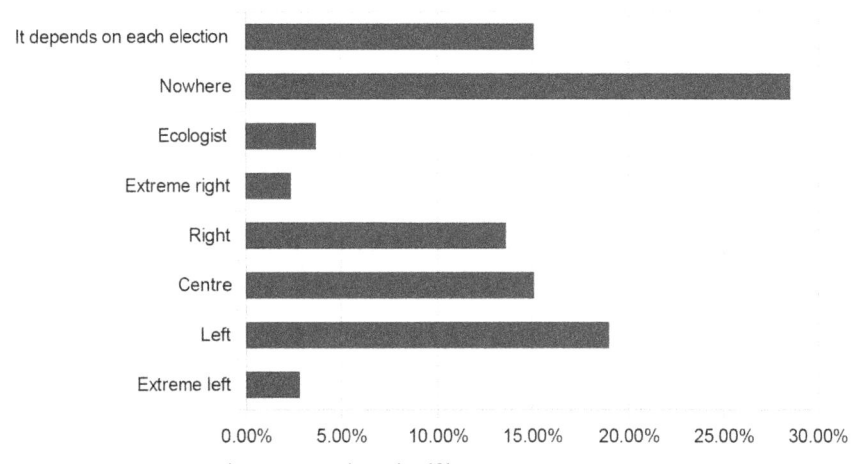

Figure 9.8 Iron Maiden Fans' Political Affiliations.

Hein has noted the issues of racism, fascism, and neo-Nazism among metalheads (2003, pp. 188–191). A quarter of our sample does not have any political affiliation, and 1 out of 7 are undecided. So, only half of the fans express a political preference, and it seems left wing leanings slightly outnumber right wing and moderate opinions. The extreme right only weighs in at 2.36%. As a consequence, even if the sample is slightly skewed to the Left, no clear overall political orientation is evident.

Substance Use

In his book, Arnett identified in the corpus of metal lyrics he studied, direct references to substance (ab)use. He implied that it was a common practice among metalheads. In her study, Fournier refutes Arnett's thesis: 'Contrary to popular belief, those affected by cultural marginality are not regular consumers of illicit substances. The association of the two is totally false and shows a simplistic reductionism. In the trends we refer to, sociability is one of the cornerstones, drug-addicts are fundamentally antisocial' (Fournier, 1999, p. 44).[12] Let us first examine alcohol consumption, then focus on drug use and then combine the two.

Table 9.8 Double Consumption of Alcohol and Drugs among Iron Maiden Fans

Alcohol consumption		Drug consumption						
		several times a day	at least once a day	at least once a week	at least once a month	at least once a year	never	totals
several times a day	n			0	2	4	11	21
	%			0.00	0.05	0.09	0.25	0.48
at least once a day	n			13	17	19	116	177
	%			0.30	0.39	0.43	2.65	4.05
at least once a week	n	11	30	71	110	271	1,384	1,877
	%	0.25	0.69	1.62	2.52	6.20	31.67	42.95
at least once a month	n	5	13	20	32	80	964	1,114
	%	0.11	0.30	0.46	0.73	1.83	22.06	25.49
at least once year	n	3	2	4	6	13	502	530
	%	0.07	0.05	0.09	0.14	0.30	11.49	12.13
never	n	0	4	2	2	10	633	651
	%	0.00	0.09	0.05	0.05	0.23	14.49	14.90
totals	n	24	60	110	169	397	3,610	4,370
	%	0.55	1.37	2.52	3.87	9.08	82.61	100.00

The results of our sample do not confirm Arnett's rather alarmist picture. Indeed, according to his perspective (daily substance use), only 4.46% correspond to this category. The 80.93% probably corresponds to social drinking among family, friends, and other fans. It would have been interesting to make a distinction between beer, wine, and spirits to further analyze this pattern. It is also worth remarking on the 14.61% of fans who declare they never drink.

In our sample, 17.39% of Iron Maiden fans recorded using drugs, some on a daily basis. The remaining 15.47% represent occasional users. Once again, it would have been interesting to ask for details of the substances taken as there are significant differences between 'hard drugs' like heroin, cocaine, crack, LSD, and amphetamines and so-called 'soft drugs', like cannabis and marijuana.

In the previous table, the cases of people using alcohol or drugs on a daily basis were highlighted, representing 6.09% of the sample. Nevertheless, distinctions need to be made among three groups: the heavy users (16 fans (0.37%) who declare they consume alcohol and drugs on a daily basis; the drug-users who are less keen on alcohol: 68 fans (1.56%) declare taking drugs on a daily basis but their consumption goes from never to once a week; and the alcohol-users who are less keen on drugs: 182 fans (4.16%) declare drinking on a daily basis but almost two-thirds of them never take drugs, while others consume from once-a-week to once-a-year. Unlike these cases, one can also find: 'ultra clean' fans (14.49%) who never drink or take drugs and 'clean' fans (65.22%) who never take drugs but who like drinking from time to time. In between these extremes, 14.22% of the sample consumes either alcohol or drugs on a variable basis. Overall only a few members of the Iron Maiden tribe exhibit what Arnett defines as 'deviant behavior' in terms of substance use; namely only 1 out of 17 members.

Unsafe Sex

In his definition of 'reckless behavior', Arnett (1996, p. 78) included two kinds of sexual activity: 'Sex without contraception' and 'Sex with someone not well known'.

Our survey combined the two questions and asked the Iron Maiden fans about unsafe sex with an unknown partner. Iron Maiden fans seem to have adopted a more careful behavior as 7 out of 10 never had unsafe sex with an unknown partner. For 1 out of 6 fans, it was a unique experience. So only 12.75% have sexual behavior that could lead to the spread of STDs. We should also note that 12 years have passed since Arnett's study during which time there have been many campaigns conducted internationally to raise awareness among populations at risk.

Suicide

A third of the fans[13] declared having thought about suicide. However, a majority, 9 out of 10, have never tried. These responses, on a difficult subject, broadly reflect the general non-metal population and are not in any way remarkable. The question was posed because of the indelible association of heavy metal music in the 1984–1991 period with youth 'suicide ideation' and the moral panic about a spate of youth suicides in this period, such as those occurring in Bergen County, New Jersey (Gaines, 1991), and cases identified with the music of Ozzy Osbourne (Walser, 1993; Weinstein, 2000) and Judas Priest (Brown, 2013).

Musicianship

To finish on a lighter note, our survey showed that 6 out of 10 Iron Maiden fans play a musical instrument.[14] Because Iron Maiden belongs to the larger metal category, it is not surprising to see that guitar, bass, and drums make up a 92.33% block with a predominance of guitar as the choice of 6 out of 10 fans.

Conclusion

Clearly, the South American continent in general and Brazil, in particular, do weigh heavily in the survey; although there are 235 North American and 871 European respondents. However, this numerical bias in the survey is only clearly a distorting factor when it comes to questions about religious belief, where in Brazil, in particular, Iron Maiden fandom is perfectly compatible with being a Catholic. Although the age range is from 10 to 60, Iron Maiden fans are usually young adults who tend to study in order to become white-collar workers, rather than skilled or semi-skilled manual workers, despite their parents' occupations. These findings correlate most closely with the research conducted in Europe, in contrast to the North American studies. This is true not only of the educational achievement data but also the 'risk taking' behaviors, as portrayed in Arnett's work. Here it is probably likely that the contrasting economic and educational circumstances of the European and Global metal fans, in comparison to the earlier North American sample population, goes some way to explaining this and other differences.

Notes

1. This chapter draws on material originally published in French (Ury-Petesch, 2010). The chapter was translated by the author, with additional editorial work by Andy R. Brown.
2. Translation from the original French by the author.
3. The survey was conducted without any external funding from research bodies.
4. Two high-school students (16 and 18), a 26-year-old Cambodian Francophone student, a 42-year-old female teacher and a 50-year-old male.
5. Despite the fact that Iron Maiden had been the first band to tour behind the 'Iron Curtain', playing dates in Poland, Hungary and the former Yugoslavia, in 1984.
6. Hyper Text Markup Language, commonly referred to as HTML, is the standard markup language used to create web pages.
7. Structured Query Language is a special-purpose programming language designed for managing data held in a relational database.

8. Figures xx-yy copyright ClustrMaps Ltd, www.clustrmaps.com, reprinted with permission.
9. It brought Iron Maiden to play concerts there in February 2011.
10. The Golden Era, for most fans, goes from *The Number of the Beast* album to the *Powerslave* album; the *Live after Death* live album can also be added.
11. *Gesellschaft für musikalische Aufführungs - und mechanische Vervielfältigungsrechte*: Society for musical performing and mechanical reproduction rights.
12. Translation: the author.
13. 1.573 observations out of 4.448: 35,36%.
14. 2.655 observations out 4.427: 59,97%.

Bibliography

Arnett, J. J. (1996). *MetalHeads: Heavy metal music and adolescent alienation*. Oxford: Westview Press.

Bénard, N. (2008). *La culture Hard-Rock: Histoire, pratiques et imaginaries*, Paris: Éditions Dilecta.

Brown, A. R. (2013). Suicide solutions? Or how the emo class of 2008 were able to contest their media demonization, whereas the headbangers, burnouts or children of ZoSo generation were not. In T. Hjelm, K. Kahn-Harris, & M. LeVine (Eds.), *Heavy metal: Controversies and countercultures* (pp. 17–35). London: Equinox Publishing.

Culat, R. (2007). *L'Âge du metal*. Rosières en Haye: Camion Blanc.

Fournier, V. (1999). *Les nouvelles tribus urbaines: Voyage au cœur de quelques formes contemporaines de marginalité culturelle*. Chêne-Bourg: Georg.

Gaines, D. (1991). *Teenage wasteland: Suburbia's dead end kids*. Chicago: University of Chicago Press.

Hein, F. (2003). *Hard rock, heavy metal, metal. Histoire, cultures et pratiquants*. Clermont-Ferrand/Paris: Mélanie Séteun/Irma.

Hennion, A. (2007). *La passion musicale: Une sociologie de la médiation*. Paris: Éditions Métailié.

Le Bart, C. (2000). *Les fans des Beatles: Sociologie d'une passion*. Rennes: Presses Universitaires de Rennes.

Roccor, B. (2002). *Heavy metal: Kunst, Kommerz, Ketzerei*. Berlin: I.P. Verlag.

Ury-Petesch, J-P. (2010). Iron Maiden: La tribu de la vierge de fer. Rosières en Haye: Camion Blanc.

Walser, R. (1993). *Running with the devil: Power, gender and madness in heavy metal music*. Hanover: Wesleyan / University Press of New England.

Wallach, J., Berger, H. M., & Greene, P. D. (2011). *Metal rules the globe: Heavy metal music around the world*. Durham, NC: Duke University Press.

Walzer, N. (2007). *Anthropologie du metal extrême*. Rosières en Haye: Camion Blanc.

Weinstein, D. (2000). *Heavy metal: The music and its culture*. New York: Da Capo Press.

10 The Social Characteristics of the Contemporary Metalhead
The Hellfest Survey

Christophe Guibert and Gérôme Guibert

Introduction

What are the social characteristics of metal music fans? Even if spontaneous opinions on this subject are widespread, the fact remains that quantitative surveys on the social origins and characteristics of metal music fans are few and far between. Yet it would seem that the images associated with metal are vivid enough that elements that seem logical may sometimes hastily be taken as proven results. After presenting the data generated by an extensive quantitative survey on those people attending an event related to metal culture in France, we can compare it with the questions often raised in studies of metal music—but rarely answered due to a lack of sufficiently reliable empirical data.

As part of this contribution, we will first focus on the social backgrounds of metal music listeners, their academic qualifications, their social status, and their genders. By measuring their level of interest in other genres, such as rock, contemporary pop, classical, and jazz, we can then qualify the cultural characteristics of metal music listeners, particularly in terms of omnivorousness (Peterson, 2004). We will also aim to measure their level of commitment to this musical culture and how involved they become, based on parameters such as their look, the age when they first became interested in metal, or whether they play an instrument. We know that metal is made up of a profusion of genres and subgenres (Guibert and Hein, 2006). This is why in the third step we will come to a more specific question. To what extent can one associate metal subgenres with the social characteristics of the listeners, especially in terms of their educational level and the social status of their fathers?

This contribution does not aim to answer every question relating to the social morphology of metal fans. It is only a step toward developing a better understanding of a phenomenon all too often overlooked, or that relies on stereotypes or images (Guibert and Sklower, 2011; Guibert C., 2012, 2015) linked to this style of music, the image[1] of which is frequently radical or rebellious (Hjelm et al., 2013).

The chosen methodological approach focuses on those people attending the Hellfest Festival, the largest metal music festival in France and one of the five biggest European metal festivals (in terms of attendance and number of bands on the bill). As such, the data collection is not based on the questioning of a group who would be asked about their musical tastes and their appreciation of metal music. This avoids obtaining results based on links to musical tastes symbolized by style labels imposed from an outside survey on a population that can be considered extremely heterogeneous, especially in the new digital age, which complicates the sources of their music and thus the classification of the musical genres chosen by listeners (Donnat, 2011). Here we are instead dealing with both amateurs and metal specialists, who are not present just by chance. When asked what style of 'extreme music'[2] they prefer, by confining the choice to subgenres associated with metal, punk, or industrial music, only 0.4% (35 people out of 8,700) said they 'did not know the styles on offer'.[3]

Methodological Approach

With the support of the event organizers (*Hellfest Productions*), those French festival-goers who had attended Hellfest at least once before were asked to complete a questionnaire comprising around 40 questions. The questionnaire was made available online via a permalink on the festival Internet site (http://www.hellfest.fr). With online purchases the most common method of obtaining festival passes, this was the method chosen to distribute the survey, directed by one of our team (C. Guibert). This also meant that the number of respondents did not need to be quantitatively limited. Over a period of two and a half months, between 15 March and the end of May 2011, over 8,700 usable questionnaires were filled in. The questions (numerical, closed, text, etc.) were designed around three main themes: relationships to 'extreme' music, life during the festival, and the social characteristics of the respondents.

Because they are attending a festival that only offers metal (and punk/hard core on the margins), the surveyed audience can already be considered a priori to be listeners, or even '*amateurs*' (Hennion et al., 2000), of the genre. But in addition, other elements from the data collecting system led us to think that the surveyed population is heavily involved in metal music, and more so than the average metal listener (you have to make the effort to attend the Festival and purchase a ticket, which costs 155 euros for a 3-day pass in 2011), and even more so than the average Hellfest participant (as they had to take part in the online questionnaire). These prejudices and methodological choices may have a tendency to slightly energize the surveyed group compared to other festival-goers, although the number of respondents was very large (with 8,700 usable questionnaires, we had access to just under a third of the daily population, which in 2011 came to 25,000 people).[4] This way of working may also tend to ignore a part of the population who listen to metal music, those who for various reasons do not attend festivals.

One last detail needs to be explained about the specifics of French metal fans compared to those from other countries, as the investigation was carried out with French participants. Can the results of the survey be used and applied outside France, too? After realizing that this type of question regarding the local characteristics of music listeners is rarely asked when talking about metal in the US, and to a lesser extent in Great Britain, we noted that the metal community at an international level shares many characteristics. According to Weinstein (2011), 'Metal is transcultural, not cross-cultural. In other words, metal is not a music tied to a particular culture, which people in other cultures happen to enjoy as outsiders; rather metal is the music of a group of people that transcends other, pre-existing cultural and national boundaries' (p. 46); other authors have already tried to understand metal as a global phenomenon (Wallach, Berger, and Greene, 2011).[5]

Once these precautions are taken into account, we can say that the data collected from our respondents gave us meaningful results, in relation to the number of answers received. In fact, the enquiry concerns people who enjoy metal and are knowledgeable about it, and they feel part of a certain community, one that is represented by metal events such as Hellfest.

Metal and Social Positions: Breaking down Prejudices

1.1 Social Origins and Categories of Metal Fans

The Father's Occupation

The father's occupation[6] is one of the most relevant variables when trying to identify the social position of those involved in an activity—especially when linked to culture (Bourdieu and Passeron, 1970; Coulangeon, 2011); the survey revealed an average but diverse range of answers from the respondents. The category 'worker' makes up 17% of the fathers of those festival-goers interviewed and occupations usually associated with the working classes account for around one-third of the population (and a little more if non-responses are removed). However, for over 30% of respondents the father's occupation came under the category of 'upper management and higher professional sectors', and the share of occupations associated with the upper grades climbs to 44% (see table 10.1). The gender of respondents has no effect on these results.

170 *Christophe Guibert and Gérôme Guibert*

If we compare these figures (excluding non-responses) to a general study of the public at another big pop-rock oriented French festival (Négrier et al., 2012), we can see that people from working-class backgrounds make up a high number of metal fans (table 10.1). If we add up those people from the working classes, we can also see that there are more of them at Hellfest than Eurockéennes (35.9 to 33.4%). While this would appear to confirm the widely held view that metal fans are drawn disproportionately from the working classes (see Brown, this volume), our data also indicates that festival-goers with fathers from the middle and upper middle classes more frequently attend Hellfest than Eurockéennes.

Table 10.1 The Jobs of Festival-Goers' Fathers

	Hellfest (2011)	*Eurockéennes (2008)*
Farmers	3.2%	3.6%
Craftsmen, shopkeepers, and company bosses	15.9%	13.0%
Upper management and higher professional sectors	35.1%	32.5%
Middle management	14.2%	21.1%
Employees	11.8%	20.3%
Laborers	19.9%	9.5%
TOTAL	100%	100%

The survey undertaken by Fabien Hein (2003), more modest in terms of the number of respondents (n=165), focused on metal musicians in the Lorraine region (France) and arrived at fairly different results from those of our study. The fathers of the metal musicians questioned in his survey came mainly from the middle and working classes (the fathers' jobs usually associated with the upper middle classes represented only 22.3% of the group, of which 10.1% were middle managers or from higher professional sectors, compared to 35.1% in our survey).[7]

Social Situation of Festival-Goers

Given the average age of the panel (26),[8] some of the festival-goers are not yet part of the national workforce, being mainly students (a quarter of the population). We did note, however, that most people were in work—more than 60%.

Table 10.2 Primary Socio-Professional Status of Festival-Goers at the Time of the Survey

	Hellfest	*Eurockéennes (2008)*
Secondary school, High school, Student	25,9%	37,9%
In work	60,4%	57%
Job-seeker or unemployed	6,3%	3,3%
Retired	0,2%	1,1%
Other	7,3%	0,7%
TOTAL	100%	100%

The Social Characteristics of the Contemporary Metalhead 171

Out-of-work people represented 6% of the entire Hellfest audience. When linked to the number of festival-goers of working age this suggested that 9.4% of them were unemployed, which was nevertheless lower than the jobless rate among the French working population in 2011, which stood at 9.8%.[9] The Hellfest audience seemed to be more employable than an average member of the national workforce (although in comparison the audience at the Belfort Festival, with an unemployment rate of 5.5% of the active workforce, revealed that it is possible to find groups with an even lower probability of being unemployed).

If we look more specifically at the 5,200 individuals who said they were of working age (excluding those unemployed), we get the table below (10.3) with distinct socio-professional categories. Compared to their fathers, the working-age audience at Hellfest is less often laborers or farmers and more often middle managers. However, we cannot equate this to social mobility as the proportion represented by the working classes has stagnated between the two generations.[10] Nevertheless, a comparison of the socio-professional categories of Hellfest-goers in relation to the active population in the same year (2011) showed that the Hellfest audience is less working class than the rest of the population (table 10.3).

Table 10.3 Hellfest Audience as Part of the In-Work Population Broken down by Professions and Social Categories (compared with the In-Work French population)

Status	Hellfest	French in-work population 2011[11]
Farmers/Producers	1%	1.7%
Craftsmen, shopkeepers and business leaders	8%	6.2%
Upper management and higher professional sectors	37%	17.4%
Middle management	19%	26.4%
Workers	18%	27.5%
Manual laborers	17%	20.8%

In addition, the proportion of those unemployed at the festival (6.2%) is far lower than that in the labor force as a whole (9.8% in 2011) even when we remove those festival-goers who say they are still at school or are students. By calculating the proportion of unemployed people among the working-age population we reach a rate of 9.4%, which is low for a working population aged 26 on average. The Hellfest audience therefore appears to be more employable than the average working-age population.[12]

Education Level

Graduates with at least 2 years of university education make up 56.5% of the Hellfest audience. This number needs to be compared with that of the

172 *Christophe Guibert and Gérôme Guibert*

French population as a whole. In the national population aged 25–34, university graduates represent 40% of the total and only 28% for those aged 25–64 years (Ministère ESR, 2011). The Hellfest audience thus appears relatively overqualified (table 10.4). This is a result that contradicts the stereotype associating metal, as a working-class style of music, with people with typically low educational attainment levels.

Table 10.4 Breakdown of Hellfest Audience by Highest Level of Qualification[13]

Qualification	
No qualification	4.9%
CAP/BEP	11.7%
Professional high-school diploma	10.1%
General High-school diploma	16.8%
General High-school diploma + 2 years of study	19.2%
General High-school diploma + 3 years of study	15.6%
General High-school diploma + 5 years of study	20.0%
PhD	1.8%
TOTAL	100%

Gender

Men make up 80.7% of festival-goers, which indicates that metal is primarily a masculine style of music preference. There is a far higher proportion of males at this festival than at events specializing in more general musical tastes (54.5% of festival-goers at Eurockéennes were male). These results are further underlined by the results of Hein's (2003) survey of metal musicians (of which only 4% were female).

1.2 Results that Refine Previous Survey Findings

Does this data reflect the results obtained in previous studies into metal fandom? At least in part, yes, because in the 1980s and 1990s research primarily linked metal to males, young people, and the working classes. In the 2000s, metal became more associated with the middle class (see Brown, this volume).

Research into metal from the 1970s in western nations suggested that metal was both an urban and working-class form of music. In the English case it was associated with the proletariat of large cities (Nilsson, 2009), or even the working classes during a period of crisis attending the contemporary decline of heavy industry in the 1970s (Moore, 2009). This calls into question the role of gender, particularly that of the male in the couple, linked to macho images in popular culture and especially in heavy metal. By the same logic, we could form a structural homology between the dominant condition and the economic crisis on the one hand and symbolism linked to the apocalypse, Satanism, and more generally the forces of evil on the other (ibid.). From the perspective of social reproduction, we could logically associate these cultural images with a low average level of education among metal fans, given the family and social environment. For Weinstein (1991), the 'heavy metal subculture (a style blend of the hippie and the biker) marks one way in which the 'liberated' youth culture of the 1960s was adopted by the demands of the blue-collar, white youth experience in the 1970s and 1980s in North America (see also Straw (1984) and Berger (1999)). Metal is therefore identified with those people with less academic skills or less cultural awareness, leading to an association with a lowness of taste and evidence of a 'distaste' toward it shown by the upper and middle classes (Bryson, 1996), and the majority of rock critics (Brown and Griffin, 2014; Pirenne, 2014). Two other elements are associated with the pervasiveness of working-class tastes and the 'arbitrary sphere' (Bourdieu, 1965): the youthfulness of its fans and the ubiquity of men. Metal is viewed as a style of music aimed at teenagers without a critical mindset (Guibert G., 2012), a musical taste that is abandoned when the person reaches adulthood. As Weinstein argues,

> Adults who continue to appreciate metal rarely use the metal media, except for playing their old albums. They do not attend many, if any concerts; do not buy new metal releases or metal magazines; and do not call in requests on the radio. Many do not even play their albums all that much, but they have not thrown them out either. Once part of the metal subculture, they are now like wistful emigrants, living a continent away in another world than their own. (2000, p. 111)

But these findings have been criticized, particularly by Bennett (2005), who shows that this phenomenon is changing, with many retaining their youthful passions into middle age. Furthermore, the view that metal is primarily a masculine taste culture has been subject to challenge (Riches, 2015; Hill, this volume). Other research, such as Kahn-Harris (2007), questions the youthful working-class stereotype:

> It is clear that the scene is not simply made up of young people [...] There are many members who have been involved since the beginning of the scene and that are now in their thirties. Hard evidence on the class background of scene members is hard to obtain. [...] Researchers have generally asserted that metal fans are predominantly young, white, working class males. My own impression is that, in Europe at least, the more affluent working classes and lower middle classes tend to dominate. (p. 70)

While Bennett (2001) argues, 'As the 1980s progressed [the] class and gender dimensions of heavy metal audiences became less pronounced as the audience base for heavy metal diversified and cross over into pop' (p. 45).

Among the reasons that might explain this structural social change is that the metal community formed in the late 1970s now encompasses several generations (table 10.5), while those who listened to metal or who attended metal concerts at the end of the 1970s have not given up this type of activity. In fact, at least some of these older metal fans are now very proud of their tastes and seek to legitimize them. This phenomenon is linked to the attachment of fans to their musical passion over time and in the context of our study, although the average age was 26, the festival attracted fans who were over 30 and a minority in their forties. All of this suggests that metal fandom is a structurally changing phenomenon.

Table 10.5 Breakdown of Festival-Goers by Age Group (Excluding Non-Responses)

Age group	Number	Percentage
20 or younger	1,176	13.6%
21 to 30 years	4,627	53.6%
31 to 40 years	2122	24.6%
41 years and over	710	8.2%
TOTAL	8,635	100%

Metal: The Level of Involvement and the Community Perspective

The level of fans' involvement in metal has been shown in numerous studies. This was notably expounded in the theory of the 'proud pariahs' (Weinstein, 1991, 2000) and echoed by many other researchers. Metal is a style of music hated by a very large majority of the population (Bryson, 1996), while a minority like it and are intensely involved. With regard to the French context, a survey on cultural activities conducted by the Ministry of Culture and Communication shows that heavy metal is certainly the most hated music style (Donnat, 2009). Using an appreciation scale, the survey conducted by Négrier et al. (2012, pp. 66–67) confirms that metal is, on average, unpopular with the public. But this average hides the greater heterogeneity of all music genres among those who really like it (a minority) and those do not like it at all (a majority). A survey conducted by G. Guibert and colleagues (2009) with secondary-school pupils shows that metal was the most disliked music style for the majority of those questioned, but the minority (10%) of those who said they preferred it spent the most time listening to music each day (p. 5).

The Festival Ritual as a Sign of Commitment and Being Together

Although the issue of how much people listen to the music was not specifically looked at within the framework of the questionnaire, several elements allow us to confirm the level of involvement with metal among those surveyed. The first is the high proportion of people purchasing a '3-day pass' (that is to say, for the entire duration of the festival) among the audience (table 10.6).

Table 10.6 Breakdown of Festival-Goers Depending on their Ticket Type

Pass length	Number	Percentage
No answer	125	1.4%
1-day pass	1,155	13.3%
2 1-day passes	266	3.1%
3-day pass	7,145	82.2%
TOTAL	8,691	100%

The festival admission price is also an indicator as Hellfest is one of the most expensive of all the various types of music festivals held in France, a fact that does not stop it from being one of the most popular each year. To be included in the survey, each recipient had to have been to the festival at least once before, but we can also measure people's commitment to the event by calculating their loyalty over the years. As such, the number of respondents who had attended at least two previous Hellfests stood at over 57%, while those who have been to at least four represented almost a quarter of all respondents (in 2011, Hellfest was taking place for the sixth time). In addition, 55% of respondents (excluding non-replies) reported that they attended one or more other metal festivals in France or abroad during the year.

How people dress according to the codes of metal culture, which is often a sign of the way this music is rejected by those outside the community, can also be used to measure people's level of involvement. 67.6% of respondents said they did indeed dress 'in metal fashion' for the festival. We also asked the festival-goers if they dressed according to metal fashion in their daily lives (table 10.7). Only 16.7% of those surveyed responded negatively. Among the 83.3% who do dress this way, nearly 40% said they do so regularly.

Table 10.7 Frequency with Which People Dress in 'Metal' Fashion (Rock-Band Tee-Shirts, Gothic Clothing, Jewelry and Accessories, Etc.)?

Yes, regularly	32.4
Yes, sometimes	28.4
Yes, but rarely	22.5
No	16.7
TOTAL	100

Finally, when we asked festival-goers to choose from a series of answers as to the main attractions of Hellfest, it was the love of music that came first, followed by two reasons that could be referred to as community-oriented—'enjoying your passion without being judged' and 'getting together with other music fans' (table 10.8).

Table 10.8 Hellfest Is First and Foremost a Way of ...

Q. Hellfest is first and foremost a way of ...	Number	Percentage
Allowing fans to listen to their favorite groups	7,429	87.4%
Enjoying your passion without being judged	5,590	65.7%
Getting together with 'extreme' music fans	5,190	61.0%
Appreciating musicians techniques	3,611	42.5%
Associating with ideas such as Satanism or death	795	9.4%
Other	660	7.8%
Participating actively in ideas such as Satanism or death	87	1.0%

Length of Time Since First Discovering Metal Music

The average age at which our survey respondents discovered metal was between 14 and 15, in their early adolescence. Given the average age of the festival-goer, most metal fans have been listening for an average of 12 years. Whatever their age, the average festival-goer has been a fan a long time. It must be said that knowledge of the genre is the main reason people feel part of the metal community (Kahn-Harris, 2007, p. 74). By comparing ages and the way in which people discover metal (table 10.9) we see that musical genres are transmitted more and more within the family unit (from older siblings, as well as from parents). While 13% of those aged 55 and above mention the family as the way they discovered metal, it is 85% for those under 15, which requires elder brothers or sisters or the parents to have a prior knowledge of metal music. Influential friends are most frequently cited among 25–59 year olds with an even higher rate for those aged 20–44. Those who say they discovered metal 'alone' are most frequently aged 50 and over, as they would have been growing up at a time when metal, still relatively unknown, was emerging as a genre in France. In addition, a comparison between the questions of 'gender' and 'where your knowledge comes from' shows that girls are proportionally more likely to have discovered metal at a young age and within a family context (Guibert C., 2014).

Another element related to socialization, the probability of dressing 'according to metal fashion' is more important when people discovered metal culture at a young age. Among festival-goers, those who discovered metal after the age of 25 are those who have the highest probability of never

Table 10.9 Pivot Table, Age against How Metal was First Experienced

	Family	Friends	Discovered alone	Other	TOTAL
Under 15 years	84.90%	33.30%	33.30%	9.10%	100%
15–19 years	47.80%	64.40%	43.00%	4.20%	100%
20–24 years	32.90%	75.00%	40.20%	3.80%	100%
25–29 years	30.1%	82.8%	33.4%	3.7%	100%
30–34 years	27.7%	81.6%	31.9%	4.3%	100%
35–39 years	24.9%	81.6%	29.1%	2.5%	100%
40–44 years	23.4%	74.5%	31.3%	3.7%	100%
45–49 years	16.30%	65.40%	45.40%	6.30%	100%
50–54 years	15.90%	44.40%	54.00%	6.40%	100%
55 years and over	13.3%	40.0%	60.0%	13.3%	100%
TOTAL	30.7%	76.8%	35.9%	3.9%	100%

dressing in line with metal fashion, while those who have been brought up in a metal culture since childhood have the highest probability of dressing regularly in metal clothing (table 10.10).

Table 10.10 Pivot Table, Age of the First Metal Experience against Frequency with Which People Dress in 'Metal' Fashion

	Yes, Regularly	Yes, Sometimes	Yes but Rarely	No	Total
Under 10 years	46,2%	25,1%	16,6%	12,2%	100%
10–14 years	36,9%	28,5%	20,4%	14,3%	100%
15–19 years	27,8%	29,2%	25,2%	17,8%	100%
20–24 years	25,5%	26,8%	25,0%	22,8%	100%
25 years and over	24,2%	26,5%	20,2%	29,1%	100%
TOTAL	32,5%	28,4%	22,5%	16,7%	100%

In a correlated way, when we compare how people discovered metal with their metal look, those who have been introduced to metal via their parents are those who have the highest probability of declaring they dress regularly according to 'metal fashion' (42.3%). As opposed to those who have discovered metal via their colleagues (and therefore much later in life) are those with the highest probability of declaring to never dress in 'metal-ware' (25.4% of this group). There is therefore a trajectory for metal fans, taking into account the adoption over time of the genre and the culture, which helps maximize its intensity, as it is likely to be passed on earlier and earlier.

A Relative Omnivorousness in Line with Social Characteristics

Does investment in metal require one to be a specialist in the genre at the expense of other genres, i.e., a type of univore-omnivorousness? The question about listening to other genres of music shows as many as 91.2% of respondents said they listen to other genres of music besides metal. The most referenced type is 'rock' in general (76.8%) followed by classical (35.4%) and jazz (27.9%). These audience figures are higher than the listening habits of the general population (Donnat, 2009). These results are consistent with Weinstein's (1991) findings, which suggest that 'The deepest pride of the member of the metal subculture is to be an appreciator of great music' (p. 143). However, listening to rap (11%) and R'n'B (2.5%) is less popular among metal fans than in the same age group of the general public (fig. 10.1).

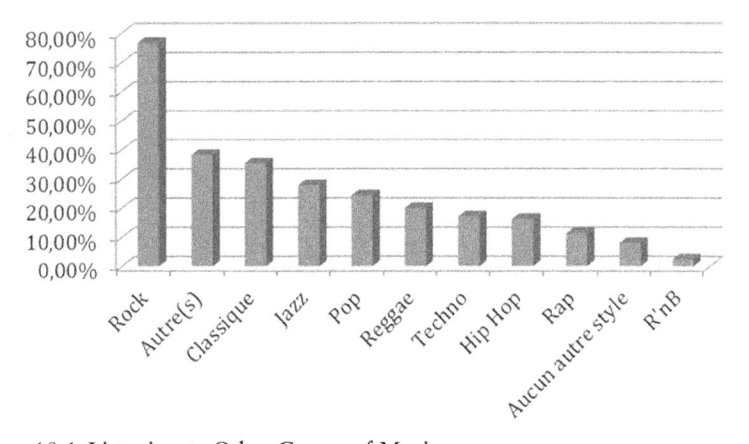

Figure 10.1 Listening to Other Genres of Music.

The high response rate for 'others' shows the claimed specificity of their musical preferences by people who appreciate metal. They also emphasize the relative omnivorousness of the metal audience's taste, a phenomenon more closely associated with the upper classes than the working classes (Coulangeon, 2011). In line with Peterson's work (2004), we could also link this relative omnivorousness to the increasing trend for middle-class participation among the Hellfest audience.

The Homogeneity and Heterogeneity of Metal Fans

We would like to conclude this presentation of the social characteristics of a large group of festival-goers with a more precise look at the differences between subgenres because metal, due to its long history, has fragmented into multiple subgenres (Hein, 2003). At the same time, it has become an independent cultural phenomenon by developing its own history, especially from the fans' perspective. As such, Meg Tze Chu (2011) speaks of an 'imaginary genealogy' in the way metal fans explain their own common history and identify with a 'metal community'. In connection with this many researchers point out that, despite the diversity of its currents, metal music is relatively distant from other music genres (Weinstein, 1991) both from the perspective of the media and listeners. Whereas subgenres have specific spaces (webzines, festivals, labels etc.), there are numerous systems that bring together the various strands of the 'metal family'. The same goes for the specialist magazines that juxtapose several subgenres and several generations of groups (in interviews, album reviews or compilations available on CD or to download). The same goes for the big festivals like the one in our survey (Hellfest).

In fact, the question (with multiple possible answers), which asks the festival-goers interviewed which types of music they prefer, generated a multitude of subgenres with varying levels of success (table 10.11). The most quoted genre is heavy metal, followed by death, thrash, and black, with respondents citing on average 4.5 different genres. As such, for Chu (2011), Metal fans attach great importance in being able to list various groups and canonical sub-genres in an encyclopaedic manner. Listening to metal is considered an art and a serious activity rather than just a form of entertainment.

Table 10.11 What Type(s) of 'Extreme' Music Do You Prefer?

Type of music	Number	Percentage
Heavy metal	4,842	55.7%
Death metal	4,593	52.9%
Thrash metal	4,367	50.3%
Black metal	3,262	37.5%
Hard rock	3,158	36.3%
Hardcore metal	2,938	33.8%
Folk metal	2,349	27.0%
Punk	2,128	24.5%
Industrial	1,929	22.2%
Doom metal	1,800	20.7%
Prog metal	1,769	20.4%
Neo metal	1,668	19.2%
Gothic metal	1,376	15.8%
Other	1,292	14.9%
Grind	1,290	14.8%
Unfamiliar with these types of music	35	0.4%
TOTAL	8,691	100%

Comparing the population of metal listeners to the population as a whole also allows us to question whether preferences for metal subgenres can be associated in a trend-related way with specific social characteristics. Although the labels of styles chosen as preferences can reasonably be discussed (we could always add more or specify them differently), offering them to the respondents can result in significant correlations between subgenres of metal and people's characteristics. Without going into too much detail, our survey reveals that gothic metal is a much more feminine than masculine genre or that the average age of those who favor hard rock, heavy metal, or punk is higher than the average age of the entire group, unlike hard-core metal, which tends to be favored by younger people.

More specifically within the framework of this chapter, we believed it appropriate to test the correlation between the preferred musical genre and the type of qualification held by the respondents, particularly because these questions are often addressed in the published literature. As such, on the subject of extreme metal subgenres, Keith Kahn-Harris suggests that 'Certainly with some exceptions, extreme metal does not seem to be the music of the 'underclass' in wealthy countries and there seems no shortage of scene members from relatively wealthy middle class backgrounds (...). Generally speaking though, in most contexts extreme metal is neither the music of the poor and dispossessed, no is it the music of the wealthy and privileged' (2007, p. 70). Following a survey in the north of Great Britain conducted among fans of black metal, (Lucas, Deeks, and Spracklen, 2011) estimated that most were from the working classes and those with a low level of cultural knowledge. Walzer found that fans of black metal who he studied in France are generally 'from the middle class, with a general high-school diploma + 2 years of study, and well integrated into society' (2011).

What does this show quantitatively? The survey shows that the level of educational attainment makes an enormous difference when applied to various subgenres of extreme music. Some are generally associated with low levels of attainment, such as hard rock or grindcore (figs. 10.2 and 10.3), while others are more linked to higher qualifications, such as doom metal (fig. 10.4) or prog metal. The case of black metal is especially interesting because it tendentiously attracts people from both extremes (low-achievers and the highly qualified), confounding those who wish to link this subgenre to a given level of cultural ability (fig. 10.5). Finally, other styles such as heavy metal, or to a lesser extent death metal or thrash metal, tend to be chosen by the majority of the respondents, regardless of their educational level (table 10.12), although these most popular of subgenres are liked more by the less-qualificated population than other genres.

Table 10.12 Pivot Table, Qualifications against Types of 'Extreme' Music

Qualification/music style	Black metal	Death metal	Doom metal	Folk metal	Grind	Gothic metal	Hard rock	Hard core metal	Heavy metal	Neo metal	Prog metal	Thrash metal	Punk	Industrial	Other
No qualification	43.5%	56.3%	18.8%	32.5%	18.5%	19.0%	43.3%	30.8%	60.0%	20.0%	17.8%	55.8%	30.8%	19.8%	20.8%
CAP/BEP (higher national diplomas)	39.5%	54.2%	14.3%	24.6%	16.9%	16.6%	44.1%	39.5%	60.0%	20.3%	12.5%	52.3%	27.0%	17.0%	12.3%
BAC PRO (Vocational qualifications)	37.6%	54.6%	16.7%	27.5%	16.7%	16.0%	37.0%	39.4%	57.0%	23.3%	15.3%	54.9%	25.2%	20.7%	12.0%
BAC (High-school diplomas)	35.3%	51.7%	19.9%	31.8%	14.9%	15.3%	34.9%	32.1%	54.6%	18.8%	21.0%	47.3%	23.4%	23.6%	17.2%
BTS (Polytechnic diplomas)	36.6%	52.2%	19,1%	24.7%	14.6%	13.6%	37.2%	34.4%	56.0%	20.5%	19.5%	50.0%	23.6%	21.6%	14.3%
Degrees	37.2%	52.1%	24.3%	29.1%	14.4%	14.9%	33.0%	35.0%	52.3%	17.1%	23.4%	49.1%	23.7%	24.4%	15.5%
Masters, Engineering and Business school diplomas	37.8%	52.7%	26.4%	23.3%	13.6%	17.7%	32.6%	30.0%	54.7%	16.1%	25.3%	50.1%	23.2%	24.4%	14.1%
PhDs	42.8%	55.2%	29.0%	28.3%	12.4%	23.5%	34.5%	28.3%	56.6%	19.3%	31.7%	49.0%	22.8%	25.5%	9.7%
AVERAGE	37.5%	52.9%	20.7%	27.0%	14.8%	15.8%	36.3%	33.8%	55.7%	19.2%	20.4%	50.3%	24.5%	22.2%	14.9%

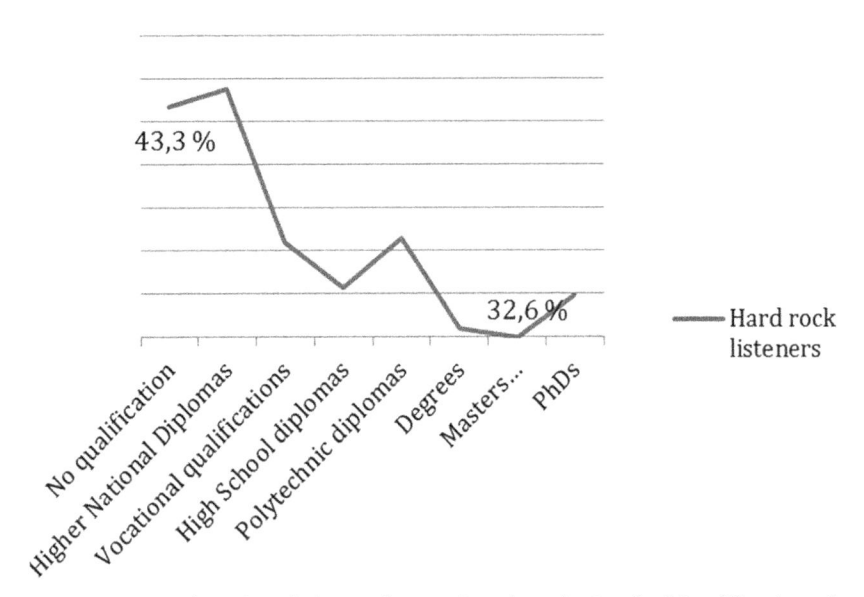

Figure 10.2 Hard Rock Relative Preference Based on the Level of Qualification of Festival–Goers.

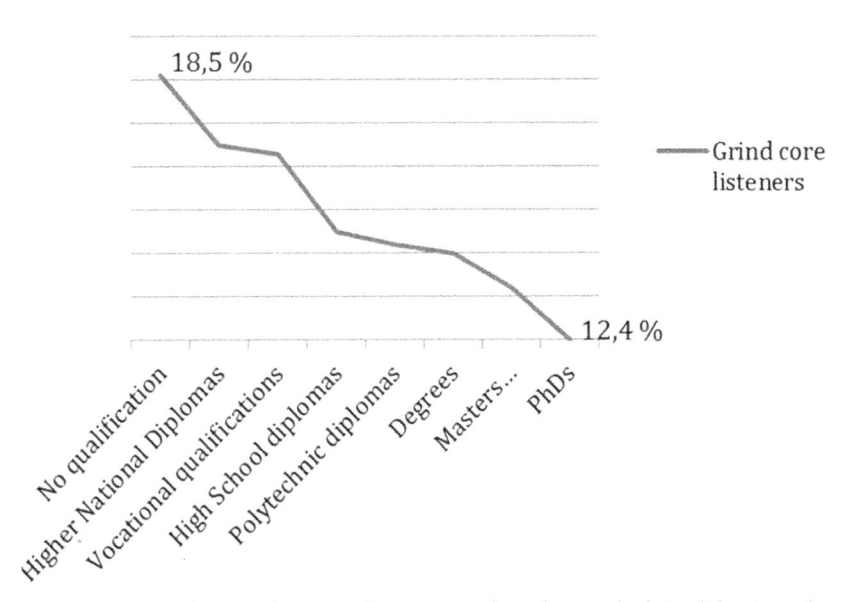

Figure 10.3 Grindcore Relative Preference Based on the Level of Qualification of Festival–Goers.

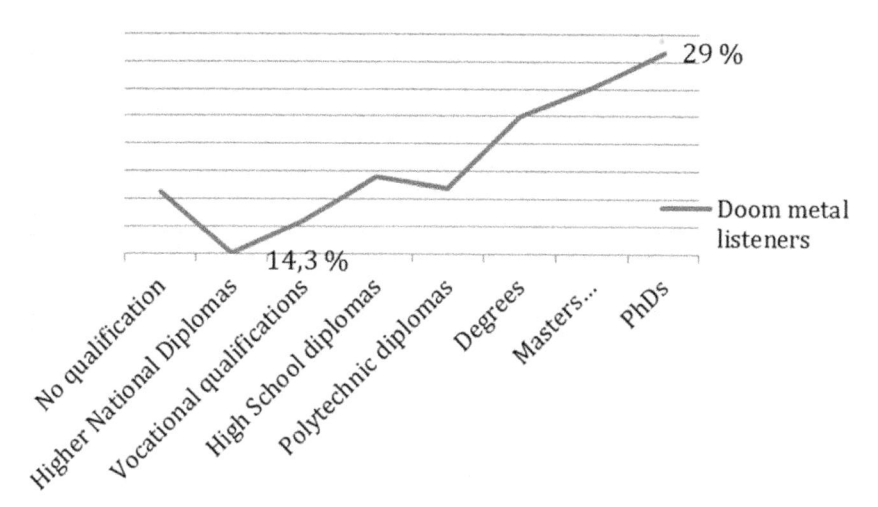

Figure 10.4 Doom Metal Relative Preference Based on the Level of Qualification of Festival-Goers.

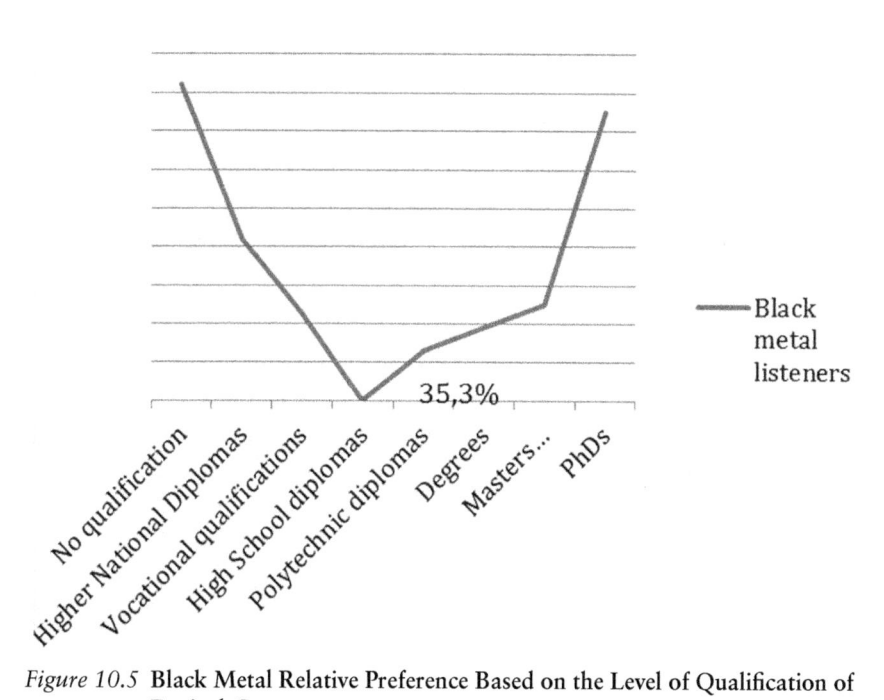

Figure 10.5 Black Metal Relative Preference Based on the Level of Qualification of Festival-Goers.

Table 10.13 The Percentage of People from the Upper Management and Higher Professional Sectors who Listen to Sub-genres of Extreme Music, as Well as the Total Number of Festival-Goers

Father profession/ music style	Black metal	Death metal	Doom metal	Folk metal	Grind metal	Gothic metal	Hard rock	Hardcore metal	Heavy metal	Neo metal	Prog metal	Thrash metal	Punk	Indus	Other	TOTAL
Farmer	35.7%	50.6%	17.0%	30.7%	17.0%	13.7%	36.9%	31.5%	52.7%	17.4%	18.3%	49.4%	26.1%	22.0%	12.5%	100%
Craftsm shopkeeper and business leaders	34.6%	53.1%	20.2%	24.5%	13.2%	13.6%	34.4%	34.9%	57.2%	19.1%	19.2%	51.8%	24.0%	21.8%	14.4%	100%
Upper management and higher professional sectors	38.9%	53.2%	23.1%	27.8%	14.0%	15.9%	34.4%	31.7%	55.1%	17.7%	23.3%	48.8%	23.7%	23.5%	16.2%	100%
Middle management	36.8%	52.0%	22.6%	26.9%	15.9%	16.0%	37.6%	34.3%	54.8%	19.2%	20.3%	50.1%	24.1%	24.6%	14.5%	100%
Workers	39.3%	53.7%	20.2%	28.3%	14.9%	15.9%	38.3%	35.5%	56.8%	18.6%	18.7%	50.1%	24.7%	20.9%	14.3%	100%
Manual laborers	36.9%	52.2%	17.6%	24.0%	15.3%	16.3%	40.5%	35.8%	57.3%	21.7%	18.5%	51.4%	26.4%	20.9%	12.4%	100%
TOTAL	37.5%	52.9%	20.7%	27.0%	14.8%	15.8%	36.3%	33.8%	55.7%	19.2%	20.4%	50.3%	24.5%	22.2%	14.9%	100%

The Social Characteristics of the Contemporary Metalhead 185

Also, when we cross-reference music genres and the father's occupation, very significant correlations are revealed (table 10.13). As such, those whose father is from the category 'Upper management and higher professional sectors' declare a preference for doom metal, prog metal, or 'other' types of extreme music (that is to say, not listed). Conversely, those whose father is a laborer state they listen less often to doom metal than the others and tick the 'other' box less frequently than the rest (we can assume that they are not challenging the typology on offer). However, they admit to being more likely than others to listen to hard rock or neo metal (nu metal). This can be illustrated by fig.10.6, which simultaneously compares the average preference of festival-goers for the different subgenres of extreme music with the number of people from both the upper management and higher professional sectors and that of workers.

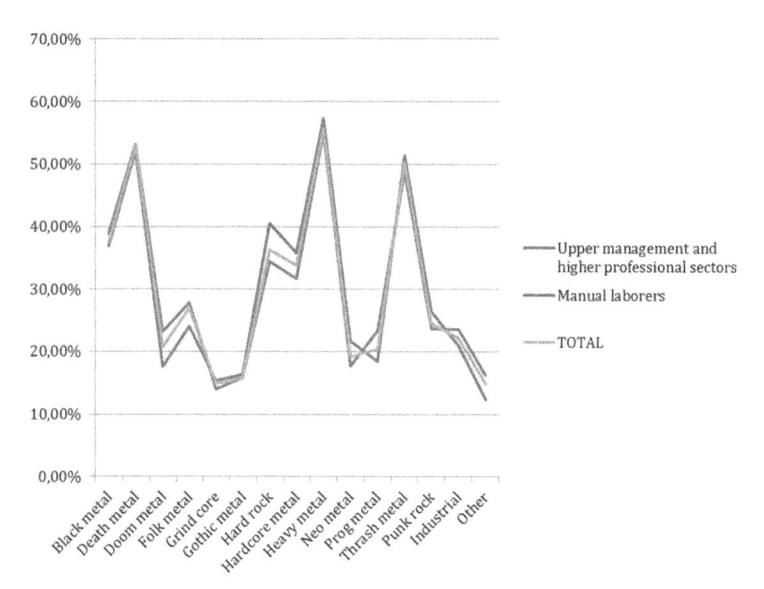

Figure 10.6 The Percentage of People from the Upper Management and Higher Professional Sectors who Listen to Subgenres of Extreme Music, as Well as the Total Number of Festival-Goers.

Conclusion

The results of this innovative survey, in France at least, testify to the fact that the characteristics of Hellfest festival-goers on the one hand and the social uses of metal music and its universe on the other cannot be reduced to spontaneous categorizations. Rather, they reflect the social complexity of the metal world and its fandom. The analyses presented in this chapter, in particular those that relate to various social origins, to high levels of educational attainment or to the omnivorousness of cultural consumption, have we hope helped to challenge some common beliefs that suggest metal fans

186 *Christophe Guibert and Gérôme Guibert*

are not socially well integrated, are deviant, poorly qualified, or predominantly working class. The 2015 quantitative survey currently underway, repeated four years after it was first conducted in 2011 for the 10th anniversary of Hellfest, will help us strengthen and consolidate these observations and analysis and help to further our knowledge of this social grouping and further develop the field of metal studies.

Notes

1. That is to say, the signs and traces objectified in bodies, on album covers, on clothing, etc. (for example the references to religion, death, etc.)
2. Hellfest was first presented as an 'extreme music' festival, but the organizers now name it an 'extreme metal music festival': http://www.hellfest.fr/fr (accessed April 28, 2015).
3. Question: 'What type(s) of extreme music do you prefer?' (several answers are possible).
4. With 8,700 usable questionnaires, we have a larger corpus than any survey of contemporary music festivals in France to date. This also shows that metal fans are 'motivated' to answer such surveys connected to the music they enjoy.
5. However, metal has local characteristics, particularly historical ones, that play a role in metal's existence as a form of culture (even though these factors are rarely studied). For example, France did not really adopt 'hair metal' or glam metal groups in the 1980s. On the other hand, in France, heavy metal was very popular following the success of the group Trust in the early 1980s, as the band had the distinction of using politically related lyrics, which was unique, even when compared to sister-groups such as AC / DC and Iron Maiden (G. Guibert, 2015).
6. The type of jobs categorized in the survey are derived from the PCS (Professional and Social categories), employed by the INSEE (French official Institute of Statistics) since 1982. This measure categorizes the working population according to social class fractions of lower, middle and upper (for a discussion, see Desrosières & Thevenot, 1996–1999). It is specific to France, partly because work on a classification scale of occupations that would converge at a European level are not yet existing (Brousse, 2008).
7. It should be noted that the survey was conducted between 1999 and 2002.
8. The average age of the population in Hein's survey was 24, with a low standard deviation of those under 17 or over 40. For the Belfort Eurockeennes survey, the average age was 27.8, therefore higher than at Hellfest. A trend of increasing the average age is consistent with the idea of rock as a genre being listened to not just by young audiences. In addition, the study of a smaller contemporary music festival (Chapiteuf, in the Aude department) by the same team of investigators gave an average age of 26.6 (p. 38). There, it was probably more the effect of the price that caused the difference, due to the cost of entrance tickets and travel (with people living farther away than at the big festivals (C. Guibert, 2008).
9. Given that the unemployment rate of festival-goers (the average age of whom is 26.8, while that of the general population is 40) needs to be put into perspective if we take into account the number of visitors per age group, the youth unemployment rate is higher than the average unemployment rate, all else being equal.

10. See Farmers+Workers+labourers in Table 10.1 (fathers) and then Table 10.3 (festival goers).
11. http://www.insee.fr/fr/themes/detail.asp?reg_id=99&ref_id=pop-act-csp-dipl.
12. However, the audience at the Belfort Festival, with an unemployment rate of 5.5% of the working age population, shows a group whose probability of being unemployed is even lower.
13. CAP/BEP: post high-school professional qualifications, BTS/IUT: higher professional qualifications obtained 2 years after high-school.

Bibliography

Bayer, G. (Ed.). (2009). *Heavy metal music in Britain*. Farnham: Ashgate.
Bennett, A. (2001). *Cultures of popular music*. Maidenhead: Open University Press.
Bennett, A. (2005). Punk's not dead: The continuing significance of punk rock for an older generation of fans. *Sociology*, 40(2), 219–235.
Berger, H. M. (1999). *Metal, rock and jazz: Perception and the phenomenology of musical experience*. Hanover: Wesleyan University Press.
Bourdieu, P. (Ed.). (1965). *Un art moyen*, Paris: Minuit.
Bourdieu, P., et Passeron J-C. (1970). *La reproduction*. Paris: Minuit.
Brousse C. (2008). ESeC, projet européen de classification socio-économique. *Courrier des Statistiques*, 125, 27–36.
Brown, A.R., & Griffin, C. (2014). A cockroach preserved in amber: The significance of class in critics' representations of heavy metal music and its fans. *The Sociological Review*, 62(4), 719–741.
Bryson, B. (1996). Anything but heavy metal: Symbolic exclusion and musical dislikes. *American Sociological Review*, 61(5), 884–899.
Chu, M-T. (2012). *L'ontologie de l'identité métalleuse face à la mondialisation – généalogie imaginaire, réseau solidaire*, Thèse de doctorat Musique, histoire, société (Antoine Hennion, dir.), Paris: EHESS.
Coulangeon, P. (2011). *Les métamorphoses de la distinction. Inégalités culturelles dans la France d'aujourd'hui*, Paris: Grasset.
Desrosières, A., & Thévenot, L. (1996). *Les catégories socio-professionnelles*. Paris: La Découverte.
Donnat, O. (2009). *Pratiques culturelles des Français à l'ère numérique. Enquête 2008*. Paris: Ministère de la Culture et de la Communication, DEPS/La Découverte.
Donnat, O. (2011). Pratiques culturelles, 1973–2008. Questions de mesure et d'interprétation des résultats. *Culture-méthodes*. Paris: DEPS.
Guibert, C. (2012). Festival Hellfest de Clisson. Les retombées économiques de la musique *metal* plus fortes que sa stigmatisation. *Espaces, Tourisme et Loisirs*, n°309, Décembre, 13–18.
Guibert, C. (2014). Les filles au Hellfest. Socialisation, goûts et usages sociaux. In G. Guibert (dir.), First French *heavy metal et sciences sociales International Conference. For an Overview of research in the Francophone World*, Angers, France, December 18 and 19.
Guibert, C. (2015). Représentations et usages sociaux de la musique metal. Le cas du festival Hellfest. *Volume! La revue des musiques populaires*, 11(2), 2015.
Guibert, G. (2008). Les festivals de musiques actuelles en Pays de la Loire. Entre logiques d'implantations locales et reconfigurations nationales. *Le Pôle, Enquête Flash*, 1–12.

Guibert, G. (2011). Médiocrité, artifices, manipulation? A propos des adolescents et de la musique à succès. Une illustration à partir du groupe Kiss. *Jeunes et médias. Les Cahiers Francophones de l'Education Aux Médias*, 1(1), 17–30.

Guibert, G. (2015). The band Trust and the curious birth of French heavy metal in the late 1970s. In G. Guibert and C. Rudent (Eds.), *Made in France: Studies in popular music*. New York: Routledge.

Guibert, G., Lambert, D., & Parent, E. (2009). Les comportements adolescents face à la musique». *Le Pôle, Enquête Flash*, 1–12.

Guibert, G., & Sklower, J. (2011). The thing that should not be? Local perceptions and Catholic discourses on metal culture in France. *Popular Music History*, 6(1/2), 100–115.

Hein, F. (2003). *Hard rock, heavy metal, metal. Histoire, cultures et pratiquants*. Paris: Seteun/Irma.

Hennion, A., Maisonneuve, S., & Gomard, E. (2000). *Figures de l'amateur. Formes, objets, pratiques de l'amour de la musique aujourd'hui*. Paris: La Documentation Française.

Hjelm T., Kahn-Harris, K., & Levine, M. (Eds.). (2013). *Heavy metal: Controversies and countercultures*. Sheffield: Equinox.

Kahn-Harris, K. (2007). *Extreme metal. Music and culture on the edge*. Oxford: Berg.

Lucas, C., Deeks, M., & Spracklen, K. (2011). Grim up north: Northern England, Northern Europe and black metal. *Journal For Cultural Research*, 15(3), 279–296.

Ministère de l'Enseignement Supérieur et de la Recherche. (2011). *L'Etat de l'Enseignement Supérieur et de la Recherche*, n°5, Décembre.

Moore, R. M. (2009). The unmaking of the English working class: Deindustrialization, reification and the origins of heavy metal. In G. Bayer (Ed.), *Heavy metal music in Britain* (pp. 143–160). Farnham: Ashgate.

Négrier E., Djakouane A., & Collin J-D. (2012). *Un territoire de rock. Le(s) public(s) des Eurockéennes de Belfort*. Paris: L'Harmattan.

Nilsson, M. (2009). No Class? Class and class politics in British heavy metal. In G. Bayer (Ed.), *Heavy metal music in Britain* (pp. 161–180). Farnham: Ashgate.

Peterson, R. A. (2004). Le passage à des goûts omnivores: notions, faits et perspectives. *Sociologie et Sociétés*, 36(1), 145–164.

Pirenne, C. (2014). Born under a (very) bad sign: Une étude de cas dans la réception de la NWOBHM. In G. Guibert (dir.), *First French heavy metal et sciences sociales International Conference. For an overview of research in the Francophone World*, Angers, France, December 18 and 19.

Riches, G. (2015). From cultural politics to pleasurable affects: Female metal scholarship's contribution to metal studies (Reviews). *Metal Music Studies*, 1(1), 171–176.

Roccor B. (2002). *Heavy metal. Kunst, Kommerz, Ketzerei*, Berlin, I.P. Verlag Jeske/Mader, GbR.

Straw, W. (1984). Characterizing rock music culture: The case of heavy metal. *Canadian University Music Review*, 5, 104–122.

Wallach, J., Berger, H. M., & Greene, P. D. (2011). *Metal rules the globe: Heavy metal music around the world*. Durham, NC: Duke University Press.

Walzer N. (2011). 'Si Nietzsche vivait aujourd'hui il écouterait du metal'. La réception de Nietzsche dans la subculture black metal', *Émulations*, 4, mai 2011 [http://www.revue-emulations.net/enligne/Walzer] (accessed May 1, 2015).

Weinstein, D. (1991). *Heavy metal: A cultural sociology.* New York: Maxwell v Macmillan International.

Weinstein, D. (2000). *Heavy metal: The music and its culture*, New York: Da Capo Press.

Weinstein, D. (2011). The globalization of metal. In J. Wallach, H. Berger, & P. D. Greene (Eds.), *Metal rules the globe: Heavy metal music around the world* (pp. 34–59). Durham, NC: Duke University Press.

11 Un(su)*Stained Class?*
Figuring out the Identity Politics of Heavy Metal's Class Demographics

Andy R. Brown

In this chapter, employing a sociological methodology (class-fraction analysis), I want to re-examine the vexed issue of the class(ed) identity of heavy metal bands and fans. There are two aspects to this. The first is the question of what are the social demographics and class profile of heavy metal's core constituency (if there is one): from its origins with bands such as Black Sabbath and their fans; its controversy-ridden commercial hiatus in the 1980s; reformation as an underground of extreme metal scenes in the 1990s; to its current formation as a global metal diaspora of bands, fans and (g)local scenes around the world. The second is the question of what follows from this class profile, in terms of the identity-politics of heavy metal music and its enduring appeal to certain groups of people (despite gender, ethnicity, and nationality) and not others. Drawing on all the available data sources, from regional and national studies, surveys, interviews, questionnaires, observations, and analysis, compiled by psychologists, sociologists, anthropologists, music scholars, and ethnographers over the life of the genre, this chapter attempts to resolve the question of the significance of the social class profile of heavy metal and the extent to which it is possible to argue for a clear and consistent relationship—over time, geography, and region—between the appeal of heavy metal music and social identities grounded in particular class(ed) cultures or whether it is time to contest, strongly dismiss, or reconfigure this claim.

A number of key 'foundational' texts in the 'mature' development of metal studies, including Deena Weinstein's (1991) *Heavy Metal: A Cultural Sociology* and Donna Gaines's (1991) *Teenage Wasteland: Suburbia's Dead End Kids*, as well as studies by Harris Berger (1999a, 1999b), published at the end of that decade, identify the genre as working class and the typical heavy metal fan as white, teenage, working-class kids from blue-collar backgrounds. Or as other studies from this period state: 'the typical heavy metal fan is an adolescent [white] male from a lower class background in an urban or suburban area' (Gross, 1990, p. 122) and Breen: 'heavy metal [...] draws its most potent audience power from working class youth' (1991, p. 194). Gross adds that heavy metal fans share a similar 'mode of dress, family background, attitude, shared symbols and slang' as well as adolescent feelings of 'isolation, anger and dissatisfaction' (ibid.). Although Gaines and Berger derive some of their evidence from ethnographic studies conducted with the sons (and daughters) of blue-collar workers in 'blue collar' or 'upper poor' towns in Bergen County, New Jersey, and Akron, Ohio, the wider evidence base is derived from a plethora of quantitative studies, conducted by social scientists in North American schools and colleges, investigating the links among youth delinquency, educational failure, and the popularity of heavy metal in the 1980s (Brown, 2011, pp. 226–231). In reference to this evidence base, Berger asserts: 'both qualitative and quantitative scholarship shows that the music's audience has largely come from a working-class youth' (1991a, p. 284), while Moore (2010) argues: 'not all metal heads are working class, but they are much more commonplace as one descends down the socioeconomic hierarchy into the ranks of white society's uneducated and unskilled, especially among 'at-risk' youth who find themselves in trouble with authority' (p. 79).

The relevance of this shared class profile argument then is how it is also linked to a wider socio-cultural and political argument about the situation of lower-class youth in this period and—by extension—to the formation of the genre in 1970s Britain. For example, as Berger suggests: 'most scholars of metal have interpreted the music as an expression of the frustrations of the blue-collar young in a de-industrialising society that neither requires their labour nor values their presence' (1999b, p. 164). Or, 'metal is primarily a working class phenomenon of the deindustrialized period, and there is little doubt that much of the rage in metal has its roots in class frustrations' (Berger, 1999a, pp. 289–290). In making this argument Berger offers an explicit connection to the genre's origins: 'Originating in the deindustrialized English Midlands of the 1970s, metal has found its most loyal American audiences in the devastated Midwest and Northeast' (p. 284). More recent scholarship, investigating these origins, has variously argued: 'The industrial geography and working-class environment of post-war Birmingham directly influenced the lyrics and sound of Black Sabbath's and Judas Priest's music [...] Feelings of anger regarding their poor, working-class experience is a sentiment that is continually expressed in band interviews and is reflected in the lyrics of both groups' (Harrison, 2010, p. 145). Or as Cope (2010, p. 97) puts it: 'The war-torn desolation of Aston, dead end prospects and boring school seemed to inspire a music that was steeped in rage'. Seeking to theorize these connections, Wallach, Berger and Greene (2011, p. 17) argue that metal and its global proliferation is both a response to and a consequence of deindustrialization in that the *industrialization* of countries such as Indonesia, Malaysia, and Singapore 'led to the emergence of a disenfranchised working class whose everyday experiences were similar in key ways to the experiences of Americans and Britain's confronting *deindustrialization*' and is therefore, as Weinstein suggests, 'a key music of the global proletariat' (op. cit., p. 16).

However, research conducted in Europe in the late 1990s and early 2000s, focusing on France and Germany, strongly contests this class profile. For example, Bettina Roccor (1998) argues that the 'social background of fans' in Germany is inconsistent with the stereotypical 'working [class] family' or 'antisocial [dysfunctional] family background' found in the North American studies; rather, such fans are now 'multifarious and heterogeneous' (p. 149). Fabien Hein (2003), citing Berger's statement (above), argues that such claims are 'difficult to support in Europe' (quoted in Smialek, 2008, p. 27). Writing about France, he goes on to assert that the majority of fans 'manifestly belong to the middle classes' and are 'strongly educated' possessing 'diplômés' (ibid.).[1] Summarizing the evidence from her survey data, Roccor claims that heavy metal has become 'bourgeoisified' (cited in Chaker, 2010, pp. 272–273). Chaker's (2010) survey of death and black metal festival-goers in Germany largely concurs with this view, particularly in terms of level of educational qualifications: '53.8% of the interviewed death metal fans and 38.1% of the black metal fans have graduated from high school' (p. 272). She concludes, 'the popular opinion that black and death metal is especially attractive for people from the lower social class has proven false. In fact, most black and death metal fans are members of the middle class' (p. 273).

Moving from Europe to the global extreme metal scene, Baulch's study of Bali states that the majority of metal enthusiasts she studied 'were distinctly bourgeois' (2003, p. 199). Other more recent studies, such as Greene's (2011) work on the Nepali metal scene, observes: 'Most listeners and musicians were middle-class Nepalis in their teens or twenties, mostly male, in school or university programs' (p. 116). Bell's (2011) study of Malta argues, 'the Maltese metalhead is typically of an upper-working class or middle-class background, possibly pursuing postsecondary education' (p. 281). This description is not dissimilar to Mursic's (2011) study of metal scenes in Slovenia, where the majority of fans are recruited from university students who, if defined in terms of the status of their parents, would 'fit into the "middle class"' (p. 307). Levine's (2008) survey of metal scenes in Morocco, Egypt, Israel, Palestine, Lebanon, Iran, and Pakistan most often describes musicians and fans as middle or upper-middle class. For example, in Egypt, metal musicians are the 'well-educated prodigal sons (and in a few cases, daughters) of diplomats, military officers, or other members of the country's elite' (p. 75). Varas-Diaz and colleagues (2015) in their study of metal communities in Puerto Rico state that, of 'self-reported social class' 67.6% defined themselves as middle class (p. 94), whereas 57.2% had completed a university degree and 17.9% an associate degree (p. 98). Attempting to summarize this changed European and global picture, Kahn-Harris (2007) observes:

> in Europe at least, the more affluent working classes and lower middle classes tend to dominate. Certainly, with some exceptions, extreme metal does not seem to be the music of the 'underclass' in wealthy countries and there seems no shortage of scene members from relatively

wealthy middle class backgrounds. This situation may vary across the globe. Anecdotal evidence suggests that extreme metal scenes in some countries in South America may have members from extremely poor backgrounds [...] Conversely, in the Islamic Middle East and some parts of Asia, extreme metal scenes appear to be dominated by the wealthy. Generally speaking though, in most contexts extreme metal is neither the music of the poor and dispossessed, nor is it the music of the wealthy and privileged. (p. 70)

This judgment is echoed in the findings from the Cultural Capital and Social Exclusion national survey conducted in the UK (Savage, 2006), which argues that heavy metal is 'not exactly the music of the socially marginal. It is certainly young men who are attracted to it, but these tend to be those in middle-income brackets, with City & Guilds qualifications, in intermediate and lower supervisory positions' (p. 170).[2]

Figuring out the Arguments: The Relevance of Class-Fraction Analysis

It is important to note that even during the 1990s there were dissenting voices that challenged the typical class-profile of the heavy metal fan in North America. For example, Jeffrey Arnett's (1996) study of 'at risk' metalheads argued that fans were 'at least as likely to be middle class as working class' (p. 172). This view, that heavy metal fandom is not primarily defined by working-class identity, is also asserted by Karen Halnon (2004, 2006) in her ethnographic research (observation and interviews) with mainly nu metal concert fans.[3] Those interviewed, 'included high school and college students, high school dropouts, service workers, blue-collar laborers, and white-collar professionals' (2006, p. 35). In an earlier account (2004), the range of occupations is even more diverse, including 'auto mechanics, nail techs, massage therapists, construction workers, nurses, lawyers, corporate managers, and other white collar professionals' (p. 749). Although she notes that the fan-base is 'approximately 80 percent males from early teens through early twenties [...] there has been an increasing representation of late boomer metal fans and college-educated middle class male youth' (ibid.).

So how do we make sense of this huge array of conflicting data? Should we conclude, as Arnett and Halnon do, that there is no relationship between social class identities and a preference for heavy metal music? Certainly, if we re-define the typical metal fan as middle class, as more recent research seems to suggest, then there is no question to answer regarding the working-classed cultural identities and outlook that many have claimed are central to understanding the persistence of the genre. What I propose is that—if a more parsimonious view is to prevail—then we need to ask the question of how social class is being defined in these various studies; more specifically, we need to ask how are the middle and working classes being defined and differentiated from one another? In other words, what are the criteria of classification operating in the various studies, and is it consistent? An obvious difference here is that between qualitative and quantitative studies (of small and large data sets) as well as how that data is collected and categorized. For example, how many of Halnon's occupational categories listed above would be defined as typical middle- or working-class jobs? First, we cannot assume that those fans in high school and college are from middle-class homes; we would need to know more about those homes.[4] Certainly, auto mechanics, nail techs, massage therapists, nurses, and construction workers (and most probably service workers) would be defined as working class, whereas lawyers, white-collar professionals, and corporate managers would be defined as middle class. Here, even at quite a crude level, we have a pattern of majority working-class and minority middle-class occupations as fans of heavy metal. But is this division satisfactory? Don't we also need to differentiate within these broad categories and typical jobs? I would argue that this is especially important as a number of studies (as we have seen) identify the typical heavy metal fan, if they are deemed to be working class, as *lower working class*; whereas those studies that define such fans as middle class do so on the basis that their respondents are *not* lower working class.

An example of the latter type of categorization is Arnett (1996): 'Among the metalheads I interviewed, few were from families where the father had an occupation that could be called working class (truck driver, factory worker); the majority were from middle to upper middle-class families (sons of insurance agents, electrical engineers, college professors, and so on)' (p. 172). Here, as we can see, Arnett defines working-class jobs as manual unskilled or semi-skilled occupations, concluding that most of the occupations he records in his study were not those kinds of jobs. It is also important to note that while Arnett defines the working class quite narrowly, he is able to make a distinction *within* the middle class, between the middle and the upper middle. The criterion that is clearly operating across these divisions is that between manual and non-manual work, which broadly differentiates the working from the middle classes, while educational accreditation at intermediate (certificates) and higher (degrees) levels enables finer distinctions to be drawn *within* the middle class. However, it is notable that Arnett does not seek to claim any significance for this *in-class* division, beyond suggesting that most of his respondents are from middle-class families. Seeking to differentiate manual from non-manual types of occupations in terms of class identity is a long-standing view that also reflects a whole host of cultural attributes that are seen to define the class identity of such groups, for example, skill levels based on apprenticeships, on-the-job training, and skill certificates, such as City & Guilds (cityandguilds.com 2015) qualifications. However, what this means is that the category of engineer in Arnett's examples of middle-class occupations is disputable; it would depend on the level of skill and, in particular, whether this was defined as an academic qualification.[5] What this points to is Arnett's narrow definition of the working class as an occupational group and, in particular, the absence of the category of skilled manual. While it is important to differentiate the category of skilled manual from semi-skilled and unskilled manual work, each of these categories is conventionally employed to define working-class occupations. What this means economically and culturally is that there is significant differentiation *within* the working class as a category and this, in turn, reflects social standing and cultural-classed identities that are widely recognized both within this group as a whole and by social scientists that have studied occupational stratification.

The standard practice is to take the occupation of the father (or head of household) as the principal indicator of social class background. This procedure, although not an 'entirely satisfactory way of measuring social class' (particularly in terms of gender) as Murdock and Phelps (1973) acknowledge in their classic study, *Mass Media and the Secondary School*:

> in the majority of cases, the broad classifications of occupations into non-manual, skilled manual, and semi-skilled and unskilled manual, does correspond to the conventional social categories—middle class, and upper and lower working class. Thus, referring to pupils as 'lower working class' is a useful shorthand way of saying 'pupils from homes where the father is employed in a semi-skilled or un-skilled manual job'. (p. 55)

The significance of this classificatory procedure is that it allows an identification of different social and cultural fractions, namely the lower and upper working class, within the broader category of the working class population. In the early 1970s this means of differentiation was very important because of the sheer size of this group, where differential location would correspond to a significant social and cultural group in terms of income, cultural identity, or what Bourdieu (1985) defines as class 'habitus'. However, this class schema is still somewhat problematic in too broadly defining the middle class as those who hold non-manual types of occupations, failing to differentiate between routine and minor supervisory jobs, professional and academic ones. This was probably satisfactory when the middle class was a relatively small 'traditional' group in comparison to the working class and when new entry into this group was relatively infrequent. However, the exponential growth in membership of this group, due to an increase in non-manual routine and minor supervisory 'office' or service-sector work, requires an equivalent distinction (which Arnett suggests) between the lower and upper middle class. What follows from this however is the question of whether we can define routine and minor supervisory positions as middle class anymore? We can if this division is perceived to be significant in the sense of cultural difference and classed distinction, as it was traditionally. However, in terms of skill level and remuneration, many routine and minor supervisory jobs could be classed as equivalent to skilled manual or indeed semi-skilled jobs. In terms of cultural standing and classed-habitus it is notable that some psephologists have identified so-called C1 (supervisory, clerical or junior managerial) and C2s (skilled manual workers), within the NRS social grade classification,[6] as a culturally significant fraction in their class identity and outlook and, crucially, their voting behavior.[7] Interestingly, Kahn-Harris in his doctoral study (2001) of the extreme metal scene, observes:

> Around two-thirds of my interviewees came from affluent working-class or lower-middle class backgrounds—the proportion was about the same in all three case-study areas. Among the scene members I interviewed, it was common for the mother to be a secretary and the father a skilled manual worker. I met very few poor scene members from educationally and socially 'deprived' backgrounds. Many scene members come from relatively wealthy middle-class backgrounds, although I met few from what could be considered rich backgrounds. (p. 152)

It is my contention that not only does this description of extreme metal scene participation depend on a version of class-fraction analysis, it is also suggestive of the key class fractions and occupational categories that could be said to constitute the genre's enduring core constituency of musicians and fans: skilled manual 'working class', intermediate and minor supervisory, and 'lower middle class'. This description seems to fit very well with Weinstein's claim that 'metal's fanbase, since its inception, tends to come from the working class and its post-industrial version, the para-professional and service-sector lower-middle class' (2004, p. 301). This is not to deny that heavy metal has lower working-class and upper middle-class fans. But, as I shall suggest, these types of fans increase and decrease according to the level of popularity of heavy metal music in various periods; that is, during periods of chart success and greater visibility, metal's lower working-class fan base increases allowing metal music to cross-over into the 'mainstream'; during periods of underground obscurity, its upper middle-class fandom increases. However, neither of these classed-cultural groups can be said to have exerted much influence on the enduring core identity of heavy metal, being rather upmarket and downmarket acts of group identification that are transitory or periodic in nature (Brown and Griffin, 2014).

I'm not sure if Deena Weinstein's (1991, 2000) class formula arose out of a similar process of reasoning, but it certainly seems appropriate at this juncture. She argues that the heavy metal audience is 'blue collar, either in fact or by sentimental attachment' (2000, p. 99). Now, strictly speaking, this is not a claim about the class composition of heavy metal but its *classed*-cultural appeal. Indeed Weinstein goes on to argue, 'in a cultural sense, heavy metal has a class signification wherever it appears' (op. cit., p. 113), which in the United States approximates to a 'blue collar ethos' (ibid). Or to put it another way, 'The class composition of the core metal audience is working and middle class, but the metal subculture is steeped in the blue collar ethos' (p. 115). The middle class identified here are the lower middle class: 'The middle-class kids who embraced metal were not from the upper reaches of their class. They were centered in the lower middle class, whose members are most insecure in their standing. There could be few things more threatening for lower-middle-class parents than to witness their sons […] espousing blue-collar values' (ibid.). Although Weinstein doesn't go on to define what these blue-collar values could be said to be (although technical ability and skill, as well as masculinity, are frequently mentioned) she does suggest that heavy metal, as a classed-cultural formation, is 'a response to the cultural marginalization of the working class' (p. 114).

So here we have an argument, similar to that of Kahn-Harris, that offers a class-fraction type model of how structural position might correlate with a preference for metal. However, this analysis does not offer an equivalent sense that the working class is internally stratified in terms of unskilled, semi-skilled, and skilled manual workers. This may be because, like a number of the key North American accounts of heavy metal, the genre and subcultural formation are seen to arise as response to deindustrialization in the 1970s, following a high point of affluence in the late 1960s (the so-called 'affluent worker' or affluent working-class thesis (cf. Savage).[8] But it could be equally argued that a key to the classed-culture that is expressed in heavy metal's blue-collar romanticism, as Weinstein perceives it, is not a valorization of the lower working class but the skilled-manual and 'tech' culture of the upper-working class and lower middle class. Dietmar Elflein (2013) makes a similar point, citing the German Sociologist Diaz-Bone's claim, that 'the central themes of heavy metal culture—the cycle of production, the work and success ethic, and the appreciation of being able to do it alone—reveal an affinity to professions like craftsperson, technician, and skilled worker' (p. 72).

At this point it is important to note that, although heavy metal is the music preference of working class fans, the majority of the working class (made up of unskilled and semi-skilled manual workers) is indifferent to or highly dislikes heavy metal (Bryson, 1996, p. 894; Savage, 2006, p. 163). Given that heavy metal is not the favored music of the working class, neither at the time of its origins nor during the peak of its popularity in the '70s and '80s—and certainly not now—we cannot reasonably entertain the veracity of sweeping claims about the structural situation of the working class to 'explain' the popularity or otherwise of metal genres, when the majority of the working class is excluded from such an equation. This problem is compounded when we also need to acknowledge that a proportion of heavy metal's audience has historically been recruited from the lower middle class. How can the class situation or circumstances of this fraction explain its fandom of metal music? How is this situation different to other middle-class youth and yet similar to a fraction of working-class youth? My argument will be that it is only a form of class-fraction analysis that can answer these questions, as it is most likely that it is the enduring structural proximity or closeness of these class fractions that allows them to share a similar classed-cultural identity, expressed in their preference for heavy metal music, which at the same time is also an act of *differentiation* within their wider class belonging.

"Rock Music, Progressive and Heavy are Fantastic": Exploring the Classed Identity of Heavy Metal Fandom in the 1970s

The first studies of age, class, gender, and musical taste that contain the categories of 'heavy rock' and 'heavy metal' are college and school-based studies conducted in the 1970s that explore changing patterns of musical taste and how they relate to 'school careers' and wider social attitudes and youth identities. Like the 1980s studies referred to in the North American research on heavy metal, these studies employ mostly quantitative techniques, conducting survey questionnaires with clusters of students selected in terms of school, neighborhood, and social class profile, followed by semi-structured interviews. The importance of these studies is that the categories of 'heavy rock' and 'heavy metal' expressed as 'likes' first emerge in them, as part of a distinction, not between a liking for pop or classical music but for 'mainstream pop' and 'underground or progressive rock' music. For example, Murdock and Phelps' study (1973) identifies just over 50% of pupils from middle-class and lower working-class backgrounds who prefer mainstream pop, whereas the remainder of the working class group (41%) chose an R&B ("Negro")[9] record and the middle class group (42.5%), an underground record (p. 109). For Murdock and Phelps 'the underground music supporters are thus more likely to be middle class than working class' (1973, p. 109). This 'statistically significant' finding also correlates with school commitment, where each group finds values in its chosen music not reflected in school life as a means of sustaining an academic 'career' or rejecting it. For the lower working-class students these are the values of a 'street culture' located in leisure time, whereas for the middle class it is more a reflection of 'critical' individualism. However, it is significant that the school conformity rejection clusters are described as lower working class and middle class, respectively. So, although the authors identify the skilled manual working class in their research design, when it comes to the analysis of the data this category is not visible.

Simon Frith's classic *The Sociology of Rock* (1978) does identify the largest group of males as the 'skilled boys', that is young males who are apprentices preparing for employment as skilled workers in industry or manufacturing or self-employed 'artisans' (mechanics, plumbers, etc.) (p. 31). However, this group's lack of commitment to music as a source of identity—it is more a soundtrack to nights out and dancing—is similar to the lower working class school rejectors who are keen to leave school as soon as possible to take up unskilled jobs. Frith's survey, of 105 14 to 18 year olds, conducted in a comprehensive school in Keighley, West Riding of Yorkshire, in 1972, reveals similar taste divisions between middle- and working-class kids (between intelligent 'thinking' music and commercial music with a 'beat'), although he is keen to note how some students did not fit this pattern, resisted it, or even rejected their traditional class cultural milieu in their choices. The significant group, who listen to music more, buy LPs, and discuss music, are the 'sixth formers' who have chosen to pursue an academic career by going on to college and university. They are mostly but not exclusively middle class (p. 40), the sons and daughters of the local professional and management class. However, working-class sixth-formers 'fitted into this culture without much difficulty' (p. 41).

> Music was a background to their lives, radio and records were always on. The records were LPs, chosen carefully and individually and often purchased by saving money after hearing a friend's copy. People listened to music together and often exchanged albums temporarily. Few people in the group had large record collections, although a crucial musical role was played by older brothers and sisters and friends who had more records, knew what was happening, and turned the group on to new sounds. The overall result was an eclecticism of taste, with individuals developing their own specialisms—folk, heavy metal, singer/songwriter, avant-garde.
>
> (Frith, 1981, pp. 209–210)[10]

However, in contrast to this 'eclectic individualism' are the group identities of the lower-fifth, divided between skins, crombies, grebos, and hairies. Notable here was 'one of the most militant groups among 15- and 16-year olds [...] the future sixth formers, the self-identified hairies and hippies, with their missionary zeal for progressive rock and a hatred of commercial pop: "Rock music, progressive and heavy are fantastic. If they were not there life would not be worth living" (quoted in Frith, 1978, p. 42). Significantly, it was from this group that 'the most assertive statements of image and shared tastes came' (ibid.). One of the contradictions of the ideology of individualism that united the progressive rock fans was when one of their musical heroes changed direction: 'This was particularly a problem for the hairies because they differentiated themselves from the masses as a self-conscious elite by displaying exclusive musical tastes. When one of their acts went commercial ('sold-out') and became part of mass taste there was great bitterness' (p. 43).

For Frith, commitment to music is not wholly reducible to social class, rather musical orientation is both a reflection of the individual situation of youth and how this informs its relationship to class-cultural backgrounds (pp. 50–51). However, in Murdock and McCron's (1973) *New Society* report on their research, the class polarization between a liking for 'reggae and soul' and progressive rock bands, has become a youth division among 'skins' and 'smooths' and 'weirdos', 'freaks', and 'scoobies' (a derisory term for college students) (p. 591). The author's comment:

> The very music which has been hailed as the lynch pin of the new "counter culture" is rapidly being incorporated into the minority culture of the middle class intelligentsia. As a result, progressive rock music is becoming less accessible and less meaningful to the majority of working class adolescents. (p. 593)

However, this class polarization thesis seems somewhat overstated, not least because in this period 'prog' rock, heavy metal, and the singer-songwriter genre are the most commercially successful rock genres (Straw, 1990), appealing across class taste groups. In addition, the research categories, seeking to differentiate within the progressive-underground category in terms of beat and rhythm (activity-potency) and lyric-meaning (understandability), reveal the categories of 'Heavy rock', 'Progressive urban blues' and the 'Singer-Songwriters'. In addition, interviews with male sixth-form clusters identify LP collecting with the latest acquisition of Led Zeppelin, mentioned by some respondents (Murdock and Phelps, 1973, p. 134). Asked to identify the qualities of the music and performers they liked, they mention 'instrumental prowess' and 'the sheer volume and energy characteristic of this type of music' along with 'adjectives such as 'loud', 'lively' and 'wild' (ibid.). So, although heavy metal will eventually become identified with a majority working-class fandom, in this period it is likely that its social class profile is predominantly made up of middle-class and aspirational working-class students, especially to the extent to which it is viewed by both its musician 'performers' and fans as part of progressive rock culture. Evidence of this cross-class cultural fandom is also to be found in youth and subcultural studies work (Brown, 2003); the most recurring descriptions identifying its fandom as made up of 'a popular alliance of scruffy students and working-class followers' (Chambers, 1985, p. 123; see also Cashmore, 1984; Hebdige, 1979). Indeed, it could be argued that it was the increasingly negative account of the genre given by influential rock critics, seeking to differentiate it from the progressive music of the counter-culture, that leads to the decline in fandom amongst middle-class rock fans. This view is certainly reflected in Frith's [1978] commentary:

> as the decade developed, it became increasingly difficult to make sense of heavy metal [...] as middle class music. Bands like Black Sabbath, Uriah Heep, and Deep Purple had their own armies of scruffy working-class fans and in America, in particular, it was obvious that a band like Grand Funk didn't appeal to the readers of *Rolling Stone*. If British fans never went as far as their American peers in their devotion

to Kiss, a heavy metal teenybop band, they did make it impossible to classify Staus Quo, one of the 1970s most successful groups, as either rock or pop. (1996, pp. 146–147)

This class-cultural shift is clearly to be found in Tanner's (1981) questionnaire-based study of 733 students from five schools in Edmonton, Canada, conducted in October 1974, which identifies a 'new' category of youth music preference, 'heavy metal rock' (p. 4), identified with the bands Deep Purple, Nazareth, Kiss, and Black Sabbath. As the author comments, 'Heavy rock is now a relatively distinct genre in contemporary popular music' not only in terms of the Top 40 Mainstream but also in relation to 'progressive rock'; that is, although, '(a)t one time enjoying the same 'underground' status as the progressive performers, these links have now been severed' (ibid.). The study goes on to identify a statistically significant preference for 'heavy metal rock' amongst working-class-identified students, which underpins a correlation between a liking for heavy rock and 'school rejection': 'students with a low commitment to school are more likely than their more highly committed peers to favour the music of the heavy metal bands' (p. 7). Seeking to explain this correlation, Tanner observes:

> The music itself is distinguished by heavy amplification, and dominated by guitar riffs (rather than extended solos). On stage, the heavy metal groups adopt a tough, aggressive, even violent stance. It can be argued that the essence of 'proletarian rage', heavy rock's appeal, rests on its ability to mirror other largely working-class adolescent core values and focal concerns—collective action and physicality, for example. (ibid.)

The findings of this study can be seen as an early template for the many North American studies that were to follow in the 1980s linking a liking for heavy metal to self-reported delinquency and risk-taking among young working class men. But what is most striking about it is how the genre's appeal, bereft of its connections to progressive rock, is described in almost identical ways to the Murdock and Phelps and Murdock and McCron studies, as articulating the 'street culture' values of lower working-class youth. What this suggests is that as soon as heavy metal becomes exclusively or predominantly identified with lower working-class students, researchers seek to explain this 'adolescent variation' in taste in terms of the 'class-based values' they identify with this group: action, toughness, physical competence, and group solidarity.

Conclusion

The significance of these early studies is not only that they are the first studies to identify a taste for heavy metal amongst students in school and college surveys but also that they identify this taste formation as predominantly but not exclusively middle class. The 'hairies', 'freaks', and 'weirdos' who passionately defend their musical tastes against mainstream pop's perceived conformity are the forerunners of the 'headbangers', 'burnouts', and 'stoners' found in the North American research of the 1980s. But what has significantly changed is the characterization of these groups as aspirational college- and university-bound 'critical individualists' to school and college 'dropouts' and educational-failures, pre-destined for insecure, poorly paid semi or unskilled work or unemployment. As Frith argues, it is the unskilled manual male group from which 'trouble' is always seen to come as its members transition from school 'floundering around for job satisfaction, a prey to bad influences (whether criminal or commercial)' (1978, p. 33). Sociologists and psychologists try to link this work 'failure' with school 'failure', distinguishing the 'integrated' from the 'alienated'. But it is changes in the labor market, the range of jobs, and opportunities available that is ultimately determinate; and this is true of the skilled manual apprentice group also. In both cases 'bored youth' whether early school leavers or on apprenticeship training are looking for fun, thrills, and excitement in their leisure time whatever the wider economic context.

While Wallach, Berger, and Greene (2011) and others are right to link heavy metal fandom with lower working-class male fans, this demographic majority is the result of a shift in class taste, away from the upper-working and lower-middle class from the mid-1970s onwards, which clearly coincides with a decline in the status of skilled manual, routine and minor supervisory non-manual occupations. The 'mainstreaming' of heavy metal in the 1984–1991 period also increases the proportion of working-class fans, while clearly the numbers of semi- or unskilled working-class fans are swelled by those from formerly skilled households who are no longer able to follow their 'fathers' into apprenticeships. This shift in classed identities, away from progressive hard rock and metal, toward a more formulaic and simplified music style (see Elflein, this volume) is symbolically exemplified by the success of the band Judas Priest in North America in the 1980s, moving from a 'hairy' or 'hippy' image[11] to a studs, chains, and leather look that became synonymous with the genre; as did the controversy that surrounded their album *Stained Class* (1978), involving the botched suicide pact entered into by two teenage boys from 'troubled' working class families in December 1985.

However, it is not clear that the rise of the sub-genres speed, thrash, and hardcore or cross-over metal and punk, in the 1984–1991 period, can be said to fit the same class profile of that of '80s mainstream metal music. Although there is certainly some overlap in fandom, the San Francisco Bay Area thrash scene is notable for the influx of ethnic minority bands and fans who viewed such scene participation as aspirational (see Fellezs, this volume), as well as the documented mix of middle- and working-class youth in the punk/hardcore scene (Haenfler, 2015; Moore, 2010). The rise of the extreme metal genres of death, black, and progressive metal thereafter, particularly in Europe, suggests an influx of lower and upper middle-class fans, who articulate their reasons for fandom and musical 'likes' in very similar ways to those of the progressive rock fans of the 1970s, particularly in respect to a sense of perceived 'superiority' to the mainstream of rock and pop music (Kahn-Harris, 2007; Chaker, 2010; Allett, 2013). For example, Allett's extreme metal 'middle-class' fans refer to the 'herd mentality' and 'sheep' of mainstream musical tastes, charactering it as 'mass conformity and a lack of individuality' against which they distinguish their 'elite' tastes (2013, p. 176).

The theme of 'individuality and intellectualism' is also to be found in a number of recent Canadian studies of progressive metal and fan reception, where the majority audience for such genres is claimed to be middle class and such values to be a defining aspect of middle-classed educational cultures (Macdonald, 2008; Smialek, 2008). However, Bowman (2002) identifies the audience for progressive rock and hard rock/metal as 'suburban working-class and lower middle-class young men born at the end of the baby boom (1955–65)' who were attracted to the technicality and complexity of the musical style and its 'message' of 'individualism and libertarianism' rather than its elite upper-middle class, classical music 'quotationalism' (p. 189). Indeed, many of these fans went on to high-tech careers in 'computer programming, astrophysics, and architecture', for example (p. 186).

It is surely not a coincidence that the North American studies that identify metal fandom with the lower working class, also identify the 'individualism' and 'libertarianism' of such fans as a form of 'false' *class consciousness*, rather than as a coherent aspect of metal-fan identities over time (e.g. Berger, 1999a, pp. 286–291; Moore, 2010, pp. 75–113). While the class stratification of global metal fandom is extremely polarized between the rich and relatively privileged and the poor, many of metal's fans in developing countries are those working in 'tech' service sectors jobs, who are predominantly viewed as a 'new' middle-class, based on their skill qualifications and positioning between rich and poor. All of this suggests that further work on metal and class identities needs to focus more on the analysis of the middle class, particularly the lower middle class.

Notes

1. These quotations from Smialek are translations by the author from the original French and German sources.
2. This survey also suggests that skilled self-employed men are more likely to be metal than rock fans.
3. Her sample also included a small number of death, thrash, doom and rap-rock fans.
4. It is interesting that many of the European surveys indicate that a significant proportion of students achieving higher diplomas are from blue collar or working-class backgrounds.

5. For example, the cityandguilds.com website describes engineering as encompassing everything 'from fabrication and welding to aeronautical engineering' and lists 31 qualifications, including 5 in electrical and electronic and 26 in mechanical engineering, which includes areas such as manufacture, maintenance and technical support (http://www.cityandguilds.com/qualifications-and-apprenticeships#fil=uk) (accessed February 13, 2015).
6. ABC1= Middle class and C2DE=Working Class.
7. In particular, this grouping has been identified with the class de-alignment thesis.
8. Interestingly, this debate engaged with the *embourgeoisement thesis* that the rising income levels of skilled workers that led to an increase in home ownership would lead to such groups' taking on the leisure and identity practices of the middle class. However, although there was some evidence of class-convergence, this did not appear to be the case.
9. This study, in common with many of the period, employed this term interchangeably with 'black'.
10. This quote re-works Frith's earlier summary (1978, p. 44), replacing 'heavy' with 'heavy metal' and adding 'avant-garde' to the genre list.
11. Vintage footage of the band appearing on the Old Grey Whistle Test (April 1975), performing 'Rocka Rolla' and 'Dreamer Decieve/Deciever', clearly show the band dressed in bell-bottom flared trousers and jeans, hats, long sleeved tops and 'hippy' smocks (Judas Priest, 2003).

Bibliography

Allett, N. (2013). The extreme metal 'connoisseur'. In T. Hjelm, K. Kahn-Harris, & M. LeVine (Eds.), *Heavy metal: Controversies and countercultures* (pp. 166–181). London: Equinox.

Arnett, J. J. (1996). *Metalheads: Heavy metal music and adolescent alienation*. Boulder, CO: Westview Press.

Baulch, E. (2003). Gesturing elsewhere: The identity politics of the Balinese death/thrash metal scene. *Popular Music*, 22(2), 195–216.

Bell, A. (2011). Metal in a micro island state: An insider's perspective. In J. Wallach, H. Berger, & P. D. Greene (Eds.), *Metal rules the globe: Heavy metal music around the world* (pp. 271–293). Durham, NC: Duke University Press.

Berger, H. M. (1999a). *Metal, rock and jazz: Perception and the phenomenology of musical experience*. Hanover: Wesleyan University Press.

Berger, H. M. (1999b). Death metal tonality and the act of listening. *Popular Music*, 18(2), 161–178.

Bourdieu, P. (1985). *Distinction: A social critique of the judgement of taste*. London: Routledge.

Bowman, D. S. (2002). Let them all make their own music. Individualism, Rush, and the progressive/hard rock alloy, 1976–77. In K. Holm-Hudson (Ed.), *Progressive rock reconsidered* (pp. 21–42). New York: Routledge.

Brown, A. R. (2003). Heavy metal and subcultural theory: A paradigmatic case of neglect? In D. Muggleton & R. Weinzierl (Eds.), *The post-subcultures reader* (pp. 209–222). Oxford: Berg.

Brown, A. R. (2011). Heavy genealogy: Mapping the currents, contraflows and conflicts of the emergent field of metal studies. *Journal for Cultural Research*, 15(3), 213–242.

Brown, A. R., & Griffin, C. (2014). A cockroach preserved in amber: The significance of class in critics' representations of heavy metal music and its fans. *The Sociological Review*, 62(4), 719–741.

Bryson, B. (1996). Anything but heavy metal: Symbolic exclusion and musical dislikes. *American Sociological Review*, 61(5), 884–899.

Chaker, S. (2010). Extreme music for extreme people: Black and death metal put to the test in a comparative empirical study. In N. W. R. Scott & I. Von Helden (Eds.), *The metal void: First gatherings* (pp. 265–278). Oxford: Inter-Disciplinary Press.

Cope, A. L. (2010). *Black Sabbath and the rise of heavy metal music*. Farnham, Surrey: Ashgate.

Elflein, D. (2013). Overcome the pain: Rhythmic transgression in heavy metal music. *Thamyris/Intersecting*, 26, 71–88.

Frith, S. (1978). *The sociology of rock*. London: Constable.

Frith, S. ([1978]1996). Youth culture/youth cults: A decade of rock consumption. In C. Gillett & S. Frith (Eds.), *The beat goes on: The rock file reader* (pp. 143–152). London: Pluto Press.

Frith, S. (1981). *Sound effects: Youth, leisure and the politics of rock 'n' roll*. New York: Pantheon.

Greene, P. D. (2011). Electronic and affective overdrive: Tropes of transgression in Nepal's heavy metal scene. In J. Wallach, H. Berger, & P. D. Greene (Eds.), *Metal rules the globe: Heavy metal music around the world* (pp. 109–134). Durham, NC: Duke University Press.

Haenfler, R. (2015). Punk rock, hardcore and globalization. In A. Bennett & S. Waksman (Eds.), *The Sage handbook of popular music* (pp. 278–295). Los Angeles: Sage.

Halnon, K. B. (2004). Inside shock music carnival: Spectacle as contested terrain. *Critical Sociology*, 30(3), 743–779.

Halnon, K. B. (2006). Heavy metal carnival and dis-alienation: The politics of grotesque realism. *Symbolic Interaction*, 29(1), 33–48.

Harrison, L. M. (2010). Factory music: How the industrial geography and working-class environment of post-war Birmingham fostered the birth of heavy metal. *Journal of Social History*, Fall, 145–158.

Hein, F. (2003). *Hard rock, heavy metal, metal: histoire, culture et pratiquants*. Paris: IRMA; Nantes: Mélanie Séteun.

Kahn-Harris, K. (2001). *Transgression and mundanity: The global extreme metal music scene*. PhD in Sociology, Goldsmiths College, University of London.

Kahn-Harris, K. (2007). *Extreme metal: Music and culture on the edge*. Oxford: Berg.

LeVine, M. (2008). *Heavy metal Islam: Rock, resistance, and the struggle for the soul of Islam*. New York: Three Rivers Press.

Macdonald, C. (2008). Open secrets: Individualism and middle-class identity in the songs of Rush. *Popular Music and Society*, 31(3), 313–328.

Moore, R. (2010). *Sells like teen spirit: Music, youth culture, and social crisis*. New York: New York University Press.

Murdock, G., & McCron, R. (1973). Scoobies, skins and contemporary pop. *New Society*, March 29, 129–131.

Murdock, G., & Phelps, G. (1973). *Mass media and the secondary school*. London: Macmillan.

Mursic, R. (2011). Noisy crossroads: Metal scenes in Slovenia. In J. Wallach, H. Berger, & P. D. Greene (Eds.), *Metal rules the globe: Heavy metal music around the world* (pp. 294–312). Durham, NC: Duke University Press.

Roccor, B. (1998). *Heavy metal. Kunst, Kommerz, Ketzerei*, Berlin, IP, Verlag Jeske/Mader GbR. Kunst, Kommerz, Ketzerei, IP Verlag Jeske / Mader GbR, Berlin.

Savage, M. (2006). The musical field. *Cultural Trends*, 15(2/3), 159–174.

Smialek, E. T. (2008). *Rethinking metal aesthetics: Complexity, authenticity, and audience in Meshuggah's I and Catch Thirtythr33*. MA Thesis, McGill University, Montréal, QC.

Straw, W. (1990). Characterizing rock music culture: The case of heavy metal. In S. Frith & A. Goodwin (Eds.), *On record: Rock, pop and the written word* (pp. 97–110). London: Routledge.

Tanner, J. (1981). Pop music and peer groups: A study of Canadian high school students' responses to pop music. *Canadian Review of Sociology & Anthropology*, 18(1), 1–13.

Varas-Díaz, N., Rivera-Segarra, E., Rivera Medina, C. L., Mendoza, S., & González-Sepúlveda, O. (2014) Predictors of communal formation in a small heavy metal scene: Puerto Rico as a case study. *Metal Music Studies*, 1(1), 87–103.

Wallach, J., Berger, H. M., & Greene, P. D. (2011). *Metal rules the globe: Heavy metal music around the world*. Durham, NC: Duke University Press.

Weinstein, D. (1991). *Heavy metal: A cultural sociology*. New York: Maxwell Macmillan International.

Weinstein, D. (2000). *Heavy metal: The music and its culture*. New York: Da Capo Press.

Weinstein, D. (2004). Rock critics need bad music. In C. Washbourne & M. Demo (Eds.), *Bad music: The music we love to hate*. New York: Routledge.

Weinstein, D. (2011). The globalization of metal. In J. Wallach, H. Berger, & P. D. Greene (Eds.), *Metal rules the globe: Heavy metal music around the world*. (pp. 34–59). Durham, NC: Duke University Press.

Part IV
Metal Markets and Commerce

12 Tunes from the Land of the Thousand Lakes
Early Years of Internationalization in Finnish Heavy Metal

Toni-Matti Karjalainen and Eero Sipilä

'Metal music from Finland?' Thirty years ago, this question would have been irrelevant, even absurd. There were hardly any Finnish bands playing abroad—hardly any recognized metal bands existed in Finland in the first place. Today, the situation is quite the opposite. Finnish metal is a recognized phenomenon within the global metal community and even outside it. Mention *Finland* to a foreign friend and she or he might have a comment or two on metal music. There are now numerous Finnish metal bands touring in different parts of the world. *Nightwish*, the biggest of them, has sold millions of records, regularly plays arenas on world tours, and at the time of writing has over five million fans on its official Facebook site.

The internationalization of Finnish metal has followed a peculiar and stony path. In this chapter we discuss how the foundations were laid during the 1980s and 1990s, how different subgenres and bands were lifted up and pushed down in the Finnish national media, and how this development was strongly influenced by wider metal trends, the emerging globalization and transculturalization of the metal scene in particular (cf. Wallach, Berger, and Greene, 2011). Finnish metal was also at times boosted by national and cultural imperatives to promote Finnish identity, allowing it to become a recognizable global/local phenomenon that could challenge the Anglo-American hegemony in heavy metal music production.

In what follows we look at the commercial aspects of the genres development, focusing on the media discourse surrounding bands that have been seen as potential exports. Our objective has not been to provide a comprehensive historical overview of the development of Finnish metal, but one more specifically focused on the main commercial movements and bands as they have been reported on in print media. This naturally means that our focus will be on mainstream developments of the metal genre rather than on underground movements, genres, or bands.

In particular, the chapter discusses how a recognized 'brand' of Finnish metal as an emblematic identity (O'Flynn, 2007)—its canonized narrative—is constructed. Within this framework, metal is deployed as a means of exporting Finnish culture, tangled around specific and strongly narrated myths. We find that there is a surprisingly consistent discourse around Finnish metal that has appeared in the media: suggesting first that Finnish metal is unique

210 Toni-Matti Karjalainen and Eero Sipilä

in sound and timbre and played by skilled musicians and second that Finnish heavy metal describes the character of the nation and its inhabitants.[1] We will review how this story was narrated and romanticized during the first two decades of Finnish heavy metal.

Approach and Data

Our aim was to identify an emergent *internationalization* framework within national rock media writing as it keenly followed the internationalization attempts of Finnish metal bands over the years. The main body of data consists of writings in Finnish rock magazines that have most consistently reported on metal bands. In the analysis we have employed a textual 'interpretative' method but one informed by the wider aim of seeking to link such texts to the emergent meanings and cultural practices of the periods under focus (Fairclough, 1997, pp. 28–29), especially within the global metal and rock music fields.

The main sources are *Soundi* and *Rumba* magazines, the two most prevalent and probably most respected magazines within Finnish rock and metal media. Our sample covers the years from 1979 to 2013, accessed via print library collections of the magazines. Within the sample, we have focused on bands seen to play a pivotal role in the internationalization trajectory of Finnish metal. In total, the data sample consists of approximately a 150 texts (consisting of features, reports, reviews, etc.). In addition, other data and studies—such as videos and documentaries, books and media—have been used as supporting contextual material.[2]

In sum, we characterize four main stages of internationalization in the history of Finnish metal: birth (early 1980s), public acceptance (late 1980s), second wave (1990s), breakthrough, and growth (2000s). In the remaining part of this chapter, we focus on the three first stages preceding this 'breakthrough'.

The Birth of Finnish Metal

When Finnish heavy metal took its first steps in the late 1970s, the genre and its public appreciation had declined from the initial popularity of *Black Sabbath* and other pioneers at the beginning of the decade, which in part was due to punk making hard rock aesthetics look old-fashioned. However, it was during this time that the first signs of domestic metal bands started to emerge in Finland.

The First Finnish Heavy Metal Band?

Sarcofagus from Helsinki has generally been regarded as the first Finnish heavy metal band (Bruun, 1998, p. 353; Juntunen, 1980). Its first album *Cycle of Life* was released in 1980. This pioneer status of Sarcofagus is, however, not indisputable—prior to it, bands such as *Apollo* and the genre-consciously named *Hard Rock Sallinen* were playing some heavy tunes. The reputation of Sarcofagus as Finland's first heavy metal band seems to have been, at least to a certain degree, a conscious marketing decision by the band itself. For example, the release of *Cycle of Life* was accompanied by the slogan: 'Finland's first heavy rock LP' (*Soundi* 2/1980).

In a musical sense, Sarcofagus was not significantly 'heavier' than many of its contemporaries. The band leader, Kimmo Kuusniemi, later admitted that the debut album was 'more progressive rock and blues than heavy metal' (Jalonen, 2009). The importance of Sarcofagus for Finnish heavy metal culture is perhaps of more of a visual and symbolic nature. The band's visual imagery was arguably influenced by heavy metal conventions, while the song lyrics were charged with typical stories of the occult and oriental imagery. But in particular, unlike other contemporaries, Sarcofagus tried to consciously *represent* heavy metal, so that *Cycle of Life* appears as a point of 'crystallization' (Weinstein, 1991, p. 7) marking a stage where Finnish metal has become a recognizable and distinctive cultural phenomenon.

At this early stage, the cultural fit of heavy metal in the Finnish environment was not obvious, not even for the musicians themselves. Answering the question of why the Finnish national phenomena and heritage, including the national epic *Kalevala*, were not used in heavy lyrics, Kuusniemi commented, 'Kalevala has been worn out in the school, and people are tired of it even though it is in itself an interesting book. Finnish language does not seem to fit the heavy metal music, which in terms of its appearance is already so far away from our country's musical tradition' (Juntunen, 1980, p. 15). Thus, heavy metal was generally regarded as a foreign and distant phenomenon.

The Slowly Growing Local Scene

The official opinion, foremost represented by journalists, was negative toward heavy metal in the early years. The growing popularity of the genre, however, inevitably led to a few heavy enthusiasts to start work at rock magazines. For example, *Soundi*'s new critics, the above-mentioned Kimmo Kuusniemi and Juho Juntunen, who would later sustain a long career in the wider media, showed a new attitude toward this music style and started to evaluate the genre on its own terms.

By the time the new generation emerged, the discourses surrounding heavy metal also started to change. While in the past the theatrical appearance and musical complexities of heavy metal were merely seen to 'cause a headache' for many, heavy enthusiasts like Kuusniemi were calling precisely for these elements in heavy metal music to be promoted: it was supposed to entail nuances and dynamics of intelligence. This appreciation planted the seeds for the technical and ambitious subspecies of metal-composition that later became particularly popular in Finland, including the likes of melodic death metal and symphonic metal.

In the 1980s, the popularity of heavy metal was steadily increasing all around the Western world. In 1984, heavy metal counted for 20% of record sales in the United States (Martin and Segrave, 1988, p. 232). The phenomenon was invading Finland, too. In March 1984 the top five places of the *Soundi* album list were taken by heavy metal bands, led by *Whitesnake* and *Judas Priest* (*Soundi* 4/1984), and in September of the same year the magazine reported on the 'heavy metal fever' (*Soundi* 9/1984) that was storming through Finland.

As heavy metal proved to be both a prevailing and also immensely popular phenomenon, the general press could no longer remain indifferent to it. Soon the biggest heavy favorites began to find their way more widely into the pages of *Soundi* and *Rumba*. *Suosikki*, another influential magazine, directed especially at teenagers and younger fans of popular culture, was also extensively featuring heavy metal bands, in particular from the blooming hair metal scene of the US west coast.

Despite the growing popularity of the genre, Finland's own heavy metal production, however, was rather minor throughout the 1980s. In the first half of the decade, the 'heavy metal fever' was purely based on foreign bands. Instead of metal, many domestic bands that gained some popularity were playing punk rock. Whereas metal was in many respects still considered risky in a commercial sense, playing punk meant a fuller gig calendar and larger audiences for the bands.

The first actual metal bands following Sarcofagus were operating in Finland on a relatively modest basis throughout the first half of the 1980s. The ones exceeding the news threshold included Tarot, Iron Cross, Outburst, Oz, and Zero Nine. Stratovarius was also formed in 1984, but its first album was released in 1989, and the band received more visibility in the 1990s.

As a rule, the bands were destined to remain on the commercial margin of Finnish music circles. Two of them, Zero Nine and Tarot, however managed to achieve small but quite longlasting popularity in Finland. Zero Nine was on a number of occasions cited as the 'number one band' of Finnish heavy metal (e.g., Juntunen, 1986a, 1986b; Bruun et al., 1998, p. 353). Tarot, in turn, became known for its pioneering stage technology for which, initially, it was difficult to find suitable venues in Finland (Juntunen, 1986b).

Some commentators were forecasting a successful career abroad for Zero Nine, with their occasional and modest visits outside the domestic borders, as well as recording visits to London, making headlines in the rock press (Juntunen, 1986a, 1986b). But such success in international markets was not forthcoming. Moreover, Tarot and Zero Nine represented a more traditional heavy metal sound that soon started to lose popularity to the newer pop metal and emerging thrash metal waves.

Authentic Hard Rock, Commercial Metal

Many hard rock bands also appeared in the latter half of the 1980s, such as Havana Blacks, Peer Günt, Gringos Locos, and Backsliders. Even though they were not labeled heavy metal, with their leather jacket and biker imagery they were openly borrowing metal aesthetics from the likes of Motörhead and Judas Priest, while their sound was characterized by guitar distortion and power chords. Of these bands, Havana Blacks was seriously knocking on the doors of international markets, but the expected breakthrough did not occur for this band, either. The same result was experienced by some Finnish glam and pop metal bands, such as Smack, Nights of Iguana, and Wild Force, who had high expectations for international sales.

Representing the Finnish hard rock scene, yet in quite a different style, the glam rockers Hanoi Rocks were already creating attention abroad in the first part of the 1980s. The band was, however, quite clearly neglected by the Finnish media, even though the band's international recognition was becoming very remarkable on the Finnish scale (Bruun et al., 1998, p. 353). Hanoi Rocks is even excluded from many later writings of Finnish heavy metal history. For example, Nikula (2002) and Juntunen (2004) do not mention a word on the band. This is strange, as Hanoi Rocks has been often cited as inspirational by the members of some hugely popular bands like Guns n' Roses, Aerosmith and the Foo Fighters and mentioned as a rare example of Finnish bands in some well-known metal history books. It is the only Finnish band that Robert Walser (1993, p. 130) alludes to in his famous study. The band is given many words also in the comprehensive overview by Ian Christe (2004, pp. 190–192), while Garry Sharpe-Young (2007, p. 121) lists Hanoi Rocks as the only Finnish band prior to the 1990s that made an international impact.[3]

Overall, heavy metal and (hard) rock were separated and treated quite differently in the Finnish media for most of the 1980s, which was perhaps based on some ideological connotations related to the genres. Such was the case with the popular Finnish rockers Peer Günt, who had both critics and the record-buying public on their side with their debut album *Backseat* (1986). 'Fortunately', Wallenius opined, 'Peer Günt, doesn't need to be diminished by calling it heavy metal. It's hard rock, heavy rock or whatever' (1986, p. 68).

Hard rock music was generally seen as authentic and powerful, while heavy metal was identified with the values of affectation and commercialism, leading to quite negative connotations. In particular, heavy metal was seen as representing the mass-culturalization and Americanization of popular culture by many 'cultured' critics. The visual shock tactics of popular L.A. metal groups, such as W.A.S.P. and Twisted Sister, were cited in moral panic-like reactions among various Finnish religious and parent groups in the early 1980s, reviving fears of American popular culture as a source of moral decadence (Bruun et al., 1998, pp. 404–405). An image of a widening chasm between a commercial 'decadent' culture and 'authentic' folk culture was reflected here and in the critical demarcation of the genres hard rock and heavy metal.

Public Acceptance

The commercial and international nature of heavy metal was, however, not seen solely in a negative light. The opportunities of metal bands to reach foreign markets were issues of great interest within the Finnish metal music scene, even in the early years. Gradually, as we shall see, the pursuit of international success of this explicitly commercial genre earned Finnish metal bands more space in the news, and this eventually led to their wider public acceptance.

Thrash and Finnish Speed

By the late 1980s, heavy metal had reached wide popularity in the Western world. The media-friendly glam/pop metal and the more unconventional and extreme metal incarnations, particularly thrash metal, had become the most popular subgenres (Weinstein, 1991, p. 21; Walser, 1993, p. 13).

The emergence of new Finnish metal bands (and perhaps Nordic metal as a wider phenomenon) was first seen in the vein of more extreme styles. Pop and thrash metal were both regarded, in principle, as US phenomena. These two genres were, however, ideologically very different. Even the thrash metal pioneers Metallica repeatedly called the whole thrash metal genre 'European', referring to its exquisite and more complex structure that created a contrast to the pop metal groups representing the stereotypically American hard rock sound (Pillsbury, 2006, pp. 25–26).

The subgenre of thrash metal, as a more intellectual and serious style accompanied by a simpler aesthetic, was widely appreciated by many young Finnish musicians. The musical intensity combined with a DIY or punk attitude was welcomed also by the Finnish rock media. The Finnish scene did not have to wait long to witness the first domestic thrash metal bands. 1987 marked a kind of a re-birth of Finnish metal, as two Finnish thrash metal bands, Stone and Airdash, grabbed the headlines simultaneously. The name of the genre was, however, in many contexts bent to 'speed metal', perhaps also to better fit the general Finnish language (*spiidi*).

The media noise around these bands was heightened and early reviews were exceptionally enthusiastic. 'The time of Finnish speed has started. And the start is handsome, persuasive [...] Rock and roll rebellion is no longer just a cliché!' began the review of the Stone debut record (Juntunen, 1988a, p. 88). Carried along by the media static, Finnish speed metal became a national trend. Between 1988 and 1989, albums were released by groups such as A.R.G., Dirty Damage, Dethrone, Warmath, and Necromancer.

The emergence of Finnish speed metal at the cusp of the 1980s and 1990s mirrored other Scandinavian metal awakenings. Heavy metal fandom had previously focused on foreign bands in other Nordic countries, with a few notable exceptions. In Sweden, a prolific death metal scene was developing in Gothenburg and Stockholm (Ekeroth, 2009), while the infamous and distinctive black metal subculture sprang up in Norway (Beste, 2008).

Compared to that of its immediate neighbors, extreme metal in Finland was, however, more mainstream. While the Swedish death metal enthusiasts formed a distinctive subculture (Ekeroth, 2009) and the Norwegian black metal scene was the focus of a mediated moral panic (Christe, 2004, pp. 318–320; Dunn, 2005), the Finnish speed metal bands immediately made it onto the pages of the largest rock magazines, even the mainstream media.

From the outset, speed metal interested journalists as both a musical and commercial phenomenon. The media was forecasting speed metal to become the first real export success of Finnish metal. Stone and Airdash became something of a subject for national pride with entry into the lucrative American market seen as only a matter of time (Juntunen, 1988a, 1988b). Stone also received contract proposals from two foreign record companies, which was widely covered in the Finnish media (e.g., Kemppainen, 1988a). In the way that thrash contributed to the wider public acceptance of metal music in the United States, the Finnish form of speed metal with Stone as its pioneer turned the same trick in the Finnish media context.

Despite the importance for public acceptance of metal in Finland, speed (or thrash) metal was not seen as something that could represent Finnish music culture as such. For example, Stone themselves did not have any desire to be marked as a Finnish band. The band's appearance in jeans and sneakers and their angular Jackson guitars was borrowed directly from their American thrash metal peers. Influences were not hidden in the music either. The musicians themselves were also understating the symbolic value of their home country. Jiri Jalkanen of Stone stated in an interview: 'Yes, speed can rescue Finnish rock. Finnishness is what pisses me off in our rock; all the bands are trying to be so special and Finnish' (Kemppainen, 1988b, p. 62). Stone was regarded as more modern and more genre-conscious and had more street credibility compared to the earlier Finnish heavy metal bands. In other words, Stone was 'international'.

The speed metal excitement faded out as quickly as it was born. The markets dried up; indeed, thrash proved to be a rather short-lived trend in the international market. Many of the commercially most successful thrash bands, like Metallica and Megadeth, distanced themselves from their extreme metal roots in the early 1990s, the former reaching massive popularity with their more mainstream 'hard rock' sound (Sharpe-Young, 2007, pp. 241, 255–256). At the same time, a new genre called grunge swarmed from Seattle all around the world, killing the popularity of many heavy metal groups in record time.

Despite the expectations, the dreams of world conquest of Finnish speed metal bands were washed away. However, the decomposition of Stone in 1991 was still very big news in the Finnish media. The position of the band as the biggest name in Finnish metal led one interviewer to ask: 'Does Stone's termination mean that metal disappears from Finland?' (Juntunen, 1992, p. 42). Certainly, after this failure to export home-grown speed metal, the media again lost interest in Finnish metal.

Second Wave

In the 1990s, the extreme metal scene started to generate new unconventional styles as a counterforce to mainstream metal; novel forms of death and black metal started to develop, marking a notable change in the metal sound as the traditional 'clean' singing was widely replaced by growling styles and an overall darker timbre (Christe, 2004, pp. 261–264, 272–273).

The new metal directions quickly found a foothold in Finland. For example, the demo plots of *Rumba* from the years 1992 and 1993 record an increasing number of death metal bands. Unlike Stone and their contemporaries, who in their early career gained big headlines without much merit, the new Finnish death metal bands received very little attention. Neither were domestic record companies interested. Many new metal bands therefore signed recording contracts with foreign companies, and most of them had released their first records before the Finnish media had even noticed a new phenomenon was being created. Of the new pioneers, Sentenced recorded for the French Thrash label, Amorphis for Relapse America, and Impaled Nazarene for the Italian label, Nosferatu.

Finnish Death Metal

Perhaps partly because of this arguably forced internationalization, the demand for Finnish metal started to slowly develop among metal fans in foreign markets. And following initial ignorance, the domestic rock media started to regard death metal as the 'next wave' of Finnish metal. For instance, *Rumba* reported on Finnish death metal comprehensively with two extensive features, one of them titled 'Death Metal—Finland's best export hope?' (Österman, 1992, 1993b). The highest hopes were directed toward Amorphis and Sentenced.

Interestingly, 1990s Finnish metal, compared to its predecessors, became much more nationally romantic in its orientation (especially in lyrics, sound, and imagery) and emblematically more Finnish. While Stone and others had borrowed aesthetics directly from the US, the themes and aesthetics of death metal bands more generally highlighted their Finnish origins. Amorphis, for example, adopted the mythology of the *Kalevala* (the Finnish national epic) for its lyrics and also included a lot of folk music influences in its sound. The band's second album, *Tales from the Thousand Lakes* (1994), became a milestone of the new wave of Finnish heavy metal, not least for its name and signature sound. Sentenced, in turn, imbued its lyrics with a certain Slavic melancholy and a type of self-destructive romanticism, which was often described as 'very Finnish' in its mood.

Media critics, who had once been worried about American influences, welcomed these references to national traditions and the romanticized Finnish melancholy, while the growing international success of Amorphis and Sentenced was remarked upon as a significant national achievement. Metal, which had previously been seen as representing an American mass culture or 'absurd devil worship' (Wallenius, 1988), began to be regarded as one of the most *authentically* Finnish popular music styles.

This symbolic change marked a fundamental shift in the export scene as well. It seemed that Finnish metal started to locate its own specific heritage. In the same way as was done in Finnish speed metal a few years earlier, Finnish death metal was treated as an original and unique musical phenomenon, something other than ordinary death metal.

Alternative Winds

Unlike in the previous decade, heavy metal trends in the 1990s were not translating into mainstream popularity; death and black metal bands, despite some initial promise, did not achieve a significant commercial breakthrough. Christe (2004) goes so far as to describe the years from the mid-1990s onwards as an 'anti-metal period' (p. 353). Nevertheless, in addition to a few commercial giants like Metallica, many successful rock bands adopted metal ingredients into their sound. For example, the North American bands, Faith No More, Red Hot Chili Peppers, and Extreme drew openly from traditional metal sources but mixed them with other pop and rock styles, leading to a plethora of new titles: funk metal, alternative metal, avant-garde metal, and others (Christe, 2004, pp. 248, 261, 295).

Finland also had its candidate for this alternative metal scene: Waltari. The band combined a heavy metal style quite freely with other music genres, like disco and prog rock. The reception of Finnish rock media was once again enthusiastic about the commercial possibilities abroad, especially after the release of the second album *Torcha!* (1992), 'Waltari has already one foot abroad and there are no obstacles—at least not reasonable sounding ones—for breaking into a broader consciousness' (Eerola, 1992, p. 21). The foreign press was also writing favorable reviews: for example, the influential European rock magazines *Metal Hammer* (UK) and *Rock Hard* (Germany) chose *Torcha!* as their CD of the month (Jortikka, 1992). The band's tours in Central Europe were also building the reputation of the band as the primary representative of Finnish musical export. The following albums increased the band's success, and it was no surprise that a *Soundi* headline announced: 'Waltari is now Finland's number one band' (1–2/1996). Although the band never managed to fully break into international markets, its success earned its members the reputation of 'pioneers' of Finnish metal (Tuomola, 2011).

Although Waltari's musical influences were taken from the world of popular music in general, the band very clearly defined itself and its music as Finnish. Like Amorphis and Sentenced before it, Waltari repeatedly made its Finnish roots visible in both its music and external rhetoric. 'In every album we must show that we are Finnish—not Americans, or anything else, but exactly Finnish', the band leader Kärtsy Hatakka announced in an interview (Eerola, 1997).

In the globalizing world of the 1990s, Finnish popular music that aimed at foreign markets was largely expected to represent the *right kind* of national identity. In the media, internationalization, and globalization often appeared as a threat to Finnish culture, so that bands that were seen to be sticking to special Finnish characteristics were seen in a positive light. In many ways, Waltari represented the Finnish cultural ideals reflected in the rock press. The band was proudly Finnish, really original, and aimed at internationalization.

The Finnishness of the 1990s Finnish Metal

With many new entrants in the 1990s, Finnish metal became an increasingly well-known phenomenon. In retrospect, it seems that the latter part of the decade was the crucial period in which the key elements of the symbolic narrative of Finnish metal were established: its local characteristics and claim to uniqueness. In the domestic media the belief in the possibilities of Finnish metal was strong; articles were written about the 'the shiny image' (Österman, 1995, p. 67) and the high level of skill (Österman, 1994) of Finnish metal bands.

Extreme metal seemed to offer a fertile breeding ground for the internationalization of Finnish music based on a different model. Bands could not build their popularity on expensive music videos or technically polished recordings. Also, the role of media was decreasing within the scene, leading new bands not to rely on media exposure as a way of gaining visibility but to seek out new ways of gaining the attention of metal fans in rapidly globalizing 'underground' markets. The best way to achieve this was to appear to be unique. In extreme metal, obscure and unique representations were actively sought out (Kahn-Harris, 2007, p. 5) and distinct death metal from an unknown country, the peripheral Finland, may have provided just the right cocktail of exoticism and familiarity for international ears.

The influences of local mythologies and folk cultures seemed to rise to the surface in many other countries, too. A type of romantic nationalism seemed to become characteristic of the Scandinavian metal culture (Kahn-Harris, 2007, p. 132). For instance, Norwegian black metal was founded on national traditions and glorification of a pre-Christian culture (Christe, 2004, p. 318).

The Troublesome Stratovarius

Despite the overall enthusiasm, the rock media of the 1990s was not treating all Finnish metal bands well. In particular, the power metal group Stratovarius, which would later be viewed as an indisputable pioneer of Finnish metal abroad, received rather negative treatment in the early years of the band's career. Stratovarius was regularly criticized as representing a too-clinical and sterile type of metal, a sort of traditional metal style that was destined to fall into unpopularity. Also, the neo-classical influences and the melodic songs of the band seemed to be difficult to digest during the turmoil of Stone and Finnish speed, while the 1990s focus on alternative music and death metal did not favor Stratovarius either. In addition, the visible lack of Finnish cultural characteristics in the representation of Stratovarius was perhaps a key factor. Unlike Amorphis, Sentenced, or Waltari, Stratovarius appeared as a purely commercial product in the eyes of the Finnish media. Without a national character, such commercialism was less legitimate.

Stratovarius, however, started to gain growing interest abroad, especially in Japan, in the first half of the 1990s. The success in Japan, though, and other 'less important' countries, was not much appreciated at home. Anglo-American influences were still dominating the music field and the U.K. and the United States were considered as the main market objectives for many bands. Even Germany and Central Europe, the first and main markets for many Finnish pioneers, were treated with less enthusiasm. Yet these were precisely the markets in which Stratovarius found a steady following, becoming an early name in the newly emerging scene of melodic 'power metal'. This genre was strongly localized as a continental European phenomenon (Dunn, 2005, 2011).

Stratovarius thus did not fit the image of Finnish metal that the media wanted to present for quite a long time. But the 1996 record *Episode* seemed to mark a turning point. At this point, Stratovarius had already sold hundreds of thousands of albums abroad, making the band probably the most successful export in Finnish music history up to that time. The album release was reported in *Soundi* with the headline 'Finland is a heavy metal country and we have a dream band' (Juntunen, 1996). The media that previously had dismissed the band began now to build Stratovarius as a visible phenomenon and the attention paid off: Stratovarius was ranked in the top four in all categories in the annual vote by *Soundi* in both 1998 and 1999 (*Soundi*, 1–2/1999, *Soundi* 1–2/2000). Stratovarius became the most reported band in Finnish metal in the second part of the 1990s.

Interestingly, as it became harder for the music press to ignore the band, attempts were made to legitimize the band's music as a cultural marker. Instead of folk music references that marked the cultural significance of Finnish death metal bands, part of the value of the 'neo-classical' Stratovarius was seen through its musical influences. In many articles and reviews, the band's technical wizardry, internationalism, and musical expertise were praised.

Breakthrough and Growth

At the turn of the millennium, the Finnish economy was experiencing an upsurge after a hard recession, which was also reflected in the rapid growth of music exports: the total value of Finnish music exports increased from four million to 12 million euros between 1999 and 2001 (Mäkelä, 2011, p. 206), a growth mainly generated by new artists. The biggest commercial success and international visibility was achieved by the dance music artists

Bomfunk MC with the hit 'Freestyler' (1999) and Darude with the 1999 'Sandstorm' single, but the general attitude that Finnish artists could conquer foreign markets was strongly held by heavy metal acts, too.

In the first years of the new millennium, numerous 'new' Finnish heavy metal bands, such as Children of Bodom, HIM, Nightwish, Apocalyptica, and Sonata Arctica started to become increasingly well known in the global metal community. All of these bands had been established during the aftermath of the second wave of Finnish metal in the latter part of the 1990s, the band members representing the new younger generation that had grown up in a more globalized music world where the Finns were already seen as offering something unique and credible.

Along with the international breakthrough, the requirements for the strong representations of the Finnish culture seemed to be loosening. Instead, attention was focused on bands' technical mastery and growing international expertise. Finland had by then redeemed its status as a credible and unique metal country, and now it was time to become more universal again—and also shamelessly accept commercialism as part of internationalization.

Through this growth, the belief in the possibilities of Finnish music export was strengthened; internationalization became a natural and logical career step for Finnish metal bands and usually occurred at an early stage. The style of press reporting also became overtly positive, and the impact of the pioneers on the development of the scene was strongly acknowledged. For example, Stratovarius functioned as a reference point when the success potential of the new entrants was discussed (e.g., Kiiski, 1998; Juntunen, 1998).

Nightwish, Children of Bodom, and HIM, in particular, started to achieve strong chart positions in different countries, regular appearances in foreign music magazines, and world tours playing to large audiences. This international success also impacted on the local scene, and metal broke into the mainstream. During this decade, Finland became one of the leading countries, if not *the* leading country, of heavy metal based on the number of metal bands per capita (Rossi & Emmerentze Jervell, 2013).

The 'heavy metal boom' in Finland—that emerged most strongly in the latter part of the 2000s—was born not only out of the bands' increasing popularity, but also by metal spreading to new areas; in addition to the music press, the bands and their members received attention across the whole media spectrum: from TV to tabloids and general magazines.

A sort of a peak was reached after Lordi's sensational victory at the Eurovision Song Contest in 2006. The winning song 'Hard Rock Hallelujah' not only brought Finnish heavy metal music into the consciousness of the general public in many new European nations, it also caused a media storm and public following in Finland. It even provoked the current President and Prime Minister to openly promote the importance of heavy metal music for the country's economy. At this point, seemingly, metal and hard rock became 'officially validated' as *the* Finnish export par excellence, as the fit between heavy metal and Finnish culture was nationally acknowledged.

The 'golden era' of Finnish metal that followed from this point, characterized by a variety of bands and styles gaining success in international markets, would require its own lengthy chapter.

The Narrated 'Canon' of Finnish Metal

The historical trajectory of Finnish metal, as described in this chapter, has consisted of a continuous balancing between international expectations and cultural ideologies sustained by the media. Alongside the internationalization, the media—together with the bands, industry practitioners, and fans—has upheld a cultural discourse that seeks to canonize Finnish metal as something unique.

National characteristics were undervalued in the first era of Finnish metal, but during the growth of 1990s and 2000s echoes of the distant folk traditions and the symbolics of national myths were positioned at the core of the narrative. This did not of course concern all the bands of the scene, but the brand of Finnish metal started to form a more consistent shape. Originally, the main intention was perhaps to battle against the Anglo-American mainstream offerings, but the identification became newly valued along with the strong globalization and trans-culturalization of the music field, particularly within metal. The country of origin and national narratives became another means of differentiation in the tight race for international visibility.

In this discourse, the narrative of Finnish metal is characterized by its romanticized origins and high level of collaborative spirit. In the writings and discussions of Finnish modern metal, the bands and musicians are presented as a firm collective community, and the music itself as expressing, in one way or another, how it stems from Finnish culture, its close relation to nature, and the specific mental characteristics of the Finnish nation. In sum, from our research, combining various sources (such as Juntunen, 2004, pp. 15–17; Kuusniemi, 2009; Nikula, 2002, pp. 6–7, 14; Riekki, 2004, pp. 139–142, 2007; Tuomola, 2007, p. 61; Schildt, 2011) the main claims of the specificity of the 'canon' of Finnish metal allow us to assert that:

- Finnish metal is unique and original.
- Finnish Metal has an essential connection to Finnish folk music and traditional culture.
- Finnish metal represents the Finnish mental landscape (esp. the stereotypes of melancholy, gloominess, sorrow).
- The popularity of Finnish metal is based on its high technical quality and the diligence of the bands' work ethic.
- Finnish metal bands are generally more skilled and proficient than those from other countries.
- The Finnish metal scene forms a strong community: musicians and other actors support each other a lot.

Overall, this narrated picture of Finnish metal seems to be very harmonious and romantic and constantly repeated by the community members. In the international context, this collaboration appears as a form of 'tribal marketing' with an objective to reinforce the Finnish national image (Karjalainen, 2014). The emblematic identity painted of the Finnish metal field is very professional and polished.

The narrated discourse reflects the internal aspirations of the media; the narrative is constructed so that it supports the current situation (Jokinen et al., 1993, p. 68) in which Finnish heavy music is a success story. As a matter of fact, however, the leading bands of the breakthrough era have made a claim to uniqueness, which is a rather plausible aspect for the media to embrace: Nightwish was a pioneer of symphonic metal, HIM created its own 'love metal' niche, Apocalyptica's cello concept was exquisite, and so forth. Moreover, the reputation of skilled and hard-working craftsmen has been attached to Children of Bodom; the band's musical skills and technical virtuosity is generally praised (e.g., Säynekoski, 1997b; Mattila, 2003). Aleksi Laiho, the leader of the band, achieved a position of acknowledged 'guitar hero', his face and skills covered in numerous music and guitar magazines all over the world.

Conclusions

In the current situation, the position of heavy metal as *the* Finnish mainstream cultural form is somewhat unique. While metal has traditionally held a subcultural position in most countries (Weinstein, 1991; Walser, 1993; Kahn-Harris, 2007), the genre has reached listeners in nearly all age and population groups in Finland. As a consequence, metal fandom does not take the same form or support the same sorts of oppositional identities as it does elsewhere. For example, the emphasis on rebellion or anti-commercialism has less importance in the Finnish context. The open commercialism of, for example, HIM and Nightwish (Lukkarinen, 2006, p. 61) is not just considered as being *evil*; at least it is dealt with humorously. The fact that metal is not only listened to by rebellious youth, but also by children, their parents, and many others appears not to be a significant problem for the credibility of bands. As stated by Children of Bodom's Alexi Laiho, Finland is the only country in the world where one can see 'six year old fans passing by in the city with their Bodom reaper shirts on' (Juntunen, 2007, p. 109).

As we have shown, this mainstream status did not develop overnight. This development though is probably unique due to the positioning of Finland in the political and cultural world. Over the period, national specificity and originality claims have been included and excluded in media discourse, either to oppose or embrace internationalization. It follows that the changes in the discourse of metal we have narrated have reflected international trends as well as cultural policy, both in Finland and abroad.

Commerciality has been closely connected, in one way or another, with the concept of the heavy metal phenomenon during its entire lifetime. The attitudes toward commercial representations, however, have varied over time. The line between the commercial (banal) and authentic (good) style in metal has been continuously defined and re-defined in an uninterrupted process. The 1980s thrash metal managed to profile a heavy rock as more intellectual yet rebellious music, which seemed to resolve the ever-present dilemma of artistic credibility and commercial potential. Stone and other representatives of Finnish speed metal were seen in this light. Similarly, the early 1990s bands Sentenced, Amorphis and Waltari were authentic enough for press acceptance, thanks to their claimed Finnish characteristics that were considered also commercially interesting. The bands highlighted Finnish identity and created new export expectations in the eyes of the media.

Now, in 2014, it is easy to see that the contribution of both the pioneers of Finnish metal and the subsequent bigger success stories have been highly significant in terms of promoting the 'brand image' of Finland. In our studies of Finnish metal bands and their fans, as well as the wider metal community, we have observed that the Finnish background of a band is almost without exception an issue of interest for the foreign fan. Hence, metal seems to function as an important representation of Finland's national popular culture.

In some cases, successful bands act as cultural ambassadors of Finland on a larger stage, whether they do it deliberately or not. In June 2013, an article in the *Wall Street Journal* (Rossi & Emmerentze Jervell, 2013) reported on a number of university students in different countries who were enthusiastic about Finnish and the other Nordic heavy metal bands, leading them to take up the study of Nordic languages. Finnish metal exports also appear to encourage tourism, academic research exchanges, and business opportunities to the country.

In this study, we have mainly focused on the commercially significant mainstream of Finnish metal, for good reason. But outside the mainstream, there exist vibrant metal subcultures with bands that are scarcely reported in the media, and for the members of these subcultures the commercial success of 'mainstream' metal or the national representations of it are not key components of their discourses.

Notes

1. This canonization process is also discussed in Kärjä (2006) and Karjalainen (2014). It is noteworthy that such a universal narrative may be generally and stereotypically valid, but it is also rather banal considering the multitude of different metal subgenres and representations that stem from the country, many of which do not readily fall under these characteristics.
2. Some sources, such as the late *Suosikki* magazine, which was extremely popular among young readers in the 1980s is not included in our analysis due to budget limitations. This and additional sources would have undoubtedly brought more

depth, perhaps even some divergence to our analysis, but they are left to discover for future research.
3. Hanoi Rocks was even awarded the 'Golden God for Inspiration' in the 2014 Metal Hammer Awards.

Bibliography

Beste, P. (2008). *True Norwegian death metal*. New York: Vice Books.
Bruun, S., Lindfors, J., Luoto, S., & Salo, M. (1998). *Suomalaisen rockin historia - jeejeejee*. Porvoo: WS Bookwell.
Christe, I. (2004). *Pedon meteli—Heavy metallin uusi ja vanha testamentti*. Helsinki: Johnny Kniga.
Dunn, S. (Dir.). (2005). *Metal: A headbanger's journey* (movie). Toronto: Banger Films.
Dunn, S. (Dir.). (2011). *Metal evolution* (tv-series). Toronto: Banger Films.
Eerola, H. (1992). Waltari: Torcha! (record review). *Rumba*, 18, 21.
Eerola, H. (1997). Waltari: Taivas yksin tietää. *Rumba*, 6, 19–20.
Ekeroth, D. (2008). *Swedish death metal*. New York: Bazillion Points Books.
Fairclough, N. (1997 [1995]). *Miten media puhuu*. Tampere: Vastapaino.
Jalonen, M. (2009). 'Mootorilintu Sarcofagissa' http://tv2.yle.fi/juttuarkisto/kakkonen/kertoo/moottorilintu-sarkofagissa (accessed April 2, 2014).
Jokinen, A., Juhila, K., & Suoninen, E. (1993). *Diskurssianalyysin aakkoset*. Jyväskylä: Gummerus.
Jortikka, J. (1992). Tanssi yli hautojen. *Soundi*, 6, 59.
Juntunen, J. (1980). Sarcofagus—Suomen ensimmäinen heavy-bändi? *Soundi*, 2, 14–15.
Juntunen, J. (1986a). Zero Nine ja muut hevihirviöt. *Soundi*, 8, 104–110.
Juntunen, J. (1986b). Heavy rämisee Suomessa. *Soundi*, 11, 54–55.
Juntunen, J. (1988a). Stone: Stone (record review). *Soundi*, 3, 88.
Juntunen, J. (1988b). Hei me lavasukelletaan! *Soundi*, 11, 32–33.
Juntunen, J. (1992). Hei Hei Hevirämpytykselle! *Soundi*, 18, 42–43.
Juntunen, J. (1996). Suomi on hevimaa ja meillä on unelmabändi—Huippumuusikot liittyvät Stratovariukseen. *Soundi*, 5, 90–94.
Juntunen, J. (1998). Viikatemiehen paluu. Children of Bodom kutsuu telttaretkelle. *Soundi*, 4, 58–60.
Juntunen, J. (2004). Raskas metalli. In P. Gronow, J. Lindfors, & J. Nyman (Eds.), *Suomi soi 2: Rautalangasta hiphoppiin* (pp. 164–179). Hämeenlinna: Tammi.
Juntunen, J. (2007). Suomi, Suloinen hevimaa. *Soundi*, 5, 108–112.
Kahn-Harris, K. (2007). *Extreme metal: Music and culture on the edge*. Oxford: Berg.
Kärjä, A-V. (2006). A prescribed alternative mainstream: Popular music and canon formation. *Popular Music*, 25/1.
Karjalainen, T-M. (2014). Thrashing tribe in Tokyo: A story about Finnish metal and cultural export. In T-M. Karjalainen, M. J. Lehtonen, & J. Niipola (Eds.), *The playing Finn—Stories on successful game development and music export* (pp. 123–174). Helsinki: Talentum.
Kemppainen, H. (1988a). Arvotaan seuraava suuri hittibändi. *Soundi*, 4, 78–79.
Kemppainen, H. (1988b). Melkein sata asiaa speed metallista, jotka olet aina halunnut tietää mutta olet ollut liian arka hypätäksesi lavalta. *Rumba*, 4, 56–62.
Kiiski, J. (1998). Nightwish—hevimiehet ja klassinen nainen. *Rumba*, 3, 13.

Kuusniemi, K. (Dir.). (2009). *Promised land of heavy metal* (film). Double Vision Ltd.
Lukkarinen, I. (2006). *Metallimusiikki paperilla—Diskurssianalyysi Juho Juntusen artikkelista raskas metalli* Jyväskylä: Jyväskylän yliopiston musiikin laitos.
Mäkelä, J. (2011). *Kansainvälisen populaarimusiikin historiaa*. Vaasa: Paino Oy Fram Ab.
Martin, L., & Segrave, K. (1988) *Anti-rock: The opposition to rock 'n' roll*. Hamden, CT: Archon Books.
Mattila, A. (2003). Children of Bodom: Hate crew deathroll (record review). http://www.soundi.fi/levyarviot/children-bodom-hate-crew-deathroll (accessed March 2, 2014).
Mattila, Z. (1983). Metallica—Kill 'em all (record review). http://www.rumba.fi/arviot/millaisen-vastaanoton-metallican-esikoisalbumi-sairumbassa-30-vuotta-sitten (accessed February 15, 2014).
Mattila, Z. (1994). Amorphis: Tales from the Thousand Lakes (record review). *Rumba*, 11, 25.
Nikula, J. (2002). *Rauta-aika—Suomi-metallin historia 1988–2002*. Porvoo: WS Bookwell.
O'Flynn, J. (2007). National identity and music in transition: Issues of authenticity in a global setting. In I. Biddle & V. Knights (Eds.), *Music, national identity and the politics of location* (pp. 1–15). Farnham, UK: Ashgate.
Österman, N. (1992). Kuolemaa juoksuhaudoissa. *Rumba*, 16, 10–11.
Österman, N. (1993a). Nallen oma nurkka. *Rumba*, 4, 12.
Österman, N. (1993b). Kalmametallin vientinimet, osa 2. *Rumba*, 6, 14–15.
Österman, N. (1994). Amorphiksella on kysyntää. *Rumba*, 17, 5.
Österman, N. (1995). Sentenced—Amok (record review). *Rumba*, 1, 67.
Pillsbury, G. T. (2006). *Damage incorporated: Metallica and the production of Musical identity*. New York: Routledge. Taylor & Francis group.
Riekki, M. (2004). From the Smithy of Ilmarinen. Kalevala and heavy metal. In J. Jaakkola and A. Toivonen (Eds.), *Inspired by tradition: Kalevala poetry in Finnish music*. Jyväskylä: Gummerus.
Riekki, M. (2007). It's so heavy to be a Finn. http://www.fimic.fi/fimic/fimic.nsf/0/127FF4006117DF3FC2257506004DC9C9?open document&cat=popular_music (accessed March 4, 2012).
Rossi, J., & Emmerentze Jervell, E. (2013). To really understand the language, it helps to know Hevibändi. *Wall Street Journal* http:online.wsj.com/article/SB10001424127887323855804578511381869336080.htm (accessed January 14, 2014).
Säynekoski, M. (1997a). HIM: Me ollaan parempia kuin. Marilyn Manson. *Soundi*, 11, 70–71.
Säynekoski, M. (1997b). Children of Bodom—Something wild (record review). *Soundi*, 11, 80.
Schildt, S. (2011). Soundi.fi 21.9.2011: Suomalaisen metallin tulevaisuus http://www.soundi.fi/jutut/suomalaisen-metallin-tulevaisuus (accessed April 2, 2014).
Sharpe-Young, G. (2007). *Metal: The definitive guide*. New York: Jawbone Press.
Soundi, 2/1980 (no author details). Sarcofagus: Cycle of Life (advertisement), 13.
Soundi 4/1984 (no author details). LP-lista, 14.
Soundi 9/1984 (no author details). Pakkanen tulee ja meistä kuuroja, 14–15.
Soundi 1–2/1996 (no author details). Vuosiäänestys 1996, 74–78.
Soundi 1–2/1999 (no author details). Vuosiäänestys 1998, 12–17.
Soundi 1–2/2000 (no author details). Vuosiäänestys 1999, 12–17.

Tuomola, P. (2007). *Ari Koivunen: Karaokebaareista hevilavoille.* Helsinki: Johnny Kniga.
Tuomola, P. (2011). *Waltari: Suomimetallin pioneerit* Helsinki: Like.
Wallach, J., Berger, H. M., and Greene, P. D. (2011). *Metal rules the globe—Heavy metal music around the world.* Durham, NC: Duke University Press.
Wallenius, W. (1986). Peer Günt—Backseat (record review). *Soundi,* 6, 68.
Wallenius, W. (1988). Eri revittäjiä: Heviii … (Niinsanottu pläjäys) (lrecord). *Rumba,* 2, 68–69.
Walser, R. (1993). *Running with the devil: Power, gender and madness in heavy metal Music.* Hanover, NH: Wesleyan University Press.
Weinstein, D. (1991) *Heavy metal: A cultural sociology.* New York: Lexington Books.
Yle. (2006).HIM myi kultaa Yhdysvalloissa: http://www.yle.fi/elavaarkisto/artikkelit/him_myi_kultaa_yhdysvalloissa_15720.html# media=15723 (accessed January 15, 2014).

13 Death Symbolism in Metal Jewelry
Circuits of Consumption from Subculture to the High Street

Claire Barratt

Death symbolism has been an enduring visible theme in the material and visual culture of heavy metal and its various related genres for several decades. Musicians and fans frequently wear jewelry incorporating the same long-established visual references to death, particularly skulls and skeletal imagery. Some makers and retailers of this type of jewelry, such as Alchemy and The Great Frog, have explicit links with a metal audience, advertising regularly in metal magazines or publicizing their famous musician clients. However, in recent years there has also been a notable increase in varieties of jewelry based on the same death symbolism (mainly skulls) within various other sectors of the fashion and jewelry industries, aimed at a mainstream customer rather than a metal audience. Examples of skull rings can be found variously within high-end luxury 'fine' jewelry ranges (such as Theo Fennell), avant-garde fashion like Alexander McQueen, and at the lower end of the price spectrum they have been available from high street fashion chains such as Top Shop and 'mass market' UK catalogue retailers Argos using non-precious materials. In addition, skull jewelry can frequently be seen adorning people completely unconnected with the metal subculture.

This chapter explores—through historical and contextual analysis and via two case studies of contemporary makers and suppliers—how such items remain desirable and relevant within metal culture and questions what makes an item of skull jewelry 'metal' when similar items are also widely available in an increasing range of mainstream jewelry retailers or worn by people who do not fit the 'metalhead' image. When an aspect of subcultural style becomes increasingly incorporated into mainstream culture but simultaneously remains central to the original subculture, then it suggests a complex relationship in which both are intertwined to some degree, continuously evolving, but also embedded within broader contexts of consumption (Hodkinson, 2002; Brown, 2007). As is well known, classic work from the Birmingham Centre for Contemporary Cultural Studies (CCCS) viewed commercial commodities adopted by subcultures and creatively re-used in an alternative way as a means to produce frequently subversive new meanings and cultural identities within their new cultural context, via a process of stylistic bricolage (Hall and Jefferson, 1976; Willis, 1978; Hebdige, 1979). Within this model, re-worked commodities would later become incorporated back into the mainstream in order to manage and neuter any new potentially rebellious connotations—a process from subversion to incorporation—that is ultimately 'a romantic story with a tragic ending' for youthful rebellion (Beezer, 1992, p. 112). Theorists such as Thornton (1997, p. 116) and McRobbie (1989, p. 36; 1994, p. 161) have challenged the tendency of earlier work to see subcultures as oppositional, arguing that they did not take into account the way subculturists frequently engaged in entrepreneurial activities and used the media and commerce in positive ways, rather than regarding this, for example as Hebdige (1979, p. 96) did, as 'selling out' and signifying the end of the subculture's authenticity through its commercial engagement with the dominant culture. Alternatively, Brown (2007) suggests that rather than viewing commerce and subcultural value as mutually exclusive, subcultural commodities can be regarded as commercially mediated artefacts that acquire meaning through a more complex set of cultural relationships of production, distribution, and consumption.

In this chapter, I adopt an object-focused approach used within contemporary fashion studies (see Steele, 1998; Breward, 1998) that shifts the primary perspective from the subculture (metal) and its participants to items of jewelry. I also draw on material from interviews I conducted with jewelry makers and retailers since 1995.[1] This gives an opportunity to examine specific items of jewelry within differing markets of consumption and locates them in relation to changes within the wider culture, rather than emphasizing them as oppositional or completely separate from mainstream styles of jewelry. Thus, selected examples of jewelry are used to illustrate transitions between mainstream *mourning* jewelry in historical funerary practice, via oppositional but non-commercialized use within early subcultural style, to forming part of a niche subcultural market that overlaps with mainstream fashion in the early 21st century. This highlights continuing questions about definitions of what subcultural style actually is (cf. Hall and Jefferson, 2006; McRobbie, 1989) when elements of that style appear within mainstream fashion and explores how the apparent commercialization of once oppositional styles may influence other aspects of the design, retail, and use of this jewelry.

Early Metal Style and Jewelry

Skulls seem to be synonymous with metal style. They are frequently seen in the dress of both metal fans and musicians and regularly appear on jewelry (Weinstein, 2000, p. 128). They feature on products in music merchandise catalogues such as *EMP* and *Grindstore* who advertise in the metal press. These items give metal consumers an opportunity to 'express their dark side' by buying jewelry or the 'Rock Skulls' range of clothing 'for real metalheads… and those who want to become one!' (EMP, Summer 2014, p. 30).

However, skulls, along with more elaborate death symbolism, did not become widely associated with metal until the 1980s when this symbolism began to visibly emerge in significant quantities within subcultures and areas of avant-garde art and design (Barratt, 2010). Indeed, during the early post-war period it was not possible to buy jewelry featuring skulls and death symbolism because the market for it did not exist or at least no one was producing for it. The first and longest established makers and retailers of this type of jewelry in Britain emerged in the late 1960s and '70s. The Great Frog, based in London's Carnaby Street, emerged out of the '60s counterculture and began making silver skull rings on request from 1972, whereas Alchemy, a Leicester-based company, started producing similar items in pewter in 1977 during the first wave of punk. Before then, someone wanting a piece of jewelry like this had limited options: to design or commission an individual piece from a maker; to purchase an antique item previously made for now obsolete funerary or mourning rituals; or to re-use military insignia that featured skulls (which will be discussed in more detail below).

Early metal musicians can be seen in contemporary photographs and film footage wearing jewelry that was available to them during that period. For example, promotional photographs of Black Sabbath, and film footage of the band performing in the early 1970s, show Ozzy Osbourne wearing a chain around his neck, an item of jewelry commonly worn by men at that time. An alternative to wearing what was available on the high street was to innovate. Ozzy describes wearing a 'hot water tap on a piece of string' around his neck in the early Sabbath days (Osbourne, 2009, p. 102). This predates the subcultural re-use of domestic items not originally intended as jewelry by punks during the mid-1970s, in their adoption of safety pins and lavatory chains as jewelry (Hebdige, 1979). Other early photographs of Sabbath show them wearing very large silver colored crosses around their necks on pieces of string, which Ozzy's father made for them out of aluminum (Iommi, 2012, pp. 81–82). Although initially worn by the band to ward off the Satanists they had begun to attract, the aluminum crosses were subsequently made in larger numbers and sold at gigs to make a bit of money, showing some early entrepreneurialism (ibid.).

This illustrates how jewelry worn within a subcultural style is shaped by the wider context of jewelry consumption and what is available during the period in which it exists. This is further demonstrated by focusing on the changing use of the skull in jewelry within metal.

Post-War Bikers and the Death's Head

Weinstein's (2000, p. 101) argument that heavy metal style emerged as a hippy-biker hybrid during the late 1960s provides a potential route to explaining the adoption of death symbolism in jewelry within metal style. The earliest use of death symbolism in jewelry within subcultures in any notable quantity was in post-war biker culture, specifically the use of metal skulls or skull-and-crossbones insignia to decorate clothing as pin-on badges. The death's head symbol was used by Nazi SS officers during World War II to adorn their uniforms (see figs. 13.1 and 13.2). The skull was also used by the British 17/21st Lancer's Brigade army regiment as part of its uniform, with the addition of a pair of crossbones and the text 'Or Glory' beneath the skull—Death or Glory. These military insignia were appropriated and reused by bikers to decorate their jackets, with symbols including the Nazi swastika, the German Iron Cross, and the skull in various forms. Contemporary photographs of bikers from the 1950s show their jackets embellished with World War II Nazi regalia, including metal death's heads (Farren, 1985; Stuart, 1987).

In Britain domestic production had been focused on supporting the war, creating shortages of civilian goods including clothing, and in the immediate post-war period the rationing of goods continued, which shaped the emerging biker's or rocker's consumer choices. Army surplus goods from both Britain and a variety of other countries were purchased by British bikers who used army surplus equipment because it was good quality, was available, and was practical for riding a motorcycle (Clay, 1988). In the United States, bikers also made use of surplus military equipment including clothing and motorcycles, and it was common for motorcycle gangs to be seen wearing Nazi insignia (Phillips, 2005), possibly brought back as war souvenirs, as many bikers had served in the army.

Figure 13.1 Cap, Service Dress (General) Waffen-SS with White Metal Death's Head Badge, 1934. © IWM (UNI 411).

This is significant for two reasons: the source of the badges and the meaning of the symbolism. As jewelry, both types of badge were originally produced as integral features of military uniforms with specific meanings for the wearers, both British and German: they signified membership of particular military groups. Later in the post-war period, they were re-used in a non-military context by bikers in a cultural context that provided a different meaning not intended when these pieces were originally made and worn. None were manufactured by a third-party for a subcultural niche market, which provides a contrast with contemporary varieties of jewelry based on skulls. It also provides an early example of subcultural bricolage that pre-dates the teds, mods, skins, and punk.

Subcultural Consumption of Death Symbolism

For bikers to co-opt or appropriate death symbolism in the 1950s or early 1960s by re-using military insignia, whether Nazi or British, can be argued as oppositional in stylistic terms because of the nature of the symbolism and the cultural and historical context in which it happened. It was adopted and worn within a context that was unrelated to the way it had been used in widespread popular funerary and mourning rituals for hundreds of years prior to the 20th century. The accepted cultural meaning of the skull as a symbol of death on jewelry was to acknowledge one's mortality (as a *memento mori*) or in mourning jewelry as a visible commemoration of personal loss following bereavement. The decline of mainstream mourning ritual and its associated material culture during the early 20th century meant that the skull no longer symbolized mortality and mourning in the way it had done previously and was therefore 'available' for new interpretations following both the disappearance of a common mourning ritual and two world wars (Barratt, 2010, pp. 7–34).

There is always a risk of over-theorizing subcultural artefacts (Breward, 2004) and thereby adding to the 'crushing weight of late twentieth century cultural analysis' (p. 136) whereby teenage style deputizes (in a post-modern form) for the absence of more lucid modes of communication, attributing meanings to objects or practices up to a point where the people being studied would not necessarily recognize or agree with the resulting analysis. With post-war subcultures, it is less of an academic leap to attribute coherent musings on mortality to beatniks, in comparison to bikers, due to perceived variables such as level of formal education, social class, and literary interests (Beezer, 1992). However, McDonald-Walker (2000, p. 1) criticizes early academic studies of bikers by Willis (1978) and Cohen (1980) for their conclusions that such groups were stylistically outrageous but inarticulate, with no apparent capacity for coherent thought. The role of semiotic analysis as practiced by Hebdige (1979) in his analysis of the swastika in punk, was to compensate for this inarticulacy, while at the same time not requiring the validation of actual wearers. However, as later work has argued (Cohen, 1980, xii; Sabin, 1999, pp. 209–212), a symbol may

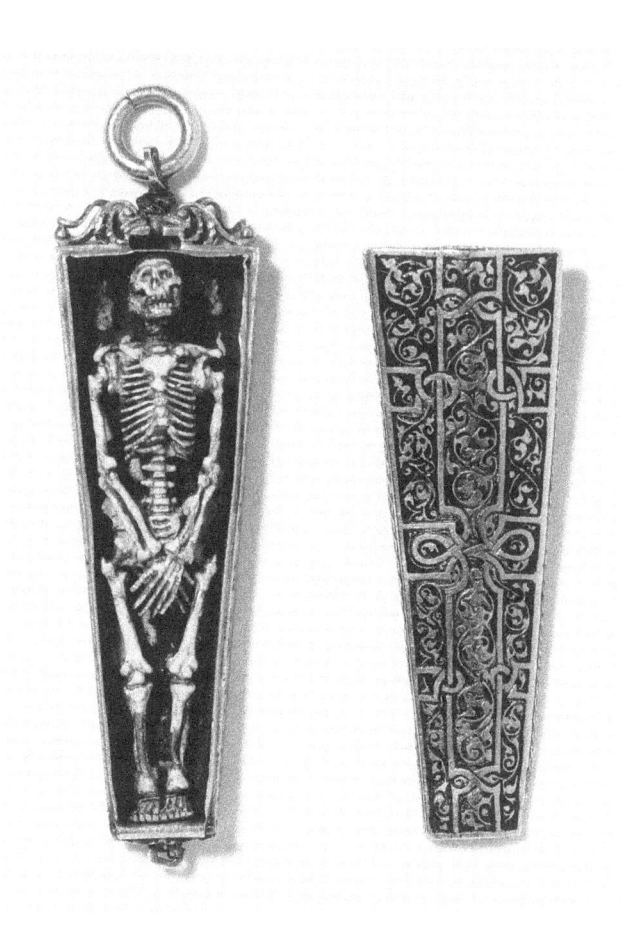

Figure 13.2 Torre Abbey Jewel, *Memento Mori* Pendant. Gold and Enamel. 1540–1550, England. © Victoria and Albert Museum, London.

Figure 13.3 Gold and Ruby *Memento Mori* Skull Ring. 1550–1575. European. © Victoria and Albert Museum, London.

have different meanings for different wearers as well as viewers if it is not reworked, but adopted intact. This suggests that assumptions derived only from a semiotic analysis, or suggesting a universal meaning for an aspect of subcultural style of dress, should be approached cautiously without supporting contextual evidence.

Regardless of the degree of meaning that can be attributed to skull jewelry, the actual practice of being a biker has explicit associations with death. Mcdonald-Walker (2000, p. 21) suggests that motorcycling has always been about risk awareness and personal assessment of potentially fatal accidents on the road, adding to the 'hedonistic image' associated with biking when confronting both a sense of mortality and of 'being alive'. Bikers confront their mortality through riding a fast motorbike, frequently in life-threatening situations, and at the same time have a 'heightened awareness' of 'living life' (McDonald-Walker, 2000, p. 22). In this context, a death's head seems an appropriate symbol to wear, although the form the jewelry takes is shaped by what was available during that period, as noted earlier.

The skull and crossbones, 'an age-old symbol of rebels and pirates', provides a visible reminder of death that may variously instill caution, act as a magic talisman, or challenge fate, as a mark of devil-may-care bravado (Stuart, 1987, p. 71). Farren (1985, p. 19) suggests that these types of insignia have always been popular with bike clubs, particularly Hell's Angels, who drew on the symbolism of darkness and power associated with the Nazis in the immediate post-war period in both Britain and the USA and were used to signify an element of 'unpleasantness' that provided 'a gauge of the collective degree of badness' (ibid.) of a club.

For death symbolism to become associated with metal style in later decades is unsurprising if it is accepted that a controversial image is an integral aspect of metal and that controversy is sometimes used intentionally by metal bands for commercial purposes and marketing, as suggested by Hjelm, Kahn-Harris, and LeVine (2013, pp. 2–5). However, this assumes that death symbolism is actually controversial and raises questions around variations in how it is depicted and the context of use.

Sam Dunn (2005) interviewed Alice Cooper for his documentary *Metal: A Headbanger's Journey* about the death symbolism in metal and related merchandise. Cooper, known for his use of gory, macabre, theatrical stage shows in which he sometimes pretended to behead babies, found the idea that the use of death symbolism in metal music could be considered in any way disturbing was slightly ridiculous. He compared the frequently low-budget horror-style graphics used in metal to Halloween imagery and asked how that could possibly be considered either scary or disturbing. This suggests that the interpretation and significance of established symbols such as the skull are not straightforward and unambiguous, but are culturally and historically specific.

Doom metal has long dwelt on the inevitability of mortality and decay, while representations of death, particularly explicit depictions of killing and mutilation, are common in the death metal genre (Kahn-Harris, 2007, pp. 34–36). Visually, the skull is either replaced by or combined with other more extreme depictions of death, suggesting that the skull as a representation of death is no longer sufficiently potent on its own. For some bands, such as the grindcore band Carcass, graphics on record sleeves and lyrics are frequently more visceral than a skull, based instead on a 'catalogue of bizarre and disgusting things that can happen to the human body' (op. cit., p. 35).

Although graphic images of death may change within metal genres and wider popular culture, increased viscerality does not translate very well into mass-produced jewelry, even for relatively small niche markets such as metal. Both designs and materials used have to be viable for either one-off designs or batch productions of a single design and in a variety of sizes, if the product is a ring. Jewelry is made to be worn and is usually purchased as a commercial product, with expectations of durability and longevity of wear, even if it is discarded in the future. These practical considerations influence aspects of the design, production, and retail of jewelry intended for a metal consumer and help to distinguish these ranges from more generic skull jewelry available on the high street aimed at a wider audience, whichever part of the price spectrum these items fall into.

Entrepreneurialism and Niche Markets

Several ranges of contemporary jewelry show a continuation of the previously cited biker examples in their use of symbols of death, particularly the skull. They also illustrate how these newer designs are more varied in ways that appear to delineate specialist markets (whether subcultural or mainstream) and show differences in each range of skull jewelry. Some are examples of collections aimed at a metal audience that illustrate how jewelry can be commercially produced but retain elements of 'subcultural capital', making them desirable within their niche market, despite looking superficially similar to an uninformed eye (i.e., also based on skulls). They are not the only examples of this type of jewelry available but are useful for discussion.[2] The following ranges occupy slightly different places in a niche subcultural market that exists outside the mainstream fashion and fine jewelry markets.

The Great Frog,[3] an independently owned jewelry shop in central London, was the first to make and sell skull-type jewelry. It sells mainly silver jewelry, sometimes set with semi-precious stones. It also makes jewelry to commission and alters any pieces to fit as required in its basement workshop on the premises. When it started up in business, there was no one else producing jewelry with deathly motifs, so it quickly gained a list of well-known customers for its specialist but niche products, including musicians such as Keith Richards of the Rolling Stones, famously photographed over several decades wearing a large silver skull ring. It is unusual from a contemporary mainstream marketing perspective in that it does not advertise, either for self-publicity or for retail, or print a glossy sales catalogue. However, word of mouth is an 'important component in the continual construction of the appearance, knowledge and tastes' of subcultural groups (Hodkinson, 2002, p. 98) and as Paterson Riley, proprietor of The Great Frog, pointed out, they don't need to advertise as people find them anyway. This suggests that it has a degree of status, whether 'cool' or otherwise, and has a reputation built up over many decades through word of mouth, rather than through advertising or high-profile media campaigns. It has become a stopping-off destination for musicians visiting London from other countries, and its informal gallery of photographs of well-known customers on its shop wall is accompanied by a list of names that constitutes a 'who's-who' of rock music history, from the above-mentioned Rolling Stones to Metallica and Motörhead. Customers receive personal service and a chat with the shop owners and staff and can have pieces altered to fit and purchase in the knowledge that they have the same taste in jewelry as rock and metal stars who also buy there.

These aspects of the way in which The Great Frog business is run can be regarded as contributing an element of value to its jewelry for the purchaser, which distinguishes it from mainstream ranges. 'Subcultural capital' can be conferred on an individual in ways that can be objectified in the products they consume to demonstrate a degree of 'hipness' or being 'in the know' (Thornton, 1997, pp. 202–203). While these values are not completely divorced from broader social values, they are specific to that group and located within complex niche value systems and distinctions of taste that do not convert easily into more conventional cultural or economic capital in the wider culture. Using this idea in relation to skull jewelry from The Great Frog, a customer may prefer to buy a silver skull ring from this shop because of its relative obscurity within mainstream jewelry (not everyone knows about it) and for its associations with the music world, which may, depending on individual tastes, also imbue an item with a degree of value in being able to wear exactly the same piece of jewelry as an admired rock star. This is not high status in conventional terms—celebrities such as David Beckham and Elton John display their economic wealth in their purchases from jewelers such as Theo Fennell, a London based fine jeweler who also makes skull jewelry and uses more expensive materials for his pieces, which cost thousands of pounds. These items of jewelry can be argued as being less attractive to a metal customer, even if they were affordable, because they do not have the long established associations with music and metal musicians The Great Frog has, an authenticity and heritage which is confirmed further within metal by collaborations with bands such as Motörhead and Anthrax on limited jewelry ranges.

As a business The Great Frog seems to have established itself firmly as an entrepreneurial success, emerging from a subculture to meet a growing demand for a very niche product—skull jewelry. Although it remains within that subcultural niche, it also overlaps with mainstream fashion as it is frequently asked to lend jewelry for photographic fashion shoots aimed at a mainstream rather than a metal audience. For example, in 2012 it did so for a UK edition of women's magazine *Elle*, on a shoot by Jan Welters. This suggests the possibility that when an aspect of subcultural style becomes used within mainstream fashion in some way, rather than becoming incorporated, subsumed or diffused, it may actually retain its subcultural authenticity as it this quality that is being 'conferred' within this changed context. Fashion commentator Caryn Franklin (2002) suggested that punk style has informed fashion at different levels since its inception in the mid-1970s, adding a touch of 'attitude' or 'edginess' to an otherwise ordinary garment by drawing on a range of design features now considered 'punk', such as fishnet, ripped and torn fabric, dayglo colors, or black leather. From this perspective, the use of The Great Frog skull jewelry in mainstream fashion shoots may be adding an element of metal 'attitude' to the styling, which it would not have gained if it had used diamond-studded skull jewelry worth thousands of pounds. This suggests that the relationship between a subculture and mainstream culture may be more complex than previously anticipated, when considering different cultures of consumption, rather than the straightforward commercial exploitation of a subculture by the mainstream.

Insider Knowledge and Entrepreneurialism

A degree of 'insider knowledge' is useful in the creation of jewelry designs that reflect the interests of a company's customers. This is more important for Alchemy, a company whose products are relatively low cost compared with The Great Frog in the materials used for its designs—pewter rather than silver—therefore needing a greater volume of sales and more variety in designs offered in order to be a viable business. Alchemy provides a level of detail and variety in its jewelry designs due to its in-depth knowledge of its customers' interests, which distinguishes the range from other skull-type jewelry available.

Examples from Alchemy's back catalogues of their product range (see figs 13.4 and 13.5) show part of its range of rings and neckwear, illustrating the variety of styles designed to appeal to either males or females within metal or goth culture. This illustrates a crossover between heavy metal and goth subcultures in music and style (Hodkinson, 2002, p. 57), which is also confirmed by the range of designs available. The imagery used moves between subcultural genres in the use of crosses, some more decorative than others, also incorporating skeletal symbolism, the pentagram, the raven, a Victorian cabinet of curiosities, and coffins and spiders and combining more elaborate, decorative Victorian gothic influences with traditional death symbolism, such as bones, coffins, and other *memento mori* iconography. Ranges are given names that refer to either historical or literary figures that address the target audience of both metal and goth fans, including references to Edgar Allen Poe, death, Satanism, Byron, Dee, Vikings, dragons, serpents, and vampire bats. The variety of detail in these pieces suggests a detailed knowledge of the potential customers, while the visual research for the range is informed by a selection of art history books containing death-related images.

This detail also distinguishes this jewelery from mainstream high street skull jewelry within a market defined more by price. UK catalogue retailer

Death Symbolism in Metal Jewelry 237

Argos has included generic skull rings resembling The Great Frog's in its jewelry range, but made from stainless steel, thus providing a very low cost way to obtain an aspect of metal style. In contrast, Alchemy provides a far more elaborate use of the skull and death-related imagery than generic skull pieces found within mainstream fashion. It also provides badges used by bikers during the post-war period, illustrating the ways in which this jewelry has moved from simple designs, using what was available for re-use, to becoming part of a more visually sophisticated commercial niche range. This suggests that the central motif—the skull—is still relevant to a subcultural market but has become modified in a way that targets a specific set of customer tastes and interests. Thus while the skull is still used, deathly references have also developed in new forms, such as preserved babies in jars, that reference anatomy museum exhibits, or skeletons in coffins that resemble traditional mourning and *memento mori* jewelry, discussed previously.

Figure 13.4 Pendants, Page from 2002 Catalogue. © Alchemy Carta Ltd.

238 *Claire Barratt*

Figure 13.5 Rings, Page from 2002 catalogue. ©Alchemy Carta Ltd.

Insider knowledge enables the company to stay a step ahead of any high street ranges that produce similar jewelry based around skulls and death symbolism. Spooner (2007) observed the way in which goth informed late 1990s fashion by reverting to visual stereotypes for the high street and the subsequent way that the actual subculture continued to redefine itself in order to remain distinguishable from mainstream fashion. In relation to commercial niche ranges, such as jewelry based on death symbolism, this suggests that either the jewelry design itself or other variables such as aspects of its retail or the way that it is worn must also change in some way in order to maintain a distance from the mainstream culture and remain a desirable purchase for the metal subculture. If the skull can be seen as a 'visual stereotype' for metal within mainstream jewelry and fashion then its design treatment by companies such as Alchemy provide something additional through its insider knowledge, which other retailers such as Argos or Theo Fennell cannot.

Different Wearers, Different Meanings?

The commercial growth and expansion of what might originally have been considered jewelry aimed at a niche metal audience, in its use of the skull as a central motif, into a variety of different retailers, provides much material for exploring boundaries and the place of consumption within subcultures. The possibility that metal might provide an element of subcultural 'attitude' to mainstream fashion, in its use of jewelry incorporating death symbolism, has already been suggested, but this interpretation may be developed further when considering age or sexuality.

Two well-known customers of The Great Frog can be seen wearing its jewelry, but neither fits the stereotype of a young 'metalhead'. The cover of a record sleeve of a solo album *Take It So Hard* by Keith Richards, released in 1988 when he was in his mid-forties, features a close-up photograph of his head and hand that shows him wearing a large silver skull ring, which he is still frequently pictured wearing today. The cover of Marc Almond's autobiography *Tainted Life* (2000) pictures him wearing a silver skull pendant and ring. He is a singer/musician who became well known during the 1980s as part of electro-pop duo Soft Cell and is also publicly 'out' as a gay man. The cover photograph is one of a series of Marc Almond taken by photographers Pierre et Gilles, known for their kitsch visual style. These examples show the way in which niche or subcultural products and the way they are used depart from established stereotypes and theories. Bennett and Kahn-Harris (2004) criticized early CCCS work for its limited focus on youth subcultures, pointing out that they 'failed to appreciate the symbolic value of style and other popular cultural resources for transforming youth into an ideological category, a state of mind rather than a particular stage in life' (p. 10), something that has become more noticeable as subsequent generations of 'youth' have reached adulthood and refused to give up their earlier preoccupations with music and style. Dunn (2005) noted the predominance of heterosexual males amongst heavy metal fans, while Kahn-Harris (2007) suggests that another genre, extreme metal, shows evidence of being sexist and homophobic. Although both of The Great Frog customers used here for illustrative purposes are established musicians with a particular public image to maintain and therefore not atypical examples of skull jewelry wearers, Keith Richards is clearly too old to be considered a 'youth' and is definitely not 'metal'. Similarly, Marc Almond gives the jewelry a slightly camp, kitsch look, which is strengthened by the photographers' style.

Conclusion

These examples suggest that such products are a niche taste that goes beyond preconceived subcultural boundaries and stereotypes, but they also raise further questions about this jewelry when worn by people who are not stereotypical metal fans or musicians: perhaps the association with metal, or through that with earlier biker subcultures, bestows certain intangible qualities on the wearer of jewelry based on death symbolism. They also highlight the complexities of contemporary consumer culture and its relation to mainstream cultures.

In this chapter I have suggested, through a historical overview of the adoption and youth appropriation of skull and death's head imagery, as well as case studies of two UK businesses that produce original skull jewelry, that the CCCS/Hebdige account of subcultural authenticity and commercial incorporation is too simplistic in failing to recognize not only the complexity of the relationship between subcultures and the mainstream but also the role of entrepreneurship and commerce within the persistence of subcultures. I have also suggested that the meanings to be found in certain items of subcultural wear, such as skull jewelry, retain a sense of authenticity and associations of edginess and danger, even when they are recontextualized in more mainstream settings or worn outside of the context of metal entirely. The extent that heavy metal culture can be viewed as a bricolage of biker and hippy cultures, at least in its formative period, goes some way to explaining the prevalence of skull and death's head jewelry within the scene over time. But as I have argued, not all death symbolism in metal is attributable to these influences, suggesting a deal of complexity to this issue. It may also be the case that such jewelry and symbolism retains a cultural and historical meaning that is 'originary' to itself, which may be its continuing source of attraction to both metal and non-metal wearers.

Notes

1. I began to investigate death symbolism in contemporary design after observing it within cultural contexts that had little to do with historical death rituals. I interviewed various people within metal and goth subcultures who were involved in the design, production, retail and circulation of designed items including graphics, magazines, music, clothing and jewelry. The Great Frog and Alchemy were two jewelry producers I spoke to about their ranges. These were variously semi-structured interviews with notes taken or recorded and transcribed and took place starting in 1995. The resulting information was used in my unpublished MA Design Studies dissertation (1997, Central Saint Martins) and PhD thesis (2010, Central Saint Martins, University of the Arts London).
2. Other generic unbranded pieces of skull jewelry are advertised in heavy metal mail order catalogues such as *EMP* (winter 2008, p. 106) alongside ranges from both Alchemy and Vince Ray, a fetish/rockabilly/hotrod culture artist who has also designed skull jewelry.
3. Paterson Riley, proprietor of The Great Frog, interviewed at their premises in 1995 and 2001.

Bibliography

Barratt, C. (2010). *An investigation into the cultural meanings of contemporary mourning and memento mori jewellery (London 1980–2008)*. PhD thesis, Central Saint Martins College of Art and Design, University of the Arts, London.

Beezer, A. (1992). Dick Hebdige, subculture: The meaning of style. In M. Barker & A. Beezer (Eds.), *Reading into cultural studies* (pp. 101–118). London: Routledge.

Bennett, A., & Kahn-Harris, K. (Eds.). (2004). *After subculture: Critical studies in contemporary youth culture*. Basingstoke: Palgrave Macmillan.

Breward, C. (1998). Cultures, identities, histories: Fashioning a cultural approach to dress. *Fashion Theory: The Journal of Dress, Body & Culture*, 2(4), 301–313.

Breward, C. (2004). *Fashioning London: Clothing and the modern metropolis*. Oxford: Berg.

Brown, A. R. (2007). Rethinking the subcutural commodity: Exploring heavy metal t-shirt culture(s). In P. Hodkinson & W. Deicke (Eds.), *Youth cultures: Scenes, subcultures and tribes* (pp. 63–78). London: Routledge.

Clay, M. (1988). *Café racers: Rockers, rock 'n' roll and the coffee-bar cult*. London: Osprey.

Cohen, S. (1980). *Folk devils and moral panics*. Oxford: Martin Robertson.

Dunn, S. (2005). *Metal: A headbanger's journey*. Momentum Pictures. [DVD].

EMP. (2014). Summer catalogue. Devon, UK: EMP Mail Order UK Ltd.

Farren, M. (1985). *The black leather jacket*. London: Plexus.

Franklin, C. (2002). *The frock and roll years*. ITV UK documentary (Off-air video recording).

Gelder, K., & Thornton, S. (Eds.). (1997). *The subcultures reader*. London: Routledge.

Hall, S., & Jefferson, T. (Eds.). (1976). *Resistance through rituals: Youth subcultures in post war Britain*. London: Hutchinson.

Hall. S., & Jefferson, T. (2006). Once more around *Resistance through rituals*. In S. Hall & T. Jefferson (Eds.), *Resistance through rituals: Youth subcultures in post war Britain* 2nd Ed. (pp. vii–xxxiii). London and New York: Routledge.

Hebdige, D. (1979). *Subculture: The meaning of style*. London: Methuen.

Hjelm, T., Kahn-Harris, K., & LeVine, M. (2013). *Heavy metal: Controversies and counter cultures*. Sheffield: Equinox.

Hodkinson, P. (2002). *Goth: Identity, style and subculture*. Oxford, New York: Berg.

Iommi, T. (2012). *Iron man: My journey through heaven and hell with Black Sabbath*. London: Simon & Schuster.

Kahn-Harris, K. (2007). *Extreme metal: Music and culture on the edge*. Oxford: Berg.

Maffesoli, M. (1996). *The time of the tribes: The decline of individualism in mass society*. London: Sage.

McDonald-Walker, S. (2000). *Bikers: Culture, politics and power*. Oxford: Berg.

McRobbie, A. (1989). Second hand dresses and the role of the rag market. In A. McRobbie (Ed.), *Zoot suits and second hand dresses: An anthology of fashion and music* (pp. 23–49). London: Macmillan.

McRobbie, A. (1994). *Postmodernism and popular culture*. London: Routledge.

McRobbie, A. (1998). *British fashion design: Rag trade or image industry?* London: Routledge.

Mudrian, A. (2004). *Choosing death: The improbable history of death metal and grindcore*. Los Angeles, CA: Feral House.

Osbourne, O. (2009). *I am Ozzy*. London: Sphere.

Phillips, L. (2005). Blue jeans, black leather jackets, and a sneer: The iconography of the 1950s biker and its translation abroad. *International Journal of Motorcycle Studies*. Available online at: ijms.nova.edu<http://ijms.nova.edu> (accessed August 10, 2014).

Sabin, R. (1999). "I won't let that dago by": Rethinking punk and rascism. In R. Sabin (Ed.), *Punk rock: So what? The cultural legacy of punk* (pp. 199–218). London: Routledge.

Spooner, C. (2007). Undead fashion: Nineties style and the perennial return of goth. In M. E. Goodlad & M. Bibby (Eds.), *Goth: Undead subculture* (pp. 143–154). Durham, NC: Duke University Press.

Steele, V. (1998). A museum of fashion is more than a clothes-bag. *Fashion Theory: The Journal of Dress, Body & Culture*, 2(4), 327–335.

Stuart, J. (1987). *Rockers!*, London: Plexus.

Thornton, S. (1997). The social logic of subcultural capital. In K. Gelder & S. Thornton (Eds.), *The subcultures reader* (pp. 200–209). London: Routledge.

Weinstein, D. (2000). *Heavy metal: The music and its culture*, (Revised ed.). New York: Da Capo Press.

Willis, P. (1978). *Profane culture*. London: Routledge.

Part V
Metal and Gender Politics

14 'Getting My Soul Back'

Empowerment Narratives and Identities among Women in Extreme Metal in North Carolina

Jamie E. Patterson

I was 14 in the early 1990s when I first heard the band Entombed blasting out of the car stereo speakers. The vocals, those echoing growls, immediately enthralled me. Combined with the raw distortion and down-tuned guitars, it sounded like a creature clawing its way through mud and filth. At the time, I deeply wanted to express myself, but I couldn't quite articulate my feelings in a way in which others could understand them. That voice on the stereo was my voice.

While I often listened to death metal with a small group of white, male, working-class friends, due to transportation limitations and our proximity in the mostly rural coastal-piedmont town of Wilson, North Carolina,[1] we had not sustained active involvement with the larger death metal community centered in Raleigh, the state capital, an hour's drive west. Therefore, most of my engagement with death metal music involved everyday listening alone, weekly visits with friends, and occasional jaunts to Raleigh, to record stores and shows.

In the late 1990s, the Raleigh shows became sparse. I moved away from the region and lost touch physically and emotionally with my 'metal friends'. Although I continued to listen to death metal and considered it part of my identity, I did not attend shows again until I returned to the region a decade later to attend graduate school for Folklore. Through coursework, I initially sought to explore how other women in the region had engaged with death metal to add to the ethnographic literature on extreme metal fans globally. Following Keith Kahn-Harris' (2007) research on everyday social practices of extreme metal fans in the United Kingdom, Israel, and Sweden, I wanted to situate research participants in everyday practice rather than focusing specifically on concert venues, which I felt, based on my background, provided a limited perspective of fan engagement.

To locate fans, I put up fliers at the University of North Carolina seeking female death metal fans and contacted the college radio station at North Carolina State University, WKNC 88.1, which, although its format had switched to indie music, aired weekend shows featuring extreme metal. Through a snowball effect, I became introduced to more women (and trans-female fans) involved in the death metal community. I conducted multiple interviews with women, asking them how death metal related to their lives. I also wanted to know what they considered important issues for a study of death metal. My questions were deliberately broad and few. I wanted to see where they took the conversation.

What emerged first were deeply personal narratives of how these women had used death metal instrumentally to instill a confidence that enabled them to make choices that improved their everyday conditions, which were often, though not always, connected to marginalized and stigmatized gender constructions in their life histories. They consistently referenced mainstream gender ideologies as practiced in the larger society of Southern America that they felt were confining and did not represent them. These involved conscriptions requiring women to be passive, nice, accommodating, physically attractive, and focusing much of their mental acuity on acquiring and sustaining heteronormative monogamous romantic relationships. Because these narratives were central to their engagement with death metal, I wanted to delve deeper to see what informed their interpretations of death metal and the death metal community and how they experienced this sense of confidence, which they termed 'empowerment', and which they internalized over years of listening. So I interacted with them not only at shows, but also in other venues, in public spaces before or after work, during radio shows, in private spaces at home, alone, with their friends, or on overnight trips to out of town venues. Through examining descriptions of empowerment and gender construction in the life narratives of female extreme metal fans in piedmont North Carolina, I argue that not only are these women obtaining power through involvement in the scene, they are using this power to do gender on their own terms in other arenas.

Previous Research on Women in North American Metal Scenes

In recent decades, metal scholars have begun to pay more attention to women in extreme metal, mostly in death metal. Recent scholarship employing ethnographic fieldwork, interviews, and questionnaires has focused on identifying modes of gender construction among female participants at shows in various American regions, particularly Houston, Texas (Vasan, 2009, 2011), the Midwest (Klypchak, 2007), areas of New York (Purcell, 2003), and the South (Hutcherson and Haenfler, 2010). Sonia Vasan (2009, 2011), Brad Klypchak (2007), Natalie Purcell (2003), Ben Hutcherson, and Ross Haenfler (2010) all report that women in American death metal scenes are adopting a set of standards and judging other members based on their gendered-presentation. In particular, female scene participants are placing other women in one of two categories: that of the 'girlfriend' or that of the 'true fan' (Purcell, 2003). According to the participants, the 'girlfriend' wears heels, tight or revealing clothes, and uses her sex appeal to gain power in the scene by attracting men. She is motivated by sexual desire rather than an 'earnest' attraction to the music. Meanwhile, the 'true fan' dresses in regular to oversized t-shirts and jeans, camouflage, or shorts, much like the men in the scene. She does not employ a discourse of 'romance' in relation to the men and instead adopts the same mannerisms and language as men in the scene. Although she may be attracted to men in the scene—most of the fans they interviewed use heteronormative discourse—she is motivated by a connection with the music. Other names are attached to these types, for example 'band whore' and 'den mother' (Vasan, 2009), or 'chickiepoos' and 'chicks with balls' (Morla, 2010). These research findings echo Krenske and McKay's (2000) ethnographic study of gender and power relations in a rural metal music venue in Queensland, Australia, implying that these folk categories may exist in other global scenes with similar economic and social contexts and mainstream gender constructions.[2]

Each of these labels reflects a dialectical relationship between the hyper feminine and the masculine, defining female participation in relation to men and dominant notions of masculinity. Robert Walser (1993) has noted how some forms of metal music *exscript* the feminine in order to eliminate it as a threat to male bonding. The women who adopt the alluring hyper feminine or 'femme fatale' identity can gain a level of power over men in the scene, but they are ultimately reduced to sexual objects and are subjugated through hyper masculine displays of dominance in the form of degrading remarks, symbolic sex with instruments, or physical sex. The women who Vasan reports 'dress and behave like men' (2009, p. 72), gain acceptance by supposedly masking their gender, but they limit their freedom of expression in the process. Klypchak (2007), who explores identity in the metal scene using the exscription model, argues that although women involved in the scene may gain a limited amount of power, it is hardly enough to boost their positions to that of the men in the scene. Ultimately, these researchers conclude that women are modifying their appearance and behavior to assimilate into a male-dominated domain. Although they may gain a limited amount of power from participating in the death metal scene, they do so at great cost.

Interviewing women in death metal mostly in Texas, Vasan's (2011) research findings argue that these women are willing to subscribe to masculinist codes as a cost-reduction strategy to experience empowerment and liberation through their involvement with the music. She repeatedly mentions how participants experienced painful events or gender-related difficulties that led to their involvement and sense of empowerment in death metal. She notes, 'If death metal does provide a certain empowerment and liberation to women, which is not available elsewhere, then it follows that women will submit to the sexist norms of the subculture in exchange for the privilege of continued participation in it' (2011, p. 344).

Although this research finding is important—women can be excluded and judged on male terms—a problem arises from this research perspective. While hegemonic masculinities and emphasized femininities exist alongside other gendered discourses in the scene, women who actively perform more masculine or feminine gendered identities become read in this light as simply subscribing to masculinist codes. Such a model tends to downplay the experiences of the women in the scene in lieu of their interpreted concert venue displays. It undermines their own interpretations of gender (or temporary refusal of it) and their personal motivations and backgrounds, which inform their participation in the scene. For example, Harris Berger (1999a), using phenomenological ethnographic methods to explore death metal fans in Akron, Ohio, notes of the live concert event:

> The participant's constitution of these [live] experiences is influenced by his or her purposes in attending the event [...] and his or her perceptual skills [...] These, in turn, are informed by past musical experience [...] and nonmusical experiences (a good day at work, local ideas about gender, a series of nonunion, service-sector jobs). Ethnomusicology includes this entire complex, all understood as experience. (p. 23)

Keeping in mind the background complexities and histories from which fans interpret their own actions and those of others within the scene, their scene identification and modes of engagement with masculinity and apparent rejection of femininity is more complex than simply accepting a set of masculinist codes. As Walser (1993) importantly notes:

> Metal replicates the dominant sexism of contemporary [American] society, but it also allows a kind of free space to be opened up by and for certain women, performers and fans alike. Female fans identify with a kind of power that is usually understood in our culture as male—because physical power, dominance, rebellion, and flirting with the dark side of life are all culturally designated as male prerogatives. (pp. 131–132)

Walser's observations may not apply to all global scenes or even all North American scenes, but they do concur with how my research participants described their involvement with the Raleigh scene. Although they coded the music as 'masculine', as Weinstein (2009) argues, this does not imply they are 'necessarily masculinist', as the genre's 'master signifier' is power rather than gender—and as a result, heavy metal devotees do not necessarily 'exult in their maleness' (pp. 27–28). Along these lines, Amber Clifford's work shows how metal can be seen 'as a queerscape that allows queer women to perform female masculinities' (2009, n.p.). Regarding fans of metal in the United Kingdom, Rosemary Hill's research argues that the women she interviewed 'find in metal a space in which the construction of mainstream femininity does not need to apply and therefore acts as haven from expectations of a gendered identity that they feel does not fit them' (2012, n.p.).

She posits that rather than constructing alternative gendered presentations, 'in metal fandom women can experience a "genderlessness" (ibid.). Vasan (2011) opens up the possibility for exploring these motivations in her concluding remarks:

> If the patterns of social exchange theory hold true for women in death metal, then their need for liberation and personal fulfillment through the music and the scene must stem as much from a lack of such empowerment in mainstream society as from a lack of empowerment in alternative groups or subcultures. (p. 347)

Accordingly, this chapter aligns itself with both Hill's discussion of 'genderless' experiences in the metal scene and Walser's readings of gender in which metal allows individuals, including women, to perform 'identity work', playing with gender, or becoming temporarily un-marked as women, and in the process obtaining power formerly only available to men. It seeks to understand how women in the death metal scene employ tropes of empowerment and belonging that contest or reject the cultural construction of the 'female' in mainstream American society. Through this process, these women gain (or regain) a sense of power, which transforms their experience of marginalization.

Such transformations occur not only within the live concert venue, but also in everyday social contexts. To examine this, it is necessary to expand the research beyond the death metal scene, to situate these women in everyday life, exploring the social roles that both inform and interact with their death metal identities. In these areas, their various identities intersect and interlace through social practice and how they construct their identities by engaging reflexively with their past and present experiences—a process that Anthony Giddens calls 'structuration' (cited in Berger 1999a, 26). Through structuration, past intentional acts, which are informed by individual and larger social contexts, 'become objectified as the context for present acts' (ibid.).

This life-narrative construction can be examined by employing Berger's (1999a, 1999b) phenomenological methodology, which addresses the continuing re-interpretation, re-constitution, and re-framing of subjective selves and experiences in relation to immediate situational contexts and broader social backgrounds and through dialogue and critique. Ethnography through this lens involves a partial sharing among subjective parties with the researcher as actor engaged in the process. Participants recognized my prior experience with death metal, but, as I had met them in a research context, they initially read me as an academic from the University of North Carolina, which is popularly referred to as an 'ivy league' public school. Framing my study around women's experiences with death metal also most likely influenced them to locate themselves within 'gendered' domains. To address these biases and gain a clearer sense of the multidimensional contexts that informed their life narratives, I conducted many long interviews in various contexts and engaged in dialogue with them repeatedly from 2010 to 2013. Over time, they learned more about my background, which encouraged them to share additional stories. Through these dialogues, I began to reflect on my own past experiences with death metal, engaging in auto-ethnography through memory re-contextualization and archival analysis of my own previous writings.

To illustrate how death metal involvement is being used to transform marginalized positions in the life narratives of these women, I specifically chose to focus on three individuals from this ethnographic fieldwork who actively adopted varying degrees of masculinity in their self-presentation but identify strongly as women.[3] First, there's Laura, a stagehand and artist, who describes herself as a 'teenage stoner dude in a middle-aged woman's body'. Then there's Louise, a social worker and radical queer activist in her thirties. And then there's me, a thirty-something graduate student revisiting myself at 15 through a researcher's lens. These narratives, though focusing on individual presentations of gender and empowerment, are not meant as anecdotal. Rather, they present themes that are representative of other participants' experiences reported in my research.

Situated in Everyday Life: Narratives of Empowerment

Laura

In my first interview with Laura, she told me that metal had 'saved her life'. We were sitting on two adjacent couches in the front room of her 1950's ranch home in Raleigh, North Carolina, surrounded on each wall by 18 years of local death metal and personal history—band posters, album covers, and hand-drawn show fliers. Munching on a pizza before her radio DJ spot at midnight, she leaned forward and told me about her life in Baltimore, Maryland, before Raleigh. She was in her mid-20s then and living in an abusive relationship with someone she described as a 'soul-sucking man' or 'John-turned-crackhead'. At the time, she was working on a degree in engineering and often used her schoolwork as an excuse to leave the house. It was during one of these jaunts that she heard White Zombie on a college radio station. She says the music transported her back to her teenage years when she had listened to punk and metal nonstop; it reconnected her to a time when she had felt power and control.

In her life narratives, Laura consistently referred to her engagement with punk and metal as methods of 'fighting back'[4] against school or family-sanctioned gendered presentations and events in which girls were supposed to be passive, feminine, and, like all students, amenable to institutional norms. In the early 1980s as a teenager living in Texas, Laura had used her senior art project to stage a boycott of prom, instead urging people to attend a Dead Kennedys show that was taking place on the same night. She had also skipped graduation in lieu of a Blue Oyster Cult concert. Her Baltimore boyfriend had hated her punk and metal past, and the two rarely discussed it. With pop metal bands saturating the mainstream market in the late 1980s, she says she was inclined to think metal was dead. At the same time, she was losing her own sense of 'aesthetic agency'. Hearing White Zombie on the radio changed all that.

In her ethnographic research on listening practices, Tia DeNora (2000) discusses how a number of her research participants had also used music associated with particular time periods in their lives to 'help them recapture the aesthetic agency they possessed (or which possessed them) at that time' (p. 143). She contends:

> In this sense, the past, musically conjured, is a resource for the reflexive movement from present to future, the moment-to-moment production of agency in real time. It serves also as a means of putting actors in touch with capacities, reminding them of their accomplished identities, which in turn fuels the ongoing projection of identity from past into future. Musically fostered memories thus produce past trajectories that contain momentum. (ibid.)

Laura's narrative reports this same process. As the days pressed on, she continued listening to metal, in a process that she called, 'getting my soul back'. Laura plotted and worked and ultimately moved to Raleigh, where she attended graduate school. Shortly after arriving in North Carolina, she volunteered to DJ for the college radio station, 88.1 WKNC, playing music on the 'heavier end' and adopting the on-air name Lucretia (after both the controversial Italian figure Lucretia Borgia and the women's rights activist Lucretia Mott). She started going to metal shows regularly. Less than a year later, she was at Snookers, a local metal bar, where she heard the death metal band Carcass playing over the sound system. She has been on what she calls 'the dark side', meaning extreme metal, ever since.

Laura's front room has no television—quoting punk band Flux of Pink Indians, she says she has no need for 'vicarious living'. Instead, there are three scratched up couches, a coffee table, and a stereo system in the corner, with crates of vinyl records stemming out toward the door. Laura's place is for socializing, and as she opens her book of drawings she has created for shows, fundraisers, album covers, and band drum heads, I can see that she even includes sketches of her friends in her artwork, as models frozen within pages of interconnected stories. She proceeds to tell me the story behind each image, where she was when she drew it (for example, working as a stagehand on the set of *Chitty Chitty Bang Bang*), what the scene invokes, and how it was received by others. Laura's identity, informed by her past and shaped in relation to those around her, is deeply intertwined with the extreme metal community

Being involved in the extreme metal community—as a DJ, artist, manager of an independent record label, and show promoter—is all part of what Laura refers to as 'wearing my soul on my sleeve'. She equates metal with the condition of 'being true', being honest to oneself, true in one's representation to others. As an example of practicing this truth, years ago, she quit her job at an office to work as a stagehand for theater productions, noting that she left the 'rat race' to be 'part of the art'. Her job provides her the freedom to work on show fliers in the rafters and adhere to a gender construction more in tune with her identity process of 'being true to myself'. Like other research participants, Laura's truth performance actively positions herself in direct opposition to social norms outside of the extreme metal community: norms of cleanliness, gender presentation, and economic status. When 'griping' about her ex-boyfriend, she invoked these oppositional associations:

> He met me at a metal show. I had just gotten off of work, so he knew I worked nights. I was dressed pretty much the way I always dress; I was in cut off camouflage shorts because it was summertime. Just got off work, hadn't showered in five days. I was on a bicycle. Everything that was me was there that night. No false advertising! My hair wasn't combed; I wasn't dressed pretty. I didn't have on makeup. I didn't talk about my office job. I didn't drive away in a car. He knew I'm not some super product hygiene queen. You caught me on a good day. I took a shower today. But it had been four days because I was busy.

Laura's oppositional identity-formations are part of a dialogic processes constructed through difference in relation to an Other. In each of our meetings, Laura seemed to speak to a specter in the room, the face of the socialized woman in mainstream American culture. She often told stories of encounters with other women in the scene, imbuing them with stereotypically 'feminine' characteristics. These women loved shoes; they played up their looks to gain men's attention; they weren't interested in the music, only the men involved. When I asked her why these women would subject themselves to what other participants had called the 'sounds of torture' just to attract men, she shrugged her shoulders, 'Maybe because of the bad boy image. They want to piss off daddy'.

Although they typically play the foils in her stories, she does not always fault these women, because they are often quite nice to her. However, they align themselves with values she opposes in practice. Citing the larger problems of female gender socialization, she complains that most girls grow up thinking they have to wear makeup. They watch television and think that's what they're supposed to look like. She says,

> If you throw away your TV and start looking around at Target and Walmart and what the average American looks like, you begin to see yourself as thin and beautiful. You're not so bad compared to the average American. But if you're watching TV all the time, sure you're going to think something's wrong with you. These girls are growing up like that. And their mothers grew up like that, and their mothers. So they just passed it on.

Following this statement, Laura launches into another oppositional identity, her motto: 'I'm evil, not pretty'. To Laura, being 'pretty' is about participating in a discourse that offers women limited and disposable power. 'But evil goes to the bone'. She replaces pretty's negation, the word ugly, with a word that in the death metal community carries power, evil. Evil in extreme metal represents freedom and choice over socialization and submission. By substituting a symbol of power for one that often demoralizes young women, Laura empowers herself in opposition. Her everyday actions and choices are informed by this trope, which is so embedded in her identity processes that it 'goes to the bone'.

Scholars may interpret Laura's actions in the scene as subscribing to masculinist codes in death metal. She admits to being judgmental of women more than men in the scene, with some of her remarks echoing what other participants have called internalized sexism. When asked about this, she cites her own experiences growing up at school where girls consistently ridiculed her. These experiences influenced her to question her own place within mainstream gender norms, just as they also led her to make generalizations about other women in the scene, often based on limited gendered cues. Laura situates her attitudes in her past. She is not simply adhering to male behavioral norms; her actions are informed by her life history, as reconstituted through everyday narrative performance. Her participation in the death metal scene enables her to find spaces where she can gain power through resisting gender normative prescriptions, power she uses in her everyday life.

Louise

Like Laura, Louise has used extreme metal instrumentally as a source of power, not only as a vessel, but also as a dialogic partner. Louise describes herself as a feminist with radical anti-capitalist values, and as a queer-identifying woman involved in radical queer organizing. Although she has never presented herself as 'fem' (hyper feminine), her involvement as a female singer within the extreme metal scene has been challenging. Through her life narrative, she discusses how she engages with the scene and uses it to strengthen and sustain her in other domains.

Louise transitioned to extreme metal in her college years from listening to punk as a teenager. In her narrative, she describes a defining moment that propelled her into extreme metal. She and her metal friend Barry were at School Kids, a local record store, and he encouraged her to buy *At the Gates' Slaughter of the Soul*. Getting into his car, they put the CD on and listened to the first song, 'Blinded by Fear'. 'And we played that and he looked over at me and I was like, 'Whoah! This is fucking intense; this is amazing!' And he looked over at me and he was like, 'Hits the spot, doesn't it?"

Louise's attraction to extreme metal follows that of other participants. She notes that she had always been intrigued by the darker side of things; the motifs in extreme metal were easily relatable. 'Dark, sad things don't scare me … It's easier for me to go into that space and feel cozy and comfortable. I don't want to live there … but it's nice to visit, you know'. Louise describes herself in school as a 'weirdo' who never fit into any 'normal scene', so she had gravitated toward other 'freaks' who shared similar musical interests and identity backgrounds.

Growing up, she wanted to perform in punk bands, but guys in the punk scene refused to be in a band with her.[5] When she moved from Durham, North Carolina, to Asheville (just three hours away) to go to college, she found the scene more welcoming to women as performers and started the grindcore crust band Resurrectum. She talks about her experiences:

> Those first few years, I was really working some shit out. I was writing some heavy stuff about family dysfunction, personal trauma, politics, feminism. We were using lots of pagan imagery to talk about feminism. One of the songs I wrote for Resurrectum, there was this feminist quote—I don't know who said it—but that one of the things that threatens men is that because women's menstrual cycle that we can bleed without pain and bleed without fear of injury, where if a man's bleeding, he's been hurt. So I was like, 'Oh my god! That's metal as shit! Right?' So I actually wrote a song about menstrual blood. And people went wild!

Louise used the tropes of 'brutal imagery' within the scene to work through gender and personal issues. Regarding the platform of extreme metal, she notes,

> Here's what I realized: being a vocalist in a metal band, you can scream at the top of your lungs about some shit that is not cool and everyone in the audience is like (in gruff voice), 'More! More!' What other setting do you have where you can literally stand there and scream about all sorts of fucked up shit and people aren't like, 'Stop!' It was amazing.

On tour, she encountered towns in which male fans at shows were not always so welcoming. In these situations, Louise used her identity as a vocalist to assert power and establish herself as an equal in the space. She shares an example.

> There was this one show in this tiny little town in Pennsylvania and it was a bunch of little young hardcore kids,[6] like doing flip kicks and all that crazy shit. Well, not when we were playing, because we got up there, and they were like, 'What the fuck is this shit?' And literally, the entire group of boys, because they were boys—they were like sixteen—moved all the way to the back of the space, like across the

entire room. Well, I had a fifty- foot mike cord, so I just walked and got like as close as we are (two feet away) and just fucking belted the entire set out. And they were literally like arms folded back against the wall scared shitless. So it was an opportunity for me to reclaim.

After the show, two teenage girls came up to her. 'And they were like, "That was awesome! We've never seen anything like it!" And I was like, 'Take some CDs. Good luck, ya'll. This place is fucked up!'

Reflecting on this story, she situates herself as a woman empowered by her role as a vocalist:

> So there were times where being a singer in a band helped me take up some space as a woman and spread some messaging. Because, when you've got a microphone and it's turned on, you get to say what you want to say. People don't necessarily agree; they might not hear it. But you get to say it. And there's power in speaking your truth. There's a lot of power in that.

Like Laura, who used extreme metal to regain power and speak her 'truth', Louise had used her involvement with extreme metal to deal with her own struggles with mainstream gender construction. But her sheer presence as a gendered performer forced her to deal with those same issues within what she called the 'counterculture'. She used this tension as a catalyst for transgressing scene norms and providing exposure for counter-attitudes and perspectives.

At what she calls her 'shining moment', she recounts visiting friends in the band US Christmas—composed of mill workers in Marion, North Carolina,—at the Scion fest in Atlanta, a large southern regional metal festival. At the merch booth, the band was selling split 7's featuring a song from her band at the time, Subramanium. The song on the split album was deeply political, for one due to the lyrics and secondly due to the fact that she was a female vocalist belting them out. Seeing teenage boys carrying that album around filled her with pride; she felt that, at the very least, it could expose them to alternative perspectives that may not be available in either mainstream or counterculture societies.

After graduating, Louise became a social worker. She reported that her experiences dealing with dark material through the extreme metal community has helped her relate to clients (including sex workers, crack addicts, and women with severe mental illness who were homeless). She notes:

> They picked up pretty quickly that I was not some scary Christian lady[7] in there to help all these poor people; that I was a freak, too. You know? It just comes across; it does. I can dress up in a suit, but it's still. I'm edgy, that's who I am. And I think I made them really comfortable with me. I think I made them more comfortably connect

with me, because they were like, 'Alright. This woman has either been through some shit or she knows about some shit and she's not some weird outsider coming in to fix me'.

The extreme metal scene has been therapeutic for Louise, but she has also used the space to regain a sense of power and has continued from this position of power. A self-described 'freak', she helps other women struggling with marginalization as a result of personal traumas and/or gendered, classist, and racist institutions. She and her sister also run a summer girls' rock camp where they provide opportunities for teenage girls to learn musical instruments and start their own bands.

Jamie

Through the course of this ethnography, as I listened to narratives from participants about their own engagement with extreme metal and mainstream gender constructions, I began to reflect on my own ambivalent experiences growing up in eastern North Carolina. I too had found power listening to death metal at a critical time in which I was dealing with gender and personal traumas.[8] But while the scene had provided a comfortable space for Laura to present her own gender construction and for Louise to work through frustrations with gender, my experiences fall more in line with Rosemary Hill's research, in which I used the death metal scene, and the live-event space in particular, to temporarily experience 'no genders'.

Growing up as a young teenager in the early 1990s, I was probably at that same show where Laura heard Carcass. And on the way to shows in Raleigh, I occasionally heard Laura's voice on 88.1. At death metal shows, I dressed in what is considered the 'male category', oversized band shirts and jeans or shorts. I felt freedom there, because for once I could feel invisible, blend into the crowd, not be looked at; I could transcend my body and the world of romance. I would stand right in front of the speakers, and with the onslaught of raw sound feel what Bogue (2004) calls 'a dissolution of self' and what Rosemary Overell calls 'brutal affect' (2011). Not only would I feel a sense of genderlessness, getting lost in the experience, I would cease to be a separate self.

The day after a show, I would walk into high school wearing a concert t-shirt and greet my two metal friends, Matt and Jon, who were still in school (my other friends had either graduated or quit), still filled with the energy from the night before. On those days, I didn't care what people thought of me, or if they were judging me. I felt confident because I had experienced a sacred event, a secret shared among death metal fans, and I felt impenetrable.

Normally I worried with makeup, fixed my hair, and experimented with my appearance. I wanted to be seen as 'attractive', but I couldn't handle the thought of being judged against some 'standard' of beauty that I knew

I could never achieve. I was particularly uncomfortable with the fact that others could view my body from behind, and I couldn't do anything about it.

Over the years, to deal with this insecurity, I started wearing a Brujeria shirt around my waist, what Folklorist Roger Abrahams would call the 'badge' of my identity (2003). The shirt featured a decapitated head, a victim of a drug cartel murder. I did not know it at the time, but by placing this image around my waist, I was engaging in a form of implicit coding, crafting a reflexive statement about the constructions of gender within my community. When I wore that shirt around my waist, I felt empowered, free to enter public domains on my own terms. I was hiding my body underneath a decapitated head, but it was more than that. The body part I had unconsciously replaced with the grotesque image was a part of the anatomy that had been objectified regularly. Growing up, my friends and I had spent our preteen years walking around the shopping mall, interacting with other kids in the local community. It was here that I first learned about being watched as I walked, becoming an object of desire. But wearing the shirt, I could refuse to participate and in the process gain strength to assert an identity of power.

I want to say that, eventually, I internalized that sense of power to the point where I no longer needed the shirt to traverse through gendered domains. But the process was not that simple, and I still grapple with what sociologist Lauraine Leblanc (2005) labels the 'femininity game', feeling pressured to be perceived as 'pretty' in a slowly aging and culturally 'marked' body. Through meeting these women and listening to their own narratives, I began to re-establish my own sense of power and voice. Like other participants, this is a dialogic process that will continue to inform my decisions, and while the shirt is no longer around the waist, its imprint remains with me.

Concluding Thoughts

The three women whose life narratives I have discussed all use tropes from death metal to empower themselves and engage in the complex process of 'identity work'. Laura uses connotations of evil to fashion a unique gender composition that puts her in control. Louise uses grotesque dark imagery and the vocal platform to speak out against injustices, imbue women's folk experiences with power, and represent queer identities in contested spaces. I used the transitory feeling of 'genderlessness' from shows to adopt tropes of inversion and regain a sense of control and freedom over my body in public domains.

With the growing body of research on extreme metal, scholars are beginning to give voice to underrepresented fans of extreme metal (Clifford, 2009; Dawes, 2012; Hill, 2012; Riches, 2011; Vasan, 2011). Much of this recent work has begun to problematize previous research on women participants and gender performance in global scenes, situating women as agents who define gender on their own terms rather than solely in relation to the men in the scene. This chapter contributes to these perspectives.

The women who participated in this study are reacting with tropes culturally labeled masculine, but they are also reframing them to make statements about gender construction and formulate identities in relation to other aspects of their lives. In practice, they are dealing with age, race, family, geographic backgrounds, education, class-affiliations, and personal histories, along with gender. It is my hope to use these examples as a springboard for further research that utilizes a more holistic ethnographic approach. Generations of women are actively taking part in the death metal scene and integrating it with their self-expression. Through experiences with the music, they may find for themselves sources of power to deal with, interpret, and reshape their multi-dimensional social contexts. Ultimately, how they re-envision themselves sheds light on gendered disparities evident in how we experience social structures. Their voices can offer researchers valuable insights on both death metal scenes and mainstream culture—if we just widen our lens.

Notes

1. Wilson's population was roughly 30,000 at the time.
2. Given that gender construction varies cross-culturally, to interpret these folk categories and their applications as universal is problematic. For one, even if the presentation is similar or utilizes the same cultural artifacts, their meaning is interpreted on not only the death metal community, but also on the larger cultural context in which the localized death metal community resides. Also, as noted in participant Louise's account, scenes within the same region may vary in these gendered categories and their coding.
3. See Patterson (2016) for an examination of feminine gendered identities among participants in the scene.
4. In their discussion of justified anger among fans in metal, Brian Hickham and Jeremy Wallach (2011) make the distinction between displays of power and aggression and what they call 'fighting back' or exhibiting strength in the face of adversity. They argue fans use the music to access strength to fight back from positions of marginalization. Harris Berger's (1999) ethnographic research also discusses the practice of using death metal as a vent for 'life anger'.
5. For information regarding gender construction in punk scenes, sociologist Lauraine Leblanc's (2005) ethnographic work provides fertile ground.
6. In the US, often extreme metal bands perform mixed bills, most recently with hardcore and metalcore bands. This can be a source of tension at shows as the two subgenres of music attract conflicting types of fans and use competing tropes in their music. Participants discuss how metalcore fans mosh using karate style methods of kicking, while extreme metal fans engage in more of a push or fist style of circle dance. Also, participants have expressed frustration with what they call a more overt, macho 'bro' posturing in metalcore scenes as opposed to the masculinity in extreme metal, which utilizes more fantasy-oriented tropes. Comparing masculine presentations between the two subgenres would be a fascinating study, as all of the participants cited these similar frustrations.
7. North Carolina is part of a southern region in the US, colloquially referred to as the Bible Belt. The social influence of Protestant Christianity had varying impacts among women's life narratives in this research.

8. My father was a veteran, a draftee in the Vietnam War, who suffered 'survivor's guilt' when most of those in his platoon were killed. He had successfully kept his symptoms at bay until 1989, when he could no longer keep them hidden. His PTSD went undiagnosed until August 2008.

Bibliography

Abrahams, R. (2003). Identity. In B. Feintuch (Ed.), *Eight words for the study of expressive culture* (pp. 198–222). Urbana: University of Illinois Press.
Berger, H. M. (1999a). *Metal, rock and jazz: Perception and the phenomenology of musical experience.* Hanover: Wesleyan University Press.
Berger, H. M. (1999b). Death metal tonality and the act of listening. *Popular Music,* 18(2), 161–178.
Bogue, R. (2004). Becoming metal, becoming death. In R. Bogue (Ed.), *Delueze's wake: Tributes and tributaries* (pp. 83–108). Albany, NY: State University of New York.
Clifford, A. R. (2009). The leather sisterhood: Heavy metal, masculinity, and lesbian fandom. *Paper presented at the First International Conference on Gender and Heavy Metal,* University for Music, Cologne, Germany, October 2009.
Dawes, L. (2012). *What are you doing here? A black woman's life and liberation in heavy metal.* New York: Bazillion Points.
DeNora, T. (2000). *Music in everyday life.* New York: Cambridge University Press.
Hickam, B., & Wallach, J. (2011). Female authority and dominion: Discourse and distinctions of heavy metal scholarship. In K. Spracklen, A. R. Brown, & K. Kahn-Harris (Eds.), Special issue: Metal studies? Cultural research in the heavy metal scene. *Journal for Cultural Research* 15(3), 255–278.
Hill, R. L. (2012). Pleasure in metal: What women fans like about hard rock and metal music. Paper presented at Metal Music and Politics Conference: Heavy Metal Generations, Prague, Czech Republic, May 9–11.
Hutcherson, B., & Haenfler, R. (2010). Musical genre as a gendered process: Authenticity in extreme metal. *Studies in Symbolic Interaction,* 35, 101–121.
Kahn-Harris, K. (2007). *Extreme metal: Music and culture on the edge.* Oxford: Berg.
Klypchak, B. C. (2007). *Performed identities: Heavy metal musicians between 1984–1991.* PhD Dissertation, Bowling Green, OH: Bowling Green State University.
Krenske, L., & McKay, J. (2000). Hard and heavy: gender and power in a heavy metal music subculture. *Gender, Place and Culture,* 7(3), 287–304.
Leblanc, L. (2005). *Pretty in punk: Girls' gender resistance in a boys' subculture.* New Brunswick: Rutgers University Press.
Morla, the ancient one. (2010). Chickiepoos vs. chicks with balls. *Feministic Headbanger,* April 25, 2010: http://feministheadbanger.wordpress.com/2010/04/25/chickiepoos-vs-chicks-with-balls/ (Accessed 28th April 2011).
Overell, R. (2011). [I] hate girls and emo[tion]s: Negotiating masculinity in grindcore music. *Popular Music History,* 6(1–2), 198–223.
Patterson, J. E. (2016) 'Blasting Britney on the Way to Goatwhore' in G. Riches, D. Snell, B. Bardine and B. Gardenour Walter (eds) Heavy Metal Studies and Popular Culture (pp. 123–144) London: Palgrave-Macmillan.
Phillipov, M. (2012). *Death metal and music criticism: Analysis at the limits.* Plymouth, UK: Lexington Books.
Purcell, N. J. (2003). *Death metal music: The passion and politics of a subculture.* Jefferson, NC: McFarland.

Riches, G. (2011). Embracing the chaos: Mosh pits, extreme metal music and liminality. In K. Spracklen, A. R. Brown, & K. Kahn-Harris (Eds.), Special issue, Metal studies? Cultural research in the heavy metal scene. *Journal for Cultural Research,* 15(3), 315–332.

Vasan, S. (2009). Den mothers and band whores: Gender, sex, and power in the death metal scene. Paper presented at 2nd Global Conference on Heavy Fundamentalisms: Music, Metal and Politics, Austria.

Vasan, S. (2011). The price of rebellion: Gender boundaries in the death metal scene. In K. Spracklen, A. R. Brown, & K. Kahn-Harris (Eds.), Special issue, Metal studies? Cultural research in the heavy metal scene. *Journal for Cultural Research,* 15(3), 333–350.

Walser, R. (1993) Running with the devil: Power, gender, and madness in heavy metal music. Hanover, NH: Wesleyan University Press.

Weinstein, D. (2009). The empowering masculinity of British heavy metal. In G. Bayer (Ed.), *Heavy metal music in Britain* (pp. 17–32). Farnham: Ashgate.

15 Gender and Power in the Death Metal Scene
A Social Exchange Perspective

Sonia Vasan

Of all the subgenres of heavy metal music, death metal is arguably the most extreme—not only in terms of sound, but also in terms of lyrics, imagery, and other musical and subcultural characteristics. While heavy metal has historically been both male-dominated and male-centric, the androcentrism of the heavy metal scene is intensified in death metal, as evinced by the subculture's codes of behavior, its aesthetic, and its reputation for having the highest male-to-female ratio of any metal subgenre (Purcell, 2003; Phillipov, 2012). Relatively few women choose to enter the death metal scene, and this is perhaps not surprising, given its masculinist culture, its subcultural barriers to female participation, and the themes of violence against women that sometimes characterize death metal songs, artwork, and even the entire *oeuvre* of particular bands and subgenres (Kahn-Harris, 2003; Barron, 2013). In previous work, I have explored the marginalization of women in the death metal scene and their reasons for continued participation in it, despite a perceived awareness of its sexism and exclusionary practices (Vasan, 2010, 2011). Here, drawing on additional research material and interviews with female death metal fans, I further explore these issues and how they can contribute to an emerging subfield within metal studies concerned with the politics of gender and female participation. I use social exchange theory as the primary framework for this discussion.

Before I further explore my own research concerning women's position in the death metal scene, I want to review the extant literature on this important topic and thus situate my research in a larger context of scholarship. Specifically, I want to examine recent scholarship on gender in extreme metal and discuss the ways in which my research offers a distinct theoretical and disciplinary perspective in comparison to this work. Given that the most prominent academic explorations of gender in metal music and subculture have been sociological and/or musicological in orientation (as indicated by the works cited here), I hope that the sociopsychological orientation of my research will contribute to a more complete understanding of gender issues in metal by providing an explanatory mechanism for some of the phenomena observed by other scholars. As Thorpe, Ryba, and Denison have noted, 'each discipline has its own set of ontological, epistemological and axiological assumptions, and theoretical, methodological and representational preferences' (2014, p. 132). As social psychology tends to identify the micro-level *mechanisms* underlying social phenomena, while sociology tends to *document* social phenomena at the macro level, social psychology has often been drawn upon to provide theoretical explanations for sociological observations (Thoits, 1995; Moola, Norman, Petherick, and Strachan, 2014; Thorpe, Ryba, and Denison, 2014). Furthermore, psychology's emphasis on empirical research methods can be (and has been) used to illuminate sociological issues (Thoits, 1995; Moola et al., 2014). Therefore, I hope that my research can function similarly to complement and enhance current metal-studies perspectives on gender from sociology and other disciplines.

Over the past two decades, several metal-studies scholars have examined gender issues. Perhaps the best-known study on women in the metal scene is Krenske and McKay's (2000) ethnographic portrait of the female denizens of a metal nightclub in Queensland, Australia. While my own findings dovetail considerably with theirs, they sought to examine the metal subculture in a general sense rather than extreme metal or death metal in particular, as I have done. Although they acknowledge that the small scope of their study (one site and 10 interviewees) limits the generalizability of their results, the larger issue is that their work does not provide a theoretical explanation for women's involvement in an androcentric subculture—only an explanation for the fact of its androcentrism. For example, they argue that:

> Without advocating notions of a conspiracy among men or that women were cultural dopes, the HM [heavy metal] texts, narratives, identities, and corporeal practices in this study constituted a complex and contradictory gendered regime of power that literally kept women 'in their place'.
>
> (Krenske and McKay, 2000, p. 303)

However, they do not provide an explanation for the 'contradictory' nature of gendered power systems—if indeed women are not 'cultural dopes', then why should they choose to participate in a subculture that keeps them 'in their place'? It is with the goal of answering such questions that I have espoused sociopsychological frameworks for my research and thus hope to provide an explanatory mechanism for 'contradictory' gender phenomena.

The marginalization of women in the metal subculture has been recognized by other pioneers in the field of metal studies, including Weinstein (1991, 2000), Walser (1993), and Arnett (1996). Weinstein observes that 'male chauvinism and misogyny [...] characterize the metal subculture' ([1991] 2000, p. 105), further noting that '[w]omen are aliens in the heavy metal subculture because of their otherness' (p. 135). While Walser is less emphatic about metal's sexism, claiming that '[i]n some ways, heavy metal reflects [...] the greatest achievement of feminist theory, the problematization of gender' (1993, p. 131), he acknowledges that '[m]etal replicates the dominant sexism of contemporary society' (ibid.). Although he asserts that metal allows women to appropriate male power, he adds that '[a]s usual, women are offered male subject positions as a condition of their participation in empowerment' (ibid.). This echoes Weinstein's observation that '[w]omen, on stage or in the audience, are either sex objects to be used or abused, or must renounce their gender and pretend to be one of the boys. The few female performers must conform to the masculinist code' (2000, p. 221). Similarly, Arnett notes that 'girls are a small and not always respected minority in the world of heavy metal [who] struggle to reconcile their enthusiasm for heavy metal with their sense of being not quite welcome in that world' (1996, p. 140). However, Arnett does not explain *why* female fans choose to remain in a world in which they are 'not quite welcome'. Thus, in order to explicate the position of women in metal, it is necessary to move beyond an examination of sexism and marginalization—the 'how' of gender—by delving into the lived experiences of female fans and their reasons for subcultural involvement—the 'why' of gender, and the aim of this chapter.

The last decade has witnessed the emergence of scholarship specifically concerned with the death metal subgenre (as well as extreme metal in the larger sense). Purcell's (2003) book-length exploration of the death metal scene is notable as a pioneering contribution to the field; however, it avoids an analysis of the complexities of subcultural identity and participation, focusing instead on validating the musical and lyrical themes of death metal to external critics, such as its relationship to the contemporary horror film text. Furthermore, it does not examine gender issues in the scene, beyond its demographics (Purcell, 2003, pp. 100–105). In contrast, Kahn-Harris (2003) has addressed death metal's misogyny directly with a discussion of the problematic nature of the Cannibal Corpse song 'Fucked with a Knife', which graphically depicts the rape and murder of a woman. However, his discussion (for the most part) does not involve female perspectives on such texts (apart from a quote from a female band manager). Instead, he focuses on a theoretical debate involving textual analysis, discussion of censorship issues, and advocacy of intellectual criticism. In his landmark book on extreme metal, Kahn-Harris (2007) briefly explores the marginalization of women in the scene but does not directly explore the experiences of women, their identities as female fans, or their perception of the scene and their place within it. He offers the idea of 'reflexive anti-reflexivity' (p. 145) to explain the scene's resistance to politics (and, by extension, feminist ideology), as well as a theorization of the scene's intolerance of the feminine and the female as 'the abject [...] that which is formless, disgusting, terrifying and threatening' (p. 29), to be 'conquered with an excessive masculinity' (p. 137). However, he does not provide a theoretical framework for understanding the unique position of women in the scene: one that takes into account the individual cognition, behavior, and affect of female fans; that addresses micro-level processes; and that is testable through empirical research methods.

Similarly to Kahn-Harris (2003), Barron (2013) has examined the blatant misogyny of porngrind bands. Barron's work is primarily a feminist critique of the scene's macro-level gender practices and ideologies, and as such, does not advance a theory that can account for the presence of misogynistic bands or explicate micro-level gender issues in the extreme metal scene. Additionally, it does not include female perspectives on porngrind and misogyny in the scene. While Barron notes that some female porngrind fans exist, and claims that misogyny can be 'negotiated or offset' by female consumption (2013, p. 78), I argue here that such a position is naïve at best, as women's acceptance of misogyny only intensifies their marginalization and reinforces patriarchal power. In another recent work on gender issues in the metal subculture, Overell (2013) examined the affective nature of 'brutality' in the grindcore scene, arguing that (male) acknowledgment of emotions is masked by masculinist and misogynistic language and behavior. While Overell comments on the gender-based barriers she encountered during her study as a female interviewer, she does not further address women's position in the scene or present a theoretical framework with which to understand their position, since her study is primarily concerned with masculinity and the male experience. Another study involving gender in extreme metal is Riches, Lashua, and Spracklen's (2014) performance ethnography of female moshers in Leeds, England. Drawing upon Riches' own experiences in the mosh pit as well as interviews with six female moshers, the authors discuss the transgressive nature of female participation in a male-dominated subcultural activity. The authors argue that female moshing can be read as an act of feminist resistance in a male-dominated scene but acknowledge that such resistance may be undermined by male fans who create physical barriers to women's involvement in the pit or grope female moshers. While their findings contribute to the current understanding of female issues in metal studies, their study involves a small sample and does not offer a theoretical framework that can be used to explain the position of other women in extreme metal (i.e., those who do not mosh).

Similarly to Purcell's (2003) work, Phillipov's (2012) recent book on death metal functions in many ways as a defense of the subgenre against those inclined to dismiss or denigrate it. Phillipov (2012) aims to critically evaluate death metal in terms of pleasure rather than in terms of politics; consequently, the orientation of her book is primarily musicological. Probably for this reason, she scarcely touches on the gendered nature of the scene and does not provide an analysis of gender in death metal (although she challenges previous research on metal's marginalization of women). However, while she asserts that 'we should not ignore the problematic aspects of metal's gendered practices and aesthetics', she neglects those very aspects in her examination of death metal (Phillipov, 2012, p. 63). Although she asks some profound questions about death metal's misogyny and the position of female fans in the last two pages of her book—for example, 'What does women's willingness to wear [a Cannibal Corpse 'Fucked with a Knife' T-shirt] say about their relationship to the music and to the scene?'—she does not attempt to answer them beyond a brief consideration of 'reflexive anti-reflexivity' (Phillipov, 2012, p. 135). However, reflexive anti-reflexivity cannot answer the questions Phillipov asks about women's relationship with death metal, their identities as fans, and their reasons for participation in the scene. As noted above, reflexive anti-reflexivity is a macro-level, sociologically oriented theory that does not take individual differences into account—including individual psychological factors—and does not examine micro-level social interactions. I believe a comprehensive explanation for such phenomena involves a more complex web of both social and individual factors and how they interrelate. While such a web may be too intricate to allow for a truly comprehensive theoretical explanation, I contend that the theoretical framework I offer here is more able to account for the unique position of female fans than previous research, including women's awareness of their own marginalization and reasons for knowing participation in a sexist subculture, as well as the resistance of the scene to feminist change.

In summary, I believe that the extant work on gender in metal does not advance a theoretical perspective that can be used as an explanatory mechanism to illuminate women's unique and 'contradictory' position in the death metal scene or to explicate the sociopsychological structure of the scene itself. Furthermore, previous studies involving female fans had certain methodological limitations—such as the use of data derived from a single site and small samples of subjects—that impact the generalizability of findings. Therefore, it is my hope that this chapter and the empirical research upon which it is based will address a gap in the current literature.

I begin my analysis with a discussion of groups, gender, and social exchange, outlining the tenets of social exchange theory and applying them to women's position in the death metal scene. In this section, I aim to provide a theoretical explanation for women's participation in the scene despite awareness of its sexism, as well as to account for the subculture's ideological uniformity and lack of feminist resistance. I follow this section with a discussion of social power, drawing upon the work of Bierstedt (1950); here, I highlight the specific nature of power, distinguishing it from related concepts, and argue that women in the death metal scene lack power both collectively and individually. I then apply classic studies on group behavior and conformity to the death metal scene, offering an additional framework for understanding subcultural pressures toward ideological and behavioral uniformity. Finally, I discuss the phenomena of loss aversion and cost reduction, which I use to further explain female conformity to androcentric subcultural codes, as well as to illuminate the paradox of women's seeming acceptance of misogyny in the scene. Here, I argue that cost reduction serves as a coping mechanism by which female fans mitigate the psychological distress that arises from submission to patriarchal demands.

Groups, Gender, and Social Exchange

My previous work (Vasan 2010, 2011) on women in death metal revealed certain patterns of identity, ideology, and behavior.[1] Women in the scene tended to divide themselves into two distinct categories based on attire and behavior: those who adopted a masculine persona and style of dress, and those who adopted a hyper feminine, highly sexualized persona and style of dress (respectively referred to as 'den mothers' and 'band whores' by one of my interviewees). The former often occupied positions of power as scene leaders (such as managers, promoters, journalists, or band members) and were accorded more respect by men in the scene, although they remained inferior relative to men; the latter were disdained by the former and viewed as pursuing sexual contact with band members or other men in the scene rather than enjoyment of the music. When asked what drew them to death metal, interviewees characterized the subculture as a space that enabled freedom from the constraints of mainstream society—including gender-based constraints, as Loana indicated in her interview comments:

> I was raised in a community that had a lot of rules. And it seemed to me that they had a lot more rules for girls. ... I mean I could definitely say that this music just grabbed me [and] gave my angst a channel... it was angst, but it was also, and I'm gonna, I am gonna put a gender on it—female anger. Because we're so socialized to not express anger that when I heard this music, it was like, 'This is what I feel'.

Laina explained her affinity for the music in similar terms:

> It's energy, it's power, it's anger, but it's also freedom. ... I can only speak for myself personally, but, you know, my everyday life, my nine-to-five, um, I think as being a *woman* [emphasis hers], that you—society does not really appreciate, um, or really allow you to really vent out your frustrations. I find this music so liberating.

Many became fans during adolescence and felt that death metal contributed to their identity formation both as individuals and as females. Several, who had histories of psychosocial turmoil or were victims of sexual violence, found the darkness and anger of death metal emotionally therapeutic.[2]

Beyond listening to the music, the women I interviewed enjoyed subcultural activities, such as interacting with other fans at live shows; however, they were conscious of the sexism that typically surfaced in such settings. Women's presence was questioned at shows, even when they were there for business-related purposes as managers, promoters, journalists, or musicians. They were frequently 'quizzed' by men about music trivia, as if to judge their worthiness to participate in the scene. They also encountered barriers to their participation in the scene as musicians. Yet they remained passionate about the music and continued their subcultural activities, taking pride in being death metal fans. Why did they maintain allegiance to the subculture despite awareness of its sexism? I have attempted to answer this question using social exchange theory (Vasan, 2011). Here, I will summarize my previous analysis, and expand upon certain points.

Social exchange theory derives largely from Homans (1958), whose economics-influenced approach to sociology presented social behavior as an exchange of goods. According to Homans, individuals engage in behaviors that will procure them the most benefits, or 'profit', following the formula 'profit = reward - cost' (1958, p. 603). Social exchange theory conceptualizes behavior as a series of exchanges by which self-interested, interdependent individuals knowingly or unknowingly behave in ways that maximize their profits (Molm, 2003; Stafford, 2008). Although the economic premise of the theory would seem to imply that costs incurred should be commensurate with rewards gained, the going rate of social exchange is not always the fair rate, as individuals are often constrained by personal or societal factors to accept unfair terms of exchange (Blau, 1964). In one of the classic studies that gave rise to the theory, Back (1950) found that social groups that held more attraction for members exerted more pressure toward uniformity of beliefs and were susceptible to less influence from individual motives. Similarly, Festinger (1950) and Emerson (1962) noted that group pressure on individuals was correspondingly greater if the individual was dependent on that group to satisfy a need or purpose, especially if other means of achieving those ends were not available. Thus, female fans of death metal will be subject to greater pressures toward conformity if the subculture addresses needs of theirs that cannot be met elsewhere, such as freedom from constraints of domesticity and femininity (Frith and McRobbie, [1978] 2000; Krenkske and McKay, 2000; Vasan, 2010).

In addition to the factors noted above, group and individual beliefs are influenced by social reality: as Festinger observed, 'where the dependence upon physical [objective] reality is low the dependence upon social reality is correspondingly high' (1950, p. 5). Schachter (1950) asserted that groups tend to preserve uniformity of behavior and opinion, and that if differences of opinion (or behavior) arise, pressures will develop within the group to eliminate those differences. Such pressures are not limited to the aforementioned group pressures on individuals, but also include pressures *within* individuals to change their own opinions to accord with the group, as well as 'the tendency to decrease dependence on the deviate [dissenting individual] as a point of reference for establishing social reality' (Schachter, 1950, p. 62). Homans commented on Schacter's work by observing that 'if the deviate, by failing to change his behavior, fails to reinforce the members, they start to withhold social approval from him' (1958, p. 600).

Thus, women who deviate from death metal's prescribed norms—whose behavior, attire, or ideology threaten group uniformity—jeopardize their social recognition by the majority, and, by extension, their membership in the subculture. The women I interviewed were painfully aware of this difficult position and reported having to fight twice as hard as men to 'earn their place' in the scene; moreover, they seemed aware of the sacrifices they made in order to do so. Viewed in terms of social exchange, women submit to the sexist demands of the subculture in exchange for the privilege of membership in it, even if they are aware that the going rate of their exchange is not the fair rate. As Loana reflected:

> One of the things that, um, I had to trade for respect was, was my sensuality, was my sexuality ... a woman who dates too many times [in the eyes of the male death metal majority] is a whore, you know? ... I resented the costs that kept coming. I had to trade it, I had to essentially be celibate. ... I had to maintain a level of respect ... that was important to me.

Explicitly noting the 'trade' and 'costs' associated with her participation in the scene, she seemed to be aware of engaging in social exchange. Jexxy-Kill, another interviewee who was particularly vocal about the sexism she encountered in the scene, spoke with an air of resignation: 'it shouldn't be this complicated, but I love the music, so, whatcha gonna do, you know?' Her statement indicates a willingness to tolerate the scene's sexism in exchange for continued participation in it.

Homans (1958) adds that individuals not only seek to maximize their own profits in social exchanges, but also attempt to prevent others in the same group from making greater profits than they themselves do. This observation provides a possible explanation for the intra-sex conflict between the two groups of women in the death metal scene. Similarly, the patterns of group behavior outlined above, particularly when viewed with a social exchange lens, go a long way toward accounting for the lack of individual feminist resistance in the death metal scene. However, an additional explanation might be found in the work of Festinger, Schachter, and Back, ([1950] 1963), who found that subgroup formation within a group tended to disrupt the cohesiveness [3] of the larger group, regardless of how cohesive the subgroups were.

Female death metal fans may be reluctant to impact the scene in such a manner by creating feminist subgroups; they may feel that subgroup formation would lead to a separate subculture (as with punk and Riot Grrrl) and have no wish to be separatists; they may be subject to the external (group) and internal (individual) pressures toward group uniformity that emerge in the face of dissent, as noted above. All such factors may play a part in the lack of feminist resistance and subgroup formation in death metal. Furthermore, just as Blau (1964, p. 203) observed that '[c]ollective approval of power legitimates that power', lack of collective disapproval of power can be said to legitimate that power as well. Thus, the power imbalance between the sexes in the death metal scene perpetuates itself through the pressures toward group uniformity that legitimate and reinforce its social reality. Such pressures are a complex web of influences that may be both subtle and overt; both informal and institutionalized (Festinger et al., [1950] 1963).

Social Power

An analysis of the position of women in the death metal scene necessitates an examination of power and its related concepts. Bierstedt (1950) distinguishes power from prestige, influence, dominance, and authority. Power is a function of social structures and requires numbers of people, social organization, and resources. Prestige, while often associated with power, is a separate concept: those with power may not have prestige, and vice versa. Influence is related to power, but is persuasive rather than coercive: as Bierstedt notes, '[w]e submit voluntarily to influence while power requires submission' (1950, p. 731). Influence can become power but is not power in itself. Dominance is a function of the individual rather than the group—it is a personal trait that may equally belong to a member of a powerful or a powerless group—but can also affect the whole: '[p]ower appears in the statuses which people occupy in formal organization; dominance in the roles they play in informal organization' (Bierstedt, 1950, p. 732). In contrast to dominance, authority is found in formal organizations as transformed social power; in less rigidly organized groups, authority may be present, but will be accordingly less defined.

In practice, social power relations are a complex matrix of the above concepts; thus, even those with authority (formal power) may refrain from exercising it due to the (informal) pressures of power in groups over which they have authority. As Bierstedt observes, 'every association is always at the mercy of a majority of its own members[...]. Given the same social organization and the same resources, the larger number can always control the smaller and secure its compliance' (1950, pp. 735, 737). One can imagine how much stronger the control of the majority becomes when the minority lacks both organization and resources, as with women in the death metal scene relative to men. Thus, while female scene leaders may have prestige, influence, dominance, or even authority, they seldom have power. This is an important distinction to make, as there are some who point to the increasing numbers of women entering the scene (both as fans and artists) as 'evidence' of gender equality. However, a review of the above social phenomena indicates that the mere presence of women, even at an equal ratio to men, would not in itself suffice to alter the sexist ideologies and practices of the subculture. Kanter (1993), speaking of power more broadly, noted that it tends to be granted to individuals resembling those already in power, as in the granting of power to men by other men (although power may also be granted to women who resemble men in appearance, behavior, or ideology). This seems to be one reason many female fans of death metal adopt masculine dress and behavior; as JexxyKill put it, 'I have to act like I'm a dude to get along'. (Interviewee comments also indicated that women who did not dress like men risked being perceived as groupies or being verbally or physically harassed.) Women needed a certain 'toughness' to survive in the scene—in the words of Samantha, an 'emotional set of balls'. Janet described men in the scene as being 'like cavemen. They walk around with, you know, the club—most of them wanna put the façade that they're unapproachable. … They don't want you approaching them, they don't wanna hear, you know, the little dumb girl talk'. The granting of power in the scene to individuals resembling those already in power is perhaps most apparent in the barriers to women's participation as artists; as Mary noted, 'Dudes don't wanna see chicks on stage, screaming. … People just expect chicks to be girls. To look pretty, to be nice, and that's it'. … Interviewees continually described the scene as an arena that men refused to share with women: Laina called it a 'man cave', while Loana likened it to a treehouse with a 'No Girls Allowed' sign. Women had to earn their place by conforming to the androcentric codes of the subculture, and they were not blind to the gender-specific difficulties they faced.

Group Behavior and Conformity

What are some other factors that account for the resistance of the death metal scene to ideological change? Beyond overt and conscious sexism, there is also the phenomenon that 'individuals possess stereotypes even though they may not often express them or feel affected by them' (Goldberg, Gottesdiener, and Abramson, 1975, 1977, p. 266). Even more striking is the following finding:

> Fishbein (1967) argues that it is a misconception to assume that an individual's attitude toward an object is a major determinant of his behavior with respect to that object. He summarizes research which indicates that attitudes were not related to behavior in any consistent fashion, but appear to be consequences or determinants of beliefs or behavioral intentions, rather than predictors of overt behavior.
> (Goldberg et al. [1975] 1977, p. 266)

Thus, while men (and women) may exist in the death metal scene who espouse nonsexist or even feminist *attitudes*, those attitudes may not necessarily result in nonsexist or feminist *behaviors*. Without corresponding behavior, such attitudes are insufficient to combat the dominant ideologies of the subculture.

In addition to the group pressures toward uniformity discussed above, classic studies on group psychology have revealed other patterns of behavior that contribute to conformity. Asch ([1955] 1977) conducted an experiment in which 123 subjects were placed in group settings and asked to judge which of a number of lines was closest in length to another, unaware that the other members of the group were instructed to answer erroneously at certain points (thus disagreeing with the subjects). Thus influenced,

36.8% accorded with the group and made incorrect choices (as opposed to fewer than 1% who did so in the absence of group influence). Nearly all the subjects claimed to value independence over conformity: an example of attitudes failing to manifest as behaviors. Interestingly, all who conformed in the experiment underestimated the frequency with which they did so. Furthermore, their conformity was consistent: having once succumbed to group pressure by changing a response, they continued to do so for the duration of the experiment. As Asch noted:

> Many of the individuals who went along suspected that the majority were 'sheep' following the first responder, or that the majority were victims of an optical illusion; nevertheless, these suspicions failed to free them at the moment of decision. More disquieting were the reactions of subjects who construed their difference from the majority as a sign of some general deficiency in themselves, which at all costs they must hide. On this basis they desperately tried to merge with the majority, not realizing the longer-range consequences to themselves. ([1955] 1977, p. 7)

While betraying one's own logic and perceptions merely for the sake of conformity to a group may seem outrageous, Firestone's (1970) classic treatise on the subjugation of women explicates such behavior: 'the distance between one's experience and one's perceptions of it becomes enlarged by a vast interpretive network; if our direct experience contradicts its interpretation by this ubiquitous cultural network, the experience must be denied' ([1970] 2013, p. 126). This observation accords with decades of social science research that indicates the use of power is determined by social structure, regardless of the intentionality of individuals or their awareness of the power structure (Molm, 1997). The above phenomena are compounded by 'institutional genderism' or the perpetuation of gender bias at the structural level: sexism is not perpetuated only by individuals, but also by groups and organizations (Goffman, 1977, p. 305). My interviewees recognized the scene's structural sexism, as Kim noted:

> I've always felt in a position of being marginalized, regardless of how the numbers [of women in the scene] have changed, because really, the scene in its origins, and even today, has always been a boys' club. And I don't know if that's ever gonna change ... there's never any question of sort of this overlying patriarchy.

However, in accordance with the social science findings discussed here, women's awareness of sexism does not alter the scene's structural inequalities.

In another study on conformity, Latané and Rodin ([1969] 1977) found that bystanders were less likely to help a person in distress or report an emergency if one or more other persons were present; the more people present, the less likely the intervention. Individuals used others to gauge whether intervention was necessary: if others did not intervene, neither did they. Individuals felt no guilt about such behavior, asserting that they would have intervened 'in a 'real' emergency' ([1969] 1977, p. 37). Latané and Rodin attributed this phenomenon to social influence processes inhibiting action that differed from the norm or was seen as disruptive, as well as to the 'diffusion of responsibility' for intervention among all those present, thus decreasing individual responsibility and leading to a state of 'pluralistic ignorance' (p. 38). The significance of such findings to the death metal scene is obvious: given the high cohesiveness of the subculture, the pressures toward conformity are likely to be even greater than those manifested in the above studies. Here we have an explanation for the lack of overt disapproval—whether verbal or physical—of concert occurrences such as sexual harassment ('Show us your tits!') and sexual assault (groping), regardless of the presence of women and nonsexist men. We also have an explanation for the other conformist practices of those who may not personally espouse (either in full or in part) the androcentric codes or sexist ideology of the subculture. Weinstein's ([1991] 2000) classic example of the young woman at a W.A.S.P. concert who cheered for 'Animal (Fuck Like a Beast)' but abstained from displaying the same enthusiasm when Blackie Lawless asked the question that traditionally opens the song ('Anyone here come to get some *pussy?*') has become the typical female at a Cannibal Corpse show who will cheer for the band's performance, but may (or may not) abstain from cheering when the song 'Fucked with a Knife' is introduced with the words, 'This song is for all the ladies out there'. As Laina opined:

> I can believe that women would stay and women would cheer [for 'Fucked with a Knife']. I can believe that. Because I think that they say, 'If I don't cheer, if I don't play along with the game, then I'm gonna look like a wimp'. I can understand that crowd mentality. ... because they're like, 'Oh, then guys are really gonna think I'm weak. Guys are really gonna think I can't take it. And I wanna fit in'. You know?

Such women may, as with Asch's subjects, interpret any personal feelings that do not accord with subcultural codes as evidence of a deficiency in themselves—such as 'feminine weakness'—that must be hidden from the male majority. If so, they doubtless do not realize the longer-range consequences to themselves any more than did Asch's subjects. It may also be the case that they do not disavow their feminist beliefs, but resign themselves to overt conformity as the price they must pay for participation in the subculture; this seems to have been true of the women I interviewed. As Firestone ([1970] 2013) famously noted, women's social legitimacy depends upon their adherence to standards of appearance and behavior imposed upon them by men. Women are able to occupy places in the death metal scene by conforming to either a sexual or a masculine ideal; while those who conform to the masculine ideal are accorded more respect and allowed participation on more equal footing than their sexualized sisters, they remain 'second-class citizens'. Whether female fans of death metal conform to the androcentric codes of the subculture deliberately or unknowingly, the result is the same: reinforcement of the very ideologies that constrain them.

Loss Aversion and Cost Reduction

While power may be exercised unknowingly, it is often used strategically, or selectively and deliberately. When strategic power is used, social exchange may be characterized by loss aversion, in which losses are perceived by individuals as having greater value than equivalent gains; in other words, the loss of one unit of something produces more distress than the gain of one unit of the same thing produces satisfaction (Molm, 1997). This phenomenon may result in a pattern of behavior known as the status quo bias: 'When the potential losses from retaliation are roughly equal to the potential gains from compliance, strategic power use is unlikely. Actors will accept the status quo of a relation rather than risk the consequences of using power to change it' (p. 119).

One can imagine how much stronger the tendency to maintain the status quo would be if the potential losses due to noncompliance were *greater* than potential gains from acquiescence, as is likely to be the case with women in the death metal scene. The women I interviewed were emphatic about the significance of death metal to their lives, one even claiming that she owed it her life. Given that women in mainstream society are still disempowered relative to men, and given that women with stereotypically 'masculine' tastes, behaviors, or identities are likely to feel out of place in the mainstream (as many interviewees reported), it is perhaps not surprising that female fans of death metal are willing to conform to the codes of the subculture. It must be acknowledged that nearly all women in society—and men as well—conform to the codes of hegemonic masculinity (Connell and Messerschmidt, 2005).

How do women—in particular, female fans of death metal—deal with the distress that must result from submission to patriarchal demands? The answer may lie in the phenomenon of cost reduction. In social exchange, an unbalanced power relation can give rise to 'a process involving change in values (personal, social, economic) which reduces the pains incurred in meeting the demands of a powerful other'—a process Emerson (1962, p. 35) calls cost reduction. Female fans of death metal may engage in cost reduction to mitigate the distress arising from various aspects of their participation in the scene. For example, a woman may alter her personal values in order to tolerate or accept misogyny in songs or artwork, so that her emotional, psychological, or moral distress will be reduced. The women I interviewed seldom adopted a hardline stance toward misogynistic death metal; while none expressed enjoyment of such bands or songs, most found some way to rationalize them (on the grounds that they are offered in jest, or that the band members do not actually rape women). Interestingly, some interviewees consciously followed certain cost-reducing paths of logic: one reported attempting to convince herself that the members of black metal bands Emperor and Dissection were not white supremacists so that she could continue to enjoy their music; another admitted that she deliberately avoided asking the members of Cannibal Corpse why they wrote misogynistic songs because she was 'afraid of the answer' and might have felt compelled to abandon the band as a fan if she knew too much. While such comments are striking, they become even more so in light of the fact that 'cost-reducing tendencies generally will function to deepen and stabilize social relations over and above the condition of balance' (Emerson, 1962, p. 35). Thus, when female fans of death metal engage in cost reduction to facilitate their participation in the subculture, such behavior only intensifies their position as subordinates.

Conclusion

In this chapter, I have sought to explicate the position of women in the death metal scene using social exchange and related sociopsychological frameworks. My aim has been to provide a theoretical foundation for understanding women's knowing participation in a sexist subculture as well as for understanding the scene's lack of feminist resistance. I have also attempted a theoretical explanation for women's seeming acceptance of death metal's misogyny—an issue that continues to perplex metal scholars (Krenske and McKay, 2000; Phillipov, 2012). As previously stated, my goal has been to account for both individual and group behavior by focusing on the 'why' of gender rather than the 'how' of gender and thus fill a gap in metal-studies literature. While I hope that my research will facilitate a more complete understanding of gender issues in metal, I readily acknowledge that my findings and theoretical perspectives represent only one piece of a very complex puzzle. Furthermore, my work does not specifically address the unique position of women of color in the scene (although this theme did emerge in certain interviewee comments) or that of lesbian women or women of non-US nationalities. In addition, my work is limited in conveying the experience of women who are groupies—let alone the potential interaction effects of the above categories (e.g., lesbian groupies who are women of color). The recent work of Dawes (2012), one of my interviewees, directly addresses the unique position of black women in the metal scene. As the field of metal studies continues to grow, I have no doubt that other such works will emerge to enable a fuller understanding of the subculture and its adherents.

Notes

1. See Vasan (2010) for information on data and use of pseudonyms. For the purpose of this chapter, I have excluded preliminary data not listed in Vasan (2010), including additional participant observation, field interviews with women, and individual interviews with male fans.

2. I wish to make it clear that none of my interviewees, including those who were victims of sexual violence, ever accorded therapeutic value to misogynistic death metal bands, even when specifically asked whether that was the case for them.
3. Cohesiveness is defined as 'the total field of forces which act on members to remain in the group' (Festinger et al. [1950] 1963, p. 164).

Bibliography

Arnett, J. (1996). *Metalheads: Heavy metal music and adolescent alienation*. Boulder, CO: Westview Press.

Asch, S. (1955/1977). Opinions and social pressure. In E. Aronson (Ed.), *Readings about the social animal* (pp. 3–12). San Francisco, CA: W. H. Freeman and Company.

Back, K. (1950). The exertion of influence through social communication. In L. Festinger, K. Back, S. Schachter, H. Kelley, & J. Thibaut (Eds.), *Theory and experiment in social communication* (pp. 21–36). Ann Arbor, MI: University of Michigan.

Barron, L. (2013) Dworkin's nightmare: Porngrind as the sound of feminist fears. In T. Hjelm, K. Kahn-Harris, & M. LeVine (Eds.), *Heavy metal: Controversies and countercultures* (pp. 66–82). Bristol, CT: Equinox.

Bierstedt, R. (1950). An analysis of social power. *American Sociological Review*, 15(6), 730–738.

Blau, P. (1964). Justice in social exchange. *Sociological Inquiry*, 34(2), 193–206.

Connell, R., & Messerschmidt, J. (2005). Hegemonic masculinity: Rethinking the concept. *Gender and Society*, 19(6), 829–859.

Dawes, L. (2012). *What are you doing here? A black woman's life and liberation in heavy metal*. Brooklyn, NY: Bazillion Points.

Emerson, R. (1962). Power-Dependence relations. *American Sociological Review*, 27(1), 31–41.

Festinger, L. (1950). Informal social communication. In L. Festinger, K. Back, S. Schachter, H. Kelley, & J. Thibaut (Eds.), *Theory and experiment in social communication* (pp. 3–17). Ann Arbor, MI: University of Michigan.

Festinger, L., Schachter, S., & Back, K. ([1950]1963). *Social pressures in informal groups*. Stanford, CA: Stanford University Press.

Firestone, S. ([1970]2013). The culture of romance. In C. R. McCann & S. Kim (Eds.), *Feminist theory reader: Local and global perspectives* (pp. 123–128). New York: Routledge.

Frith, S., & McRobbie, A. ([1978] 2000). Rock and sexuality. In A. McRobbie (Ed.), *Feminism and youth culture* (pp. 137–158). New York: Routledge.

Goffman, E. (1977). The arrangement between the sexes. *Theory and Society*, 4(3), 301–331.

Goldberg, P. A., Gottesdiener, M., and Abramson, P. R. (1975/1977). Another put-down of women? Perceived attractiveness as a function of support for the feminist movement. In E. Aronson (Ed.), *Readings about the social animal* (pp. 262–267). San Francisco, CA: W. H. Freeman and Company.

Homans, G. (1958). Social behavior as exchange. *The American Journal of Sociology*, 63(6), 597–606.

Kahn-Harris, K. (2003). Death metal and the limits of musical expression. In M. Cloonan & R. Garofalo (Eds.), *Policing pop* (pp. 81–99). Philadelphia, PA: Temple University Press.

Kahn-Harris, K. (2007). *Extreme metal: Music and culture on the Edge*. New York: Berg.
Kanter, R. M. (1993). *Men and women of the corporation*. New York: Basic Books.
Krenske, L., & McKay, J. (2000). Hard and heavy: Gender and power in a heavy metal music subculture. *Gender, Place and Culture*, 7(3), 287–304.
Latané, B., & Rodin, J. ([1969] 1977). A lady in distress: Inhibiting effect of friends and strangers on bystander intervention. In E. Aronson (Ed.), *Readings about the social animal* (pp. 28–41). San Francisco, CA: W. H. Freeman and Company.
Molm, L. (1997). Risk and power use: Constraints on the use of coercion in exchange. *American Sociological Review* 62(1), 113–133.
Molm, L. (2003). Theoretical comparisons of forms of exchange. *Sociological Theory*, 21(1), 1–17.
Moola, F. J., Norman, M. E., Petherick, L., & Strachan, S. (2014). Teaching across the lines of fault in psychology and sociology: Health, obesity and physical activity in the Canadian context. *Sociology of Sport Journal*, 31, 202–227.
Overell, R. (2013). [I] hate girls and emo[tion]s: Negotiating masculinity in grindcore music. In T. Hjelm, K. Kahn-Harris, & M. LeVine (Eds.), *Heavy metal: Controversies and countercultures* (pp. 201–227). Bristol, CT: Equinox.
Phillipov, M. (2012). *Death metal and music criticism: Analysis at the limits*. Lanham, MD: Lexington Books.
Riches, G., Lashua, B., & Spracklen, K. (2014). Female, mosher, transgressor: A 'moshography' of transgressive practices within the Leeds extreme metal scene. *IASPM@Journal*, 4(1), 87–100.
Schachter, S. (1950). Deviation, rejection and communication. In L. Festinger, K. Back, S. Schachter, H. Kelley, & J. Thibaut (Eds.), *Theory and experiment in social communication* (pp. 51–82). Ann Arbor, MI: University of Michigan.
Stafford, L. (2008). Social exchange theories: Calculating the rewards and costs of personal relationships. In L. Baxter & D. Braithwaite (Eds.), *Engaging theories in interpersonal communication: Multiple perspectives* (pp. 377–389). Thousand Oaks, CA: Sage.
Thoits, P. (1995). Social psychology: The interplay between sociology and psychology. *Social Forces*, 73(4), 1231–1243.
Thorpe, H., Ryba, T., & Denison, J. (2014). Toward new conversations between sociology and psychology. *Sociology of Sport Journal*, 31, 131–138.
Vasan, S. (2010). *Women's participation in the death metal subculture*. PhD Dissertation. Houston, TX: University of Houston.
Vasan, S. (2011). The price of rebellion: Gender boundaries in the death metal scene. *Journal for Cultural Research*, 15, (3), 333–349.
Walser, R. (1993). *Running with the devil: Power, gender, and madness in heavy metal music*. Middletown, CT: Wesleyan University Press.
Weinstein, D. (1991/2000). *Heavy metal: The music and its culture*. New York: Da Capo Press.

16 Masculine Pleasure?
Women's Encounters with Hard Rock and Metal Music

Rosemary Lucy Hill

The broad genre of hard rock and metal is often described as male-dominated (Walser, 1993) and 'masculine' (Weinstein, 2000, p. 106; Bayton, 1998, p. 40). The former is not difficult to critique, as the line-up of any hard rock or metal festival or a glance through any of the genre's magazines will show (Brown, forthcoming). The latter, however, is not so straightforward, even though there is well-known academic work that highlights the misogyny and exclusionary musical and non-musical practices. Such common sense and academic ideas about the music bring forth questions about why women would enjoy it; yet it is clear that some do. A number of influential studies have engaged with the question of women's pleasure in popular culture, even when it has been thought to be damaging for them, in many cases reinforcing a destructive ideal of femininity (see for example Radway, 1984; Ang, 1985; Geraghty, 1991; Stacey, 1994; Skeggs, 1997). These authors show that the pleasures women experience are complicated for a variety of reasons and that textual readings produce a multiplicity of meanings. These include resistant readings that allow texts to be reconceived so that messages that women find difficult to identify with become more palatable and even enjoyable (Fetterley, 1978). In this chapter I discuss women's 'readings' of hard rock and metal via critical discourse analysis of what the British women fans I spoke to during my doctoral research said about the music of the genre and their favorite bands. From their responses, it is clear that the genre has much more to offer listeners than simple expressions or celebrations of masculinity: the music has more nuanced meanings than that, and I argue that the women's descriptions mount a challenge to that perceived masculinity.

This chapter should be read in the broader context of popular music studies and the field of the phenomenological experience of music (Hesmondhalgh, 2013). It should also be read in the context of metal studies in which research around gender and musical experience (such as that by Fast, 1999; Clifford-Napoleone, 2009; Vasan, 2010; Patterson, 2011; Riches, 2011; Vasan, 2011; Overell, 2012) forms a vibrant and forceful critique of assumptions about hard rock and metal and about women's participation in male-dominated cultures. In particular, this chapter sits alongside Gabrielle Riches' work that examines pleasure and gender: where she describes the experiences of live performance, I focus on more private listening practices; where she discusses behaviors thought of as masculine and challenges that assumed masculinity, I examine un-gendered and feminine qualities. I see our work as a two-pronged interrogation of the gendered assumptions about metal. Riches argues that,

> Failing to incorporate pleasure into music and leisure discourses obfuscates the ways in which we can explain why women, appearing to consent to dominant and patriarchal practices and expectations, engage in contradictory activities within forms of popular culture.
> (Riches, 2011, p. 327)

Riches is arguing for a consideration of pleasure as a necessity in any work that looks at gender and popular culture: if pleasure is overlooked then the ways in which gender works cannot be fully examined, nor can we gain a rich understanding of women's participation in male dominated spheres. Furthermore, as Radway (1984) shows as regards romance readers, examining pleasure is a successful means to challenge devaluing stereotypes of women's cultural engagement. One thing that has been striking in metal studies is the way that discussions of gender have been limited to examinations of misogyny and problems of access for women fans (e.g., Kahn-Harris, 2007, pp. 71–76; Vasan, 2010, 2011) or women fans have been reduced to unhelpful stereotypes (e.g., Walser, 1993; Weinstein, 2000) or their particular experiences have been ignored (e.g., Purcell, 2003). Where does women's pleasurable engagement with the music fit in?

Sonia Vasan (2011) hints at the pleasures that women derive from their engagement with the music but does not explore them in depth. Her focus is on the ways in which women engage in 'cost reduction' mechanisms in order to reduce the personal impact of the misogyny at live 'gigs' (pp. 345–346). Keith Kahn-Harris' discussion of pleasure in music is brief and focuses on how fans are, perhaps purposefully, inarticulate about what they like (2007, pp. 51–54). In the main, his discussion of women death and black metal fans focuses on their marginal status. While such a focus is important, the emphasis on sexisms results in it being difficult to understand why women would enjoy death metal. The allusion to pleasure serves as a tantalizing glimpse of some other story, but this is not told. In fact, focusing solely on problems of access women fans face does an injustice to those fans. Kahn-Harris, Vasan, Walser, and Weinstein's accounts sell women fans short by not considering how women love the music as well, because female fans are always positioned by their gender. Thus loving the music, whilst taking their gender for granted, becomes a position that is only available to male fans, to the extent that such fandom is presented as 'normal' and 'general', whilst female fandom is reduced to that of gender, as Wittig argues: 'the masculine is not the masculine but the general. The result is that there are the general and the feminine, or rather, the general and the mark of the feminine'

(1992, p. 60). Such a thesis produces women as extraordinary, so that the ways in which they are *different* become the focus of study, rather than any potential similarities. Women's engagement with the music is therefore forgotten or treated as having lesser importance. Although it is vital to sort out the structural matter of women's marginalization, I think the problems of access are only part of the way that women are positioned as second-class fans in a genre in which their musical engagement is considered suspect.

In this chapter I prioritize women fans' experiences of the music and examine how they discuss the pleasure they derive from their favorite bands.[1] I employ discourse analysis to consider the language that women use to describe hard rock and metal music and their favorite bands, and in doing so offer a complex picture of women's musical pleasure that challenges previous accounts. In particular, I argue that although the women I spoke to use language that echoes ideas about the genre, which in some ways reinforce the dominant understanding of it as masculine music, they also use unexpected and creative language that challenges understandings of the genre as only enjoyed as a masculine pleasure.

Hard Rock and Metal as a 'Masculine' Genre

Robert Walser's (1993) work on heavy metal and gender centers around the way that the genre 'exscripts' women, writing them out and creating a fantasy world for men in which women don't exist. Musically, he characterizes heavy metal as masculine music due to its 'virtuosity and control', articulation of 'a dialectic of controlling power and transcendent freedom', 'vocal extremes, guitar power chords, distortion; and sheer volume of bass and drums' (p. 109). This conception of the music as masculine is evident in Kahn-Harris' (2007) analysis of fans' descriptions of what they like about the music. He concludes that fans are 'inarticulate' (p. 54) and that they have limited language available to them. The lexicon they do use is bounded by the extreme metal scene, which values 'aggression, brutality, energy, etc'. (p. 53). He moves on to consider other (non-musical) aspects of extreme metal fandom, but I do not think we should leave our understanding of musical pleasure to rest with responses such as 'I just liked it' (quoted in Kahn-Harris, 2007, p. 54). The opacity of this speech proves an obstacle to greater understanding and 'just' works to foreclose any follow-up questions. We cannot afford to allow such a wall to remain in place; to do so means relying on received ideas about the music and about women fans' involvement in hard rock and metal.

In my interviews with women fans, I asked how they would describe heavy metal. Like Kahn-Harris, I found that they employed words that echoed notions of warrior masculinity and ideas of authenticity. They used terms such as: 'loud', 'heavy', 'hard', 'severe', 'raw', 'power', 'grunty', 'strong', 'faster', and expressions related to anger or aggression; adjectives such as 'fiercer' and 'angry' were also employed. Such terminology is reminiscent of the warrior aesthetic in metal (Hill, 2011) in which physical power and intimidation are celebrated. My interviewees also talked about guitars, more specifically, electric guitars. Monique Bourdage (2010) has shown that electric guitars are constructed as masculine, reinforcing the symbolic construction of hard rock and metal musicians as male; Mavis Bayton (1997) has shown how valuable the guitar is for maintaining the masculinity of rock. Hard rock and metal were contrasted with pop by a number of my interviewees, with all the attendant language of the pop/rock divide: pop was manufactured, formulaic, throwaway fluff, and it was inauthentic, but rock and metal were 'real'. Its lyrics were more poetic and meaningful; instruments were more 'real' and musicians more talented; virtuosity was in evidence, and song structures were more complex. These descriptive terms owe much to the way in which pop and the mainstream is feminized (Thornton, 1995, p. 52).

All of these sorts of descriptions parallel the symbolic framing of hard rock and metal as masculine. In doing so, it would appear that my interviewees were rejecting the femininity associated with pop music whilst celebrating masculinity. This reading looks problematic: by asserting rock's value to the detriment of a pop culture that is associated with women and is positioned as being less valuable (Huyssen, 1986, p. 55), women as producers, artists, and enjoyers of culture are seen as less important. Thus, the idea that only men have something important to say, be it artistically or politically, is maintained and feeds into the persistence of women's subordination. Furthermore, it positions women fans as involved in the disparagement of their own gender as they align themselves with a masculine culture that writes out the feminine. However, this is a simplistic reading that does not take into account the more complex ways in which women understand their relationships with the music they love. Any assertion that women who like hard rock and metal are somehow traitors to their gender needs to be questioned.

Problems in Understanding Hard Rock and Metal as Only Masculine

Common sense understandings of hard rock and metal as masculine owe much to the ways in which certain sounds are *construed* as 'masculine'. However, it is important to remember that 'masculine' sounds are only 'masculine' because they have been understood as such: they have no inherent masculine qualities. In his description of metal as masculine, Walser (1993) clarifies his position by asserting that the description is not due to any essential gender qualities of the music:

> Underpinning all semiotic analysis is, recognised or not, a set of assumptions about cultural practice, for ultimately music doesn't have meanings; people do. There is no essential, foundational way to ground musical meaning beyond the flux of social existence. (p. 32)

In ascribing these qualities to masculinity, Walser makes it clear that these meanings are constructed rather than inherent (p. 113), a perspective derived from Susan McClary in the foundational feminist musicology text *Feminine Endings* (1991). McClary investigates the way in which music has been divided along gender lines so that, for example, major keys are linked to the masculine and minor to the feminine (p. 11). Throughout traditional musicology, she finds that gendered binaries abound. Whether or not composers are consciously choosing to musically construct femininity or masculinity, the gendered codes are 'taken to be "natural"', by them (p. 9). Moreover, they are *heard* as natural by the listener, too (ibid.). Gendered interpretations of music therefore affect our understandings of and pleasure taken in the music, as well as our thoughts and feelings about musicians and about fans. This is clear from my interviewees' descriptions of music where their language choice emphasizes the *masculinity* of hard rock and metal. Their gendered hearings of the music were part of their experience and part of their pleasure. However, that pleasure has not been treated as neutral and has been politicized by groups of non-fans.

The perceived hyper masculinity of heavy metal and the virulently misogynistic lyrics to be found in some rock and metal songs (Grant, 1996) have led to criticism of the music from conservative quarters, particularly in the USA, including the powerful PMRC campaign that led to the famous 'Parental Advisory' stickers,[2] and also from feminists in the early days of the Women's Liberation Movement (e.g., Wise, 1984; Baumgardner, 2005; Rat, 2013). Some feminists in the 1970s assumed that rock music was 'bad for women' and contributed to oppression via negative representations of women, their sexual objectification; images of women as deserving victims of male violence or as out to deceive and harm innocent men; or as sexually passive (for an overview of these 'repressive representations' see Whiteley, 2000, pp. 32–43). In her introduction to the compilation of the Chicago and New Haven Women's Liberation Rock Bands' recordings, Jennifer Baumgardner states that there was a general feeling of rock as a problem:

> Rock was part of the revolutionary language, and feminists were squeezing out the sexism there too. They were challenging the Rolling Stones – or at least talking back to their lyrics—She's "under your thumb"? Oh, yeah? Screw you, sexist pig! (2005, n.p.)

This was reflected in a comment made by a male friend of one of my interviewees. He was confused that as a *Spare Rib* reader and feminist she could enjoy the music of Led Zeppelin and other heavy metal bands:

> I can remember having a conversation with a friend who said, 'you know I find it really uncomfortable that you like this sort of music'. A male friend. [...] Yes, he said 'because it seemed to me to epitomise everything that you stand against'.
>
> (Susan)

The conversation, although it had occurred in the 1970s, had clearly stayed in Susan's memory and had made an impact upon her, although it did not stop her from listening to Led Zeppelin, Deep Purple, and other 1970s heavy metal bands. More recently, Vasan's (2010) feminist research is underpinned by incomprehension, causing her to: 'Ponder why women are drawn to death metal in general: why women choose to associate themselves with a male-dominated and overtly misogynistic subculture' (p. 70).

These kind of criticisms place women who enjoy hard rock and metal music, despite its sexisms, in a minority amongst feminists and have led to criticism of those women who want to make rock music (Baumgardner, 2005, n.p.) or listen to it (Willis, 1977). Sue Wise (1984) felt pressure from feminist friends to drop her fandom of Elvis, as if being an Elvis fan and being a feminist were incompatible: liking Elvis was a state of false consciousness to be rejected (p. 394). Norma Coates (1997) draws attention to this problem when considering her own attachment to The Rolling Stones, but for her it is not only the misogynist attitudes or lyrics that are problematic, but the music itself:

> A feminist fan of the Stones and rock like myself is faced with an immediate conundrum: if indeed it is the phallic power of the sound that draws me to it, then I am complicit in my own submission to that power. I accept and at the same time reinforce it. Some might say that when I describe the Stones' sound as sexy, I am operating under 'false consciousness', simply accepting and reinforcing hegemonic tropes of male and female sexuality. This is an unsatisfactory explanation. (pp. 50–51)

False consciousness may be an unsatisfactory explanation for her Stones fandom, but she does not offer another. The argument that rock is bad for women is rooted in the construction of rock and pop as dichotomously oppositional, which results in a cyclical relationship: thinking of metal and rock as 'masculine' means thinking in ways that are inevitably compelled to hang upon the gender binary. Furthermore, interpreting metal as masculine misses out on some of the more interesting aspects of the genre, such as the queering discussed by Whiteley (2006, pp. 257–259). When hard rock and metal is thought of as 'masculine', its more 'feminine' attributes are hidden: the high voices of bands like Led Zeppelin and Budgie; the make-up of, for example, My Chemical Romance and many glam metal bands; the ubiquitous long hair. When these elements are considered, the heteromasculinity of hard rock and metal looks more complicated, as Sheila Whiteley argues:

> In essence, metal is about men being manly, and while Walser relates this to the codes of misogyny, exscription and the fraternalistic culture of bands and fans, problems arise when connecting the sweaty gods to their often androgynous images—the long hair, mascara, spandex, and leather. (2006, p. 257)

Whiteley also makes an important point about the dangers of interpreting metal *only* as masculine: that is, the genre is more open to gender play for its male musicians than critics allow, and this needs to be taken into account.

Susan Fast (1999), too, finds a good deal to worry about in conceptions of rock music, Led Zeppelin in particular, as masculine. She argues that leaving the masculinity of rock assumed and unquestioned misses an opportunity to engage with the ways that both female and male fans make sense of Led Zeppelin's music (pp. 246–247). She writes that in the assumption of the masculinity of the music and the fans there is no place for her own fandom of the band (ibid.). Similarly, the identification of Elvis as 'butch god' by feminists did not correlate with the Elvis beloved of Sue Wise (1984, p. 395). Wise argues that this macho Elvis rejected by her feminist friends was the Elvis of 'men who depicted this phallic hero as having worldwide cultural significance' (p. 397). As Fast (1999) argues in her discussion of how the 'masculinity' of Led Zeppelin and their music has been maintained, the key players in the media and academia who have contributed to this reading are male (p. 247). Representations of hard rock and metal music are written and sanctioned by men (music journalists, the musicians, editors) or by those whose job it is to ensure the ideological perspective of the genre is maintained (albeit with some female industry workers or musicians) (Bayton, 1998; McDonnell and Powers, 1995). For this reason, Fast argues, it is vital that women's perspectives on rock and metal be considered. Picking up on Coates' notion of the gender binary of rock/pop and the effect of interpreting rock as masculine, she writes, '[i]n reading these words I felt enormous sorrow that her pleasure had been compromised by an essentialist view of how gender might work in music' (op. cit., p. 252). Considering hard rock and metal as exclusively masculine eclipses women fans' own interpretations that challenge the notion that the genre is only an arena for hyper masculine posturing, which excludes or demeans women. For this reason, I now consider how my interviewees described their pleasure in hard rock and metal in ways that did *not* fit in with the ideology of this imaginary community.

Articulating Pleasure in Music

When describing their enjoyment of their favorite bands, only five women used the same kinds of language employed in their descriptions of heavy metal. More women invoked 'dissimilarity' between the music of their preferred bands and others. In addition, my interviewees used quite novel and imaginative descriptors, so that they were able to articulate why their favorite bands moved them in language that often contrasted sharply with the sort of terminology that is typically associated with hard rock and metal. They described the music as allowing transcendence, as enabling shared experiences; they also used romantic terms, and two women discussed their simultaneous love of pop musicians alongside their hard rock and metal fandom.

Transcendence and Transportation

Three of the women articulated the ways in which the music allowed them to transcend their immediate surroundings. For instance, Aime described Avenged Sevenfold's unusual musical choices in order to elucidate her listening experience:

> In 'Beast and the Harlot' they go verse chorus solo verse chorus chorus so that's weird: I found it weird that they put the solo within the first half of the song and that's how they experiment. And it's like one of the greatest riffs of all time and they don't just do the riff, they do things in the background, which makes it even more interesting. You're listening to it and the bass is different; it's not just going along with the chords and it's an adventure to listen to in a way.
>
> (Aime)

At first Aime was specific about the construction of the song, determining that the format was 'weird' in order to emphasize the difference between this song and more traditionally constructed songs. What I found most intriguing, however, was her use of 'adventure' to describe her listening experience. Listening to the band was akin to going on a journey. Sections of the song led her through the musical landscape: the positions of the instruments and other effects in the mix meant that there was much of interest to experience each time the voyage was made, and the unusual bass melody meant that the passage was an extraordinary one in comparison to other musical journeys. Here 'Adventure' does not just mean 'journey'; it also connotes excitement, quests, and tasks to be accomplished, with potentially the thrill of meeting wizards and the risk of encountering dragons! 'Adventure' is romantic, and in describing 'Beast and the Harlot' in this way Aime created a sense of the song as able to transport the listener to another world that was more exciting than everyday life in 21st century Britain.

Jeanette described seeing her favorite band, Red Sparowes, and the effect of the political images of China that they were using as the backdrop combined with the music:

> It was visually absolutely stunning, but it was also very disturbing images at the same time. Together, combined with extremely melodic, beautiful music in front of you, so it transports you as well. I mean I certainly didn't, during that show I didn't think political thoughts, but makes you think very creatively, erm. Yes, it just opens up, erm, it lets your mind flow.
>
> (Jeanette)

Jeanette's use of 'visually stunning' and 'together combined' provide a sense of the concert as more than simply an aural event; it was a fuller sensual experience. The strong adverbs, 'absolutely', 'very', 'extremely', 'certainly', all signify how powerful the effect of the concert was for her. The beautiful music had the impact of allowing her mind to 'flow' in ways that she considered as creative. Hard rock and metal are not generally thought of as allowing space for *thinking*. As I infer from Overell's work on the way in which grindcore 'blows away' its listeners (2012, p. 202), the genre is often thought of as allowing the listener some sense of obliteration. Hard rock, in particular, is not associated with the intellect. Rather it is often associated with the life of the body: sex, drugs, and alcohol. This attitude is epitomized in Hebdige's off-the-cuff denunciation of 'heavy metal rockers' as being distinguishable by their 'idiot dancing' (1979, pp. 109, 155), in which the movement of bodies in time to the music is the notable characteristic. In Jeanette's remarks, there was an impression of images crossing her consciousness, as if in a meditative state, and that this kind of creative thinking was not the kind of thinking she could access easily in her daily life. Red Sparowes' music and imagery enabled this, and it was extraordinary and central to her pleasurable experience. Furthermore, Jeanette used 'melodic' and 'beautiful', words that are not usually associated with hard rock and metal. Hard rock and metal are not typically thought of as 'beautiful': common sense understandings of the genre by non-metal fans sometimes interpret the music as harsh and ugly (See, e.g., Weinstein, 2000, p. 1). The density and pace of the songs can make listening a difficult experience for new listeners, and in these cases they may not hear a melody at all. Furthermore, these terms do not fit into the ideological language of the genre, as they do not refer to speed, heaviness, hardness, or aggressiveness; in fact they are more associated with femininity and with art.

Susan described listening to Led Zeppelin as enabling a feeling of being different from normal when normal is 'mundane': 'it lifts you out of the mundane. I mean cleaning or ironing can't be anything but mundane, can it? So a well-chosen piece of music just lifts you above that' (Susan). Susan used the verb 'lifts' to describe the way in which music can affect someone doing housework. In this, she implicitly placed cleaning and ironing in the position of bringing one down, i.e., that such tasks are depressing. 'Mundane' lent an air of transcendence to the way in which music functions. This presentation of music as enabling transcendence of boring tasks is a view shared by Lawrence Grossberg. Grossberg (1984) argues that rock enables young people to find some sense of empowerment in their adolescent powerlessness (p. 228), but Susan's description of the way music 'lifted' her was rooted in her experience of being a single mother with young children. For Susan, it was not powerlessness that needed to be overcome, but the boring and endless task of housework. Susan was not alone in finding that hard rock and metal music helped with housework: Ruby found that energetic metal helped her with the gardening, and Jessica said that it aided her in cleaning. However, for Susan the music's power to 'lift her above' the mundane was not just to motivate her to engage in house or garden work, rather it meant that she could feel outside of the tasks.

Musical beauty was credited with the power to expand the women's minds, enabling them to think more 'creatively', lifting them above mundane employments, or taking them on a journey into a fantasyland. All of these descriptions give an impression of pleasure in hard rock and metal that is quite different from those descriptions that characterize the genre as masculine or negative. My interviewees described positive elements that enhanced their thinking and meditative lives.

Shared Experiences

Ruby found that sharing the emotions or experiences with the musicians was an important component of her musical experience. She enjoyed the ways in which she could relate to what the musicians were singing about.

> It's an affiliation. [...] when I got divorced [laughs, but a little forced], probably a bad example, er, but obviously it was a highly emotional time, I think, you know, that a lot of, a lot of the metal music I listened to at the time was, especially with Killswitch Engage, was about heartbreak and sorrow and it kind of makes you feel like you're not the only person in that situation. It's almost like having a heartbreak buddy there on your iPod.
>
> (Ruby)

Ruby used 'affiliation' in the sense of sibling-love and friendship. This was signified also through her use of 'not the only person', 'buddy' and 'there on your iPod'; all terms which worked to create a sense of how Ruby felt about the music at the time of her divorce: that the music could provide intimacy, friendship, and stability in a time of difficulty. Ruby's vocabulary—which is readily found in pop music—brings forth the question of to what extent does vocabulary cross genre boundaries? Ruby called Killswitch Engage her 'heartbreak buddy' as she found that the songs resonated with her own feelings at the time of her divorce. She felt that she was not alone, even when she was alone with her iPod headphones.

Jenny gained happiness from what she saw as the enthusiasm and enjoyment of the band; in this case in the gig environment when she went to see/hear Slabdragger:

> Really like enthusiasm and commitment and energy. And particularly if their lead singer's got that, I mean I don't necessarily make out the words they're singing, but I like commitment, and that respect and they played really well as a band, you could really see they were all enjoying themselves and it's nice when it works both ways.
>
> (Jenny)

Jenny ascribed her affection for Slabdragger to the merits of the band in performance. The three qualities that she liked about the performance were not musical merits, rather they were about the attitude of the performers. For Jenny, the enthusiasm was combined with what she interpreted as the commitment of the band and 'that respect'. The phrase 'it's nice when it works both ways' implied that the audience gained pleasure from hearing and witnessing the band's performance and the band too gained satisfaction and enjoyment from their own performance. In the words 'both ways' Jenny intimated that the band's joy was also inspired by seeing their audience's enthusiastic response.

Jenny made the suggestion that bands can convey their own feelings of exuberance and enthusiasm to fans: that music has the power to transmit emotions. This idea of joy in the performance implies that there are times when bands are unable to enjoy the music they perform. On these occasions the performance itself may be note-perfect, but there is some *je ne sais quoi* missing. The joyous performance is therefore very important: happy, socially shared, and overwhelmingly positive. This brings to the fore ideas about music as a communal experience that allows for personal feelings to be explored in musical companionship. These pleasures do not necessarily fit in with the language that echoes the ideology of hard rock and metal, particularly in the myth of the warrior. However, the women were not describing a whole-community experience: Ruby and Susan in particular were feeling a quite personal communion with the band.

Romance Language

Aime told me that her first encounter with Avenged Sevenfold had been via music television. This occurred after having just read a review of the band:

> It was just a review of a gig, and I thought, 'oh that gig sounded cool; [I] might go on YouTube and have a find out a bit' and er just before then I was watching Kerrang! on TV and I flipped over the channel and just that second a song of their's came on and it was this kind of like husky bit where he sings and I was like ah! It was just I felt [breathy] that moment and I was like, it was really nice, it was kind of like a fairytale.
>
> (Aime)

Aime began by saying 'it was just a review', where 'just' ascribes little importance to her encounter with the piece (it came to have more significance later). The synchronicity of reading the review and then seeing the band on television seems to have suggested a magical or romantic relationship between herself and the band, as indicated by her use of the word 'fairytale' (she seems to have forgotten that she was intending to 'go on YouTube' where she may very well have chosen to watch the same video). The romance came from her somewhat erotic response to the 'husky' quality of the singing. 'Husky' is associated with throatiness and can be read as 'sexy', particularly if used about women (Churcher, 2007). Aime struggled to put her response into words, using instead 'ah!', sighing breathily and intimating a short time of arousal, 'that moment'. The use of 'fairytale' with Aime's narration of the story, which presents it as an encounter like love at first sight, relying on magical synchronicity, works within a discourse of romance language. There is a distinct sense that Aime's musical experience of Avenged Sevenfold was a romantic one. Although Aime's storytelling might well work to bolster ideas of young women fans as groupies by ascribing a romantic relationship to her attitude toward the band, her response to Avenged Sevenfold is not as 'straightforward' as a passion for particular band members; her previous comments signaled that it was a relationship with the music *and* how she imagined the musicians. It was a complex affection that intertwined her intellectual musical pleasure with her erotic musical response and with her imaginative thoughts about the band.

Upheaval at the Pop/Rock Divide

As discussed above, many of my interviewees made generalizations about pop music and its fans that contrasted pop unfavorably with hard rock and metal music and its fans. Most did not describe the ways in which pop music and rock music can both defy their ideological construction as separate spheres. Yet although the women tended to be invested in the notion of difference between rock and pop, ambiguity remained in delineating that difference. Thus, the rock/pop dichotomy impacted on their thinking in some ways, but not in others. For instance, Gwen insisted that she rarely knew the name of songs or the bands that were singing them, thereby showing little interest in the accumulation of band-related knowledge so important for demonstrating 'real' fandom. Nor was she uncomfortable about this lack of cultural knowledge.

Two women, Alexa and Aime, both spoke of their passion for pop singers (Adam Lambert and Britney Spears, respectively) and acknowledged how this was unusual. Alexa said she felt slightly guilty about her passion for Adam Lambert, and I asked why. She responded:

> I don't know, I think it's just because, with him being erm, like an *American Idol* runner up and loads of people are like, 'oh it's all manufactured and it's not real music, it's just processed'. I think that's the problem with it that a lot of people have, but I think he is actually one [of] the few that has defended his position and he is quite unique and original from it and he does actually sing live and put on a good show [laughs].
>
> (Alexa)

Alexa's presentation of the terms that she imagined were used about Adam Lambert very much fit in with ideas of a rock/pop divide ('manufactured', 'not real', 'processed') and she summed up that it was these set ideas belonging to others that caused her guilt: 'I think that's the problem'. In acknowledging these criticisms of Adam Lambert, Alexa deftly positioned herself outside of such concerns. Her defense of the singer may in some ways have paid homage to ideas about what 'counts' as authentic music ('unique', 'original', 'sing live'), but Lambert remains a pop musician. In openly discussing her love for his music and in challenging stereotypes about pop she shook the divide between pop and rock. Perhaps not to its foundations, but certainly with the effect of worrying its 'truth' claims.

For Aime, also, liking hard rock and metal *and* pop was not always easy:

> You don't often find someone like me [...], I like such a massive group of bands and different types of music and stuff like that and I suppose I'm just a part of a lot of communities in a way, depending on who I'm going to see. Avenged Sevenfold it's all moshers and then I like erm Britney Spears. I love Britney Spears, I got her album on my phone and [My Chemical Romance] and then both get criticism and I'm like 'oh I feel bad now!' but I like the bands or the singers so they can get over it.
> (Aime)

She posited herself as unusual and explained that a wide range of eclectic tastes marked her out as different within her peer group. Aime's taste was clearly unusual, and she saw herself as shifting between different groups of music fans. She was initially tentative about naming Britney Spears, but then she announced confidently that 'I love Britney Spears', adding as an exemplum of her passion that she had 'got her album on my phone'. She carried her phone with her everywhere, so this indicated that the album was always available to listen to. However, when Aime found that others could not understand her genre-crossing, she employed a rock 'n' roll 'fuck you' non-conforming attitude to fend off criticism and bolster her wavering self-esteem. So whilst she enjoyed music from the 'wrong' genre, the 'right' attitude made sense of her tastes.

These young women transgress the boundaries of rock and pop so that they are able to enjoy the music they chose. In my semiotic readings of *Kerrang!* magazine's letters pages, I found that in the early 2000s a number of letters contained an ethos of 'just like what you like', meaning that one should not feel bound by genre classifications, and one should feel able to enjoy any music (Hill, 2014). This worked within a framework of authenticity and equality in which being true to musical taste was valued and equality translated into respecting other fans. In practice, however, the letters pages demonstrated numerous occasions when fans *did* denounce other fans for genre-crossing musical pleasures. These squabbles over preference and genre work to reinforce the myth of authenticity because ultimately enjoying pop music marks out a hard rock and metal fan as not really an authentic fan. That these women broke through the anti-pop prejudice was remarkable, and it indicates the straitjacket that the ideology of hard rock and metal places fans in, particularly women fans who are more in need of proving their fandom, being seen generally as second-class fans or groupies. For a woman hard rock and metal fan to admit to enjoying pop music was to lay herself open to criticism from other fans as not being serious about hard rock and metal. In speaking openly and without (much) shame about their preferences, Aime and Alexa challenged the myth of authenticity.

Conclusion

Coates (1997) meditates on whether being a feminist Rolling Stones fan is a state of false consciousness, a concept that Fast (1999) finds problematic. However, women's fandom cannot be reduced to understandings of women hard rock and metal fans as cowed by the music or as 'betraying' women or feminism. Deeper consideration of women's pleasure in hard rock and metal music is vital in challenging assumptions about the genre and its fans. Kahn-Harris (2007) notes that extreme metal fans, when describing or explaining their love of the music, use language that is limited by the scene itself. I too found that amongst women fans the use of language that fits neatly within the ideology of the genre *was* prominent in their descriptions of heavy metal. Terms such as 'fierce' and 'heavy', the emphasis on noisy electric guitar, the love of virtuosity and musical ability, and the comparisons to pop music that stressed hard rock and metal's authenticity against pop's manufactured nature are intrinsic to the ways in which hard rock and metal music are understood as symbolically masculine. When particular qualities are ascribed a gender, the male dominance of the genre is maintained via the reification of male-associated qualities and the denigration of those linked to femininity. The result is the alienation and exclusion of women from the genre and the presumption of an underlying male norm for musicians and for 'real fans'. When only these 'masculine' qualities are taken into account, metal appears to be 'naturally' associated with men, but as Riches (2014) shows, such qualities are not exclusively available to men: aggression is a human quality not a male one.

However, my interviewees' language was not limited by these conventions. When asked about their favorite bands they were able to extend their descriptive lexicon beyond those conventions in unusual and persuasive ways. Descriptions of the music as beautiful, as allowing transcendence and the opening of the mind; interpretations of musical performances as joyous; and feelings of companionship between musicians and fans all challenge notions of hard rock and metal fandom as a reification of warrior masculinity. Moreover, the pop fandom of some women undermines the rigid boundaries and assumptions that underpin the myth of authenticity. My participants' expressions move our understanding away from a strict notion of the genre as 'masculine' because they highlight how pleasure is also found in aspects of the music that are not associated with masculinity, some of which are linked to what is considered feminine. This wider consideration of women's pleasure in the music draws attention to the fact that when qualities are ascribed a gender this is a social process: the qualities that are associated with masculinity are not 'essentially' masculine (and similarly those linked to femininity are not 'essentially' feminine). Therefore, when hard rock and metal are thought of as masculine this is the result of constructed understandings of gender, not the cardinal qualities of the music. The importance of considering these elements, therefore, is not just a matter of giving a fuller picture to women's rock and metal pleasure. It is necessary in order to challenge the orthodoxy of the genre as masculine and therefore the naturalized hierarchy that places men upon the stage and/ or positioned in the audience as the 'real fan' whilst women are relegated to the subordinate role of the groupie.

Notes

1. Between 2008 and 2012, I spoke to 19 women living in Britain, predominantly in Northern England, aged between 16 and 69, though clustering around the mid-30s. The women were all white and either working or middle class. They liked a range of subgenres of hard rock and metal, including emo, extreme metal, classic rock, and metalcore. I selected women using the snowball method and conducted semi-structured interviews lasting, on average, one hour and covering such topics as favorite bands, listening practices, the male dominance of the genre, the groupie stereotype, musical endeavours and relationships with family and friends.
2. For example, the Parents Music Resource Centre in the 1980s. See Weinstein for some discussion of this (Weinstein, 2000, p. 249).

Bibliography

Ang, I. (1985). *Watching Dallas: Soap opera and the melodramatic imagination.* London: Methuen.

Baumgardner, J. (2005). Aural history: The politics of feminist rock. Sleevenotes to Papa, don't lay that shit on me: The Chicago and New Haven Women's Liberation Rock Band and Le Tigre. *Rounder,* 82161–4001–2.

Bayton, M. (1997). Women and the electric guitar. In S. Whiteley (Ed.), *Sexing the groove: Popular music and gender* (pp. 37–49). London: Routledge.

Bayton, M. (1998). *Frock rock: Women performing popular music.* Oxford: Oxford University Press.

Bourdage, M. (2010). A young girl's dream: Examining the barriers facing female electric guitarists. *IASPM@Journal (Journal of the International Association for the Study of Popular Music)* 1(1).

Brown, A. R. (forthcoming). 'Girls like metal, too!': Female reader's engagement with the masculinist culture of the tabloid metal magazine. In F. Heesch & N. W. R. Scott (Eds.), *Heavy metal, gender and sexuality: Interdisciplinary approaches.* Ashgate: Farnham; Surrey: Ashgate.

Churcher, M. (2007). What is a sexy voice? *Voice and Speech Review,* 5(1), 260–262.

Clifford-Napoleone, A. (2009). Leather sisterhood: Metal, masculinity, and lesbian fandom. Paper presented at *Heavy Metal and Gender International Congress,* Cologne, Germany, October 10.

Coates, N. (1997). Rock and the political potential of gender. In S. Whiteley (Ed.), *Sexing the groove: Popular music and gender* (pp. 50–64). Abingdon: Routledge.

Fast, S. (1999). Rethinking issues of gender and sexuality in Led Zeppelin: A woman's view of pleasure and power in hard rock. *American Music*, 17(3), 245–299.
Fetterley, J. (1978). *The resisting reader: A feminist approach to American fiction.* London: Indiana University Press.
Geraghty, C. (1991). *Women and soap opera: A study of prime time soaps.* Cambridge: Polity.
Grant, J. (1996). Bring the noise: Hypermasculinity in heavy metal and rap. *Journal of Social Philosophy*, 27(2), 5–30.
Grossberg, L. (1984). Another boring day in paradise: Rock and roll and the empowerment of everyday life. *Popular music*, 4, 225–258.
Hebdige, D. (1979). *Subculture: The meaning of style.* London: Routledge.
Hesmondhalgh, D. (2013). *Why music matters.* Chichester: Wiley-Blackwell.
Hill, R. L. (2011). Is emo metal? Gendered boundaries and new horizons in the metal community. *Journal for Cultural Research*, 15(3), 297–313.
Hill, R. L. (2014). *Representations and experiences of women hard rock and metal fans in the imaginary community.* PhD thesis, University of York.
Huyssen, A. (1986). *After the great divide: Modernism, mass culture, postmodernism.* Basingstoke: Macmillan Press.
Kahn-Harris, K. (2007). *Extreme metal: Music and culture on the edge.* Oxford: Berg.
McClary, S. (1991). *Feminine endings: Music, gender, and sexuality,* Minneapolis: University of Minnesota Press.
McDonnell, E., & Powers, A. (Eds.). (1995). *Rock she wrote: Women write about rock, pop, and rap.* New York: Delta.
Overell, R. (2012). [I] hate girls and emo[tion]s: Negotiating masculinity in grindcore music. *Popular Music History*, 6(1), 198–223.
Patterson, J. (2011). When Jane likes cannibal corpse: Empowerment, resistance, and identity construction among women in death metal. Paper presented at *Home of Metal Conference: Heavy Metal and Place*, Wolverhampton, UK, September 1–4.
Purcell, N. J. (2003). *Death metal music: The passion and politics of a subculture.* Jefferson, NC, London: McFarland.
Radway, J. A. (1984). *Reading the romance: Women, patriarchy, and popular literature.* Chapel Hill: University of North Carolina Press.
Rat. (2013). Cock rock: Men always seem to end up on top. In T. Cateforis (Ed.), *The rock history reader* (pp. 119–124). Abingdon: Routledge.
Riches, G. (2011). Embracing the chaos: Mosh pits, extreme metal music and liminality. *Journal for Cultural Research*, 15(3), 315–332.
Riches, G. (2014). "Throwing the divide to the wind": Rethinking extreme metal's masculinity through female metal fans' embodied experiences in moshpit practices' Paper presented at *IASPM UK & Ireland Conference*, Cork, Ireland, September 12–14.
Skeggs, B. (1997). *Formations of class & gender: Becoming respectable.* London: Sage.
Stacey, J. (1994). *Star gazing: Hollywood cinema and female spectatorship.* London: Routledge.
Thornton, S. (1995). *Club cultures: Music, media and subcultural capital.* Cambridge: Polity.
Vasan, S. (2010). Den mothers and band whores: Gender, sex and power in the death metal scene. In R. L. Hill & K. Spracklen (Eds.), *Heavy fundametalisms: Music, metal and politics* (pp. 69–78). Oxford: Inter-Disciplinary Press.

Vasan, S. (2011). The price of rebellion: Gender boundaries in the death metal scene. *Journal for Cultural Research*, 15(3), 333–349.
Walser, R. (1993). *Running with the devil: Power, gender, and madness in heavy metal music.* Hanover, NH: University Press of New England.
Weinstein, D. (2000). *Heavy metal: The music and its culture.* New York: Da Capo Press.
Whiteley, S. (2000). *Women and popular music: Sexuality, identity, and subjectivity.* New York: Routledge.
Whiteley, S. (2006). Popular music and the dynamics of desire. In S. Whiteley & J. Rycenga (Eds.), *Queering the popular pitch* (pp. 249–262). London: Routledge.
Willis, E. (1977). Beginning to see the light. *Village Voice.*
Wise, S. (1984). Sexing Elvis. In S. Frith & A. Goodwin (Eds.), *On record: Rock, pop, & the written word* (pp. 390–398). London: Routledge.
Wittig, M. (1992). *The straight mind and other essays.* Boston: Beacon Press.

Part VI
Metal and Cultural Studies

17 Retro Rock and Heavy History
Simon Poole

Since the past occupies me as if it were the present, and the present seems to me infinitely far away, for these reasons I cannot separate the future from the past as sharply as is usually done.

(Hesse cited in Lachman, 2009, p. 126)

Heavy metal is a progressive genre, with a long, tangential and complex development. This development has been the topic of much critical, academic and fan debate, and yet it is a genre marked by a consistent musical and ideological practice of return and revision. The 'evolution' of heavy metal, notable by the growth, fracture and splintering over time into myriad subgenres—the multiplicity of successive and concurrent 'metals'—masks retro-progressive engagements with heavy metal histories, with retrospective fan and musician practices, with its relationships with past classics and canons, failures and fads. Whilst heavy metal has not entirely escaped the perceived cultural, and specifically musical, collapse into perpetual nostalgia, described by Simon Reynolds[1] as 'retro-rock leeching off ancient styles' (2011, p. 1), the genre's continuous development and consistent and deferential relationship with its own past has meant that it has not succumbed to mere nostalgic pastiche in the way that Reynolds suggests, but continues to investigate, construct, and deconstruct its own pasts and 'origins'.

In this sense, heavy metal's nostalgias are nostalgias in the name of progress. They are peculiarly bohemian nostalgias that drive heavy metal forward through engagements with possible 'pasts'. '[B]ohemia is always yesterday' (Cowley in Wilson, 1999, p. 14), and, as such, the past is constructed and narrated, as both more authentic and therefore more bohemian than the present. It is also, at least in part, through these bohemian retrospections, as with previous bohemian cultures, at odds with mainstream or mass cultural production. As such, heavy metal's development seems far from 'obvious and well coded' (Fabbri, 1981, p. 55) and also, as a series of stories, analyses and narratives, arguably important 'given the longevity of heavy metal's appeal in a sphere of popular culture notable for fads and fashions' (Bennett, 2001, p. 42).

The Problem of Heavy History

> The past has gone and history is what historians make of it when they go to work.
>
> (Jenkins, 1991, p. 6)

The progressive narrative of heavy metal is often depicted in linear family tree models such as those created by Pete Frame in the 1970s for the British music press and subsequently used by the BBC in the mid-1990s in the 'Rock Family Tree' television series; or again by Sam Dunn as a map to guide viewers through the *Metal Evolution* (2011) television series. In this graphic model, a point of origin is presented at the head of the map and then followed by the familial-spawned new branches of the genre, which in turn are followed by the next unfolding linear musical generations beneath it, and so on. This linear narrative of generations that spawn new generations belies both the complexity of the development of heavy metal and the lack of a specific agreed point of origin. As Deena Weinstein (2000) suggests 'Heavy Metal has many histories. There is no consensus on its precursors, basic influences, first full-fledged songs and bands, or developmental stages' (p. 14) and yet there is also the persistent notion that 'the family begins with Black Sabbath' (Frimodt-Moller, 2013, p. 81).

With no agreed-upon origin, only suggestions of pre-metal, proto-metal, or early metal leading up to heavy metal itself, building a linear history is problematic: to whom can we attribute the genetic code of the genre? And beyond this complex problem of historical origin, there are further historiographical problems. How, for instance, do we locate bands such as Pentagram, whose early unreleased or marginalized work has been reissued into the contemporary metal sphere in multiple volumes? Pentagram, a (now) highly influential band that formed in the early 1970s but whose multiple line ups, name, and location changes meant that their 'debut' album only saw the light of day in incremental stages—a CD demo in 1982; self-released vinyl in 1985; followed by an official release almost a decade later (Peaceville Records, 1993)—are problematic to heavy metal histories. Where, given their relatively recent growth in stature, should they be placed in such a linear, generational model of generic development? At their point of formation, valorization, or canonization? To write—or over write—them into an already existent linear history of heavy metal development in the 1970s alongside historically anchored acts such as Black Sabbath, would be problematic, as would writing them into existence only in the 1980s or '90s. Although their prolific song-writing and demo recording meant that a small number of metal fans were able to hear Pentagram material through the late '70s and early '80s,[2] their entry into a broader journalistic and fan discourse of heavy metal and subsequent influence happened much later and continues to grow with each issue, reissue, documentary, and article. It is now impossible to imagine heavy metal history without acts such as Pentagram. Not in the sense of the weight of influence or subjective critical worth of their contribution to the broad or niche musical culture, rather in the sense that now they occupy a place in the cultural memory of heavy metal; they, and the substantive history, line-up changes, stories, and demos accumulated before their debut release, *cannot be unimagined*. They are part of heavy metal memory, a memory that is ascribed by the culture rather than prescribed to the culture.

> [C]ultural memory signifies that memory can be understood as a cultural phenomenon as well as an individual or social one [...] cultural memorization as an activity occurring in the present, in which the past is continuously modified and redescribed even as it continues to shape the future.
> (Bal, 1999, p. vii)

The collective writing and memorization into genre history of Pentagram, or any other previously marginalized heavy metal act, by fans, musicians, and journalists, or the fading from memory of other once musically influential acts such as Vanilla Fudge, suggests a different way of approaching the story, development, past, and present of heavy metal as both fluid and *non* linear. An approach that is not concerned with creating a methodology to irrefutably identify the chronological key points of a singular becoming of heavy metal, or uncovering the archaeological site of its birth, but one that celebrates the multiplicity, the overlapping, argumentative, impossibility of the heavy metal narrative. Here, I propose three ways that may facilitate the imagining of the genre's relationship with its own and other equally complex pasts. First, the idea that heavy metal history might be explored as a complex, multilayered model—as a palimpsest (as discussed by Dillon, 2007)—rather than a linear, orderly, and sequential map. Second, the notion that the lack of agreed origins of the genre mean that, within this bottomless narrative web, there are multiple available histories, routes back and routes from points of influence that continue the progression and development of the genre. They do so by facilitating the exploration that these rhizomatic trails present, rather than being stifled through the complexity and multiplicity of narrative webs. And third, that a genealogical approach to this genre without origin—genealogical in the sense that Foucault (1977), via Nietzsche (1996) explores it—is part of the story of the genre; that is, it is what fans and musicians have practiced through the decades of the genre's shifting development in spite of historical, journalistic, and academic attempts to fix a definitive narrative where '[t]he history of a musical movement is often told as a series of dramatic beginnings, when disparate musical and social trends come together in a creative fusion. These moments are usually mythologized and are often established well after the fact' (Hegarty and Halliwell, 2011, p. 31). These moments also, as evidenced in Deena Weinstein's (2014) recent article on the naming of the genre, create false information—demonstrated through the frequent citation of Burroughs' use of 'heavy metal' in *Naked Lunch* (1959) rather than the

300 Simon Poole

Nova Trilogy[3]—rumor and myth (often perpetuated by bands themselves that they were the ones the term was first applied to) that then, once published, are repeatedly presented as truth, as a mythical origin, cited by journalists and academics alike (Walser, 1993, p. 8).

The Heavy Palimpsest

If these linear historical narratives cannot accommodate the ways in which the heavy metal community approached and continues to approach the genre, how can its generic development be explained or imagined? Rather than a linear heavy metal history with discreet, near biblical, unfolding of neat generations and layers, the stories of heavy metal can be read as a memorative palimpsest—a multi-layered writing over writing, memory over memory, practice over practice—a complex web of overlapping, competing, and contradictory stories. As Dillon (2007) defines it, 'The palimpsest is a space in which two or more texts, often different and incongruous, coexist in a state of both collision and collusion' (p. 52). The palimpsest is thus a fittingly appropriate metaphor for heavy metal's genealogy: allowing multiple understandings of multiple histories, as well as differing genre origins, competing or complimentary understandings of the present and of the past. It also allows for differing depths of reading; for example, the emboldening of particular proto-metal styles and privileged influences within the cultural memories of subsets of the heavy metal community. Of course, with the slow emergence of heavy metal as generically definable—given that Nova Express was published in 1964 and a general consensus that 'one cannot talk about metal as a genre before 1970' (Waksman, 2009, p. 10)—the initial texts of heavy metal were not recorded as heavy metal history per se, but rather within a popular cultural history and critical discourse of rock and pop. And as much as the phrase 'heavy metal' exists in popular cultural discourse in this pre-metal decade, its imagining as a genre label relies on more contemporary imagining: the phrase 'heavy metal' predates the music 'heavy metal', and yet the music 'heavy metal' predates the genre label 'heavy metal'. As such, various pre-metal and non-metal musical forms and artists as well as technological, ideological, or broader cultural references may well feature in other colluding palimpsestic narratives: narratives of film, politics, youth culture, fiction, and fashion. These narratives are fundamental and/or unimportant in the development of these oxidizations and contribute to differing and multiple metal memories. As Andrew Weiner (1973) suggested in an exploration of Black Sabbath's and heavy metal's popularity: 'Earth became Black Sabbath at the tail-end of a fairly spectacular boom in the black magic business. Polanski's Rosemary's Baby, itself based upon a best-selling creapocreapo novel. Exposés in the News of the World, full frontal nudie witches in the television night. Thrills for a jaded nation' ([1973] 1996, p. 22). These are the 'different and incongruous' tales exposed in the appearance of the heavy metal palimpsest awaiting the curious heavy metal reader.

Palimpsests are both actual and figurative texts. They, as historical documents, date back to the third century BC (Dillon, 2007), usually vellum, parchment, or in early cases, papyrus, where the original text was, due to the scarcity of writing material, erased so that new texts could be inscribed on their surfaces. Unlike other textual recycling, such as the reuse of old vinyl in new record production, this erasure was not wholly successful, and the original writing, through the process of oxidization would, over time, reappear through the subsequent overwriting. In the late 19th and early 20th centuries these 'reappearances' began to be chemically induced as the search for past texts underneath more recent writing increased, much like the rush to uncover, curate, and reissue the output of marginalized or erased groups from the early 1970s (the aforementioned Pentagram's oxidization leads to other appearances from Bang!, Fire, Dust, Icecross, Sainte Anthony's Fyre, etc.). As such, these discovered palimpsests have become important historical, philosophical, and ideological documents; in the most part because of what was initially erased, rather than what was then written over. Of course, an original text, once dismantled from a complete manuscript into any number of individual pages, can appear in many newly produced texts and in new locations without the narrative cohesion or cultural context of its creation or without the other pages that complete the narrative. This is particularly problematic in the case of heavy metal because, as mentioned previously, the original texts were not framed by the generic understanding of the music, culture, or practices or even name—heavy metal—and so its traces are scattered throughout numerous histories, archives, and narratives. The paradox of preserving the texts of the past by erasing them and writing over them with the texts of the present creates a figurative use of the palimpsest that has been used as 'a psychological, historical and social model' (Dillon, 2007, p. 3). The further privileging of the original erased texts over the newer writing complicates this paradox and furthers the bohemian idea that the past is more authentic than the present. It has been used as a model in and across a variety of disciplines, including literary theory where: 'The palimpsest becomes a figure for interdisciplinarity—for the productive violence of the involvement, entanglement, interruption and inhabitation of disciplines in and on each other' (op. cit., p. 2).

In using the palimpsest as a metaphor for heavy metal's genealogy, a number of ways of thinking about the genre can be explored. First, the idea of many, seemingly competing and contradictory stories and ways of engaging with the genre—journalistic, musicological, historiographic, academic—written over and entangling each other, enables the creation of multiple narratives that then cease to be competitive, that can then only be complementary, non hierarchical texts that seek not to create order but to celebrate the multiplicity of styles, forms, influences, and trajectories. Second, the web of metal that is created through these sometimes disparate, sometimes clustered narratives allows for different moments of historical focus, both stylistically and chronologically—Bathory, Napalm Death, Venom, Judas

Priest, or Mountain for example—as key for different readers, musicians, and fans, as pivotal points of influence within a seemingly endless narrative where they go 'back to music that does certain things for them, or has certain typical traits' (Frimodt-Moller, 2013, p. 77). And third, it removes the linearity, singularity, and point of origin focus of authenticity-focused historical narratives. This allows, at any given moment, contradictory pasts of heavy metal to be simultaneously celebrated in 'a polysemic space where the paths of several possible meanings intersect' (Barthes quoted in Dillon, 2007, p. 82). These celebratory subsets of the genre coexist without contradicting the central core of heavy metal ideology, sound, and style. Nor do they challenge or threaten the heavy metal narrative as a whole. This is notable in the last decade of heavy metal where the subgenres of doom, thrash, black, and death metal flourished, not in competition with each other but in complementary metal retro-progressive 'new waves', revivals, and re-imaginings. All of these subsets are quintessentially metal. All subsets and their bands exist side-by-side on festival bills, all share common ideological and stylistic points and the 'sufficient conditions for being a metal band' (Frimodt-Moller, 2013, p. 79). But all emphasize and amplify aspects of the genre, of the *palimpsestuous* trajectory of heavy metal's 'non written poetics' (Fabbri, 1981, p. 54) through their different routes and readings through the web-like narrative. All take different pages from some historically dismantled text and traverse through and write over the existing and emerging texts. Whilst there are distinct sonic differences between say, Saint Vitus and Municipal Waste, for example, they are both understandable as heavy metal in a broader sense. As Fabbri (1981) suggests, 'no one is willing to accept a style of genre as an identity document any longer' (p. 54). In either case Saint Vitus and Municipal Waste, as present bands amongst the strands of the heavy metal palimpsest, are only understandable in relation to the past. Saint Vitus in particular has been party to both erasure *and* oxidization in the palimpsestuous metal narrative.

> The 'present' of the palimpsest is only constituted in and by 'presence' of texts from the 'past', as well as remaining open to further inscription by texts of the 'future'. '[...]' the palimpsest does not elide temporality but evidences the spectrality of any 'present' meet which always already contains with it 'past', 'present' and 'future' moments.
> (Dillon, 2007, p. 37)

Whilst Saint Vitus has an intricate and complex relationship with the palimpsest, the relationship is perhaps most obviously evidenced by the primary rupture in heavy metal's development. The new wave of British heavy metal (NWOBHM) was both a new and progressive musical departure and yet a return to the past (Brown, 2012, p. 9; 2015, p. 272). Its newness was reliant on a return to heavy metal's beginnings; it could only be new because of its recognition of, and departure from, the old. It acknowledged its own past whilst writing over it, leaving the original text in place, not only visible but newly acknowledged by its departure. This 'palimpsestuous logic' (Dillon, 2007, p. 8) is a constant in the 40 plus years of the development of the genre. New 'waves', new subgenres, and movements can only announce their newness through the writing over and acknowledgement of the old. 'The palimpsest is thus an involuted phenomenon where otherwise unrelated texts are involved and entangled, intricately interwoven, interrupting and inhabiting each other' (op. cit., p. 4). In this logic, recent movements or labels such as 'the new wave of traditional metal'—itself a self-conscious return to the 1980s and the influence of the 'new wave of British heavy metal'—become, not an oxymoron, but an embodiment of heavy metal's retro-relationship with its own past.

Heavy Origins

Much of the historical investigation and study of heavy metal has been concerned with its beginnings, with the origin of the genre. Whether geographically discussing the importance of Birmingham (Bayer, 2009; Harrison, 2010; Cope, 2010), or Detroit (Carson, 2006), or musicologically (Walser, 1993), historically (Brown, 2012; Frimodt-Moller, 2013), linguistically and journalistically, critically (Weinstein, 2000, 2014; Brown, 2015), or stylistically, in an unfolding narrative of genre after genre '[t]he origins of the heavy metal sound can be traced back to the decline in popularity of psychedelic music at the end of the 1960s' (Bennett, 2001, p. 43). Within this literature, there has been both consensual agreement and wildly differing opinion. Whilst Black Sabbath's position in critical, academic, and genre-community narratives appears consistently stable, beyond this there is little agreement, much myth-making and multiple 'truths'. Psychedelia, the Blues, Rock, Hard Rock, Devil Rock, Downer Rock, Progressive Rock, Holst, Wagner, The Kinks, MC5, Blue Cheer, Cream, Hendrix, Steppenwolf, Iron Butterfly, Sir Lord Baltimore, Grand Funk Railroad, Atomic Rooster, Black Widow, Hapshash and the Coloured Coat, William Burroughs, Lester Bangs, and the omnipresent Beatles have all made appearances—voluntarily or otherwise—in these whodunit genealogical paternity tests, or what Andy R. Brown critically calls 'the smoking gun' (2012). This kind of journalistic investigation relies on there being a linear historical narrative, an 'explanation that links a chain of events to their cause or point of origin' (op. cit., p. 4) a proud mother and father at the head of the rock family tree. With a palimpsestuous imagining of heavy metal, however, there can be no origin, no birth, no miraculous metallic conception of the genre, only multiple and equally miraculous conceptions of metal goddesses and gods:

> The lofty origin is no more than a 'metaphysical extension which arises from the belief that things are most precious and essential at the moment of birth'. We tend to think that this is the moment of their

> greatest perfection, when they emerged dazzling from the hands of a creator or in the shadowless light of a first morning.
>
> (Foucault, quoting Nietzsche, 1977, p. 143)

And whilst Black Sabbath may, communally, fulfill the role of the first born in Foucault's 'shadowless light', the role of creator is *unattributed* and arguably *unattributable*. This, it could be suggested, is a central nodal-point in both the myriad metals that currently coexist under the umbrella of the 'heavy metal' meta-genre whilst also offering a possible reason for the astonishing longevity of the genre. That is, the heavy metal community—collectively at least—is 'less concerned with origins conceived as single punctual events' (Smith, 1996, p. ix) and more concerned with authenticity of sound, of ideology, and of context as it pertains to their own understanding of subgenres, subsets, tastes, and narratives. Whilst individual fans or subgroupings may search for a mythical singular source of style—musically, semiotically, and/or ideologically within the maze-like structure of the palimpsest, the bands or albums that 'capture the imagination with their spectral power' (Dillon, 2007, p. 13), these strands have themselves, of course, a questionable heritage. Each new individual or collective reading of the heavy metal palimpsest creates its own authenticity narrative, which may result in new musical production or new imaginings of history, where 'authenticity is assured by 'reflecting back' to an earlier authentic practice' (Moore, 2002, p. 213).

The draw of origins does not necessitate a return to the 1960s or '70s, for there is no true origin to return to, only a narrative web and as such the 1970s is no more an authentic origin than the 1980s (indeed the 1980s are becoming an increasing subject of interest), depending on the subset of metal under discussion. The search for beginnings, creators, and origins can be in terms of subgenre, or in terms of early periods in later developments of the genre or for some kind of imagined *golden age*. An age that may include spatially or chronologically disparate acts—Judas Priest and/or Metallica, Hellhammer and/or Mayhem—with little regard for the sanctity of chronological or historical similarity.

Heavy Genealogy[4] (Slight Return)

> A genealogy of values, morality, asceticism and knowledge will never confuse itself with a quest for their origins.
>
> (Foucault, 1977, p. 80)

This lack of chronological respect for origins is the third area where a palimpsestuous model of heavy metal's development may be useful. Rather than seeing these fan fixations and musical and cultural influences on various performers as randomized or lacking in respect or proper historical regard, these engagements with the narrative of heavy metal can be read in geneaological terms. Not genealogical in the sense that I first mentioned in this chapter—in terms of the family tree and its use by Pete Frame or Sam Dunn—but genealogical in the sense that Foucault, in his readings of Nietzsche, uses the term. For Foucault and for Nietzsche, genealogy uncovers '"something altogether different" behind things: not a timeless and essential secret, but the secret that they have no essence or that their essence was fabricated in a *piecemeal fashion from alien forms*' (Foucault, 1977, p. 142, emphasis added). This genealogical practice is in diametric opposition to the practice of historiography, where '[w]e want historians to confirm our belief that the present rests upon profound intentions and immutable necessities. But the true historical sense confirms our existence among countless lost events, without a landmark or point of reference' (op. cit., p. 155). Yet this approach to its own past could be responsible for its longevity. For if there is no definitive landmark, the differing visits through the 'entangled and confused parchments, on documents that have been scratched over and recopied many times' (p. 139) will uncover innumerable influences, none of which can be real, true, or definitive historical points. These innumerable influences, in turn, create any number of authentic heavy metals.

Fans of these multiple heavy metals, collectively articulate some of Nietzsche's ideas about historiography, about history as they relate to the Platonic modalities of history. First, once an area of the palimpsest has made itself culturally visible via any number of routes, there is a clamor to understand it. That is, fans wish to engage with musical 'history' in a way that expands it, as evidenced through the collecting of early or first vinyl pressings, vintage shirts, original concert tickets, and memorabilia as well as wider contextual ephemera—films, fashions, magazines, badges, posters, books, and so on. However, their 'unrealization' through the excessive choice of identities offers more, rather than fixes, historical ideas or narrative. Second, these collective metal histories make history almost impossible—that is the metal community shows an 'orientation towards the eternally valid examples of the past' (Smith, 1996, p. ix) that allow, encourage, and embrace newly emerging, 'old' examples of 'heavy', or celebrations of those artists, songs, etc., that demonstrate proto-metal sensibilities. Third, the fans, journalists, and musicians of metal have an unending approach to history; 'a passion for knowledge' (Foucault, 1977, p. 96) that fears no end (or beginning in this case). The emulation of styles, sounds, tunings, configurations, instrumentation and surrounding visual styles of the past, is not specific to heavy metal but is a practice that is a constant cyclical force in the genre and its approach to history. This, of course, can be seen through the continued new waves of traditional, black, death, doom, or other extreme forms of metal, as well as more general returns to earlier styles.

To return, by way of example of this palimpsestuous logic, to the earlier quote by Andrew Weiner discussing Black Sabbath's and heavy metal's surprising popularity: the group not only emerged during the decline of psychedelia (Bennett, 2001), along with contemporaneous heavier style of bands and forms of amplification, such as Vanilla Fudge, Blue Cheer and Deep

Purple, but during 'a fairly spectacular boom in the black magic business' (Weiner, [1973]1996, p. 22). This boom, as well as including film, tabloid, and underground newspapers, novels, and comics also included 'full frontal nudie witches in the television night', creating a palimpsest of 'different and incongruous' texts and allowing a narrative built from 'alien forms'. As such the oxidization of the contextual palimpsest for heavy metal fans and artists leads not to an origin but to a plethora of popular culture, the cultural context of the period between the end of Burroughs' *Nova Trilogy* and the eponymous Black Sabbath debut. The musical output of this period, as it pertains to the mythical birth of heavy metal, has been, and will continue to be, discussed across fan and journalistic discourses, across the terrain of The Kinks' guitar sound and Mars Bonfire's use of the phrase 'heavy metal thunder'. Some of this historical material appears crisp and clear in the narrative, whilst other musical contributions have oxidized and continue to oxidize through, and much like the boom in interest in palimpsests in the late 19th century, there is an attempt to induce the oxidization of texts to see what lies beneath. Either way 'retroactive memory is an important aspect of rock's relationship to occultism' (Bebergal, 2014, p. 111). The work of Coven, with its LP *Witchcraft Destroys Minds and Reaps Souls* for instance (1970), or Black Widow's *Sacrifice* (1970) has arguably impacted on more recent heavy metal output by way of the community's genealogical engagement with the heavy metal palimpsest. The female fronted Coven is cited as influential on a host of female-fronted occult rock acts such as Devil's Blood, Jex Thoth, Blood Ceremony (Kelly, 2011), and more recently Jess and the Ancient Ones, Mount Salem, et al. The imagery from Black Widow's elaborate stage show was used on the cover of Electric Wizard's 'Demon Lung' single (1995). Electric Wizard is, in this respect, an exemplar in the engagement with this kind of palimpsestuous logic, with its approach to heavy metal histories, contexts, and traces. Numerous musical and non-musical contextual citations appear amongst the titles, credits, and artwork accompanying their recorded and live performances: from German leftist group Baader Meinhof to the comic book *Weird Tales*, from actress Brigitte Bardot to film score composer Bruno Nicolai. Their live shows are accompanied by a light and film show supplied by the same team that provides visuals for *Hawkwind*, a show where 'the band are silhouetted in turquoise, purple and red lights, while Jus Oborn's collection of VHS cult horror plays on the screens at the back of and flanking the stage' (Horsley, 2012). The 'Without Whom' credits on the 2010 album, *Black Masses* contain more non-musical references than they do musicians or bands (although they are there too: The Pretty Things and Serge Gainsbourg, sitting alongside Alice Cooper and Venom). The films *Defiance of Good* (Costello, 1975) and *Terror at Orgy Castle* (Rotsler, 1972), the actress Susan George, and film director Jess Franco are listed on the inner sleeve, whilst the outer sleeve is a psychedelic take on a promotional film photograph as featured on the 1975 cover of film journal *Cine Revue*. Witchcult Today (2007), the predecessor to Black Masses, similarly utilizes poster art and cultural references throughout. The cover features a stylized rendition of the poster art for Terence Fisher's 1968 film adaptation of Dennis Wheatley's novel *The Devil Rides Out*, (with the American film title *The Devil's Bride* providing a title for a track on the 1994 self-titled album). Mention is also given to exploitation movie directors Jose Larraz and Jean Rollin. Rollin's movie *Frisson Des Vampires* provides the only cover version on the album with a song of the same name originally performed by Acanthus. The liner notes also contain a nod to fashion house 'Biba' as well as infamous '60s cult—The Process Church of the Final Judgement.[5] The latter, via one of their '60s pop-culture-evangelist magazines—in this instance the notorious 'Death' issue—also proved a source of artwork for the 2008 limited 12-inch single 'The Processean'. Whilst 2014's *Time to Die* breaks with this growing tradition and contains no credit list, it does use the photograph that adorned Peter Cave's (1971) biker pulp novel *Chopper* on the inner sleeve.[6] 2004's *We Live* contains a track named in homage to Sergio Martino's movie *Tutti i Colori del Buio* and credits the film's star—Edwige Fenech—in the inner sleeve as well as the director. 1996's *Come My Fanatics* is housed in a sleeve featuring a still of Anton Lavey from Oliver Hunkin's 1971 BBC television documentary *The Power of the Witch,* and although there are fewer direct mentions of influences on the sleeve, the track 'Wizard in Black' begins with a sample from George Grau's 1974 movie *The Living Dead at the Manchester Morgue* (*Let Sleeping Corpses Lie* in America) where the investigating police officer damns the hippy protagonist with the line 'You're all the same, the lot of you, with your long hair and faggot clothes. Drugs, sex, every sort of filth ... and you hate the police, don't you', to which George, replies 'You make it easy'. The artwork for the soundtrack to Grau's movie (composed by Giuliano Sorgini) has also been used by the band as a T-shirt design. Other shirt designs have featured the artwork for Paul Wendkos's 1971 movie *The Mephisto Waltz* and Luigi Scattini's *Witchcraft '70*.

These last two designs are important to mention as both have since been used by other heavy metal groups: the *Mephisto Waltz* artwork turned up again in a t-shirt design for Japan's Church of Misery, themselves notorious trawlers of the palimpsest, searching for stories, images, and samples of serial killers. The *Witchcraft '70* artwork appeared again on the cover of Bloody Hammers' 2014 LP *Under Satan's Sun*. In fact, the use of underground film and comic horror imagery for album artwork, to advertise shows and for t-shirt designs, is now common practice. The more obscure and hard to find, the better, demonstrating subcultural capital (Thornton, 1995) through engagement with the heavy metal palimpsest's content and context. Church of Misery's further engagement with the palimpsest is regularly demonstrated through their use of cover versions on their albums, including May Blitz, Blue Oyster Cult, Cactus, Captain Beyond, and perhaps most obscurely a cover of Cindy and Bert—German Eurovision song contest perennials' 'Der Hund Von Baskerville'—itself a reworking of Black Sabbath's 'Paranoid'.

308 Simon Poole

The artwork for more contemporary groups, such as Satan's Satyrs, liberally use '60s biker movie stills, while their songs contain horror and biker movie samples and references. Swedish group Salem's Pot similarly demonstrates this historical fascination. The band shares its name with an exploitation novel and used an image of the aforementioned director Jess Franco's movie—*The Devil Came from Akasava* (1971) featuring the actress Soledad Miranda for their 2014 album … *Lurar ut dig på prärien*. Beyond these examples, fan-produced videos that combine the audio from heavy metal songs with clips from horror movies have also become commonplace, to the point that the style has been used in official video releases.

Conclusion

Each new act of writing over this continuous palimpsest propels heavy metal forward and yet brings the very past it over writes forward with it, giving it renewed interest. This retro-progressive discourse is arguably a central trait in heavy metal's longevity and, in part, responsible for the lack of what Byrnside [1975] calls the exhaustion phase of a genre, where 'artists repeat the success formulas of the glory days in a mechanical fashion, boring audiences and critics' (quoted in Weinstein, 2000, p. 43). However, this constant writing of heavy metal—musically, critically, and historically—constantly defining and redefining the core and the peripheries of the genre, changes our understanding of what heavy metal is and what heavy metal was. Each new discovery, be it musical, filmic, comic or book, local or global, shifts the narrative of heavy metal. This constant shifting of the past of heavy metal arguably has more impact on the discourse of the genre than the cultural context of the progressive present. This impossibility of origin and these ambiguous beginnings have meant that heavy metal's cultures and narratives have been and continue to be, built on 'resurrective sorcery' (Dillon, 2007, p. 19).

Notes

1. Simon Reynolds's recent 'anti metal' confession in *Pitchfork* where he claimed that in the 1970s he 'was appalled by the resurgent metal's misogyny and machismo, its phallic-ballistic imagery and warrior-male wank fantasies' (2014) should be taken into account here.
2. Pentagram did release one official single under the name Macabre in 1972. Be Forewarned B/W Lazy Lady was issued on intermedia in two pressings of 500 copies. This is now a highly collectible record, particularly the first 500 copies where the name of the band is spelled incorrectly.
3. The Nova Trilogy consists of The Soft Machine (1961), The Ticket That Exploded (1962) and Nova Express (1964).
4. Heavy Geneaology is the title of a 2011 article by Andy Brown that, utilizing Foucault's archaeological method, explores the parameters of heavy metal as a subject of academic enquiry.
5. The Process Church of the Final Judgement was (initially) a UK based religious organization founded by disillusioned scientolgists Robert de Grimston

and Mary-Ann Mclean. It developed into a highly visual and visible 'cult' with branches across America and Canada (as well as the UK). The members 'disdained flower power, tie-dye and patchouli oil. On the streets they wore black cloaks with hoods and Goat of Mendes patches, selling literature with titles like Death and Fear and Humanity is the Devil' (A. Parfey, 2009, p. 80). Their engagement with, and influence on, popular culture was prevalent at the time—their writing appearing in the liner notes of the first two Funkadelic albums and their magazines, including interviews with stars of the day such as Mick Jagger, among others. Their alleged association with Charles Manson and, by association, the Tate/LaBianca killings, through two books—Maury Terry's 'Ultimate Evil' and Ed Saunders 'The Family: The Story of Charles Manson's Dune Buggy Attack Battalion' damaged their reputation at the time but has led to increased interest in the intervening years. Since its eventual disintegration in the mid-1970s it has been a source of material and influence for a number of bands including Skinny Puppy, Psychic TV, Integrity and Sabbath Assembly, as well as Electric Wizard.

6. This image also appears on the 2005 Japanese tour edition of Orange Sunshine's 'Homo Erectus' released on Leaf Hound records, itself an homage to the British proto-metal group of the same name, which has reformed and are touring again.

Bibliography

Bal, M. (1999). Introduction. In M. Bal, J. Crewe, & L. Spitzer (Eds.), *Acts of memory: Cultural recall in the present* (pp. vii-xvii). London: University Press of New England.

Bayer, G. (2009). *Heavy metal music in Britain*. Farnham: Ashgate.

Bebergal, P. (2014). *Season of the witch: How the occult saved rock and roll*. New York: Penguin.

Bennett, A. (2001). *Cultures of popular music*. Maidenhead: Open University Press.

Brown, A. R. (2011). Heavy genealogy: Mapping the currents, contraflows and conflicts of the emergent field of metal studies, 1978–2010. *Journal for Cultural Research*, 15(3), 213–242.

Brown, A. R. (2012). The speeding bullet, the smoking gun: Tracing metal trajectories, from Sabbath to Satyricon. In A. R. Brown & K. Fellezs (Eds.), *Heavy metal generations:(Re)generating the politics of age, race, and identity in metal music culture* (pp. 3–14). Oxford: Inter-Disciplinary Press.

Brown A. R. (2015). Explaining the naming of heavy metal from rock's 'back pages': A dialogue with Deena Weinstein. *Metal Music Studies*, 1(2), 233–261.

Cave, P. (1971). *Chopper*. London: Nel.

Carson, D. (2006). *Grit, noise and revolution: The birth of Detroit rock 'n' roll*. Ann Arbor: University of Michigan Press.

Cook, P. (2005). *Screening the past: Memory and nostalgia in cinema*. London: Routledge.

Cope, A. (2010). *Black Sabbath and the rise of heavy metal music*. Farnham: Ashgate.

Costello, S. (1975). *The defiance of good*. New York: S.P.S.C. Productions.

Dillon, S. (2007). *The palimpsest: Literature, criticism, history*. London: Continuum.

Dunn, S. (2011). *Metal evolution*. VH1 August 11, 2011.

Fabbri, F. (1981). A theory of musical genres: Two Applications. In D. Horn and P. Tagg (Eds.), *Popular Music Perspectives* (pp. 52–81). Göteborg: IASPM.

Foucault, M. (1977). *Language, counter-memory, practice: Selected essays and interviews*. Ithaca, NY: Cornell University Press.

Frimodt-Moller, S. R. (2013). Black Sabbath and the problem of defining metal. In W. Irwin (Ed.) *Black Sabbath and philosophy: Mastering reality* (pp. 76–86). Chichester: Wiley Blackwell.

Frith, S. (1996). *Performing rites: On the value of popular music.* Oxford: Oxford University Press.

Harrison, L. M. (2010). Factory music: How the industrial geography and working class environment of post-war Birmingham fostered the birth of heavy metal. *Journal of Social History*, 44(1), 145–158.

Hegarty, P., & Halliwell, M. (2011). *Beyond and before: Progressive rock since the 1960s.* London: Continuum.

Horsley, J. (2012). Live review electric wizard, London forum. *Decibel Magazine*: [online] available from: http://www.decibelmagazine.com/featured/live-review-electric-wizard—london-forum/ (accessed October 12, 2014).

Irwin, W. (Ed.). (2013). *Black Sabbath & philosophy: Mastering reality*. Chichester: Wiley Blackwell.

Jenkins, K. (1991). *Re-Thinking history*. London: Routledge.

Kelly, K. (2011). Into the coven: Women of occult rock. *MetalSucks* [online] available from: http://www.metalsucks.net/2011/10/21/into-the-coven-women-of-occult-rock/ (accessed August 10, 2014).

Lachman, G. (2009). *Turn off your mind: The Dedalus book of the 1960s.* Sawtry: Dedalus.

Lawson, D. (2011). Occult rock: Do you believe in black magic. *The Guardian*. [online] available from: http://www.theguardian.com/music/2011/nov/24/occult-rock-black-widow-ghost (accessed August 9, 2014).

Moore, A. (2002). Authenticity as authentication. *Popular Music*, 21(2), 209–223.

Nietzsche, F. (1996). *On the genealogy of morals*. Oxford: OUP.

Reynolds, S. (2011). *Retromania: Pop culture's addiction to its own past.* London: Faber and Faber.

Reynolds, S. (2014). Worth their wait. *Pitchfork*. [Online] available from: http://pitchfork.com/features/tpr/reader/worth-their-wait/ (accessed October 25, 2014).

Rotsler, W. (1972). *Terror at Orgy Castle*. New York: Satyr IX.

Smith. (1996). Introduction. *On the genealogy of morals*. Oxford: OUP.

Strong, C. (2011). *Grunge: Music and memory*. Farnham: Ashgate.

Thornton, S. (1995). *Club cultures: Music, media and subcultural capital*. Cambridge: Polity.

Waksman, S. (2009). *This ain't the summer of love: Conflict and crossover in heavy metal and punk*. Berkley: University of California Press.

Walser, R. (1993). *Running with the devil: Power, gender and madness in heavy metal music*. Middletown, CT: Wesleyan University Press.

Weiner, A. ([1973] 1996). Doom patrol: Black Sabbath at the rainbow. In C. Gillett and S. Frith (Eds.), *The beat goes on: The rock file reader* (pp. 19–28). London: Pluto Press.

Weinstein, D. (2000). *Heavy metal: The music and its culture*. New York: Da Capo Press.

Weinstein, D. (2014). Just so stories: How heavy metal got its name—A cautionary tale. *Rock Music Studies*, 1(1).

Wilson, E. (1999). The Bohemianization of mass culture. *International Journal of Cultural Studies*, 2(1), 11–32.

Wylie, T. (2009). *Love sex fear death: The inside story of the process church of the final judgement*. Port Townsend: Feral House.

18 Transforming Detail into Myth
Indescribable Experience and Mystical Discourse in Drone Metal

Owen Coggins

> We can't describe this experience: it is loud, dark, violent, meditative, powerful.
> (Survey respondent description of SunnO))) performance)
>
> Is mystical discourse possible? [...] the 'ineffable' itself structures language. It is not a hole in language or a source of leakage. It becomes, rather, something in relation to which language is redefined.
> (Michel de Certeau, 1995, p. 52)

Drone metal's vast, repetitive, and overwhelming dirges produce experiences that are reportedly indescribable. Yet they provoke description, in entertaining, hyperbolic, and creative language often referencing mysticism, religion, and spirituality. In this chapter, I outline the history of drone metal's emergence in the 1990s as a distinctive subgenre with associated conventions and listening practices. I examine the question of genre, formed in the forging of symbolic links to the history of metal (especially Black Sabbath). Touching upon drone metal's institutions and locations (that do not form a local scene), I suggest understanding genre as a constellation of points and interpretations. Given the significance of mystical rhetoric in drone metal discourse, I then trace an outline of the 20th century study of mysticism, noting its reliance on problematic concepts of (religious) 'experience', before examining metal scholarship's engagement with religion and the mystical. Then, I show how Michel de Certeau's work on productive readings of popular culture, and on mysticism as a mode of communication, can offer ways of understanding drone metal as mystical discourse, produced by listeners as well as musicians, in reviews, commentary, and conversation, as well as in recordings and live performances. Specifically, I investigate how drone metal listening practices and experiences are described in terms of altered senses of time, space, and the body and how these themes are often portrayed in rhetorically religious or mystical tropes, highlighting in particular the figure (both metaphorical and iconic) of pilgrimage. In addition to analyzing sound recordings and performances, I draw on ethnographic material gathered from participant observation fieldwork at drone metal concerts, listener survey responses, in-depth interviews, and online and print materials.[1]

Emergence and Development

If doom metal's orthodox homage to Black Sabbath resists the acceleration characteristic of other extreme metal genres, drone metal (or drone doom) is a yet more extreme exploration of slowness and low distortion. Slow to the point of tense stasis, tracks extend to the limits of recording media, and performances stretch beyond the endurance of some audience members: minimalist structures at maximum volume. Key recordings begin with Seattle band Earth's 1991 EP *Extra-Capsular Extraction* and their first full album *2: Special Low Frequency Version* (1993), containing extended tracks of layered, down-tuned, distorted guitars and very slow riff cycles.

Two recordings then extended this template, with single-track, hour-long albums both emphasizing monotony, feedback, and guitar noise. California band Sleep graduated from their Sabbath-style *Holy Mountain* (1992) to produce an epic hymn to marijuana and pilgrimage in gradually evolving slow riffs. Due to record company difficulties, this emerged in several versions titled either *Jerusalem* (1996, 1999) or *Dopesmoker* (2003, 2012). Meanwhile Tokyo band Boris released *Absolutego* (1996), which opened with 10 minutes of feedback, amplifier fuzz, and slow bass rumble before trudging through slow, repetitive riffs for the remainder of the single 65-minute track before dissolving back into noisy sludge.

These recordings contrasted starkly with contemporary trends in heavy music. Grunge and mainstream alternative rock gradually converged throughout the '90s; while nu-metal turned toward rhythmic and vocal influences from hip hop, achieving wide commercial success. During the same period, extreme metal was marked by acceleration in (perceived) tempo, in death metal and in the frenetic lo-fi sound of second-wave black metal (Christe, 2003, pp. 239–247, 270–273). Bands such as St. Vitus, Cathedral, and Candlemass continued to play "classic" doom metal, although toward the mid-'90s Thergothon, Skepticism, Funeral, and others further dragged tempi and added more sludgy distortion and lower-pitched vocals, with Electric Wizard amongst the most successful in this new style of doom.

Since the late 1990s, a small number of bands developed their own more radical drone styles. Among the most notable of these are Om, a band emerging from the defunct Sleep, and SunnO))), who have become the best-known and most commercially successful drone metal band, together with various related projects featuring overlapping personnel (Gravetemple, Burial Chamber Trio, Pentemple, and Nazoranai, to name just a few).

Throughout the development of the subgenre, sonic, verbal, and visual references have frequently been made to mysticism, spirituality, and esoteric religion. These range from Earth's repeated mentions of angels in song and album titles, to Om's recitation of religious texts and sounds, to SunnO)))'s ritualized live shows shrouded in smoke and robes, to British band Bong's invocation of fictional deities. In conversations, album or concert reviews, and online comments, listeners' experiences and practices are articulated through these and other figures, continuing and constituting a discourse on mysticism surrounding drone metal.

Forging Genre Connections and Conventions

While extreme, unusual, and significantly departing from existing metal genres, early drone metal recordings acknowledged influences from the history of metal, and from Black Sabbath in particular. Bands also drew deliberate links to similar-sounding contemporary musicians and thus began to develop the sonic, formal, and symbolic conventions of an emerging subgenre. Sleep highlighted their adherence to Black Sabbath's style in covering 'Lord of this World' and 'Snowblind' and replicating the design of Sabbath's *Volume 4* with their *Volume 2*, while Sleep's *Holy Mountain* was an extension of Sabbath's sound.

Figure 18.1 Front and Back Cover of *Sleep Vol. 2* (1992), with Design, Font and Title Referencing Black Sabbath Vol. 4 (1972). The back lists a Sabbath cover version recorded live, and 'Special Thanks to Black Sabbath'.

The band name Earth was taken from the original name used by Black Sabbath, as well as implying weighty foundations (Carlson in Richardson, 2008). In a sleeve photograph on Earth's 2, founding member Dylan Carlson wears a Morbid Angel death metal band shirt, asserting a visual association with metal and its extreme offshoots. Original Earth bass-player Joe Preston later joined The Melvins, who also experimented with a slower, sludgier sound, especially on *Lysol* (1992). Boris, in turn, was named after a slow, repetitive Melvins track, and on its own first album made a connection with Earth by using the same subtitle 'Special Low Frequency Version'. Later, SunnO))) took its name from its own amplifiers as well as punningly nodding toward Earth, and recorded a song named 'Dylan Carlson' after that band's guitarist (1999). They also collaborated with Boris and recorded highly abstract cover versions of heavy tracks by Melvins, Metallica, and Immortal (2000, 2002, and 2006, respectively). These bands and others toured together or performed at special events, developing personal and generic links among the bands. In addition, other personnel such as producer Randall Dunn (who has worked with SunnO))), Boris, and Earth amongst others) and Stuart Dahlquist (who formed drone metal group ASVA and has also played in SunnO))) and Burning Witch) have contributed to these connections. As well as similar sounds, these symbolic and personal links between groups helped to establish codes that constitute drone metal as a subgenre, while the use of images and titles associated with Black Sabbath and other groups firmly situate drone metal within heavy metal.

Even with a small number of recordings extant, the close network of mutual influences, and the difference from contemporary metal meant that a subgenre became recognizable. However, due to dispersed interest and influence there has never been a drone metal 'scene' based in a particular geographic region (compared with, for example, death metal in Tampa or Stockholm; black metal in Norway), despite the loose, internationally connected milieu fulfilling many conditions for scene formation (see Wallach and Levine, 2011). Nevertheless, other bands from the UK (Bong, Ommadon, Bismuth, Urthona, Moss, Greg(o)rian), Canada (Nadja, Menace Ruine, Gates, Northumbria), the USA (Barn Owl, Robedoor, Horseback, ASVA) and elsewhere (Orthodox from Spain, Corrupted from Japan, Monarch! from France, Black Boned Angel from New Zealand) have received some mainstream critical interest while still on the margins of the wider metal industry.

Southern Lord, set up and run by members of SunnO))), has become the most influential record label releasing and promoting drone metal recordings, and the Roadburn festival in Tilburg, Netherlands, often has several drone metal bands performing alongside doom, black metal, and psychedelic musicians. The city of Montréal, Canada, is home to several drone metal musicians (Menace Ruine, Aun, Thisquietarmy) as well as scenes for related musics such as black metal, post-rock, and experimental electronic music; a record label that has released several drone metal recordings (Alien8 Recordings); and at least one record shop (Cheap Thrills), which sells drone metal recordings and is decorated with concert posters and other promotional images of international drone musicians. However, one Montréal artist maintained that there were not enough concerts to sustain a drone metal scene based on frequent musical and social interaction. Even these prominent institutions do not survive through producing solely drone metal events or recordings: drone metal and its audience remain marginal.

Genre as Constellation

Despite these sonic and other affinities, there are difficulties in delineating the boundaries of this subgenre, particularly as it is marginal, non-scene-based, and deliberately strains the possibilities of metal forms. Deena Weinstein writes that:

> the term 'metal' refers, at most, to a 'super-genre' comprehending all sorts of musical styles and hybrid genres which bear little resemblance to each other musically or in their cultural and social contexts, yet bear some connection with what has been called 'metal' in the past. (2011, p. 244)

Genre terms change with usage, and a relation with the past is important in situating music as metal. This deliberately fostered relation with metal's history is evidenced in the sonic and symbolic references to Sabbath and other bands and also in how much a listener's own history of listening has incorporated these references.

In framing this research, I began with the genre label 'drone metal' from my own usage, having listened to this music for many years. However, genre names used by other listeners were varied; many musicians distanced themselves from generic categories; and understandings of the terms 'drone' and 'metal' were contested. In conversations during fieldwork, and in interviews, rather than trying to elicit genre definitions, I asked about related experiences, which led to a network of claimed similarities between bands and other experiences.

Fredric Jameson notes the necessity of genre categories: 'not in order to drop specimens into the box bearing those labels, but rather to map our coordinates on the basis of those fixed stars and to triangulate this specific given textual movement' (1982, p. 322). Jameson's genre co-ordinates (see also Walser [1993, p. 27]) might imply too much fixity, given that the connotations of genre labels gradually change. To develop Jameson's stellar metaphor, however, I suggest thinking of genre as a constellation, recognizing these gradually shifting geometries between points and that a plurality of frames represents the different but intersecting usages and understandings by varied communities of listeners. Understanding genre in this way means situating drone metal around bands mentioned almost ubiquitously, such as SunnO))), Earth, and Om, while also including, more obliquely, frequently mentioned bands like Swans and Godflesh, and connecting yet more distantly to occasionally referenced musicians such as Pink Floyd or Miles Davis. Specific recordings by these latter artists were mentioned in relation to drone metal by some listeners and explained as sharing certain sonic, structural, or experiential characteristics.

Genre labels also appear as constellations online. For example, on the Last.fm website, bands are tagged with multiple genre labels by listeners. All tags attributed to an artist can then be displayed, with darker shading emphasizing those most frequently used.

In this example for SunnO))), 'drone', 'doom', 'metal', 'experimental', 'ambient', and 'avant-garde' are frequently tagged and also combined (such

316 *Owen Coggins*

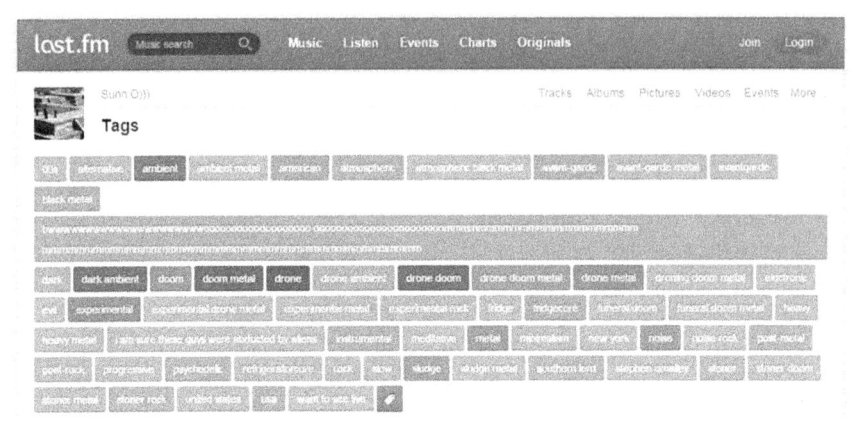

Figure 18.2 Last.fm Website, Genre Tags for SunnO. Screengrab, 5th November 2014.

as 'drone doom metal'). Other tags denote categories less immediately recognizable as musical styles: 'fridgecore', 'fridge', and 'refrigeratorcore' are variations on the joke that SunnO)))'s monotonous noise sounds like amplified refrigerators. While these and others may be meant satirically or humorously, in practice they function like any other tag. Clicking on the 'fridgecore' tag leads to a page collecting other artists so tagged, such as Earth and Boris, who are in turn also tagged 'drone', 'drone doom'. 'drone metal', and so on.

Listeners' descriptions also provide similarly interlinked constellations. Features most frequently mentioned in interviews were repetition, slowness, extension, monotony, or a limited tonal range, down-tuned or bass-heavy guitars, loudness, use of feedback, distortion and gain, and inclusion of drones (in the technical sense of a continuously pitched sound extending throughout a track). The terms drone, droney, droning, and droniness emerged to describe assemblages of these characteristics, often including but not requiring the technical sense of drone. These sonic characteristics were often used in combination with more affective, experiential descriptors such as endurance and difficulty; meditative, cathartic or transcendental qualities; evocations of journeys; ritualistic atmosphere; or, drone metal as spiritual, religious, or mystical experience. Never clearly distinguishable from ostensibly strictly sonic elements (endurance bearing close relation to extension and loudness, for example), these descriptors, mystical, and musical alike, were sought-after and valued aspects of listening experience.

Mysticism and Experience in the Study of Religions

Framing language or practices as religious is controversial, nowhere more so than when attributing the word 'mystical'. Much of the 20th century study of mysticism has been predicated upon psychological conceptions of religious experience, which in turn often rely upon an assumed universal subjectivity beyond culture. In this kind of view, humans in vastly different conditions and contexts have experiences that are axiomatically assumed to have been the same mystical experience, subsequently reported imperfectly in mystical texts (see, in particular, James [1902] and Huxley [1945]). Discrepancies between texts are explained away as inevitable inconsistencies or corruptions due to linguistic and cultural variation and the impossibility of accurate description, while the supposed purity of the experience is maintained. A version of this idea underpins many vernacular differentiations between religion and spirituality, with religions conceptualized as flawed institutions that have perverted a supposedly pure spirituality founded in individual experience.

In her critique of the concept of experience, Joan Scott (1991) suggests that use of the term is too ingrained to abandon: instead, she calls for usage with greater consciousness of the potentially problematic implication of a universal notion of subjectivity through which 'experience' can be compared (p. 797). This critique is especially salient in the study of religious experience, as Richard Sharf has noted, even for constructivist scholars who argue for more contextualization of mystical writings than their perennialist opponents (1995, p. 229). The refusal to acknowledge differences in such universalizing essentialism risks authorizing epistemic violence, in projects that suggest neo-colonial underpinnings, by asserting that particular phenomena adhere (in greater or lesser degrees of purity) to a particular author's theory of transcultural mysticism.

Despite these ingrained issues, it remains important to engage with the language of mysticism as it forms such a prominent feature of listeners' discourse surrounding drone metal. In line with Michel de Certeau, I understand 'mysticism' as a mode of communication that happens in and between texts, in reading and writing; and in the case of drone metal, in listening to recordings and performances and reading, writing, and conversing about them. Drone metal is experienced, and it is often described, as 'experiential' in contrast to, for example music 'just for listening'. While some reviews and reports can lapse into the problematic Orientalist tropes that plague the study of mysticism (see Coggins, 2014, pp. 38–39), an understanding of mystical discourse in drone metal should attempt to avoid this ideology of pure experience imperfectly related in texts.

Approaches to Metal, Religion, and Mysticism

Scholarly treatments of metal and religion have not as yet provided adequate frameworks for understanding the language of mysticism in drone metal; although writers that have mentioned drone metal—or more often, mentioned the band SunnO)))—have emphasized ritual (Partridge, 2013, p. 69; Lucas, 2013), the sacred (Partridge, 2013, p. 69), sonic and bodily transgression (Kahn-Harris, 2007, p. 131; Piper, 2013, p. 68; Riley, 2010, p. 67), or overwhelming and extraordinary experience requiring commitment or endurance (Morton, 2013, p. 192; Scott, 2014, pp. 27–28; Ishmael, 2014, pp. 138–140; Thacker, 2014, p. 192; Shvarts, 2014).

Elsewhere, religion in metal has often been studied as a background social and moral framework contested by metal musicians, fans, and other stakeholders (in relation to Islam, in Wallach, 2008; Levine, 2009; Hecker, 2012; and Catholicism in France in Guibert and Sklower, 2011) or as an expression of either side of a binary opposition between anti-Christian and Christian metal, which nevertheless share styles, symbols, and audiences (as in Glanzer, 2003; Luhr, 2005; Cordero, 2009; Moberg, 2009; James, 2010; Jousmäki, 2011). Some have attempted to 'rescue' metal from Satanism by declaring it anti-Christian but not Satanic (Weinstein, 2000, p. 262; Walser, 1993, p. 143; Faulkner, 2009). Others have examined the nuances of various interpretations of Satanism (Dyrendal, 2008; Baddeley, 2010) and their subsequent development toward paganism, especially in black metal (Hagen, 2011; Granholm, 2011). Some attention has been paid to heavy music having analogous functions with aspects of religion, in numinous experience (Sylvan, 2002), liturgy (Scott, 2014), or communality (Stewart, 2014).

Mysticism has been mentioned in relation to metal, though often vaguely and without analysis. Often the notoriously contested term is implied to have a straightforward, common-sense meaning, as in Walser's description of Iron Maiden as 'mystical' due to lyrical references to mythologies and the devil (1993, pp. 151–158). In Natalie Purcell's surveys, death metal fans were invited to check whether they 'agreed with' metaphysical theories including 'mysticism, deism, rationalism or Cartesianism, existentialism, skepticism, and chaos theory' (2003, p. 122), and in Susan Fast's survey, Led Zeppelin fans used the term in describing what appealed to them, with Fast then implying synonymy with mythology or mystery (2001, pp. 50–52). Elsewhere, mysticism in metal is associated with empowerment (Moore, 2009, p. 148; Olson, 2011, p. 146). Christopher Partridge describes a SunnO))) performance as 'mystical', employing scare quotes to underline the controversial nature of the word (2013, p. 69). Mystical experience, specifically, appears infrequently in scholarship on metal, though it has been mentioned in relation to black metal, albeit with an implicitly universalist conception of 'experience' (Olson, 2008, p. 37). Some references in relation to black metal more closely approach my understanding of the term, particularly Steven Shakespeare's description of mysticism as 'the ruin and fulfilment of language' (2012, p. 10). Discussions of mysticism in Black Metal Theory writings often themselves tend toward an impenetrable and self-consciously mystical style (see contributions to Masciandro, 2010; and the pseudonymous Saheb and Abaris, 2014).

These attempts at understanding connections between metal and religion are reminders of the necessity, outlined by Marcus Moberg (2012, pp. 121–122), of empirical substantiation and working with listeners' own concepts and language in relation to mysticism, ritual, religion, and spirituality.

Reading/Writing Popular Culture and Mysticism: Michel de Certeau

Michel de Certeau has much to offer a theorization of drone metal mysticism. In *The Practice of Everyday Life* (1984), Certeau suggested understanding the consumption of popular culture texts as a creative activity, locating a kind of 'silent production' in reading (p. xxi) or walking in the city (pp. 93–97), where users appropriate or utilize aspects of text and environment for their own purposes in '*another* production, called 'consumption'" (Certeau, 1984, p. xii, original emphasis). This approach has been adopted by a number of cultural studies scholars (Fiske, 1989; Jenkins, 1992; and notably Brad Klypchak, 2014, in relation to metal). However, Certeau notes that this fluid consumption-as-production, momentary 'poachings' on the hegemonic territory is difficult to grasp (1984, p. xii)[2] but crucial for undermining an assumed division between consumption and production, between reception and creation, and, in a broader sense, reading and writing. Here, Certeau's example of walking in the city chimes with listeners' rhetoric of journeying amidst or through the texts of drone metal's recordings, performances, reviews, and reports.

Certeau's work frequently engages with the mystical; *The Practice of Everyday Life* refers to religious language, belief, texts, and practices (1984, pp. xiii, 4, 128, 133–138, 172, 180–196), despite appearing as a secular project. For Certeau (1992), 'mystics' is a mode of communication or manner of speaking, which draws attention to the materiality of opaque signifiers, using oxymorons and ruined and contorted phrases to highlight the limits of what is sayable. These kinds of symbolic operations, Certeau argues, take place at the margins of a tradition, simultaneously heretical and ultra-orthodox. Consistent with Joan Scott's admission that the use of the word 'experience' shouldn't or couldn't be abandoned (1991, p. 797), Certeau's treatment of mysticism does not attempt to deny experience, but shifts the focus of the study of mysticism toward productive, creative acts within traditions of writing and interpretation.

Altered and Imagined States: The Body, Space, and Time

In this section, I examine how accounts of listening connect to an existing network of drone metal's discourse and practices, referencing and sustaining an ongoing conversation around musical sound and noise, and in turn contributing to the structuring of expectations and conventions for future listening. The range of characteristics (from sonic to affective and experiential) are drawn together in reviews, online comments, survey responses, and interviews as the music is described as having extreme, extraordinary effects on listeners' perceptions of time, space, and their own bodies.

> Survey Respondent: It was very visceral, I could feel the vibrations in different parts of my body at different times. At times, I felt the textile of my pants vibrating against my legs, other times, my teeth were

chattering or the drink in my cup was vibrating in my hand. The repetitive nature of the music, together with the fog & the anonymous forms on stage had an impact on my perception of time (and space, but to a lesser degree). (Describing a *SunnO)))* performance)

The physicality of live drone metal is repeatedly stressed by listeners and is heightened by performance practices, such as playing in the dark or with smoke-machines. In asking listeners about experiences similar to drone metal concerts, other non-musical experiences were mentioned, foregrounding bodily experience:

> OC: What other experiences (musical or other) are comparable or similar in any way?
> Sauna.
> Very good marihuana :)
> Sex, rollercoaster, horror movie.
> A big fat chili with lots of red peppers and hot sauce.
> I guess extreme forces of nature.

Listeners characterize drone metal as an extreme form of metal and popular music, distancing it from the normative by discussing it in terms of unusual physiological and psychological effects and in relation to sleep, drugs, and non-ordinary states of consciousness.

Listening to recorded drone metal also has important physical aspects. Vinyl is overwhelmingly preferred, the medium described by two respondents as 'the way the music is meant to be heard', despite the album under discussion having also been released on CD, cassette, and digital formats. In addition to the analogue sound, ritual was frequently mentioned in explaining the appeal of vinyl. The importance of ritual and the body in listening to and interacting with recordings was underscored by listeners describing the tactile qualities of vinyl (and even the smell), while physically miming the actions associated with playing records.

> It's the whole ritual, you know, you can't skip tracks, you put the needle on the record, you need to not fall asleep so you can keep listening to the record. It's big, its physical [*mimes dimensions of record with hands*] like you *get* something, you know'.
>
> 'It's very ritualistic. [With] vinyl, you constantly have to get up and open up the double gatefold tome [*mimes opening record sleeve*] and put this monolithic heavy black SunnO)) vinyl on your platter. There's a much more focused, ritualistic feeling to it for me'. (Comments about vinyl from Gravetemple interviews)

As well as this tactile and physical emphasis, these excerpts also show how listeners consciously set aside and separate time and space. The careful marking of the boundaries of experience, as well as repetition, are key features of ritual (Turner, 1969; also Fast, 2001, p. 56; Partridge, 2013, p. 158 with specific reference to vinyl).

Perceptions of time and space were frequently reported to have been altered by the effects of extreme sound on the body, with respondents frequently describing losing track of time while listening. Listeners also reported making specific temporal or spatial preparations for drone metal listening, whether on recordings or at concerts. One interviewee related the length of a particular track to the long process of coming to appreciate drone metal, which he also later connected to his own spiritual practice and development.

> OC. Why did it take a long time to like Nadja?
> Just listening to it. [Nadja album] *Thaumogenesis*, it's 64 minutes long, so it needs a lot of effort. It took a long time to be open to it, and you need to when it's long. The length is important for the effort required.
> OC. What is it about length?
> I like long songs! [...] With drone ... You get more patient. When I put on a record I know what I'm getting into. I make an effort to listen to the whole thing, with no breaks. You need a certain time to feel what it does with you. [...] It's a ritual, you need to allocate enough time, after I have done everything for the day, my head is free. I spent a lot of money on my stereo, you know, to hear the records how they were intended. I move this chair into there [*gestures to other room*], I have my headphones, I turn up the music. ...
> (Interview about Gravetemple)

Some listeners mentioned that, when listening on headphones on public transport or while walking, drone metal affected their perceptions of and relation to public space. While this kind of listening has been criticized as a reactionary effect of capitalist culture and a withdrawal of the alienated individual from community, straightforwardly detrimental to both (Bull, 2007; Labelle, 2010, pp. 97–98), I understand listeners to be deliberately changing their interaction with the social world, often as a way of retrieving value from commuting or work time. However, several listeners also eschewed listening to drone metal in such contexts, sometimes in strong terms. One listener, who said he listened to music on headphones '95% of the time' while out and about, said that listening to drone metal would be 'distressing' in that situation.

While some people considered live and recorded drone metal (even by the same artists) to be so different as to be hardly comparable, in other cases there was a sense that continuity was at least sought, if not fully achieved, between public and private listening.

> We didn't go out after the gig, we were both kind of not wanting to socialise, we almost wanted to continue with that sort of feeling. [...]

I just wanted to get on the bus, listen to more music, get home and just have some time to myself. It was good, it was definitely helpful. (Interview description of Nazoranai concert)

Here a listener reports attempting to sustain continuity of feeling among three forms of listening (at a public concert; in public space but with personal headphones; and in private space) together with a particular 'helpful' function.

This movement between public and private listening spaces is also manifested in the exchange and distribution of material culture, with listeners buying physical musical media, posters, and t-shirts, practices familiar to many metal music cultures (Brown, 2007). Listeners preferred to buy music-related commodities at concerts as a way to support artists directly, access otherwise unavailable items sometimes before official release dates, and save on postage costs, while also an opportunity to publicly display their support and discuss music with the artists themselves. Aspects of packaging and production are emphasized in terms of their tactile qualities, especially in terms of weight: vinyl and cardboard sleeves are advertised as 'heavyweight': implying higher quality, foregrounding the sense of touch, and distancing them from digital images and sounds. Even digital music files, heralded by some for their departure from physical media, are sometimes sold with original drawings or other objects providing a physical component. Posters advertising concerts are also frequently removed from the inside and outside of venues toward the end of shows, the actual components of the ritualized event space removed and then reinstalled in private space together with other such salvaged items, reconstructing a ritualized listening space.

Drone Metal Pilgrimage: Rhetoric, Metaphor, and Iconicity

In combination with these efforts to construct and manage the spaces of listening for perceived optimal sonic/musical experience, a rhetoric of imagined spaces, times and journeys is used to talk about the experience of listening to drone metal. These imaginary traversals relate to the specific sonic qualities of the music, including the sense of endurance and distance involved in extended and often loud pieces, as well as drawing on thematic aspects of artwork, titles, and references to other texts. Performance practices, particularly SunnO)))'s use of smoke, robes, and numerous amplifiers, evoke description in terms of ritual and the sacred, in scholarly as well as listener descriptions (Partridge, 2013, p. 69; Lucas, 2013; Saheb and Abaris, 2014, p. 33).

Connections with attending church are made from different perspectives. A Christian attendee at an Om performance in a secular venue and an atheist attendee at a drone performance in a church both drew parallels between the feelings and atmosphere of each event.

It's similar in a way to the reverence you feel when you're at a prayer meeting or at church at a certain part where … what you would describe as the Holy Spirit is being manifest in the room. (Interview comment about Om performance at the Brudenell Social Club).

I'm not really into religion for the dogmatism and the mind control, but at the same time I think the ritual aspect, the spirituality aspect is something that is appealing to me. [...] It's like this church is now being used for something I like, and without me having to sit through something that I wouldn't enjoy, like sit through a mass. (Interview comment about drone performances in churches in London)

Although Christian religious buildings (churches, cathedrals, crypts) have often been used as evocative and perhaps transgressive venues for drone metal events, performances in ordinary concert halls and bars, and even recordings, are described in relation to religious sites: 'Like a Stonehenge of amplifiers … a vision of hell …' (Survey respondent describing SunnO))) performance). 'It's like the church of stoner' (Interview description of Sleep *Dopesmoker/Jerusalem*). While touching upon physical aspects of a concert venue, such as amplifiers arranged in a formation reminiscent of a stone circle, such descriptions often move toward less tangible architecture perceived to be religious or ritualistic: feeling, atmosphere, and sound.

The themes of time, space, and the body, as modalities of describing experience and in the rhetoric of ancientness and distance, are combined in the trope of pilgrimage. Journeys, relating to holy mountains, deserts, or other sacred landscapes are figured in lyrics and artwork: Sleep's *Holy Mountain* album, Om's tracks 'Gebel Barkal', 'Sinai', 'Annapurna', but also Bong's album artwork for *Mana-Yood-Sushai*, and arguably their band logo itself.

But the trope of journeys (perhaps sacred, often arduous) in drone metal description is far more widespread than can be explained by recordings that make explicit reference to travel. Each listener description, and each choice of artwork and lyrical theme by musicians, emerges into an existing network of influences and ways of talking about drone metal. It seems, though, that it is the endurance of repetitive sound for long periods that prompts descriptions of listening as journey or pilgrimage, rather than such descriptions merely resulting from visual or verbal references to travel: 'It's perfect for the invocation of a journey, you've got no choice but to just keep on listening, it's so repetitive. It's not just a journey from A to B, it's a pilgrimage' (Interview description of Sleep, *Dopesmoker/Jerusalem*); 'An enchantingly spaced-out aural pilgrimage' (Review of Bong, *Mana-Yood-Sushai*). 'There are certain songs like 'Sinai', which sound very much like the kind of music pilgrims would listen to in a Hindu temple' (Review of Om, *Advaitic Songs*).

In these reports, drone metal is described as soundtrack or invocation to journey; as similar to a journey; and as a journey; or the music is imagined to be like what pilgrims would listen to, while also being a pilgrimage; sometimes these semantic shifts occur in adjacent sentences. Rather

Figure 18.3 Bong, *Mana-Yood-Sushai* (2012).[3]

than simply representing choices between rhetorical modes in talking about music 'about' journeys, I suggest that such responses offer an insight into the iconicity of drone metal discourse. The experience of listening actually shares certain formal properties with journeys: endurance, physical difficulty, and long duration, allowing drone metal to be described *as* pilgrimage; as well as like pilgrimage and about pilgrimage.

Conclusion: Drone Metal's Mystical Discourse

As descriptions of drone metal pilgrimage slip between the metaphorical and the iconic, the various texts that make up drone metal's discursive formation similarly effect subtle deferrals and displacements. Oxymorons or paradoxical constructs, described by Certeau as the smallest unit of mystical discourse (1995, p. 443), are a kind of short-circuiting or ruining of rational language, in order to demonstrate its limits and turn attention to the materiality of the mystic sign, the perceptual experience of the sign's opaque material presence in the absence of an impossible referent. These formulations are present in much drone metal language, in titles (such as 'The Absence of Presence', 'The Presence of Absence', and 'Beyond Opposition' on Ommadon's 2012 albums *III* and *IV*) and in listener descriptions (such as 'chapel of apprehension' or 'satanic sermon' in a review of a SunnO)) recording). Further, if the riff is 'one of the primary units of meaning' in metal (Fast, 2001, p. 116), then drone metal's excessive repetition of riffs performs a similar mystical deconstruction of the symbolic code, such that their status as riffs are simultaneously affirmed and questioned, in repetitive structures reminiscent of mantra or recitation. 'Bong immerses the audience in slow and heavy walls of sound that can't even be called riffs;' while Om's instruments 'make something it feels almost blasphemic to describe simply as 'riffs"(Lines from drone metal reviews).

Similarly, concerts are described as more than concerts; drone metal as both metal and beyond metal; and even as music that is something more than music: 'It's hard to look at Om as a 'metal' band at all, although their approach seems to be pursuing the Sabbathian ethos much more intricately and determinedly than most of their contemporaries' (Line from Om review); 'It's more like an experience or mass rather than a 'concert';' 'the air became solid, it's not only music, it's air morphology' (Survey descriptions of SunnO))) performance).

The focus on amplification (signaled in Boris' album *Amplifier Worship*, 1998), and SunnO)))'s eponymous amplifiers) is a turn away from the virtuoso lead guitar, a turn from semantic meaning to materiality, to the experience of corporeal vibration itself as mystic sign. As well as a questioning and subversion of the functions and structures of language (and, by extension, music), Certeau understands mystical discourse as undermining and challenging the institution that authorizes it. Drone metal can similarly be understood as an interrogation, at once radical and orthodox, of its own tradition, heavy metal (itself often read as somehow religious, even if sometimes ironically). This interrogation and renewal is effected symbolically, in the identification with Black Sabbath and other icons of metal in artwork and titles, and also in musical terms, in the interplay between riffs extended to drones, between repetition and tense stasis, and in review and commentary texts that describe the extension to breaking-point of metal riffs and conventions.

Drone metal's sonic productions also dissolve the entrenched and problematic conceptual text/experience division in studies of mysticism. Performances especially are referred to as experiences, though can be read as texts; while sound recordings are also texts to be experienced and, together with reviews, commentary, and conversation, are full of references to previous sounds, texts, and experiences of texts. John of the Cross and St. Teresa denied mystical status in their own writings, while appealing to anterior mystical texts; those same writings are now widely designated as mystical in later texts (Certeau, 1992, p. 78), while Certeau's own writing style in turn could be described as a mystical manner of speaking. Similarly, drone metal bands pay homage to previous mystical texts in the tradition: Om named its 2006 album after the mystical Sufi poem *Conference of the Birds* and subsequently both poem and record are designated mystical by reviews of the album; elsewhere musicians speak of Black Sabbath's recordings as holy grails or religious texts that have prompted others to make recordings (such as Sleep's *Dopesmoker*) in turn described as sacred.

In minimalist structures experienced as overwhelming, physical sound in concert, or in the repeated and ritualized practices of listening to recorded sound, drone metal's mystical sonic, verbal, and visual discourse 'transforms [...] detail into myth; it catches hold of it, blows it out of proportion, multiplies it, divinizes it' (Certeau, 1992, p. 10). A mystical tradition is constituted through recordings and concerts performing extreme, radical extensions of metal's foundational sounds, in combination with an array of connotations to established, if obscure, religious traditions and spiritual practices. No less constitutive of drone metal as mystical are listeners' ongoing and collaborative exegeses of their own profound experiences of bodies vibrating with such sounds. The paradoxically deconstructive yet fundamentalist extensions of heavy metal's symbolic codes return to a performatively contradictory ineffability, where statements denying the possibility of description not only foreshadow and call into question actual descriptions, but are themselves descriptive. Experiences of texts are reported in new texts to be experienced, as drone metal's discourse on mystical experience is itself mystical discourse, tradition, and experience.

Notes

1. Participant observation took place at more than 50 concerts and 11 music festivals, across the UK, Belgium and the Netherlands, featuring drone metal and related music, September 2012 to December 2014. Over 400 responses were collected from nine surveys relating to specific events or tours, by drone metal and related musicians: SunnO))), Bong, Dylan Carlson, Om, Gravetemple, Nazoranai, Ufomammut and Tim Hecker. The latter three perform music styles related to drone metal and with significant audience overlap (experimental improvisation, psychedelic doom metal, and electronic ambient/drone, respectively). Interviews were arranged by requesting contact information from survey respondents, then arranging in-person, telephone or email interviews. Online reviews of concerts and recordings were compiled from music websites and blogs, together with comments from forum discussions and streaming sites.
2. Certeau has been criticized for assuming a too fixed opposition between dominant culture and transitory uses by the dominated (Hills, 2002, p. 39). However, scholarly applications of Certeau's poaching (that which 'does not keep what it acquires' (1984, p. 176) tend to focus on examples that have already been reabsorbed into dominant modes, such as fan fiction that is successful enough to be published (Jenkins, 1989, pp. 177–184).
3. The album cover image is derived from a painting of the sacred mountain Kanchenjunga by Nicholas Roerich, a visionary artist who often portrayed mountains and mythical religious figures.

Bibliography

Baddeley, G. (2010). *Lucifer rising: Devil worship and rock 'n' roll*. London: Plexus.

Brown, A. (2007). Rethinking the subcultural commodity: The case of heavy metal t-shirt culture(s). In P. Hodkinson & W. Deicke (Eds.), *Youth cultures: scenes, subcultures and tribes* (pp. 63–78). Oxford: Routledge.

Bull, M. (2007). *Sound moves: iPod culture and urban experience*. New York and London: Routledge.

Certeau, M. de (1984). *The practice of everyday life* (S. Rendall, Trans.). Berkeley, Los Angeles, London: University of California Press.

Certeau, M. de (1992). *The mystic fable (Volume 1: The sixteenth and seventeenth centuries)* (M.B. Smith, Trans.). Chicago, London: University of Chicago Press.

Certeau, M. de (1995). History and mysticism (A. Goldhammer, Trans.). In J. Revel & L. Hunt (Eds.), *Histories: French constructions of the past, postwar French thought (Volume 1)* (pp. 437–447). New York: The New Press.

Christe, I. (2003). *Sound of the beast: The complete headbanging history of heavy metal*. New York: HarperCollins.

Coggins, O. (2014). Citation and recitation in mystical scholarship and om's drone metal. *Diskus*, 16(1), 30–47.

Cordero, J. (2009). Unveiling Satan's wrath: Aesthetics and ideology in anti-Christian heavy metal. *Religion and Popular Culture*, Volume 21(1), n.p.

Dyrendal, A. (2008). Devilish consumption: Popular culture in satanic socialization. *Numen*, 55, 68–98.

Fast, S. (2001). *In the houses of the holy: Led Zeppelin and the power of rock music*, Oxford: Oxford University Press.

Faulkner, F. (2009). 'Get your kicks on Route 666' or why the devil has all the best tunes: Trekking through the darker side of heavy metal music. In C. Balmain & L. Drawmer (Eds.), *Something wicked this way comes* (pp. 183–198). Amsterdam, New York: Rodopi.

Fiske, J. (1989) *Reading the popular*. London, New York: Routledge.

Glanzer, P. L. (2003). Christ and the heavy metal subculture. *Religion and Society*, 5, 1–16.

Granholm, K. (2011). 'Sons of northern darkness': Heathen influences in black metal and neofolk music. *Numen*, 58: 514–544.

Guibert, G., & Sklower, J. (2011). Hellfest: The thing that should not be?: Local perceptions and Catholic discourses on metal culture in France. *Popular Music History*, 6(1/2), 100–115.

Hagen, R. (2011). Musical style, ideology and mythology in Norwegian black metal. In J. Wallach, H. M. Berger, and P. D. Greene (Eds.), *Metal rules the globe: Heavy metal music around the world* (pp. 180–199). Durham, NC: Duke University Press.

Hecker, P. (2012). *Turkish metal: Music, meaning and morality in a Muslim society*. Farnham: Ashgate.

Hills, M. (2002). *Fan cultures*. London and New York: Routledge.

Huxley, A. (1945). *The perennial philosophy*. Oxford: Chatto & Windus.

Ishmael, A. (2014). Black metal in the white tower: Metal's formless presence in contemporary art. In S. Wilson (Ed.), *Melancology: Black metal theory and ecology* (pp. 119–151). Winchester, Washington: Zero Books.

James, W. (1902). *The varieties of religious experience*. New York: Longmans.

James, C. A. (2010). The common vernacular of power relations in heavy metal and Christian fundamentalist performances. In R. Hill & K. Spracklen (Eds.), *Heavy fundamentalisms: Music, metal and politics* (pp. 19–29). Oxford: Interdisciplinary Press.

Jameson, F. (1982). Towards a new awareness of genre. *Science Fiction Studies, 9*(3), 322–324.

Jenkins, H. (1992). *Textual poachers: Television fans and participatory culture*. New York, London: Routledge.

Jousmäki, H. (2011). Epistemic, interpersonal, and moral stances in the construction of us and them in Christian metal lyrics. *Multicultural Discourses, 6*(1), 53–66.

Kahn-Harris, K. (2007). *Extreme metal: Music and culture on the edge*. Oxford: Berg.

Klypchak, B. (2014). Authenticities, anomalies, and animetal USA. presentation at *Metal and Cultural Impact Conference*, University of Dayton, Ohio, USA. November 7, 2014.

Labelle, B. (2010). *Acoustic territories: Sound culture and everyday life*. New York: Continuum.

Levine, M. (2009). *Heavy metal Islam*. New York: Three Rivers Press.

Lucas, O. (2013). MAXIMUM VOLUME YIELDS MAXIMUM RESULTS. *Journal of Sonic Studies, 7*. Available online at http://sonicstudies.org/jss7.

Luhr, E. (2005). Metal missionaries to the nation: Christian heavy metal music, "family values", and youth culture, 1984–1994. *American Quarterly, 57*(1), 103–128.

Masciandro, N. (Ed.). (2010). *Hideous gnosis: Black metal theory symposium I*. Oxford: CreateSpace.

Moberg, M. (2009). *Faster for the master!* Turku:Åbo Akademi University Press.

Moberg, M. (2012). Religion in popular music or popular music as religion? *Popular Music and Society, 35*(1), 113–130.

Moore, R. (2009). The unmaking of the English working class: Deindustrialization, reification and the origins of heavy metal. In G. Bayer (Ed.), *Heavy metal music in Britain* (pp. 143–160). Farnham: Ashgate.

Morton, T. (2013). *Hyperobjects: Philosophy and ecology after the end of the world*. Minneapolis: University of Minnesota Press.

Olson, B. H. (2008). I am the black wizards: Multiplicity, mysticism and identity in black metal music and culture. MA Thesis, Bowling Green: Bowling Green State University.

Olson, B. H. (2011). Voice of our blood: National Socialist discourses in black metal. *Popular Music History, 6*(1/2), 135–149.

Partridge, C. (2013). *The lyre of Orpheus: Popular music, the sacred and the profane*. Oxford: Oxford University Press.

Piper, J. (2013). Locating experiential richness in doom metal. PhD Thesis, San Diego: University of California: http://escholarship.org/uc/item/7bq7387s

Purcell, N. (2003). *Death metal: The passion and politics of a subculture*. Jefferson, NC: McFarland.

Richardson, D. (2008). Dylan Carlson comes to terms. … *SFGate*, June 12, 2008.

Riley, A. (2010). *Impure play: Sacredness, transgression, and the tragic in popular culture*. Lanham, MD: Lexington Books.

Saheb, N., & Abaris, D. X. (2014). *Bergmetal: Oro-Emblems of the musical beyond*. London: CreateSpace.

Scott, J. W. (1991). The evidence of experience. *Critical Inquiry, 17*(4), 773–797.

Scott, N. W. R. (2014). Seasons in the abyss: Heavy metal as liturgy. *Diskus, 16*(1), 12–29.

Shakespeare, S. (2012). Of plications: A short summa on the nature of Cascadian black metal. *Glossator,* 6, 1–45.
Sharf, R. H. (1995). Buddhist modernism and the rhetoric of meditative experience. *Numen,* 42(3), 228–283.
Shvarts, A. (2014). Troubled air: The drone and doom of reproduction in SunnO)))'s metal maieutic. *Women and Performance,* Dec 2014, 1–17.
Stewart, F. (2014). Straight edge punk: Religious mutation or over-reaching? *Diskus,* 6(1), 49–67.
Sylvan, R. (2002). *Traces of the spirit: The religious dimensions of popular music.* New York: New York University Press.
Thacker, E. (2014). Sound of the abyss. In S. Wilson (Ed.), *Melancology: Black metal theory and ecology* (pp. 179–194). Winchester, Washington: Zero Books.
Turner, V. (1969). *The ritual process: Structure and anti-structure.* Ithaca, NY: Cornell University Press.
Wallach, J. (2008). *Modern noise, fluid genres: Popular music in Jakarta, Indonesia 1997–2001,* Madison: University of Wisconsin Press.
Wallach, J., & Levine, A. (2011). 'I want *you* to support local metal': A theory of metal scene formation. *Popular Music History,* 6(1/2), 116–134.
Walser, R. (1993). *Running with the devil: Power, gender and madness in heavy metal Music.* Hanover, NH: University Press of New England.
Weinstein, D. (2000). *Heavy metal: The music and its culture.* New York: Da Capo Press.
Weinstein, D. (2011). How is metal studies possible?' *Journal of Cultural Research,* 15(3), 243–245.

Discography

Black Sabbath. (1972). *Vol. 4.* Warner Bros.
Bong. (2012). *Mana-Yood-Sushai.* Ritual Productions.
Boris. (1996). *Absolutego.* FangsAnalSatan.
Boris. (1998). *Amplifier worship.* Mangrove.
Boris. (2003). *Akuma No Uta.* Diwphalanx.
Earth. (1991). *Extracapsular extraction.* Sub Pop.
Earth. (1993). *2: Special low frequency version.* Sub Pop.
Melvins. (1992). *Lysol.* Boner/Tupelo.
Om. (2006). *Conference of the birds.* Holy Mountain.
Om. (2012). *Advaitic songs.* Drag City.
Ommadon. (2012). *III.* self-released.
Ommadon. (2012). *IV.* self-released.
Sleep. (1991). *Vol. 2.* Off the Disk Records.
Sleep. (1992). *Holy mountain.* Earache.
Sleep. (1996/1999). *Jerusalem.* London Records/Music Cartel.
Sleep. (2003/2012). *Dopesmoker.* TeePee/Southern Lord.
SunnO))). (2000). *The grimmrobe demos.* Hydra Head.
SunnO))). (2000). *ØØVoid.* Hydra Head.
SunnO))). (2002). *3: Flight of the behemoth.* Southern Lord.
SunnO))). (2006). *Black one.* Southern Lord.
SunnO))) & Boris. (2006). *Altar.* Southern Lord.
Venom. (1981). *Welcome to Hell.* Neat Records.

Part VII
Metal Futures

19 The Future of Metal Is Bright and Hell Bent for Genre Destruction
A Response to Keith Kahn-Harris

Tom O'Boyle and Niall W.R. Scott

At the 2011 Home of Metal conference in Birmingham, a question was asked following Deena Weinstein's keynote speech by an audience member: 'What will happen to metal when the old guard go?' This comment carries with it the idea that metal will reach a point of crisis and it is only the 'true' originators who are capable of keeping its flame burning. It is flawed, but an interesting question nonetheless. The idea that an old guard is not just respected but is somehow necessary to keep the metal movement alive, fails to recognize its growth and diversification; it can also halt its creative growth as metal perpetually refers back to a canon of work rather than be future oriented.

The idea of metal being at a 'point of crisis' is how Keith Kahn-Harris opened a series of essays on his view of the current state of metal. Parts of the essays were delivered at the *Heavy Metal and Popular Culture* conference at Bowling Green State University, Ohio, in 2013, and he then promised to produce a series of seven short instalments, duly fulfilled, on the subject of metal in crisis and the future of metal under the heading 'Metal Beyond Metal' (Kahn-Harris 2013a, b, c, d, e; 2014a, b). Slightly earlier, when work had started on this collection we were in the mood to finish with an epilogue on the future of metal, so it seemed ideal to combine the two and offer a response to Keith's essays and give him a further right to reply.

It must be mentioned from the outset that to talk about the future of anything in predictive terms is notoriously problematic and left to nothing but guesswork. However, the arguments that Kahn-Harris presents are about a concern regarding the future of heavy metal, a concern that is very much situated in the present. Most writing on the future, unless it is science fiction, usually involves a way of managing the present so that one is attentive to the direction one steers into the winds of change. Who the old guard is, too, may very well depend on one's present subjective outlook on the past. For some it will be Black Sabbath, for example, for others Iron Maiden, but then for some it might be Mayhem or, believe it or not, it may very well be My Chemical Romance. We can distil Kahn-Harris' arguments into four phrases that capture why according to him, metal is in crisis: the first is its abundance; the second concerns scarcity and quality; the third, immediacy of access; and the final one concerns metal's dissipation held in tension with its ossification. It must be recognized that Kahn-Harris is expressing his views to a general audience and making some claims to stimulate debate, rather than to hold fast to them. In this sense, his essay is polemical and in some parts rhetorical; it is not filled with empirical data to support his claims, for example. But in the spirit of debate, we have decided to take on the challenge his ideas pose to metal fans and metal theory.

Too Much Metal: A Bad Thing?

Kahn-Harris begins the first essay entitled 'Too Much Metal' with the claim that metal is in a crisis because of its abundance, leading to an unawareness of metal being in a crisis. In the opening essay, he writes:

> Metal today is in crisis. Metal's crisis doesn't feel like a crisis. In fact it sometimes feels like quite the reverse. This is a crisis in which most are unaware that there is a crisis—and that is the crisis. The crisis is one of *abundance*.
>
> (Kahn Harris, 2013a)

In other words, if there is so much of it about, then how can it possibly be in a state of crisis? For Kahn Harris, there was value in the scarcity of metal; the crisis of abundance he articulates on a personal level as experiencing a sense of deflation (Kahn-Harris, 2013a) where the abundance of metal is asking to have all his dreams fulfilled. He importantly sees abundance as distinct from diversity. The latter describes the breadth of music available, in terms of sub-genres, styles, and forms, but abundance he claims has to do with depth—the sheer quantity of metal that is available to the listener, fan, and scene member. He expresses disappointment concerning both the abundance of the music and the growing abundance of metal scholarship, because its existence has removed the pleasure (he) had of searching and discovery. So the crisis in metal that he observes has to do with so much of it being about and it being so easily accessible, as opposed to a feeling of value attached in the past to metal's scarcity. He sees scarcity as a counterweight to the domination of what he calls metal's 'dinosaurs' and the fragmenting effect of its diversity. For Kahn-Harris, the crisis of abundance is a threat to the 'balance'… 'achieved by change and stability, by homogeneity and heterogeneity' (Kahn-Harris, 2013c).

'Almost everything that I ever wanted in metal now exists', continuing: 'I could never get my hands on enough metal recordings to satisfy my thirst for metal knowledge' (Kahn Harris, 2013a). We would be interested in what Kahn-Harris means by metal knowledge. Accumulating knowledge of a scene—the bands' biographies, listening to the music produced and so on—is always a reflective activity on what has already happened: the recorded past or reflection on the present, but it is not something that can be strongly future oriented. If one finds a metal gem, one might hope that it will generate more, one may be thinking of what is to come next. But 'metal knowledge' is more likely to be reflective, the anticipation of the new being a present tense preoccupation. Of course, there is a qualitative difference between the way in which one accessed and consumed music in the past and the multitudes of ways in which it is accessed and consumed now. This has to do with a difference related to the aesthetic perception of the music mediated through changing technologies over time. This aspect of the consumption of music does not necessarily affect the quality of the music itself. Where Kahn-Harris laments the passing of the days when one could eagerly search for rare metal output, it is sadly a feature that has been manipulated by the market. The anticipation that the consumer expresses is precisely what the market preys upon leading to ever more music being produced in order primarily to be consumed, rather than music being made to be appreciated on its own terms. In other words, one needs to distinguish between abundance that comes from the creative output generated by musicians and abundance that comes from serving the profit motive of the market. These two kinds of abundance have different qualities—the latter being produced despite the inefficiencies of the market, the former's artistic abundance more akin to natural abundance. One would for example never have cause to complain about an abundant tomato harvest, but the inefficiencies of the market may very well overproduce a product that is reminiscent of the Marxist complaint that 'there is too much civilisation, too much means of substance, too much industry, too much commerce' (Marx, 1848 [1978], p. 478).

But there is a further complaint about desire and availability, which is worth noting: what makes a sound, band, album, song worth pursuing? It may be based on previous listening experience, but it might be the rarity of a recording. In other words, it is that obsessive journey made by a collector, where having the object matters in a way that is significant beyond the mere listening experience. Kahn-Harris is relating the contemporary abundance of availability with a previous age where the sheer work one had to do to be able to afford or even find a recording, say in the case of tape trading, leads to a special relationship with the object; even a relationship that affects one's listening experience. Here we think Kahn-Harris has a point but a more general one: that is with music being so ubiquitously available in so many formats, but especially in its digital form, one's relationship to recorded music has changed. When downloading a track, the music is not owned or possessed in the same sense as one used to be, so there may well be a change in the listening experience. Indeed Kahn-Harris talks of the relationship among obscurity, the discovery of the music object, and the sense of anticipation and searching for things that has been removed by metal's abundance; with a nod to Walter Benjamin, its 'aura' has been lost. Kahn-Harris speaks of a strange sense of deflation accompanying this abundance in heavy metal, that his dreams fulfilled are now disappointing, that the current abundance does not satisfy: waiting for a demo in the mail from an obscure Pakistani metal band is just not the same as googling the name and finding it online (Kahn Harris, 2013a).

The internet *has* made it easier for artists to disseminate their material, to get it out to listeners, to be discovered. We do not think one needs to lament a past golden age of metal discovery. We happen to have the privilege of experiencing both states of affairs. But those born in the Internet age have no point of reference to the past that Kahn-Harris refers to, so his position is in danger of sounding like a 'they don't know how good they've got it, these kids' kind of argument. It is a familiar form of argument containing an inductive error: one cannot forge a necessary link between what has been the case and what will be the case. Something important is only lost on the transfer from old formats to new ones for those who have experienced both. The sense of anticipation, excitement, the thrill of searching and discovery for the collector and fan remains. But now the individual can act as critic, sieve through the vast amount of material and alight on something he or she considers to be worthwhile, rather than waiting for a journalist to do so. Rooting through to the coalface to eventually uncover a shiny diamond simply takes place in a wider range of formats. For example, one could consider the dedication required to access and research all the European recordings listed at www.metalunderground.com. Perhaps in an age of metal abundance it is even more of a challenge. The metal underground is very much alive and direct in its dissemination of music through websites, forums, live events, and yes, tape trading, as well as a resurgence in vinyl; are all testament to a healthy abundance of metal.

It is important to pay attention to what Kahn-Harris does by using the term abundance. As an adjective, paired with the term scarcity, there is a problem in the manner in which it is used. He writes of abundance and scarcity as if metal music is a natural resource. The exploitation of this ambiguity in the meanings of these terms can allow abundance and scarcity to be misdefined in the context of music, leading to erroneous conclusions regarding metal's current state and its future. Thus, we do not see metal as threatened by either abundance or scarcity. Music is not like a necessary natural resource—its scarcity does not lead to death nor does its abundance lead to gluttony in the same manner that a food would. So to speak of scarcity and abundance of metal in this way as if it were some kind of resource that could run out seems to us to force the issue in a particular direction. It may well be a resource in a sense, where it has a certain utility to the listener and fan for the sake of entertainment or its employment in identity formation, or for the metal studies researcher in the production of knowledge. But it is not the case that it is a resource that is going to run out or be used up; rather it is an artistic product that is of its time; it will manifest itself in different forms and change. What counts as metal today is certainly not what it was in its early formative days of the 1970s or in its development into the '80s and '90s. So we do not agree that abundance and the expanding availability of the music points to a crisis; it may well point to changes in direction. There is likely to be a day in the future where metal is no longer produced, of course, but that is part of change and only a cause for lament

The Future of Metal Is Bright and Hell Bent for Genre Destruction 337

and concern for those who have a rather conservative disposition for the things that they like to be always available. But the beauty of digital storage makes even that possible.

He continues in the second and third essays (Kahn-Harris, 2013b, c) to make a case for the relationship between scarcity and quality; that is, prior to the current abundant period, not everything managed to get through to a metal fan's ear. For music to get to the fan's ears significant barriers needed to be overcome, logistical barriers that he cites as 'recording, releasing, circulating and publicising metal recordings' (Kahn-Harris, 2013b). Further he writes of this process concerning the production and distribution and marketing of the music also needing to link to the fans' capacity for acquisition of it, including the accumulation of 'scene knowledge' (Kahn-Harris, 2013b). Although he sees this as a filtering process that could, in equal measure, have led to the loss of promising bands and new material, such a filtering process delivered a manageable volume of music; in other words, the scenic system of production and capital acted as a cap on production. He further claims that metal had its own built-in obsolescence, citing the emergence of grunge, leading to what he calls the 'mass extinction event' of 1980s style heavy metal. The main point that Kahn-Harris makes, though, is that the manageability of quantity and discernibility of style was predicated on scarcity claiming that in 'today's abundance nothing ever becomes truly obsolete'. (Kahn-Harris, 2013b) There are several complex issues here that need be teased out. We respect Kahn-Harris enough to recognize that he knows that scarcity and abundance do not correlate with quality. However, it is impossible to identify the filtering process that eventually allows those diamonds to shine through without some considerable historical distance. The challenge today is to recognize each individual's role in the judging and consumption of metal. If music recordings in their abundance do not become obsolete or scarce because of digital storage and access, the more pertinent point is whether such recordings remain relevant. Something may not become obsolete, but it may well lose its relevance. We hope this loss of relevance is driven by novelty and creativity.

Rather than abundance and scarcity, the marker for metal's future ought to be its quality of creativity and, as he mentions later on, its transgressive voice. In what sense has that been damaged by abundance, apart from the challenge for the listener to be more discerning? You can only listen to one piece of music at a time. But then he claims that metal is not artistically dead, just that metal has no shape or movement and that it is stuck between ossification and dissolution (Kahn-Harris, 2013b, d). But arguably it is this tension where metal's creativity is to be found and Kahn-Harris's essays a jolt to remind metal musicians to use that tension to their advantage is a welcome one, a point we will expand on below. Perhaps we need to work harder to follow the fault lines or instead just sit back and bathe in metal's crucible.

Metal is arguably a postmodern music form, as asserted by Goodwin in its *bricolage* of iconography (2006, p. 448). It is replete with paradoxes and is comfortably detached yet respectful of its origins, so it is odd that

Kahn-Harris is worried about its lack of reflexivity. The abundance of immediate access and loss of reference to the original in the Baudrillardian (1994) sense is, we will suggest, required for its future: for metal to grow it needs to forget (but more on that below). Wallach and Levine (2013) have coherently theorized metal's scene formation at the local level, arguing that it is the 'underground' that drives and sustains the genre-formation. They note that, in their research, metal scenes in non-western context emerge before other music scenes, for example before punk, and draw on both the global and the local in their formation. Scene knowledge and change we claim happens at a pace that only some connoisseurs and well-informed journalists manage to keep up with for a given period of time.

Metal Has a Future

Kahn-Harris states that metal is not dying but rather that it has become incoherent (Kahn- Harris, 2013d). Metal is suffering from dissipation by which he means that it is moving in many different directions and is thus losing its overarching cultural identity. On the one hand, either this means that he is unable to keep up with the abundance and wishes he could, or on the other hand, the claim is that there may as well be an atomic one-to-one relationship between a band/artist and a genre or style. The claim is resting on the view that there are so many different forms of metal that identifying and critically teasing out strands has become impossible. It has fragmented into so many parts that nothing recognizable keeps it together. In part, this is also because metal's musical identity has been incorporated into other musical styles, such as hip hop and rap. The second worry that he cites concerning metal's future is that it will become static, as mentioned above, that it will become 'ossified'. This sets up a dilemma for Kahn-Harris, as these two poles—dissipation and ossification—seem to condemn metal. But this only holds true if one wishes to classify and categorize, in the manner a collector would. The fragmentation of metal is precisely the threat that it maintains: it cannot be controlled by the Garden of Eden's Adamic act of classifying and naming. Metal is never what one says it is: this is its satanic charm—it escapes definition and thus always retains the potential to be transgressive. So where Kahn-Harris is concerned that metal has lost its transgressive edge, we think it still has the capacity to be transgressive, as it always manages to escape definition, and in his words, escape 'ossification'. We thus reject any idea that there is some core sound or value to metal that is aesthetically diluted as different forms emerge and merge in exploration of the genre. To argue thus is to maintain a rather conservative view of what metal might be and fail to recognize the movements and currents at work in the underground scene and in other fields. If it is a certain kind of transgression that Kahn-Harris is after then yes, maybe that effect has dissipated in some areas of the music. For example, the anti-religious sentiment in death and black metal does not carry much weight in a western context. But that is not unique to metal. It would be better perhaps to encourage metal to find new transgressive ground and get something to aim at either politically or ethically. There are even those areas of metal that are transgressive by being resistant to change and keep on doggedly generating the same sound regardless of popular or scene opinion. Consider the sound generated by Airborne, for example, as a reworking of AC/DC's path or doom metal's expansion on Black Sabbath's riffs. Yet even here, we find new and novel offshoots being generated. However, what the music and culture *is* has always been in transition and cannot be easily defined. It is a fluid movement. Thus, his claim recognizing that 'metal is part of a fast changing world in which no institution or cultural practice can ever be guaranteed to endure' is important. We hold that one can either step back and reminisce on what it used to be or be at the center of it, participating in its change, as recognized in Nicola Allett's (2013) research on the extreme metal connoisseur.

The claim made by Kahn-Harris concerning the erosion of the status of the critic (2013d) is in our view a good thing in that it frees up the individual as the determinant of taste. Much like the proclamation of the 'death of the author' by Roland Barthes (1993) and Michel Foucault (1984), the music fan has been liberated to develop his or her own critique and vote with his or her ears and feet. Devin Townsend's recent crowd-funding campaign is a paradigm example of fans' relationship to an artist they like and are willing to support. Someone who is known for a Bowie-like chameleon character in the metal world chose to develop and release an album ('Casualties of Cool') using crowd funding; he managed to exceed the total needed by 544%. Furthermore, he comments on the capacity for this form of funding to open new avenues that the traditional music industry could not:

> Ultimately, the audience, the labels, the artists, musicians and performers that help make these visions come to life are together in this. It's a 'common goal' in my mind that we can strive to make things that are awesome, funny, serious, uncompromising and ultimately a compliment to daily life for all of us, the likes of which the standard 'music industry' would never ever allow.
>
> (Townsend, 2015)

Although Townsend's output is predominately metal, this recording project is firmly rooted in the country/folk music tradition and would seem to be an example of metal's dissipation: an artist who maintains his fan base, receives financial support for a side project that opens up an entirely different genre of music. But we would argue, that this can only serve to enrich metal and stretch musical tastes into new fields. A further example of metal's reach can be seen in the hip hop material produced by Odd Future, combining hip hop and extreme metal aesthetics. Odd Future is a group of skateboard loving teenagers from Los Angeles that have used the Internet to supreme effect. By making records at home and releasing them as free downloads, combined with their innate puerile charisma, they rose from unknowns to one of the hottest things in the hip hop scene in 2011/12. Their leader goes by the name of Tyler, the creator, or Wolf Hayley—the alter ego he adopts when speaking about some of the darker aspects of his personality. Tyler writes nihilistic rhymes about serial killers, rape, and violence, rapping about Satan and 666, about packs of wolves and deals with some of the darker sides of human psychology one would normally associate with a Shining album. On the cover art for 'Goblin' (2011), he appears with an inverted crucifix upon his forehead, and the video work accompanying the album's releases would sit well in a death or black metal aesthetic.

Moving further into the world of fine art, metal is expressing itself through the arts in general not just in the moment of musical performance; see, for example, the work of Locrian's Terrence Hannum (2014) in relation to black metal. In this case, metal shows its capacity to inject new life into stagnated forms of music and beyond. These are examples of metal's dissipation. However, unlike ossification, dissipation does not have to equate with dilution of quality. Far from it; it can open up new horizons.

Our position is that metal can rise to the challenge of being even more future oriented than it perhaps is. For this to work, metal needs, in paying due respect to its origins, to also be in a position where artists are willing to forget. We leave it to the artist exactly which qualities in metal can or even ought to be forgotten to allow its move forward. Even acting 'as if' something has novelty involves a certain kind of forgetting (Mullarkey, 2013). Mullarkey's words on the future of continental philosophy are highly appropriate: 'Any new movement acts as if it has real novelty, and this as if involves an act of forgetting (of the past) and fabulation (of the future) that creates its own starting point in an act of fidelity with this future and infidelity with this past' (2013, p. 275).

He further maintains that a youthful fundamentalism needs to pretend that others in the past got it wrong or that they never existed in order to get something new started. This is the challenge that besets each new musical formation, every present second, around the globe in any scene, including metal. What could be more transgressive *within* metal than to declare, with the arrogance of an Italian futurist the irrelevance of Black Sabbath, to condemn Iron Maiden as being merely of archaeological interest, to condemn the Big Four (Metallica, Megadeth, Anthrax, and Slayer) as bearing no relevance to the now? Such eliminative transgression is creatively present even where, for example in black metal, it means being true to humanity's oblivion. Metal culture is not just confined to its music, and as such heavy metal is a movement that embraces traditions and counters antiquities in its opportunity to reconfigure progression. At its heart, it is a subversive movement that is capable of shining a dark light on musical and cultural stagnation.

So Kahn-Harris can remain comfortably assured that the loss of historical baggage as he puts it will, and probably is, happening. Metal has always been at the cultural vanguard of calling the status quo institutionalization and establishment into question. Its fluid movement into musical genres speaks to a future where heavy metal continues to evolve. But instead of subgenres rising and fading out of popularity, heavy metal allows genre fusion—much like jazz has done in the past—yet toward a future where genre becomes meaningless, with the effect of both frustrating and weakening commodification and definitional oppression. Features of this are found in heavy metal's focus on the live music event, the use (although not unique to metal) of music distribution that bypasses traditional modes of output. The openness of heavy metal to transformation is dialogical, where music movements are feeding off heavy metal's sound and aesthetic as well. This is pointed in Kahn Harris' final two essays 'Breaking Metal's Boundaries' and 'Metal Beyond Metal' (Kahn Harris, 2014a, b) where he shows that it is not easy to pin down what 'metal' means and refers to. 'It does not just mean genre affiliation. It connotes a certain kind of social value, at least when metal fans use the term'. (Kahn-Harris, 2014b) The lists of suggestions—five for metal musicians and five for metal listeners (Kahn-Harris, 2014b) are already being pursued, as he recognizes, and are exemplars of shape and movement in the scene.

Metal is something that evolves continually, as one witnesses subgenres rise and fade in and out of popularity. Change and evolution see both the emergence of complexity and simplicity in equal measure but not necessarily in the same repeating patterns. This is true of biology as well as the arts. The lament Kahn-Harris expresses in his essays seems to be one affected by generational perspective. At one stage we of a certain age might have been on a speedboat heading toward an unending horizon, but when the fuel runs out and the other side is visible, it is time to face the opposite direction, grab the oars, and row, enjoying the sunset over the vast expanse of the opposite horizon, occasionally looking over one's shoulder to be sure we are headed in the right direction.

Metal is beginning to escape from the oppressive effect of superlatives. It is no longer the case that metal has to be louder than everything else, faster, darker, heavier … The establishment of heavy metal as a culture takes its future beyond the musical affect, shedding layers of skin that could have infected the movement with sameness. Theodor Adorno and Max Horkheimer's (2002) condemnation of mass culture as infected with sameness extends to the sameness of the very idea that there may be something new on the horizon; this too has been thought before. Heavy metal genuinely has the capacity to embrace progress, held in tandem with tradition yet bypassing sameness and repetition. But to do so it needs to take advantage of forgetting. In this metal is well placed: it is devoted to histories but disinterested in time; it embraces individualism, community, and tribalisms, yet it is critical of the self-effacing 'inauthentic' ego commonly found in pop music and mass culture. Its appeal in part is a consciousness that is true to itself—its roots and its future. This is an oddly dark bright future, hell bent on genre destruction.

Bibliography

Adorno, T., & Horkheimer, M. (2002). *Dialectic of enlightenment*. Redwood City, CA: Stanford University Press.

Allett, N. (2013). The extreme metal 'connoisseur'. In T. Hjelm, K. Kahn-Harris, & M. LeVine (Eds.), *Heavy metal: Controversies and countercultures* (pp. 166–181). London: Equinox.

Barthes, R. (1993). The death of the author. In R. Barthes, *Image-Music-Text* (pp. 142–148). London: Fontana Press.

Baudrillard, J. (1994). *Simulation and simulacra*. Ann Arbor: University of Michigan Press.

Foucault, M. (1984). What is an author. In M. Foucault & P. Rabinow (Trans.) *The Foucault Reader: An introduction to Foucault's thought* (pp. 101–120). London: Penguin.

Goodwin, A. (2006). Popular music and postmodern theory (3rd ed). In J. Storey (Ed.), *Cultural theory and popular culture: A reader* (pp. 440–453). Harlow: Pearson Longman.

Hannum, T. (2014). http://www.terencehannum.com/ (accessed March 3, 2015).

Kahn-Harris, K. (2013a). Too much metal. *Souciant*: http://souciant.com/2013/11/too-much-metal/ (accessed November 29, 2013).

Kahn-Harris, K. (2013b). Invisible metal. *Souciant*: http://souciant.com/2013/12/invisible-metal/ (accessed December 6, 2013).

Kahn-Harris, K. (2013c). Music at a standstill. *Souciant:* http://souciant.com/2013/12/music-at-a-standstill/ (accessed December 12, 2013).

Kahn-Harris, K. (2013d). The metal future. *Souciant*: http://souciant.com/2013/12/the-metal-future/ (accessed December 20, 2013).

Kahn-Harris, K. (2013e). Slow metal. *Souciant:* http://souciant.com/2013/12/slow-metal/ (accessed December 27, 2013).

Kahn-Harris, K. (2014a). Breaking metal's boundaries. *Souciant*: http://souciant.com/2014/01/breaking-metals-boundaries/ (accessed January 10, 2014).

Kahn-Harris, K. (2014b). Metal beyond metal. *Souciant*: http://souciant.com/2014/01/metal-beyond-metal/ (accessed January 17, 2014).

Marx, K. (1848 [1978]). The manifesto of the Communist party. In R. Tucker (Ed.), *The Marx-Engels reader* (pp. 469–500). New York: Norton.

Mullarkey, J. (2013). The future of continental philosophy. In J. Mullarky & B. Lord (Eds.), *The Bloomsbury companion to continental philosophy* (pp. 259–275). London: Bloomsbury.

Townsend, D. (2015). http://www.pledgemusic.com/projects/casualties-of-cool (accessed February 1, 2015).

Tyler the Creator. (2011). *Goblin*. Los Angeles: XL recordings.

Wallach, J., & Levine, A. (2013). "I want *you* to support local metal": A theory of metal scene formation. In T. Hjelm, K. Kahn-Harris, & M. LeVine (Eds.), *Heavy metal: Controversies and countercultures* (pp. 117–126). Sheffield: Equinox Publishing.

20 A Reply to Niall W.R. Scott and Tom O'Boyle

Keith Kahn-Harris

I am grateful to Niall W.R. Scott and Tom O'Boyle for taking my ideas seriously and engaging with their implications. As they recognize, my keynote at the 2013 conference, together with the selection of essays that followed it (Kahn-Harris, 2013; 2014), was intended to be a provocation and a stimulus to debate. While Niall and Tom take issue with some of my arguments, their piece is very much in the spirit of what I was aiming for. In some ways, Niall, Tom, and I are very much on the same page. In the final part of my series of essays, I suggest the concept of 'Metal beyond Metal' (Kahn-Harris, 2013g). This refers to taking *metalness* beyond the confines of what we currently understand as metal. Metalness here connotes the following:

> It refers to something that is hard, intractable and resilient. It refers to something that is defiant, inexhaustible and unashamed. To be metal is to be unafraid to explore darkness and transgression, but to do it in such a way that one retains one's sense of selfhood. To be metal is to possess a certain ebullient wit and playfulness that those outside metal often mistake for crassness. To be metal is to value fellowship, to commit to supporting and celebrating the bonds between like-minded people. (2013g)

I don't know if Niall and Tom would necessarily sign up to this particular articulation of metalness, but I think we are reaching for the same thing: a future in which metal reaches out simultaneously in myriad different (Deleuzian) directions at once. I found myself both excited and moved by the passionate way in which they uphold the possibilities of a transgressive and radical metal future. Yet, although I am struck by the similarities between our respective projects, I think there are significant and revealing differences in our relationship to metal today. Niall and Tom point out that my works to which they are responding are 'not filled with empirical data to support his claims' but I want to argue that, in fact, my piece is more grounded in an analysis of contemporary metal culture than may at first be apparent.

Even if my latest work seems very different from my more solidly sociological *Extreme Metal: Music and Culture on the Edge* (2007), it actually stems from observations made during the research for that book and during my earlier PhD work (1996–2001). The period between 1996 and 2006—during which I was the most intensely active in sociological research on metal scenes—coincides roughly with the period when Internet use moved from marginal to ubiquitous. Certainly, at the start of this period, most of my interaction with scene members was by letter and phone, and by the end, it was by e-mail and occasionally mobile phone. Similarly, whereas at the start of this period, metal websites were highly erratic and incomplete in their coverage, by the end of the period it had become unusual for a metal band not to have some kind of web presence. In 1996 the spine of the metal underground was letters, flyers, demo tapes, distros, and fanzines; by 2006, all these institutions had undergone varying levels of decline or transformation (demo tapes most noticeably) in favor of forms of web-based communication.

What impressed me both now and at the time was not how much changed and how quickly, but how little changed and how slowly. This impression was, in part, based on my contacts and relationships with scene members who seemed to take a remarkably long time to get online and evidently relished the letter-writing process. Admittedly, this perspective could be seen as overly impressionistic. What is much more difficult to dismiss is the persistence, both between 1996 and 2006 and subsequently, of the foundational structures through which metal scenes have long been reproduced.

Simply put, the standard model of what it means to be a metal band and what it means to be a metal scene member is still strongly wedded to practices that could (should?) be obsolete. The scenic career of averagely 'successful' metal bands still tends to be: rehearse-play live/record demo—get signed to label—record and release album—do interviews—tour—record another album, etc., etc. Some of these elements have changed (for demo tape, read mp3; for fanzine interview, read blog interview) but the basic pattern has not. Even when artists challenge one element of this model, it is remarkable how they often keep the model as a whole alive: Job for a Cowboy may have come to attention through Myspace, but it is now a regular part of the metal industry; Devin Townsend and Obituary may have *Kickstarted* albums, but they retain relationships with traditional metal institutions.

This model faces pressures from a number of sources—illegal downloads, free music, and streaming dramatically reduce record sales; the ease of recording makes the number of metal recordings proliferate, leading to the problems of abundance I have pointed to—yet it persists. Bands and labels may complain continuously about reduced revenues, but they still somehow keep going. There is no shortage of innovation in metallic scenic practice, but the 'standard model' remains standard. Metal has neither abandoned itself to a free-floating virtual space (although some scene members have) nor to a reactionary 'meatspace' ghetto (although some have tried to do so).

Today's metal scene would, give or take some component parts, still be recognizable to a time-traveling metal scene member of 20 or even 30 years ago. Yes, few people still receive photocopied flyers and C90 tapes in the mail, but the basic contours of scenic reproduction remain very similar to those of the past. Indeed, as Deena Weinstein has pointed out in her keynotes at various conferences in the last few years, the biggest metal acts from 20 years ago are mostly the same as today: the pantheon of major acts, such as Iron Maiden and Metallica, remains small and aging, even if the likes of Slipknot have added to them to some extent.

The difference from 20 or 30 years ago—which would probably not be immediately visible to our time traveler—is that while the practices of scenic reproduction in metal remain very similar to those of before, the wider context has changed radically. In a world with an instantly accessible abundance of virtual symbolic goods, the persistence of record labels whose entire purpose historically was to attempt to achieve the mass circulation of physical record media 'product', at the very least raises many questions. That isn't to say that record labels are necessarily an anachronism today, but that to continue with well-worn strategies from a different era certainly is anachronistic. And yes, anachronism can be a virtue—those metal labels who are dedicating themselves to releasing cassettes are doing so very much aware of the wider context—but it isn't much of a virtue when anachronism is clung onto because one can simply not see any other way of continuing.

The reason I think this anachronism is problematic for metal is because innovation in metal cannot, historically speaking, be disengaged from the thick scenic infrastructure within which it has taken place. Niall and Tom look forward to the continuing reproduction of metal's transgressive power into the future, without grasping the ways that this metallic transgression has always been embedded in and nurtured within metal scenes. Perhaps metallic transgression can survive once dis-embedded from scenic infrastructure or perhaps not. What may be the case is that we currently have the worst of both worlds—metal that remains scenically embedded, but within a scene caught up in anachronism.

I don't believe, therefore, that Niall and Tom have a sufficient appreciation of the importance metal scenes have in generating metallic transgression and innovation. They offer a paean of praise to the agency of individual metal fans and the possibilities of curating one's own journey through the metal firmament, without fully recognizing the sociality of taste. There is a neo-liberal, consumerist tinge to their piece that, while I am sure is not intended, needs to be better thought through.

Niall and Tom are of course correct that musical innovation can and will continue to happen. But whereas they see metal today as forging a path into the future—in a process that will take care of itself in some unidentified way—I am much less sure of metal's continuing vitality. Without a concomitantly robust process of innovation in metal's scenic infrastructure, it is an open question of how metal's musical innovation will unfold. I am well aware of the dangers of nostalgia and particularly of members of an older generation—of which I am a part—disparaging youth. But while it is dangerous to assume that the younger generation is a lesser reflection of one's own, the corollary is also true—that it is dangerous to assume that today's generation is simply the same as one's own generation.

Here it's important to acknowledge how central music has been for those who grew up in the post-World War II period in much of the world. Not only has music provided a generational marker and a potent force for social transformation, the production, consumption, and dissemination of music has created new and innovative social practices. Metal is part of this history, particularly underground metal. The metal underground as it developed in the 1980s and 1990s (in tandem with the punk and hardcore scenes) was at the bleeding edge of social innovation: in creating complex global networks for the creation and dissemination of metal music, the metal underground was not only an early harbinger of today's tightly integrated global culture, its radical decentralization and relative egalitarianism provided a potent demonstration of how to form resilient communities. Indeed, it was in part a desire to share these extraordinary achievements of metal culture that motivated my postgraduate work on metal in the 1990s.

There is much in metal today that continues this remarkable legacy. Aside from the ever-expanding diversity of music, it remains a potent source of community, empowerment, and meaning. In non-western countries metal is a still-growing source of connection into a global culture. But whereas metal was once one of the few sources of such transformative and empowering practices, today there are many others and there are few reasons to accord metal any particular status among them. While a cliché, it is certainly true that online communication and social media have been a powerful engine of innovation and change. There are many different sources of global communication and community. Movements such as Occupy, while their long-term impact may be uncertain, have pioneered ways of mobilization and politicization that are predicated on the new ways of bringing people together afforded by new technology. Music is often a part of such movements, but it is rarely as pivotal as was the case in the 1960s, for example.

There is no reason music 'has' to be 'important'. Historically speaking, the centrality of music in post-war social change may prove to be a transient phenomenon. Concomitantly, there is no reason metal will always have the transgressive mobilizing power it has had until now. My argument, then, is not against innovation and change but the reverse: metal today is saturated with nostalgia, despite its ongoing musical innovation. Belief in the continuing transgressive power of metal relies on a nostalgic belief that metal's illustrious history will provide a stable basis for its development into the future.

In another sense though, my argument that there is a crisis in metal does indeed depend on a kind of nostalgia: there is only a crisis if one believes that metal has, can, and should be significant in some way beyond being 'just another' way of passing time between birth and death and that this requires a certain coherence as a social form. Not only is this a vision of metal that I personally hold to, I suspect that it is a vision that is widely shared amongst many of those involved in metal culture (and certainly most of those who have a long involvement in underground metal's scenic infrastructure). I would suggest then, that there is good reason to think that it is precisely the kind of vision of metal that is most under threat that is the one that is (and has been) most central to the reproduction and motivation of metal's scenic vitality.

So perhaps the choice that those of us who uphold the power of metal's history are confronted with is between two possible kinds of nostalgia: one that reveres metal's past and believes that this reverence provides a firm basis for metal's present and future; the other, which I hold to, a nostalgia that reveres metal's past but believes that it cannot effectively undergird the sustainability and power of metal into the future. At the moment, the first kind of nostalgia dominates. It is striking how far those sections of the metal world who are most committed to the threatened aspects of metal culture are *not* afflicted by a sense of crisis. It is absolutely correct to point out (as Niall and Tom hint at, although they are too polite to come out and say it directly!) that my argument that contemporary metal is in crisis is not reflected in the research emerging from the burgeoning field of metal studies. Metal scene members are, on the whole, concentrating on doing what they have always been doing, and certainly not making dark pronouncements about the fate of the scene (although gripes about finances, record sales, and the like are not uncommon).

It is precisely this gap that convinces me that crisis is a good way to describe the contemporary state of metal. There has been a radical transformation in the context within which metal scenes operate and the infrastructure through which metal is reproduced, but metal's responses to such profound changes have been piecemeal, contingent, and sometimes highly conservative and reluctant. To use more conventionally sociological language, there is a disjuncture between the deep structural changes that metal has undergone and the limited exercising of agency that metal scene members have wielded to meet the resulting challenges. The ability to mediate between structure and agency is embedded in the workings of reflexivity within the scene. As I have argued elsewhere (Kahn-Harris, 2007), metal scenes have been highly reflexive communities, with members constantly monitoring the structures within which they operate and adapting their practices accordingly. The emerging gap between structure and agency in metal today represents a weakening of reflexivity. Note here though that I am *not* saying this is another instance of what I have termed 'reflexive anti-reflexivity'—in which reflexive techniques are used to limit reflexive challenges to certain kinds of practice—so much as a much less artful incapacity.

Even if metal's reflexivity is not currently proving equal to the challenges it faces, that isn't to say that it can never be so. Labeling a situation a crisis does not always imply that it is necessarily negative. Crisis also implies opportunities and possibilities. Niall and Tom do implicitly recognize this in the examples they cite of innovation in metal, and I have cited other examples elsewhere. I think we can go further. In a world undergoing extraordinarily rapid change, it is both necessary and exciting to rethink some of the most of fundamental aspects of metal culture. This is why I talk about 'metal beyond metal'—metal that goes beyond entrenched understandings of what metal is and could be.

In reading the contributions to this collection, I am struck by how well and how rapidly metal studies has interrogated metal culture in all of its diversity. We know more than we ever did about what metal is and what it has been. Thinking about what metal could be is a much more difficult task, as it would seem to depart from accepted rules of empirically grounded scholarly practice. Yet the distinctiveness of metal studies is that it has a closer relationship to its topic of study than is the case in most scholarly fields. That offers opportunities for influencing practice and, I would argue, even imposes an obligation to do so. Metal criticism that proceeds from a solid basis in scholarship of what metal currently is and historically has been, can work to envision a different metal future.

One of the most valuable things that metal scholarship can do is to denaturalize some of the assumptions that are entrenched in metal culture. Certainly, there have been considerable efforts to this end—for example, metal studies is leading the way in showing that metal need not be (and often is not) male, hetero-normative, and white. Yet other unacknowledged assumptions remain and need to be understood as provisional and constructed. One such assumption is that metal is important, valuable, and that it has a future. This is ripe for challenge, however painful it might be. I hope that my own recent work has provided at least a modest impetus for this process to begin.

To conclude by referring back to Niall and Tom: I think we share a similar vision of what metal could be (and sometimes is). What we don't share is faith that the future of metal will necessarily unfold in this direction. It is perhaps ironic that I, a sociologist—in a profession so often accused of describing how the world is rather than the world as it could or should be—should be making the case for a forceful intervention in metal culture that, at the moment anyway, flies in the face of how many metal scene members view the culture that they love. Nevertheless, it is an irony that I am happy to live with.

Bibliography

Kahn-Harris, K. (2007). *Extreme metal: Music and culture on the edge*. Oxford: Berg.

Kahn-Harris, K. (2013a). Too much metal. *Souciant*: http://souciant.com/2013/11/too-much-metal/ (accessed November 29, 2013).

Kahn-Harris, K. (2013b). Invisible metal. *Souciant:* http://souciant.com/2013/12/invisible-metal/ (accessed December 6, 2013).

Kahn-Harris, K. (2013c). Music at a standstill. *Souciant:* http://souciant.com/2013/12/music-at-a-standstill/ (accessed December 12, 2013).

Kahn-Harris, K. (2013d). The metal future. *Souciant:* http://souciant.com/2013/12/the-metal-future/ (accessed December 20, 2013).

Kahn-Harris, K. (2013e). Slow metal. *Souciant:* http://souciant.com/2013/12/slow-metal/ (accessed December 27, 2013).

Kahn-Harris, K. (2014a). Breaking metal's boundaries. *Souciant:* http://souciant.com/2014/01/breaking-metals-boundaries/ (accessed January 10, 2014).

Kahn-Harris, K. (2014b). Metal beyond metal. *Souciant*: http://souciant.com/2014/01/metal-beyond-metal/ (accessed January 17, 2014).

Notes on the Editors and Contributors

The Editors

Andy R. Brown is Senior Lecturer in Media Communications at Bath Spa University, UK. His teaching/research interests include popular music, music journalism, global music industries, media and youth consumption, with a specific focus on metal music culture(s). He was one of a nucleus of scholars that got together to imagine the idea of 'metal studies' and out of which ISMMS emerged. He has published widely on metal and subculture; the metal magazine; gender, class and metal; metal and moral panics; metal and rock criticism and metal and cultural legitimation. He co-edited a special issue of the *Journal for Cultural Research* on 'Metal Studies?: Cultural Research in the Heavy Metal Scene' (July 2011), and the *Heavy Metal Generations* e-book (2012). Recent publications include 'Everything Louder than Everyone Else': The Origins and Persistence of Heavy Metal Music and its Global Cultural Impact' in *The Sage Handbook of Popular Music* (2015).

Keith Kahn-Harris is the author of Extreme Metal: Music and Culture on the Edge (Berg, 2007). He has published extensively on metal and has written for the magazine *Terrorizer*. His website is kahn-harris.org.

Niall W.R. Scott is Senior Lecturer in Ethics at UCLan in Preston. He is editor of *Helvete: A Journal of Black Metal Theory* and co-editor of *Metal Music Studies* (Intellect). He is currently the Chair of the International Society for Metal Music Studies (ISMMS) and has published widely and spoken internationally on heavy metal, politics, philosophy and cultural theory. He headed up the Heavy Metal and Place conference in collaboration with Capsule's Home of Metal project in Wolverhampton and Birmingham in 2011 and with Interdisciplinary.net and Rob Fisher, brought together the first gathering of Metal Scholars in Salzburg in 2008.

Karl Spracklen is Professor of Leisure Studies at Leeds Beckett University, UK. He is interested in the ways in which leisure forms and spaces might be used to construct social identities and inequalities of power. He has been researching heavy metal for over 10 years and has written mainly about black metal, folk metal and related genres such as goth. He is the

Vice-President of Research Committee 13 (Sociology of Leisure) of the International Sociological Association. He has published extensively on the sociology of leisure and sociology of music, including four monographs (The Meaning and Purpose of Leisure; Constructing Leisure; Whiteness and Leisure; and Digital Leisure). He is the Principal Editor of Metal Music Studies and one of the founders of the International Society for Metal Music Studies (ISMMS).

The Contributors

Claire Barratt is an Associate and sessional Lecturer in cultural and contextual studies at University of the Arts London and Ravensbourne. Her research interests are jewelry and visual and material cultures of death. She has contributed to *Fashion Studies* and *Mortality* journals and holds degrees in Social Sciences and Design Studies. She was awarded her PhD from Central Saint Martins for her interdisciplinary theoretical study of contemporary jewelry, death and memory, which she is currently developing for publication, alongside projects that combine cultural theory with design practice.

Owen Coggins is currently completing his PhD on mystical rhetoric and religious practices surrounding drone metal, in the Religious Studies and Music departments at the Open University, Milton Keynes, UK. After studying Philosophy at King's College London and Religions at SOAS, he has presented and published work on various topics relating to popular music, noise and religion. These include book chapters on urban monstrosity in industrial music, nationalist tropes in black metal and an article on Blind Willie Johnson's gospel blues in the journal *Altre Modernitá*. He has published research relating to drone metal, reception and religious language in the *Journal of Implicit Religion*, the *International Journal for the Study of Religion in Society*, and edited a special issue of *Diskus,* on music and religion.

Dietmar Elflein is an ethnomusicologist and lecturer on popular music at the Technical University Braunschweig, Germany, with teaching assignments at the Hdpk Berlin, Popakademie Mannheim and HfMT Köln, amongst others. He is a member of the advisory board of the German Society for Popular Music Studies. His dissertation in musicology (Schwermetallanalysen, transcript 2010) deals with analyzing stylistic norms of heavy metal music. Besides Metal Studies, he has published on German popular music history and the analysis of popular music. His research interests include national popular music history, applying actor-network theory and actor-media-theory to popular music, popular music analysis and post-colonial studies. For further information including a complete list of publications, visit www.d-elflein.de.

Kevin Fellezs is Assistant Professor of Music at Columbia University, where he shares a joint appointment in the Institute for Research in African-American Studies. His work is primarily concerned with the relationship between music and identity. His book *Birds of Fire: Jazz, Rock, Funk and the Creation of Fusion* (Duke University Press) was awarded the 2012 Woody Guthrie Book Award. Fellezs has also published articles on African-American musicians in heavy metal as well as enka (Japanese popular music genre), Asian-American jazz musicians, and Hawaiian slack key guitar.

Christophe Guibert is a sociologist and Senior Lecturer at the University of Angers (UFR ESTHUA Tourism and Culture, where he is the deputy director for scientific research) and a member of Espaces et Sociétés laboratory (UMR CNRS 6590). He worked for nearly five years on the social properties of the Hellfest festival, the premier metal and 'extreme' music event in France. He has published several articles in French scientific journals (*Volume !, Revue Espaces, tourisme et loisirs*) and communicated in academic seminars on the subject (French Sociological Association, International Association of French-speaking sociology, EHESS, etc.). He also participated in organizing the first French-language international conference Heavy metal and Social Sciences, an overview of the Francophone research, led by Gérôme Guibert, December 2014 in Angers, France.

Gérôme Guibert is Senior Lecturer in sociology at La Sorbonne Nouvelle, Paris 3 University and researcher at the CIM-MCPN laboratory (EA n°1484). His work is linked with cultural sociology and the cultural economy of popular music. He has published several books, including *La Production de la Culture* (2006) regarding the popular music field in France and Musiques Actuelles, ça Part en Live (2013), on the French live music sector. He is also the co-editor of *Made In France: Studies in French Popular Music* (Routledge, 2015). He is the editor-in-chief of *Volume*! The French popular music studies journal and has published widely on the subject of heavy metal and music since 2002. In particular, he co-edited with Fabien Hein the Metal Scenes special issue of *Volume!* (2006) and was a contributor (with Jedediah Sklower) to the Popular Music History special double-issue (2011) on Heavy Metal: Controversies and Countercultures. He is also a member of the Metal Music Studies advisory board.

Gareth Heritage is completing his PhD in the department of Sport and Leisure Studies, Leeds Beckett University, UK. His thesis critiques the hyper realization of '80s heavy metal and defends its hyper masculine aesthetic. A former high school music teacher, Gareth continues to teach music and guitar at schools in London and privately from his studio in South East England. He is also an instrumental grades examiner for Trinity College London. Gareth holds several postgraduate qualifications, including

PGCE, PGCert, PGDip and MMus and is Fellow of the London College of Music. He also works as an editorial assistant for the *Metal Music Studies* journal.

Rosemary Lucy Hill, University of Leeds, gained her PhD in Women's Studies at the Centre for Women's Studies, University of York (2013), focusing on the representations and experiences of women hard rock and metal fans. She co-edited the conference volume, *Heavy Fundametalism* (2010) and has published research in the *Journal for Cultural Research* and the *International Journal of Community Music* on the ideology of metal, the moral panic around emo, imaginary community and the media representation of women fans. In 2014, she co-organized the Metal and Marginalization symposium with Gabrielle Riches and Caroline Lucas, papers from which will be published as a forthcoming special issue of *Metal Music Studies*. Rosemary has been interviewed for the BBC Radio 4 programme, *Thinking Allowed* on the topic of subcultural theory. She is currently writing a book *Gender, Metal and the Media*, to be published by Palgrave Macmillan. She also researches how big data visualizations make data understandable for non-specialists.

Toni-Matti Karjalainen is a devoted metal head from Espoo, Finland. He holds the degrees of Doctor of Arts (Art & Design) and MSc (Econ.) and is Academy Research Fellow at Aalto University, Helsinki. Toni-Matti also works as lecturer, seminar and workshop facilitator, and supervisor in a number of universities and schools in different countries. He has also worked in collaboration with several Finnish and international companies and institutions. His publications include over 100 articles in books, journals, international conferences and other forums; the topics ranging from design management, visual communication, branding and product development to, most recently, popular music industry and heavy metal. The metal studies of Toni-Matti concern visual communication, cultural narratives, global fandom, Finnish music exports and creative management. Toni-Matti was the coordinator-in-chief of the Modern Heavy Metal: Markets, Practices and Cultures international conference, held in Helsinki in June 2015.

Mark Mynett is a record producer, live music engineer, and Senior Lecturer in Music Technology and Production at the University of Huddersfield, UK. He holds a Bachelor of Science in Popular Music Production from Manchester University and completed his PhD on contemporary metal music production in 2013. Mark has had an extensive career as professional musician with six worldwide commercial album releases and several years of high-profile touring. This was followed by a 10-year career as self-employed record producer and front-of-house sound engineer, the highlights of which include Download Festival. In addition to teaching music technology, and his own production work, Mark is frequently invited to write articles on the subject for various publications, such as Sound on Sound (including November 2009's cover feature), as well as *Guitar World* magazine. He is currently completing the world's first book on producing contemporary metal music, to be released in January 2016.

Tom O'Boyle is an independent scholar, freelance journalist and writer. He has published widely in heavy metal journalism, including publications such as *Metal Hammer*, *Iron Fist* and the *Quietus*, for whom he has interviewed an array of artists, including Devin Townsend, Arcturus and Goatsnake. He recently appeared on an international panel of judges in Iceland, there to determine the victor of the Wacken open air metal battle, the winning act going on to perform at the festival itself. As well as a music journalist, Tom is an aspiring screenwriter presented with the Matt Greenhalgh award by the University of Central Lancashire in 2012 for screenwriting excellence.

Jamie Patterson is currently completing her Masters thesis in Folklore at the University of North Carolina, Chapel Hill. Her research examines gender, race, class, and identity-work in folk life-narrative construction among female-identified death metal fans in Raleigh, North Carolina, and the American South. Her work has been presented at several academic conferences, including the International Conference on Heavy Metal and Popular Culture in Bowling Green, Ohio. She is also interested in music and rural landscapes, ritual studies, and trauma narrative research. A long-time extreme metal fan and musician, she teaches Cultural Anthropology at Western Carolina University.

Simon Poole is Senior Lecturer and course leader for BA (Hons) Music, Theatre and Entertainment Management, Falmouth University, UK. Simon has been studying, selling, collecting, managing and writing about heavy music for 30 years. During this time he has written for magazines and the underground press, produced music videos, worked as a freelance in A&R and set up and managed an independent record label specializing in all things heavy. He is also a practicing musician. During his career, he has recorded numerous albums as well as radio sessions for Radio One and Six Music, toured Europe and America and played many of the international heavy metal festivals.

Gabby Riches is currently completing her PhD within the Research Institute for Sport, Physical Activity and Leisure, Leeds Beckett University, UK. Her research explores the role and significance that mosh pit practices play in the lives of female fans in Leeds' extreme metal music scene. Gabby's research interests include the socio-spatial constructions of underground music spaces, women's participation in male-dominated leisure practices, non-representational theory, intersectionality, and subcultural embodiment. She has also written about alcohol use, the affective dimensions of music-making practices, and reconceptualizing women's marginalization in heavy metal. Her research has been published in: Metal Music Studies, the journal of the International Association for the Study of Popular Music, International Journal of Community Music and the Journal for Cultural Research.

Eero Sipilä studied Musicology at Helsinki University, achieving his MA in 2014. He has researched the history of Finnish metal music and its treatment in the media. The paper 'Unique roots of Finnish Metal?', based on his master's thesis, was presented to the Modern Heavy Metal conference in Helsinki, June 2015. Eero is also the bass player for the Finnish metal band Battle Beast, with whom he has toured extensively in their home country, as well as in continental Europe and Japan. Battle Beast has released three albums, the last of which, *Unholy Savior* topped the Finnish national album chart in January 2015.

Eric Smialek is a doctoral candidate in musicology at McGill's Schulich School of Music where his research combines the study of fan and media discourses with close music analysis. His dissertation, 'Genre and Expression in Extreme Metal Music', offers an interdisciplinary overview of extreme metal through the lenses of genre theory, semiotics, music theory, and phonetics. He recently served as the graduate student representative of the Canadian branch of the International Society for the Study of Popular Music (IASPM-Canada) and is a three-time winner of their Peter Narvaez Memorial Student Paper Prize. Eric is currently completing articles on musical expression in extreme metal vocals, self-exoticism in the music of Icelandic band Sigur Rós and the role of music at hockey games to promote regional forms of nationalism. Prior to graduate school, Eric enjoyed a brief stint playing electric guitar, keyboards and bass for black and death metal bands in Vancouver, BC.

Jean-Philippe Ury-Petesch was born in Lorraine, France, in 1978. He learned sound engineering in Dublin from 1998 to 2002 while playing guitar in local bands and studying British Civilization through Nancy 2's distance learning centre where he graduated in 2001. He moved to Cambodia in 2002 to teach and he founded indie production house KHLAKHMUM, which produces bands and music films. Meanwhile he prepared a PhD about Iron Maiden's discourse (focusing on the way the band uses cinema and literature to write songs, a process that he defined as 'lyrical intertextuality') and their fans that he designated as a 'tribe' in the light of Michel Maffesoli's work. He gained his PhD in aesthetics and science of arts from Sorbonne Nouvelle university in 2009. Then he moved to Bangkok to focus on music and film production.

Sonia Vasan is Adjunct Professor of Research at the University of St. Thomas, Houston, Texas, USA. A former teacher, she holds a PhD in Educational Psychology, an MEd in Curriculum and Instruction (both University of Houston) and was a Visiting Graduate Student at the University of

Helsinki, Finland. A lifelong metal fan, she was a metal DJ at college radio for many years, including a stint as Music Director of WZLY at her alma mater, Wellesley College; she also contributed song lyrics to the first two albums by prog-metal band Anubis Gate. Her wide-ranging research interests include gender, adolescent alienation, Finnish education, Japanese culture, media studies, art, architecture and religion. Her recent work includes publications on Asian masculinity in Japanese anime and American film, as well as on national identity in the Finnish metal scene (in press).

Deena Weinstein is Professor of Sociology at DePaul University in Chicago and specializes in cultural sociology and social theory, with a focus on rock music. Her books include *Heavy Metal: A Cultural Sociology* (1991), *(Post)-Modernized Simmel* (1993), and most recently *Rock 'n America: A Social and Cultural History* (2015). Among her metal-relevant publications are: 'Neil Peart versus Ayn Rand' (2011), 'The Globalization of Metal' (2011), 'Metallica Kills' (2013), 'Pagan Metal' (2013), and 'Birmingham's Post-Industrial Metal' (2014). Her latest journal articles include: 'All Singers Are Dicks' (2004)', 'How Is Metal Studies Possible?' (2014), 'Rock's Guitar Gods—Avatars of the Sixties' (2013), 'Just So Stories: How Heavy Metal Got Its Name—A Cautionary Tale' (2014), and 'La nostalgie construite; L'âge d'or du rock ou 'I believe in yesterday' (2014). Beyond academic discourses, she is also a long-time rock journalist, concentrating in metal.

Index

Abrahams, Roger 257
"*Absolutego*" (Boris, 1996) 312
"*Ace of Spades*" (Mötörhead, 1980) 90
"*Adagio in G minor*" (Albinoni, 1708) 58–59
Adler, Chris 81
aesthetic agency 251
age: of heavy metal fans 157; when discovering metal music 176–8
agency of heavy metal music 98
aggressive vocal techniques 78
Airborne 339
Airdash 214, 215
Alchemy 227, 229, 236–7
Allett, Nicola 203, 339
Allom, Tom 12
Almond, Marc 239
American Indians as musicians 100–1
Amorphis 216
Amott, Michael 41
"*Amplifier Worship*" (Boris, 1998) 325
anarchist philosophy of grindcore 129
anarcho-punk 125–6
'A National Acrobat' (Black Sabbath, 1973) 42
"*And Justice for All*" (Metallica, 1988) 108
androcentrism of heavy metal music scene 261, 262
'Angel of Death' (Slayer, 1986) 45
Anselmo, Phil 90
Anthrax 89, 90
Apocalyptica 220, 222
Apollo 210
Argos 237, 239
Arnett, Jeffrey 91, 97, 157, 163, 164, 165, 193, 194, 195, 262, 263
artist-audience directness 106–7, 113
Asian musicians 99–100
audio experience 80

audiotactile 80
authenticity 7, 291; of metal jewelry in subculture 235–6, 240; of Metallica 106–7
Avenged Sevenfold 284, 287–8

Bach, Johann Sebastian 54–55, 58
"*Backseat*" (Peer Günt, 1986) 213
badge of identity 257
bands. *See also* names of individual bands: by country 5–6; Finland's hard rock 212–13
band whore 247, 266
Baroque music correlated with rock music 50
Barratt, Claire 14–15
Barron, L. 264
Bashe, Philip 24
bass distortion 77
bass guitar 83–84
Baulch, Emma 7, 192,
Baumgardner, Jennifer 281
Bayer, Gerd 2
Bayer 16
'Beast and the Harlot' (Avenged Sevenfold, 2006) 284
Beethoven, Ludwig van 60
Behemoth 79
Bell, A. 192
Benjamin, Walter 335
Bennett, Andy 94
Bennett 173, 174, 239, 297, 303
Bennett and Peterson 7
Bennett and Kahn-Harris 239
Berger, Harris 8, 190, 191, 248, 249
Berger 13, 27, 35, 36, 97, 99, 173, 192, 203, 258,
Berger, H. and Fales 35
bikers, post-war and skull jewelry 229–31, 233
Billy, Chuck 100

360 *Index*

Binder, Amy 97
Birch, Martin 12
Birmingham (England) 1–2, 125, 303
Birmingham Centre for Contemporary Cultural Studies (CCCS) 227
"*Black Album*" (Metallica, 1991) 26, 107–8
Black Country (England) 2
'Blacken the Cursed Sun' (Lamb of God, 2006) 80
Black Masses 306
"*Black Masses*" (Electric Wizard, 2010) 306
black metal fans and their educational level 180, 183
black metal music 7, 26–27, 216
Blackmore, Ritchie 53
Black Sabbath 2, 16, 25–26, 52–53, 210, 303, 305, 333; 'Black Sabbath' (1970) 39–42; and drone metal music 312, 313, 325–6; and metal jewelry 229; song structures of 36–47
'Black Sabbath' (Black Sabbath, 1970) 39–42
'Black Star' (Bowie, 1984) 59–60
black-white binary music genres 91
"Bloodstone and Diamonds" (Machine Head, 2014) 69
blue collar 13, 146, 173, 190–3, 197
blues music influence 52–53
bodily performances of grindcore 133–5
body experience with drone metal music 319-2
Bong 312, 323, 324, 325
books on metal music 24
Boris 313, 325
Bourdage, Monique 280
Bourdieu, Pierre 91, 106, 112–17, 119–20, 169, 173, 195
'Bourrée' (1708–1717) 58
Brackett, David 108
'Breakin the Law' (Judas Priest, 1980) 44
bridge section in songs 43–46
"*British Steel*" (Judas Priest, 1980) 37
Brown, Andy R. 3, 10, 14, 22, 52, 90, 97, 102, 120, 126, 127, 131, 132, 165, 191, 200, 228, 276, 302, 303, 308, 322
Brown and Griffin 196
brutal affect 256
Burnside, R. L. 40

Cannibal Corpse 263
"*Canon in D*" (Pachelbel) 55–58
capitalism: depicted in grindcore 131–2; promoted by heavy metal music 4
'Caprice No. 5' (1809) 61
Carcass 234, 251
Carlson, Dylan 313
carnival-grotesque 132
Case, Alexander 68, 71
"*Casualties of Cool*" (Townsend, 2014) 339
Certeau, Michel de 16, 311, 317, 319, 324, 325, 326
Chaker, S. 192, 203
chickiepoos 247
chicks with balls 247
Children of Bodom 220, 222
Christgau, Robert 39
Chu, Meg Tze 179
Church of Misery 307
Clarke, Eric 70
Clark, Steve 53
classed-cultural groups 196–8
class-fraction analysis 193–8
social class fractions (measure) 186
class-fraction analysis 14, 190,
classicization of heavy metal 50–64
class polarization 200
class profile of fans 190–8
Clifford, Amber 9, 248
Clifford-Napoleone 9, 276
Clifford 257
Coates, Norma 282
Coggins, Owen 16, 352
"*Come My Fanatics*" (Electric Wizard, 1996) 3–7
commerce and metal jewelry 209–40
compression in signal processing 82–84, 117
"*Conference of the Birds*" (Om, 2006) 326
conformity to group behavior 269–73
consumption-as-production in popular culture 319
Cooper, Alice 233
copresence 80
corporeal brutality 132
corporeal politics: of grindcore 133–5; of resistance 136
cost reduction in social exchange 273–4, 278
Coven 306
cultural imperialism 3
cultural populism 23
cultural production theory 112–17, 119–20
cultural studies of heavy metal 16

Index   361

cultural theory 23
culture, democratization of 23
"*Cycle of Life*" (Sarcofagus, 1980) 210, 211

Dahlquist, Stuart 314
Darkthrone 80
'Davidian' (Machine Head, 1994) 81
Davis, Miles 315
Deafhaven 82
Death Angel 92, 100
"*Death Magnetic*" (Metallica, 2008) 116, 117–20
death metal music 5, 7; in Finland 216–17; gender and power in 261–74; in Sweden 213–14
death's head symbol. *See* skull
death symbolism: in metal jewelry 15, 227–40; subcultural consumption of 231–4
Def Leppard 53
Deep Purple 36, 47, 64, 200, 201, 282
deindustrialization influencing rise of heavy metal music 191, 197
Deluze, Gilles 28
democratization of culture 23
'Demon Lung' (Electric Wizard, 1995) 306
den mother 247, 266
density impacted by harmonic distortion 74
Derrida, Jacques 28
deviance in heavy metal youth subculture 13, 97–98, 164, 186
diffusion of responsibility 272
digital clipping 117–18
direct injection (DI) signal 72–73
dissolution of self 256
distortion. *See also* harmonic distortion: and ecological perception 70–71
distortion paradox 12, 68–85
DJs 24
Dome, Malcolm 24
domestic items re-used for jewelry 229
doom metal 339; and representations of death 233–4
doom metal fans and their educational level 183
"*Dopesmoker*" (Sleep, 2003, 2012) 312
Dorrian, Lee 131
Downing, K. K. 45
dressing in metal fashion 175, 176–7
drone metal music 16, 311–26; amplification in 325; emergence and development 312–13; experience of listening as a pilgrimage 322–4; as a genre 314–16; impacting altered and imagined states 319–22; mysticism in 317–18, 325–6; physicality of 319–22
drum samples 82–84
drums and punchiness 78–79
dual song structures 41–43
Dunn, Randall 314
Dunn, Sam 233, 298
'Dylan Carlson' (SunnO))) 1999) 313
dystopia in grindcore 130–33

Earth 313, 315
"*Earth 2:Special Low Frequency Version*" (Earth, 1993) 312
ecological perception and distortion 70–71
education of heavy metal fans 158–9, 171–2, 180–3
electric guitar maintaining masculinity of rock 280
Electric Wizard 306, 309, 312
Elflein, Dietmar 11, 197, 352
employment of heavy metal fans 159, 170–1, 184–5
empowerment. *See also* power: by women heavy metal fans 245–58
Encyclopedia Metallum 5
Entombed 245
entrepreneurialism in metal jewelry 234–9
"*Episode*" (Stratovarius, 1996) 219
ethnography: of females in metal music scene 262; of gender and power relations in metal music 246–50
"*Evangelion*" (Behemoth, 2009) 79
evil connotations for gender identity 253, 257
'Evil Eye' (Ferdinand, 1984) 58
'Exciter' (Judas Priest, 1978) 41
exscription of women 247, 279, 282
"*Extra-Capsular Extraction*" (Earth, 1991) 312
extreme metal music 35–36; dual song structures in 42–43; and female empowerment 245–58; in Finland 214–16; and social class of fans 192–3; subgenres 179–85; and women empowerment narratives 245–58
Extreme Noise Terror 126, 127, 131, 132–3

'Fade to Black' (Metallica, 1984) 43
false consciousness 282, 290

false start in song writing 41
fans: classed identity of 198–203; class profile of 190–8; female 15–16; homogeneity and heterogeneity of 178–85, 192; level of involvement in metal music 174–8; survey of Hellfest fans 167–86; survey of Iron Maiden fans 145–65
'Far Beyond the Sun' (Malmsteen, 1984) 60
Fast, Susan 9, 283, 318
father's occupations of heavy metal fans 169–70, 184–5
Fellezs, Kevin 12, 116, 202
female anger 266
female gender socialization 246, 252
female scholars in metal music 15–16
feminine weakness 272
femininity and masculinity in metal music scene 247–9, 261–74
femininity game 257
feminists' criticism of heavy metal music 281–2
femme fatale identity 247
Ferguson, Jason 113
Filipino musicians 100
film imagery for album artwork 306–7
"*Final Frontier, The*" (Iron Maiden, 2010) 148
Finnish alternative metal music 217–18
Finnish death metal 216–17
Finnish heavy metal music 209–23; birth of 210–13; breakthrough and growth 219–21; Finnishness of 218, 221–2; internationalization of 210, 216–18, 220; national characteristics 221; public acceptance of 214–15; second wave of 216–19
Finnish speed metal 214–15
Foucault, Michel 28, 299, 304, 305, 308, 339
Fournier, Valérie 145, 146, 163
Frame, Pete 298
Franklin, Caryn 236
freedom of expression by women in heavy metal music scene 15, 247, 253, 256, 266
'Freewheel Burning' (Judas Priest, 1984) 45
frequency content of electric guitars 72–74
Frimodt-Moller 299, 302, 303
Frith, Simon 79, 113, 127, 129, 134, 198–9, 200, 202, 204
Frith, S. and McRobbie 267

Frith, S. and Zagorski-Thomas 68
"*From Enslavement to Obliteration*" (Napalm Death, 1988) 131, 136, 140
'Fucked with a Knife' (Cannibal Corpse, 1994) 263

Gaines, Donna 8, 13, 15, 25, 99, 165, 190
Galeon, Andy 93, 100
gender: in death metal music scene 261–74; empowerment of extreme metal women fans 245–58; femininity or masculinity of music 281; of heavy metal fans 157–8, 172; and metal politics 15–16, 135–9; perpetuation of bias at structural level 271; and pleasure 277–8; and power relations in metal music scene 246–7; transcendence 15
gender binary of rock/pop music 280, 282, 283
genderless experience in metal music scene 15, 249, 256–7
geographic location and origin of thrash metal 89–101
Gibson, James J. 70
globalization of metal music 2–7, 26–27
"*Goblin*" (Odd Future, 2011) 340
Godflesh 315
'Goodbye to Romance' (Osbourne, 1981) 55–58
Greene, P. D. 192
grindcore 125–40; corporeal politics and bodily pleasures 133–5; dystopia and extreme realism in 130–33; educational level of fans 182; origins of 125–7; participation by women 134–9; as protest music 128–30; sociality 127
Gross, Robert L. 99, 190, 285
grotesque realism in grindcore 130–33
Grossberg, Lawrence 285
group behavior and conformity 270–3
grunge 215
Guibert, Christophe 14, 353
Guibert, Gérôme 14, 30, 353
Guibert, G. and Sklower 318
Guibert, G. and Hein 8, 25
guitar: bass 83–84; harmonically distorted 68–74; heaviness of timbres 78–79; maintaining masculinity of rock 280; twin guitar sound 43
Guitar Hero 3 (video game) 117–18
guitar riff. *See* riffs
guitar riff sonograms 72–76

Haight-Asbury district 96
Halford, Rob 36, 43
Hall, Stuart 93
Halnon, Karen 15, 127, 132, 133, 136, 139, 193, 194
Hammett, Kirk 89, 100, 101, 109
Hannum, Terrence 340
Hanoi Rocks 213
hard rock bands in Finland 212–13
hard rock fans and their educational level 182
'Hard Rock Hallelujah' (Lordi, 2006) 220
hard rock-metal music continuum 35–36
hard rock music: as masculine music 279–83; women's experiences with 277–91
Hard Rock Sallinen 211
harmonically distorted guitars 68–74
harmonic distortion 68–70; impact on proximity and density 72–74; and note definition 76–77; and signal stability and volume 75–76
harmony and neo-classical aesthetic 53–58
Harrigan, Brian 24
Harris, Steve 152
Hatakka, Kärtsy 217
Havana Blacks 213
heaviness of metal music 11, 12, 68, 69, 77–79; correlated with definition and intelligibility 79–82; of Metallica 109; related to frequency content 74; and technological mediation 82–84
Heavy Fundametalisms conference 8–9
heavy metal music 201; audience demographics 13–14, 145–203; cultural impact of 3; dissipation of 339–40; encouraging deviancy 97–98; history of 297–308; increasing popularity of 212; mainstreaming of 12–14, 94–97, 128, 202–3; as masculine music 279–83; neo-classicization of 50–64; origins of 303–4; as a palimpsest 299, 300–3; as reflection of British regional identity 1–2; song structures 38; subgenres 179–85; surveying fans 145–65, 167–86; underground 4–5, 94, 99, 107–8, 196, 198, 336–8, 346–7
Heavy Metal Parking Lot 13
Hebdige, D. 200, 227, 228, 229, 231, 240, 285

Hein, Fabien 9, 146, 157, 158, 159, 161, 163, 170, 172, 178, 186, 192
Hellfest Festival 167–9
Hellfest Festival fans: dressing in metal fashion 175, 176–7; education level 171–2, 180–1; father's occupation 169–70, 184–5; gender 165, 173; length of time since discovering metal music 176–8; level of involvement in metal music 174–8; listening to metal subgenre music 179–85; listening to other genres of music 178; omnivorousness of taste in music 178; social origins 169–72; social situation of festival-goers 170–1
Heritage, Gareth 12, 353
Hesmondhalgh, D. 119, 120, 277
Hetfield 109
Hickam, Brian 8, 9, 10, 27
Hickam and Wallach 15
high art 52
Hill, Rosemary 15, 248–9, 256, 257, 354
HIM, 220, 222
Homans, G. 267
Home of Metal project 1–2
Hooker, John Lee 40
"*Human Error*" (Unseen Terror, 1987) 130–1
human error in grindcore 130–33
hyper feminine 247, 263, 266

"Icarus' Dream Suite Opus 4,' 58–61
'Ignorant Scene' (Unseen Terror, 1987) 137
"*III*" (Ommadon, 2012) 325
individuality: expressed by Metallica 107–8, 113; of fans 199, 203
industrial capitalism depicted in grindcore 131–2
insider knowledge in metal jewelry 236–9
institutional genderism 271
intelligibility: of metal music sound 79–82; of music 68
internalized sexism 253
International Society for Metal Music Studies (ISMMS) 10
Internet based survey 147–8
Internet increasing awareness of metal music 26–27
Iron Maiden 3, 186, 318, 333, 340, 345; song structures of 45, 46

Iron Maiden fans 13, 145–65; age of fans 157; concentration in South America 152, 155; distribution by geographic location 154–7; distribution by nationality 153; education 158–9; employment 159; gender 157–8; marital status 161; musicianship 165; political affiliation 162–3; social background 159–61; social morphology 157–65; substance use 163–4; suicidal thoughts 164–5; unsafe sex practices 164
'Iron Man' (Black Sabbath, 1970) 40, 53
Ironthesis survey 145–65
Irwin, William 9
"*IV*" (Ommadon, 2012) 325

Jalkanen, Jiri 215
Jameson, Fredric 315
Jasper, Tony 24
jazz 96, 99; influence 52
"*Jerusalem*" (Sleep, 1996, 1999) 312
jewelry: metal 15, 227–40; re-used in non-military context 229–31
Judas Priest 2, 202, 213; song structures of 36–47
Juntunen, Juho 211

Kahn-Harris and Bennett, A. 239
Kahn-Harris and Hein 10
Kahn-Harris, Keith 4, 5, 7, 8, 9, 10, 11, 16–17, 77, 107, 126, 128, 137, 138, 173, 176, 180, 192–3, 196, 218, 234, 239, 245, 261, 263, 264, 278, 279, 290, 317, 333–41, 351
Kalevala 211, 216
'Killing Yourself to Live' (Black Sabbath, 1973) 42
Killswitch Engage 286
King, Kerry 114
Krenske, L. 247, 262, 274
Kuusniemi, Kimmo 211

Laiho, Aleksi 222
Lambert, Adam 288–9
Lamb of God 80
Larraz, Jose 307
Latina/o musicians 96, 99–100
Leblanc, Lauraine 257
Led Zeppelin 40–41, 46, 52, 282, 283, 285, 318
Leeds (England) 126, 135
Levine, Alexandra 90
Levine, M. 4, 192, 318
Levi-Strauss, Claude 28

Lilker, Danny 89
Lipsitz, George 91
listening space for drone metal music 321–2
listening to other genres of music 178
"*Load*" (Metallica, 1996) 110
lo-fi approach 80
'Lord of this World' (Black Sabbath, 1971) 41
Los Angeles and origin of thrash metal 89–90
loss aversion in social exchange 273–4
loudness: and harmonic distortion 75–76; wars with Metallica 117–20
low art 52
"*Lulu*" (Metallica, 2011) 116
Lynch, George 61
Lyotard, Jean-Francois 28
"*Lysol*" (The Melvins, 1992) 313

Machine Head 81
Maffesoli, Michel 28
magazines on metal music 24
mainstream culture incorporating metal jewelry 227–8, 234–6, 238–9
Malmsteen, Yngwie 58–61
'Mamma Said' (Metallica, 1996) 111
"*Mana-Yood-Sushai*" (Bong, 2012) 324
Manowar 54–55
Management: company 118; band 26; venue 4; professional 199; upper 169, 170, 171, 184, 185; middle 170, 171, 184
marginalization of women in metal subculture 261–74
marital status of heavy metal fans 161
Martinez, Silvia 8
masculinist codes in death metal 247–8, 253, 263
masculinity: in grindcore 136; of heavy metal music 15–16, 279–83; relationship with femininity in metal music scene 247–9, 261–74; and women's pleasures 277
mass culture, independent from 106–7, 113
"*Master of Puppets*" (Metallica, 1986) 108
"*Master of Reality*" (Black Sabbath, 1971) 37
Mastodon 77, 79
Matikevic, Miljenko 62
Mayhem 333

McClary, Susan 281
McKay, J. 247, 262, 274
Megadeth 26, 41, 42–43, 89, 90, 215
melody in neo-classical aesthetic 55–58
Mephisto Waltz, The (film) 307
metal demographics 13–14, 145–203
'Metal Gods' (Judas Priest, 1980) 44
metal jewelry 15, 227–40; early style 228–9; entrepreneurialism and niche markets 234–6; insider knowledge and entrepreneurialism 236–9; interpretation influenced by wearer 239
metal knowledge 334–5
Metallica 94, 101, 215; being authentic 106–7; *Black Album* 26; crossing over to mainstream music 12–13; dual song structures 42–43; lost of symbolic capital 114–16; and negative associations with mass culture 106–7, 113–15; and origins of thrash music 89–90; sell-out accusations against 108–12, 117–20; song structures of 45, 46; subcultural consecration of 107–8; suing Napster 106, 112
"*Metallica*" (Metallica, 1991) 108–9
metallization of Western High Art 12
metal musicology 11–12
metal music: anachronism of 344–5; awareness of 26; crisis of abundance in 334–8; definition of sound 79–82; in Finland 209–23; future of 16–17, 333–41, 343–8; and gender politics 245–91; globalization of 2–4, 26–27; -hard rock continuum 35–36; heaviness 11, 12, 68, 69, 74, 77–79; markets and commerce 14–15; and punk music 90, 92; scenes 12–13, 94–97; women's experiences with 277–91
metalness 343
metal studies 8–10, 22–30; advent of 26–28; and cultural studies 16; history of 23–24
Metal Studies Bibliography Database (MSBD) 10
middle class: defining 193–8; as metal fans 191–3, 198–203
lower-middle 14, 196, 197, 202
upper-middle 13, 14, 192, 203
Middleton, Richard 38, 71
Midlands (England) 126, 191
military insignia appropriated as metal jewelry 229–31

misogyny 262–4, 274, 278, 281–2
'Misty Mountain Hop' (Led Zeppelin, 1971) 40, 46
Moberg, Marcus 318
'Monkeybats' (Jurassic 5, 1991) 62
Montréal, Canada and drone metal music 314
Moore, Alan 36–7, 44, 70, 71, 74, 79, 304
Moore, Ryan 94, 172, 191, 202, 203, 318
mosh pit 98, 133–5, 264
Mötörhead 90, 213
mourning jewelry 228, 229, 231
Moynihan, Michael 27
multiple choice question survey 147, 149
Municipal Waste 301
Murdock, G. 195, 198
Murdock, G. and McRon, 199–200
Murdock and Phelps 195, 198, 200
music. *See also* specific types: commitment to 198–200; gendered interpretations of 281
musicianship of heavy metal fans 165
My Chemical Romance 333
Mynett, Mark 12, 354
mysticism 16, 316–17; in drone metal music 312, 317–18, 325–6

Napalm Death 126–7, 129, 131, 132, 136, 140
Napster 106, 112
neo-classical music 12
neo-classicization of heavy metal 50–64
Newsted, Jason 114
New Wave of British Heavy Music (NWOBHM) 5, 90
Nightwish 209, 220, 222
Nilsson, M. 129
Nordic countries and popularity of heavy metal music 214
North Carolina and female death metal fans 245–58
Norway: mayhem in 26–27; and popularity of heavy metal music 214
note definition and harmonic distortion 76–77
Nova Trilogy (Burroughs) 300, 306
"*Number of the Beast*" (Iron Maiden, 1982) 148
nu metal 114, 116
Nu Pogodi! 128, 135–6

O'Boyle, Tom 16–17, 343
occupations as indicator of social class 194–6
Occupy movement 346
Odd Future 339–40
Oliver, Derek 24
Om 215–6, 312, 315, 325
Ommadon 325
"*Once More 'Round The Sun*" (Mastodon, 2014) 77, 79
'One' (Metallica, 1988) 108
oppositional identity formations 246, 249, 252–3
Osbourne, Ozzy 55–58, 229
Osegueda, Mark 100
Overell, R. 15, 126, 127, 128, 130, 134, 139, 256, 264, 276, 285,

Pachelbel, Johann 55–58
Paganini, Niccolò 60–61
Page, Jimmy 41
"*Painkiller*" (Judas Priest, 1990) 46
'Painkiller' (Judas Priest, 1990) 46
palimpsest as metaphor for heavy metal music genealogy 16, 299, 300–8
palm-muting 109–10
Pantera 26
"*Paranoid*" (Black Sabbath, 1970) 40
'Paranoid' (Black Sabbath, 1970) 40–41
Parents Music Resource Center 25
participant observation research method 146
Partridge, Christopher 318
'Peace Sells' (Megadeth, 1986) 43
Peel, John 126
Peer Günt 213
Peer, Ralph 91
Pentagram 298–9
performance complexity 79–80
Peterson, Richard A. 94, 167,178
'Phantom Lord' (Metallica, 1983) 45, 46
Phelps, G. 195, 198
Phillipov, M. 2, 3, 15, 79, 127, 137, 139, 261, 264–5, 274
Pillsbury, Glenn 9, 11, 94, 107, 108, 109, 110, 111, 112, 113, 114, 117, 120, 121, 214
Pink Floyd 315
pleasures by women engaged with music 277–9, 283–91; romance language 287–8; shared experiences 286–7; transcendence and transportation 284–6

pluralistic ignorance 272
PMRC 25
political orientation: of grindcore 125–6, 128–30, 133–5, 137; of heavy metal fans 162–3
Poole, Simon 16
pop music: dichotomy with rock music 280, 282, 283, 288–9; song structures 36–38
'Postmorten' (Slayer, 1986) 43
power. *See also* empowerment: in death metal music scene 261–74; social 269–70
power chords 53–54
Presley, Elvis 282, 283
Preston, Joe 313
producer, role of 12, 68, 122; of the year 122
progressive rock music 198–203
protest music of grindcore 128–30
proud pariahs theory 174
proximity impacted by harmonic distortion 74
punchiness 78–79
punch in metal music 78–79, 82–83
punk music 90, 92
Purcell, Natalie 263, 318

queer identity in heavy metal music scene 250, 253, 257
questionnaire survey of Iron Maiden fans 145–65
Quintana, Ron 24

race diversity influencing origin of thrash metal 90–91
racialization of thrash music 92–94, 99–100
racialized music industry 91
radical EQ boosts 82–83
rap music 97, 98
Rasmussen, Flemming 109
Reagan, Ronald 25
realism, grotesque in grindcore 130–33
Red Sparowes 284
Reed, Lou 116
reflexive anti-reflexivity 263, 265, 347
religion in drone metal music 318
"*Reload*" (Metallica, 1997) 110
retro-progressive nature of metal music history 302–8
retro rock 297
Reynolds, Simon 297
Rhoads, Randy 51, 55–58

Richards, Keith 234, 239
Riches, Gabby 13, 15, 173, 257, 264, 277–8, 290
"Ride the Lightning" (Metallica, 1984) 108, 116
riffs 11, 38–47, 81, 235, 312
riff sonograms 72–76
Riley, Paterson 235
"Rising Force" (Malmsteen, 1984) 58–61
Roadburn festival 314
Roccor, Bettina 8, 15, 25, 159, 192
Rock, Bob 109–10, 116
Rockett, Rikki 62
rock music 99–100; dichotomy with pop music 280, 282, 283, 288–9; song structure 37
Rollin, Jean 307
romance language impact of heavy metal songs 287–8
Rubin, Rick 118–20
Rumba (magazine) 210, 212

"Sabbath Bloody Sabbath" (Black Sabbath, 1973) 41–42
'Sabbath Bloody Sabbath' (Black Sabbath, 1973) 42, 53
'Sabra Cadabra' (Metallica, 1973) 42
'Sad But True' (Metallica, 1991) 109, 110
Saint Vitus 301
Salem's Pot 308
Sanders, Troy 77
San Francisco Bay Area: music scene in 94–101; and origins of thrash metal 12, 89–101
Sarcofagus 210–11
Satan's Satyrs 308
Schenker, Michael 24
Schippers, Mimi 9
Scott, Joan 317, 319
Scott, Niall W. R. 9, 10, 16–17, 133–4, 136, 140, 318, 343
'Seek and Destroy' (Metallica, 1983) 41
selling-out 12–13, 107–12, 228
Sentenced 216
Sepultura 7
sexism 15, 262–3, 266–8, 281; internalized 253; structural 271
Shakespeare, Steven 318
shared experiences impact of heavy metal songs 286–7
Sharf, Richard 317

Shepherd, Ian 117
Shirley, Kevin 43
signal stability and harmonic distortion 75–76
skeletal imagery in metal jewelry 227
skull: changing use in metal jewelry 229–31; in metal jewelry 227, 228–9; used as jewelry by post-war bikers 229–31
skull jewelry 236–8; entrepreneurialism and niche markets 234–6
skull rings 227, 229, 232, 237
Slabdragger 286
Slagel, Brian 24
slam dancing 98
Slayer 42–43, 89, 90; song structures of 45, 46
Sleep 312, 313
"Sleep's Holy Mountain" (Sleep, 1992) 313
slogan songs 131
Smialek, Eric 12–13, 192, 203
social characteristics of metal music fans 159–61, 167–86
social class: categorizing 194–8; defining 193–8
social exchange theory 261, 267–9
social morphology of heavy metal fans 157–65
social power 269–70
Soderlind, Didrik 27
"Some Kind of Monster" (Metallica, 2004) 114
song structures 35–47, 284; dual 41–43; of heavy metal 38; of Judas Priest 43–46; in popular music 36–38; in rock music 37
Soundi (magazine) 210, 212
sound production 68
Southern Lord record label 314
space altered with drone metal music 321–2
Spears, Britney 288, 289
spectral masking 68, 77
speed metal in Finland 214–15
'Spiritual Black Dimensions' (Dimmu Borgir, 1999) 80
Spracklen, Karl 10
Spracklen, Brown and Kahn-Harris 10, 28
Spracklen, Lashua and Wagg 2
Spracklen, Lucas and Deeks 180
Spracklen, Riches and Lashua 264

Springsteen, Bruce 36
"*Stained Class*" (Judas Priest, 1978) 202
'Stained Class' (Judas Priest, 1978) 44
"*St. Anger*" (Metallic, 2003) 114
status quo bias 273
'Steeler' (Judas Priest, 1980) 44
Stephenson, Ken 37
Stone 214, 215
Stone Vengeance 101
Stratovarius 212, 218–19, 220
Straw, Will 25
structuration 249
subcultural bricolage 28, 147, 222, 231
subcultural capital 235
subcultures and commercial engagement with dominant culture 227–8, 234–6
substance use by heavy metal fans 163–4
suicidal thoughts of heavy metal fans 164–5
"*Sunbather*" (Deafhaven, 2013) 82
Sunn O))) 312, 313, 315, 325
Suosikki (magazine) 212
survey: of Hellfest Festival 167–86; of Iron Maiden fans 145–65; methods of 145–7
Swans 315
Sweden and popularity of heavy metal music 214
Symphony No. 5 (1808) 60

"*Tainted Life*" (Almond, 2000) 239
"*Take It So Hard*" (Richards, 1988) 239
tape trading 5, 7, 335, 336
"*Tales from the Thousand Lakes*" (Amorphis, 1994) 216
Tarot 212
Taylor, L. Wiebe 16, 127, 129, 130, 131, 137
technicality of music composition 79–80
technological mediation 82–84
Testament 100
'The Crown and the Ring' (Manowar, 1988) 54–55
The Great Frog 227, 229, 234–6, 239
The Melvins 313
Theo Fennell 235, 239
The Rolling Stones 282
'The Unforgiven II' (Metallica, 1997) 111
thinking man's metal 107
Thin Lizzy 53
Thornton, Sarah 107, 228

thrash metal music 5, 7, 26; dual song structures in 42–43; in Finland 214; origins in San Francisco Bay Area 89–101; racial autonomy in 92–94
timbral heaviness. *See* heaviness of metal music
time altered with drone metal music 321–2
"*Time to Die*" (Electric Wizard, 2014) 307
"*Toccata and Fugue in D minor, BWN 565*" (Bach, 1708) 54–55
"*Torcha!*" (Waltari, 1992) 217
Towle, Phil 114
Townsend, Devin 339
transcendence and transportation impact of heavy metal songs 284–6
transgression of grindcore 128, 133, 264
'Transilvanian Hunger' (Darkthrone, 1994) 80
translocal music scenes 7
Trilling, Daniel 2
"*Trilogy*" (Malmsteen, 1986) 61
'Trilogy Suite Opus 5' (Malmsteen, 1986) 61
Trujillo, Robert 94, 101
twin guitar sound 43
two-handed tapping technique 53
'Tyrant' (Judas Priest, 1976) 44

Ulrich, Lars 108, 116, 118–19
"*Under Satan's Sun*" (Bloody Hammers, 2014) 307
Underground: radio 24; markets 218; network 4; newspapers 306; scenic-infrastructure 347; progressive-underground 200; tape-trading 7; Satanic Metal Underground 27; global metal extreme underground 12; of extreme metal scenes 190; underground champions (Metallica) 13; underground metal 108, 346; underground methods 126; underground movement 99; underground movements 209; underground music 198; underground obscurity 196; underground opposition 107, 113; underground phenomenon 94; underground prestige 106; underground reputation 108; underground subculture 108; underground scenes 97; underground scene 338; underground scenic

infrastructure 128; underground status 201; metal underground 336, 346; extreme metal underground 1; extreme metal global underground 5
unsafe sex practices by heavy metal fans 164
Unseen Terror 127, 130–1, 137
Ury-Petesch, Jean-Philippe 13
'Use Your Mind' (Extreme Noise Terror, 1989) 132–3

Van Halen, Eddie 53
Vasan, Sonia 15, 278
Venom 90
vernacular cosmopolitanism 92–94
vocals 36; aggression 78; distortion 77–78; intelligibility 81–82
"*Vol. 4*" (Black Sabbath, 1972) 313
"*Volume 2*" (Sleep, 1992) 313
volume and harmonic distortion 75–76
"*Voodoo Violence*" (Wood, 1991) 62
'Voracious Souls' (Death Angel, 1987) 92

'Wake Up Dead' (Megadeth, 1986) 41
Waksman, Steve 92
Wallach, Jeremy 4, 68, 71, 80, 90, 318
Wallach & Levine 95, 314, 338
Wallach, Berger and Greene 5, 8, 89, 92, 146, 169, 191, 202, 209
Wallach and Clinton 91
Walser, R. 8, 50–51, 55, 63, 71, 99, 213, 262–3, 279, 280–1
Waltari 217
Wang, Grace 100
'War Pigs' (Black Sabbath, 1970) 40–41
warrior aesthetic in metal music 279–80
Wayne's World 13
Weiner, Andrew 300, 305–6
Weinstein, Deena 3, 4, 8, 10–11, 13, 35, 99, 106, 157, 158, 159, 173, 178, 179, 190, 196, 197, 262, 278, 291, 298, 315, 333, 345
"*Welcome to Hell*" (Venom, 1981) 90

"*We Live*" (Electric Wizard, 2004) 307
Werbner, Pnina 93
Western High Art music influence 50–64
West Midlands as home of heavy metal 1–2
'Where Eagles Dare' (Iron Maiden, 1983) 45, 46
white genre of music 91
Whiteley, Sheila 282–3
White Zombie 250, 251
Wise, Susan 282
Witchcraft '70 (film) 307
"*Witchcult Today*" (Electric Wizard, 2007) 306–7
women: empowerment narratives in extreme metal 245–58; experiences with hard rock and metal music 277–91; fans 15–16; as girlfriend in metal music scenes 246–7; and group conformity 270–3; lack of feminist resistance and subgroup formation in death metal 268; lack of social power in death metal scene 269–70; marginalization in death metal music scene 261–74; as masculine persona in heavy metal music scene 247–50, 253, 266; participation in grindcore 134–9; as true fan in metal music scenes 246–7
Wood, Mark 12, 62–63
working class: defining 193–6; expressed in grindcore 126, 129–32; as metal fans 191–2, 198–203; stereotype of heavy metal fans 159, 172–3; lower-working 14, 194, 195, 196, 197, 198, 199, 201, 202, 203; upper working 14, 192, 195, 197, 202; un-skilled manual 195; semi-skilled manual 195; skilled-manual 14, 197
World Tours 1, 3, 148, 209, 220

Zagorski-Thomas, S. 71, 74
Zero Nine 212